M000198247

PEOPLE POWER

PEOPLE POWER

The Community
Organizing Tradition
of Saul Alinsky

Edited by

Aaron Schutz and Mike Miller

VANDERBILT UNIVERSITY PRESS ■ *Nashville*

Copyright for the reprinted selections resides with the author, agent, or original publisher. For more information, see the credit that accompanies each selection.

© 2015 by Vanderbilt University Press
Nashville, Tennessee 37235
All rights reserved
First printing 2015

This book is printed on acid-free paper.
Manufactured in the United States of America

Library of Congress Cataloging-in-Publication Data on file
LC control number   2014012672
LC classification number   HN90.C64P46 2014
Dewey class number   303.30973—dc23

ISBN 978-0-8265-2041-8 (hardcover)
ISBN 978-0-8265-2042-5 (paperback)
ISBN 978-0-8265-2043-2 (ebook)

To my wife, Jessica,
and my daughters, Hiwot and Sheta.

—Aaron Schutz

To all those
who have invested themselves
in the art/craft/science of organizing
as a way to fight for social and economic justice
and make democracy a living reality.
And to the memory of Herb White,
organizer extraordinaire.

—Mike Miller

Contents

Part I: Introduction

Part II: Alinsky's Colleagues

Section A: Nicholas von Hoffman: The Woodlawn Organization and the Civil Rights Movement in the North

Part III: Different Directions

Section A: Heather Booth, Midwest Academy, and Citizen Action

Section B: Wade Rathke and Association of Community Organizations for Reform Now (ACORN)

Part IV: Concluding Commentaries

Acknowledgments

We would like to thank the following people for reading and commenting on portions of the book, being interviewed by us, and otherwise helping move this book to completion: Frank Bardacke, John Baumann, Heather Booth, Luke Bretherton, Molly Corbett, Don Elmer, Ken Galdston, John Gaudette, Michael Gecan, Arnie Graf, Stephanie Gut, Dick Harmon, Stan Holt, Lester Hunt, Bud Kanitz, Gretchen Laue, Spence Limbocker, Richard March, Craig Merrilees, Mary Ochs, Gilbert Padilla, Bill Pastreich, Gregory Pierce, Frank Pierson, Karen Ramos, Miles Rapoport, Wade Rathke, Fred Ross Jr., Danny Schechter, Ed Shurna, Tom Sinclair, Margery Tabankin, Madeline Talbott, Gabriel Thompson, Nicholas von Hoffman, Michael Westgate, and Herb White. Thank you to all the authors, estates, and owners of the included texts for permission to reprint them, including many of the individuals named above, as well as Noëlle McAfee, *Presbyterians Today*, Johnny Ray Youngblood, and Kathy Trapp. Without their participation, this book could not have been completed.

In addition to the wonderful University of Wisconsin-Milwaukee interlibrary loan department staff, who went beyond the call of duty in accessing many materials, we would like to thank the archives of the following institutions: the Archdiocese of Chicago, the Chicago History Museum, DePaul University, East Tennessee State University, the Highlander Center, Loyola University-Marymount, the University of Notre Dame, Stanford University, and the University of Illinois at Chicago.

The Farmworker Movement Documentation Project website (*farmworkermove ment.com*), put together by LeRoy Chatfield, was invaluable for the Fred Ross section.

We apologize if we have missed anyone who assisted us with this effort.

Aaron would like also to thank his family: his wife, Jessica, who put up with numerous long and loud phone discussions with Mike, and his daughters, Hiwot and Sheta, always annoyed at the time their father spends on his computer.

While thanks are due, the final responsibility for what has been done with these contributions rests with us.

Preface
Why Is Alinsky Important Today?

■

MIKE MILLER

Millions of people demonstrated in Egypt and toppled a dictator. But the people responsible for that mobilization were unable to elect a government to fill the vacancy. A careful analysis of "people power" in the country would have made the outcome predictable. When the elected president exceeded the military's definition of what was acceptable, it dumped him. A careful analysis of the power structure of the country would have made this outcome predictable as well. I think the organizers of the liberation struggle in Egypt would benefit from a reading of Saul Alinsky.

Occupy Wall Street lifted up the vast economic inequalities that exist in the country and made them the topic of everyday conversation. Opinion polls agreed: the vast majority of the American people opposed the growing income and wealth gaps. They wanted politicians to do something about it. Nothing has been done, nor is anything likely to be done. I think the organizers of Occupy Wall Street would benefit from a reading of Saul Alinsky.

Barack Obama's election lifted the hopes of millions that something might fundamentally change in Washington. When he ran, he was attacked as a radical Saul Alinsky community organizer. While he was a community organizer for three years, he abandoned that path to social change and chose an electoral one. Here's what I wrote elsewhere shortly after his election:

> What Obama does with the electoral organization that was put together for his campaign is separate from what people who want a small-d democratic agenda in the country must do. Obama's agenda is a presidential one. Community organizing's agenda should be to push the president. There will be plenty of people pushing him from Wall Street, the auto industry, and other elite circles. If there is not a countervailing push, organized independently of Obama, hopefully with his blessing, we will be disappointed in him as a president—and will have ourselves to blame.[1]

By his second term, the disappointment with Obama was palpable. But it was also the case that there was no countervailing push, organized independently of him, to make him be better.

In his younger days, in a special issue of *Illinois Issues* titled "After Alinsky," Obama wrote:

> In theory, community organizing provides a way to merge various strategies for neighborhood empowerment. Organizing begins with the premise that (1) the

problems facing inner-city communities do not result from a lack of effective solutions, but from a lack of power to implement these solutions; (2) that the only way for communities to build long-term power is by organizing people and money around a common vision; and (3) that a viable organization can only be achieved if a broadly based indigenous leadership—and not one or two charismatic leaders— can knit together the diverse interests of their local institutions.[2]

This means bringing together churches, block clubs, parent groups and any other institutions in a given community to pay dues, hire organizers, conduct research, develop leadership, hold rallies and education campaigns, and begin drawing up plans on a whole range of issues—jobs, education, crime, etc.

Once such a vehicle is formed, it holds the power to make politicians, agencies and corporations more responsive to community needs. Equally important, it enables people to break their crippling isolation from each other, to reshape their mutual values and expectations and rediscover the possibilities of acting collaboratively—the prerequisites of any successful self-help initiative. . . .

Organizing teaches as nothing else does the beauty and strength of everyday people. Through the songs of the church and the talk on the stoops, through the hundreds of individual stories of coming up from the South and finding any job that would pay, of raising families on threadbare budgets, of losing some children to drugs and watching others earn degrees and land jobs their parents could never aspire to—it is through these stories and songs of dashed hopes and powers of endurance, of ugliness and strife, subtlety and laughter, that organizers can shape a sense of community not only for others, but for themselves.[3]

The idealistic supporters of Barack Obama who now bemoan his failures would benefit from a reading of Saul Alinsky. So, too, would the idealistic supporters of Hillary Clinton, who wrote a senior thesis on Alinsky and was asked by him to direct his new "Proxies for People" effort. She chose law school instead, deciding to be an insider rather than an outsider. The electoral path followed for her as well.

Saul Alinsky devoted his working life to teaching the poor, the marginalized, the powerless, the discriminated against, the working class, and toward the end of his life, the middle class, as well as those who generally cared about democracy and social and economic justice, how to realize their hopes and aspirations. He was an idealist who believed passionately in the capacity of everyday people to be self-governing. He was a small "d" democrat who knew that if people were to participate effectively in a democracy they had to have the latent power of their numbers brought forth and made manifest in effective people power organizations. He was a hardheaded realist who fully appreciated the maxim from abolitionist Frederick Douglass that "power concedes nothing without a demand. It never did and it never will." He was a social inventor who developed and fine-tuned two instruments of people power—the broad-based community organization and the professional community organizer—that are as relevant today as when he and Joe Meegan organized the first of his "mass-based" organizations in 1939.

This book provides an introduction to Alinsky's ideas and practices. It ranges from an analytic look at his core concepts to detailed stories about their implementation in a variety of contexts, and includes an introduction to some of the organizers who in one way or another implemented their understanding of what he had to teach.

Aaron Schutz and I raise critical questions about the work and thinking we present. But make no mistake: I think the people in these pages are American heroes and heroines, and the work they did and do has been vital to American democracy and the now-necessary fight to regain it. My own life is deeply indebted to three major connections—the early student movement at UC Berkeley, the Student Nonviolent Coordinating Committee and the civil rights movement in the Deep South, and Alinsky—along with the work and thinking of many of the people who appear in these pages.

Alinsky has much to say to our current situation. By the end of this book, I hope you will agree.

Notes

1. Mike Miller, *A Community Organizer's Tale: People and Power in San Francisco* (Berkeley, CA: Heyday Books, 2009).
2. The money Obama is talking about would come from membership dues, grants from relatively small foundations, and other contributions to finance an organization.
3. Barack Obama, "Why Organize? Problems and Promise in the Inner City," *Illinois Issues,* September 1988, *illinoisissues.uis.edu.*

PART I

INTRODUCTION

1

Editors' Introduction

■

MIKE MILLER AND AARON SCHUTZ

In the pages that follow, we have assembled a range of articles, documents, organizational papers, and interviews about the tradition of community organizing that began with Saul Alinsky and the Industrial Areas Foundation (IAF). From its origins in Chicago in the late 1930s, Alinsky's approach spread across the country, increasingly diffusing into other parts of the world.

The book is structured around the work of five of his most important colleagues—Ed Chambers, Tom Gaudette, Dick Harmon, Fred Ross, and Nicholas von Hoffman—supplemented with speeches by leaders and documents from the organizations they built. We also include pieces by organizers who either worked directly with Alinsky or followed in his footsteps, and who, in ways we will discuss, diverged from his path. Together, these texts show how different organizers and leaders have adapted and elaborated Alinsky's theory and practice in their work.

Many of these items appear in formal publication here for the first time; they were previously available only on untranscribed audiotapes or in early, mostly obsolete, and often difficult-to-read formats, such as mimeographed, dittoed, Thermo-Faxed, or Xeroxed pages. A few have remained well known among organizers, passing from hand to hand in flyspecked photocopies of photocopies. Others have mostly been forgotten. We drew some of them from university archives and the extensive collection of papers preserved by Miller during his long organizing career, and learned about others through citations in reference lists and discussions with other organizers. From a broad corpus of possibilities, we selected what we believe represent the best or most important examples of this shadow literature of organizing.

Mostly created by practitioners for audiences already deeply interested in the field, there is a directness to these texts—a vibrancy and sense of urgency often lacking in many of today's more abstract or textbook-like introductions to organizing. As we explain in introductions to each section, because these documents were created for particular purposes at particular moments of history, many reflect the issues and circumstances of the time they were written and should be read with this in mind. We hope you find them as interesting as we have.

What Is Community Organizing?

In an interview with T. George Harris, Alinsky said, "When people are organized, they move in . . . to the central decision-making tables. [They] say, 'This is what we want. . . . We are people and damn it you are going to listen to us. . . . ' They are admitted to the decision-making tables . . . on the basis of power."[1]

Community organizing brings powerless and relatively powerless people together in solidarity to defend and advance their interests and values. Through their organizations, they speak with people power to established power on matters that affect them in their daily lives. They speak on major issues that might affect tens of thousands (or even millions), and on small but important issues like a stop sign at a dangerous intersection.

Community organizing groups typically start by trying to negotiate with decision-makers who have the authority to make the changes they want: elected officials, private sector owners, executives and administrators in bureaucracies, and the like. Decision-makers, however, are used·to making unilateral decisions. They feel accountable only to those who already have substantial influence, wealth, or power. They rarely need to respond to everyday people and their concerns. As a result, decision-makers often simply ignore the people's requests to meet with them. Even when they do sit down, they generally try to defuse concerns without really listening or negotiating real change.

Action, at this point, inevitably involves conflict.

In fact, community organizing welcomes conflict as a tool to build people power. Only when adversaries recognize that there is power on the other side do they enter into real negotiations.

For example, tenants in a rat-infested, high-rent, no-services apartment building might organize themselves and seek changes from their landlord. When the landlord refuses to meet with them, they might start picketing him at a place where their presence will embarrass him, or engage in a rent-strike that will affect his profits. If they are wise in their choice of strategy and tactics, these actions will lead to substantial gains in their cause, reflected in an agreement that will recognize the tenant association as the collective voice for the tenants. Even after an agreement is reached, however, the tenants must stick together to prevent the landlord from backsliding, or evicting tenant leaders, or otherwise trying to ignore or undo what he has agreed to. This is why they need a long-term organization, not simply a momentary mobilization. Similar stories could be told about negotiations with plant managers, public administrators, politicians, corporate and financial executives, and others who hold the power to make decisions that affect people's lives.

Community organizing is a thoroughly *practical* process. Organizations are successful only when they clearly identify their power in relationship to their potential adversaries. In the vernacular, they don't pick fights they don't have a chance of winning. Early on, when an organization's membership is relatively small and it faces greater skepticism, it tackles smaller issues. Over time, small victories increase the competence and self-confidence of participants and help them recruit skeptics. The formula is simple: more people + more power = a growing capacity to address issues that are more deeply rooted in the status quo. Through organizing, communities that were marginalized, excluded, oppressed, and discriminated against increasingly gain the capacity to foster effective change.

In the most general sense, community organizing seeks to change the relations of power between existing institutions and the formerly powerless. Community organizers, including most of the writers of the essays included in this volume, build these community organizations. They identify leaders and potential leaders in communities and do their work through them.

In his short book *Community Organizing: A Brief Introduction* (Milwaukee, WI: Euclid Avenue Press, 2012), Mike Miller provides a detailed view of how institution-based community organizing was implemented in a small Presbyterian church that was a member of what he calls "American City Community Organization (ACCO)." The book presents a composite story of the development of this congregation and the larger organization of which it is a part. The portrayal of fictional organizer "Jeanne Steuben" carefully demonstrates what a community organizer working in this tradition does.

A Brief History of the Alinsky Tradition of Community Organizing

Alinsky's first organizing project led to the creation of the Back of the Yards Neighborhood Council (BYNC) in Chicago. He borrowed from the tough approach of the 1930s industrial union movement, grafting its strategy and tactics onto the poor, working-class Back of the Yards neighborhood next to Chicago's vast industrial stockyards (an area infamously described in Upton Sinclair's novel *The Jungle*). Drawing on local traditions and values, Alinsky built community power on the strength of long-standing formal and informal social relationships. His organizations were rooted in existing institutions within these communities and built new associational life as the situation required.

As Alinsky noted in an interview many years later, Back of the Yards

> was the nadir of all slums in America. People were crushed and demoralized, either jobless or getting starvation wages, diseased, living in filthy, rotting unheated shanties, with barely enough food and clothing to keep alive. And it was a cesspool of hate; the Poles, Slovaks, Germans, Negroes, Mexicans and Lithuanians all hated each other and all of them hated the Irish, who returned the sentiment in spades. . . .

I knew that once they were provided with a real, positive program to change their miserable conditions, they wouldn't need scapegoats anymore. Probably my prime consideration in moving into Back of the Yards, though, was because if it could be done there, it could be done anywhere.[2]

Whether this long-after-the-fact explanation really reflected what he was thinking at the time, the poverty and interethnic conflict he faced in this neighborhood are well established by historians.

The BYNC established the pattern for Alinsky's subsequent organizing. Catholic parishes and the Packinghouse union were the BYNC's most institutionalized anchors, but it also included every type of organization that Alinsky and his partner, Joe Meegan, could identify and draw in: block clubs, sororal and fraternal organizations, mutual aid societies, athletic clubs, interest groups, merchants, and so on. And, where appropriate, new groups were formed. The goal was to get every group that had any real following among local people to be part of the organization—including groups that had previously believed they could never work together, like the Communist-led local union and the often-warring Catholic parishes that reflected the ethnic tensions of the neighborhood.

Without Meegan, the local Irish Catholic lay leader in Back of the Yards, Alinsky could not have proceeded. Meegan was widely respected and trusted in the neighborhood; he "credentialed" Alinsky. But after the creation of the BYNC, its co-organizers took different paths. Meegan became the director of the BYNC. The BYNC became his life's work, and persists today—albeit with a great deal of controversy surrounding it (to Alinsky's disappointment and frustration, its later efforts included the goal of keeping African Americans out of the neighborhood—an issue we address elsewhere).

Alinsky, in contrast with Meegan, saw the possibility for a larger agenda. With support from high-level Catholic clergy, key people in the industrial union movement (specifically in the Congress of Industrial Organizations, or CIO)—and the wealthy department store owner Marshall Field III, he started the IAF. Under its umbrella, and with the legitimacy his supporters provided, Alinsky sought to spread this work across the Midwest, particularly in places with sympathetic bishops and strong locals of the Packinghouse Workers union.

World War II brought an abrupt halt to Alinsky's local organizing, and he joined the Roosevelt administration to provide productivity assistance in wartime industries. At the end of the war, Alinsky resumed his work, but soon had to contend with the anti-Communist hysteria of the McCarthy era. Divided by anti-Communism and increasingly co-opted by a relatively narrow collective bargaining and political agenda, labor's support for Alinsky's work withered.

Catholic support grew, however, especially where there were bishops in the tradition of Catholicism's social encyclicals, which said the church should engage the world on behalf of social and economic justice, and in the National Conference of

Catholic Charities, a service and action arm of the national church. Soon joining the Catholics, particularly in previously white but now African American communities, were mainline Protestant churches with an institutional interest in dealing with the problems posed by largely vacant church buildings, and a new breed of inner-city pastors with a moral commitment to racial and economic justice. These Protestant churches sought ways to translate the sometimes conflicting social gospel and Richard and Reinhold Niebuhr's approach to social justice (Protestantism's equivalents to the Catholic social encyclicals) to the problems of the ghetto. Catholic and Protestant leaders spread the word about Alinsky through their official church bodies, which mostly responded favorably when local church leaders decided they wanted Alinsky to organize in their communities.

Nicholas von Hoffman

Among the most imaginative of Alinsky's early lead organizers was Nicholas von Hoffman, whose work with African Americans on Chicago's South Side led to The Woodlawn Organization (TWO), returning Alinsky to national prominence in the 1960s. For the most part, the core of the IAF's work in the early post–World War II days had been in white ethnic, working-class neighborhoods. The impact of the Deep South Freedom Riders on TWO led von Hoffman and Alinsky to conclude that they were in a rare moment in history when a social movement moves significant numbers of people into action. They hoped to draw on this energy in more "movement-like" actions while still working to build durable local power organizations. TWO's slogan was "self-determination through community power." As Minister Franklin Florence, an African American leader of the IAF's later effort in Rochester, New York, said of his group, "When you say 'black power,' in Rochester, you spell it 'F.I.G.H.T.' (Freedom, Integration [later Integrity], Goals, Honor, Today).[3]

Fred Ross

Somewhat separately from all this, Alinsky heard about Fred Ross just after World War II. Louis Wirth, one of Alinsky's University of Chicago sociologist poker-playing partners, complained that Ross was supposed to be doing research but was always getting distracted by social action. Alinsky's ears perked up. After further checking, he offered to take Ross off his friend's hands. Ross's engagement with poverty went back to the 1930s; in fact, Ross had worked in the Farm Security Administration camp depicted in John Steinbeck's *Grapes of Wrath*. There he had developed a democratic tenant body, and the farmworkers had used lessons from their experiences governing a camp to deal with local politicians and growers.

After the war, working with Mexican Americans, Ross developed an organizing methodology that used informal house meetings as the key building block for chapters in what became the statewide Community Service Organization (CSO). Ross, and later other organizers, identified informal leaders or potential leaders whom they would meet with one on one and ask to host house meetings. By agreeing to be hosts, these people agreed to get "their people" to attend. Thus, the house meeting tested whether someone could deliver. After a critical mass of house meetings demonstrated local interest, an area-wide meeting would give birth to a CSO chapter.

The CSO became a powerhouse organization for Mexican Americans in California. For example, it was largely responsible for the election of the state's first Mexican American member of the U.S. Congress—Ed Roybal—and it was the frontline fighter in battles against urban renewal, job discrimination, police harassment and brutality, and other problems.

The individual membership approach to building CSO chapters contrasted with the "organization of organizations" approach of Alinsky's BYNC, in which organizations were the formal members, though in both cases the organization was built around local leadership. In the CSO, individuals joined geographically-based (town or urban neighborhood) chapters, and the chapters were members of the statewide organization. To create an institutional anchor, CSO chapters typically established "service centers," which offered an array of services to members and the larger community.

Ross involved people like Cesar Chavez, Dolores Huerta, and Gil Padilla in the CSO, where they became leaders and then full-time organizers. In the early 1960s, they became key organizers, joined by Ross, in a newly forming farmworker organization initiated by Chavez in the area around Delano, California, which eventually became the United Farm Workers of America (UFW).

Ross's vision represents a different strand of the Alinsky tradition. And Ross's individual membership strategy remained influential in the years to come. It informed a range of important efforts, from Cesar Chavez's farmworker organizing to the Association of Community Organizations for Reform Now (ACORN), formed by Wade Rathke in 1970. And Ross's boycott operation was the school for many organizers who went into both labor and other community organizing work.

Tom Gaudette

Tom Gaudette was famously needled by Alinsky in 1961 into quitting his position of vice-president at Admiral Corporation to become an organizer. He worked with Alinsky on a number of projects before striking out on his own. Gaudette's own work focused on neighborhood organizing with congregations and other neighborhood institutions, but he did not focus on the internal life of the churches themselves to the extent that the later IAF would. He mentored Shel Trapp, who developed an approach to block club organizing, and who, along with the leader Gale Cincotta, created National People's Action (NPA) and its training arm, the National Training and Information Center (NTIC), which won major changes in national housing laws, among many others. Gaudette also trained Fr. John Baumann and Fr. Jerry Helfridge, who created what became People Improving Communities through Organizing (PICO) when they went to California.

The Birth of the Institute and the Challenges of the 1960s

One problem with Alinsky's approach to building organizations of organizations was that he didn't have enough skilled organizers to respond to the demand for them. This demand rose sharply as the civil rights movement exploded in the North and the visibility of The Woodlawn Organization grew nationally.

In the early days of the IAF, Alinsky would find creative and talented people who were already at work in poor communities and seeking to address powerlessness and the social and economic justice issues. He would develop a one-on-one relationship with them, engaging in conversations about organizing and sharing anecdotes drawn mostly from his study of the CIO and his Back of the Yards experiences. When Alinsky thought someone had the talent to put together a mass-based organization, he would try to recruit him.

(Mike Miller was recruited by Alinsky in this way. Alinsky and Miller met in 1961. A tutorial relationship developed between them in San Francisco airport meetings; in Miller's visits to Alinsky's summer home in Carmel, California; and in the rides Miller gave Alinsky to the San Francisco airport. Alinsky would tell Miller organizing stories, using them to illustrate principles, and then ask Miller questions to learn his responses. In 1966, Alinsky hired Miller to direct his Kansas City, Missouri, project.)

Once recruited, the organizer immediately began work in the field. He was required to file regular tape-recorded or written reports, which Alinsky would review and comment on. It was an informal approach to recruitment and training, but Alinsky's initial conversations and subsequent commentaries on reports were filled with insights about how people and power worked. Alinsky also began conducting ten-day workshops around the country, typically sponsored by religious bodies that had given their blessing to his work. Attended primarily by clergy and potential organizers, these were a precursor to the formal workshops later offered by all the organizing networks.

This one-on-one approach was limited in the number of new organizers it could develop. By the mid-1960s, Alinsky was under pressure from his religious supporters to start a more formal organizer training institute. With the support of Midas Muffler heir Gordon Sherman, Alinsky's training center opened in Chicago in 1968. Thus began a new era in the Alinsky tradition.

The emergence of the organizing institute, however, came at the same time as a confluence of other complicating factors for Alinsky's organizing. The black power movement pushed back against the idea that a white man could be an agent of black liberation. The federal government's War on Poverty and a proliferation of foundation-funded "community-based nonprofits" increasingly co-opted and tamped down the conflict created by organizing groups and other social movements of the time. And Alinsky was becoming increasingly concerned about what was happening to two major white constituencies. He saw the "white ethnics" (Irish, Italians, Poles, Slavs, and others), with whom his organizing work had begun, drifting to the political right (he called them "the have-a-little-want-mores"). At the same time, he worried that the liberals and moderates in the suburban churches who had been supporting organizing in minority poor neighborhoods were becoming alienated by the militant rhetoric of many organizations in these communities. They were themselves experiencing powerlessness as they dealt with more-and-more distant and bureaucratized institutions and saw the war in Vietnam continue.

In an effort to connect with young organizers emerging from student movement organizations like the Student Nonviolent Coordinating Committee (SNCC), the Northern Student Movement, and Students for a Democratic Society, Alinsky hired Staughton Lynd. Lynd had codirected the Mississippi Freedom Schools, a major civil rights effort in 1964 that had been organized by the SNCC (nicknamed "snick"). Lynd joined two veteran Alinsky organizers, Ed Chambers and Dick Harmon, as the core personnel for the Institute.

The connection was a tenuous one from the outset, however. A number of criticisms were emerging from the New Left regarding Alinsky and his approach. They weren't all new. Some of the same criticisms had come previously from some in the Old Left and from some liberals. Some Old Left radicals complained that Alinsky didn't identify capitalism as the core source of injustices in the world. They also thought he was too antagonistic to electoral politics. Depending on the source, Alinsky's political problem was either his failure to speak out for a third party or his unwillingness to endorse the Democratic Party as the lesser of two evils. From the perspective of some liberals, in contrast, Alinsky's emphases on self-interest, conflict tactics, and people power were unnerving. These liberals favored discussion, reason, and an appeal to altruism or at least a more enlightened notion of self-interest. Alinsky's New Left critics thought him too pragmatically focused on power; they wanted a broader moral and analytic critique of American power from him. They also saw his approaches to leadership as too hierarchical, both within the IAF and in the pattern of organization he developed within communities.

Alinsky was usually dismissive of these critics. Let them get their hands dirty in the actualities of organizing, he generally said, and then we'll have a discussion. At the same time, however, he did present nuanced responses to all these critics on occasions when he thought it appropriate. We will explore these responses as we dig deeper into his thinking and work.

"Proxies for People"

Alinsky participated in some of the seminars of the newly established organizer training institute, but his interest had largely shifted to a new effort he called "Proxies for People." He proposed that churches and others give the votes attached to their retirement fund stock portfolios to a new organization that Alinsky would start. With proxies in hand, the organization would begin to make the modern corporation accountable to its communities and workers in addition to major shareholders.

Alinsky had no illusions about the concentration of ownership and control in the modern corporation. But as he said when he used proxies to bring Eastman Kodak to the negotiating table in Rochester, New York, he did think that proxies could provide leverage for antitrust and other political action.[4] The combination of direct action (aimed at the corporation and its key personnel) with political action (aimed at breaking up concentrated economic power) would have been the key to his approach, but this notion of combining these two thrusts was largely lost to later users of the proxy vote tactic, in part because in 1972, before this project could be launched, Saul Alinsky quite unexpectedly keeled over and died of a heart attack.

A New Face and New Emphases

Under Ed Chambers's direction, the organizing institute began, with missteps and experimentation, to institutionalize community organizing. As the hip-pocket operation that was Alinsky's IAF expanded, the new IAF formalized the relationship of both local organizations and organizers to it so that all three stayed connected over time. From this came the idea of organizing "networks." There are now six national networks—the IAF, People Improving Communities through Organizing (PICO), the Direct Action and Research Training Center (DART), the Gamaliel Foundation, National People's Action (NPA), and USAction. Training organizations like Midwest Academy and a number of regional organizations (some representing the reconstitution of ACORN) are also at least partially legacies of Alinsky's original work. There are independent local efforts and regional networks as well. There is also a continuing, though in many cases sadly diminishing, commitment from much of American mainline Protestantism, the Catholic Church, major Jewish institutions, and other religious leaders to Alinsky-tradition community organizing. And one can find a growing presence of his thinking and work throughout the world.

An Alinsky adage was that the vital life span of one of these community organizations was five years. After that point, he believed, it would either decline and die or, in most cases, become simply another co-opted organization. In the late 1970s and early 1980s, the IAF added important new dimensions to community organizing, including Ernesto Cortes Jr.'s revival of San Antonio's Communities Organized for Progress and Services (COPS). The organizers who inherited the IAF introduced major new thinking into the Alinsky approach.

The new IAF vision focused more attention on the internal dynamics and renewal of the congregations IAF was working with. If the organizations that made up a community organizing group were not strong, then the organizing group itself would be weak as well. Further, congregations were vital to restoring an autonomous civil society, separate from political, government, and economic institutions. This approach worked to codify, more than Alinsky had been willing to, the intersections between organizing and Judeo-Christian language and visions, as well as the IAF's overall approach to organizing. For unions or other civil society institutions willing to find parallels, this new approach was applied to them and their traditions and language.

The new thinking was consistent with Alinsky's notion that organizing had to respond continuously to new conditions. The focus on congregational renewal, especially, was driven by several important changes in churches and society that created conditions quite different from those in which Alinsky had developed the BYNC:

- The reforms prompted by Vatican II in the Catholic Church changed relationships among laity, clergy, and its hierarchy, sometimes disrupting the infrastructure of parishes. There was parallel erosion in the internal life of mainline Protestant churches.
- The federal War on Poverty, private foundations, and other external groups poured money into minority communities, creating what Alinsky called "welfare colonialism."[5] As we noted above, these resources supported the emergence of what some have called a "community-based nonprofit industry complex" in impoverished areas.[6] These new nonprofits increasingly crowded out the more autonomous civic associations prominent during Alinsky's BYNC years. While specific programs may have contributed to alleviating poverty and other positive goals, they also had the negative effect of undermining independent civic associational life.[7]
- The erosion of civil society by mass media, an expanding culture of consumerism, dramatic shifts in the economy, and other forces deepened alienation in large sectors of American society.

Most of the other networks picked up on these ideas, modifying or elaborating them according to their own experience and understanding, and followed in the direction taken by the IAF.

Ross and the Organizing Individuals Approach

During this time, Ross went his own way, developing a nationally important cadre of organizers when he teamed with Cesar Chavez to organize farmworkers, and creating a national boycott organization that was essential to their initial successes. The farm worker boycott used Ross's house-meeting approach to build farmworker support organizations in every major metropolitan area of the country. There was a key difference between the boycott approach and the CSO, however. The boycott organizations sought to support the farmworkers' union effort in California and did not attempt to develop local people power vehicles that could address multiple local interests. Ross's trainees and subsequent generations of organizers trained by them now are present in numerous union organizing departments and hold leadership and staff positions in a range of labor organizations. Still others work in a wide variety of advocacy and other community organizations. Boycott training, however, prepared organizers to be mobilizers rather than organizers—a distinction we will later elaborate.

After Alinsky

What we do here is provide key texts from the early years of what is now among the most promising approaches to social change in the country and world—whatever the differences among its practitioners, and whatever their limitations.

Amoeba-like, organizing has spread. If we attempted to describe it we would run the risk of a series of begats, as in the Bible stories of who begat whom. In fact, the intersecting influences are too complex and individual to describe without elaborate detail. In a more general sense, the begats in these pages take form in the writings and ideas of Ernesto Cortes, Arnie Graf, Dolores Huerta, Shel Trapp, Heather Booth, Wade Rathke, and an array of lesser-known organizers, as well as in the documents from the organizations in which they worked.

Learning the Craft

Organizers learn the craft of organizing on the job. As the tradition advances, journeymen and journeywomen organizers recruit and mentor new organizers. Because we do not believe you can learn organizing from books, for those new to organizing this volume is meant as an incitement—not just to go out and organize, but to find a good mentor from whom you can learn the work. In the case of experienced organizers, we hope that these pages will challenge established ways of thinking, provide new ways of understanding old truths, and spark ideas for moving forward into an always uncertain future.

It is important to stress, however, that more than journeyperson work is involved in becoming an effective organizer. Creating or remaking an organizing group is not like opening a new franchise of McDonald's. Given the complexity of human cultures, the unique history of particular communities, and differences among regions and individual human beings, one cannot simply replicate a static model from one location to another, or one time to another. Organizers are also architects, or even painters, working with a human drawing board or canvass. In an organizing project, a skilled organizer—sometimes working with a small group of committed others, sometimes in the recesses of his or her imagination—designs and redesigns the scope and method of the project. Intuition and knowledge about the history, character, culture, politics, and social patterns of the people involved all come into play as an organizer thinks about what is to be built.

Appreciating the Craft

This is also a book for members of the general public who are concerned about the present drift to the right in the political world, the continuing growth of consumer culture, the concentration of wealth and power among an ever-smaller number of people in the world, the erosion of a vital and independent civil society, and the general growth of poverty and powerlessness, especially in the United States.

Barack Obama put "community organizing" on the lips of millions who had never heard of it. That was both a service and disservice to the work. It is good that it be known. It is not good that so few people understand what the "organizing" is and are told (mostly incorrectly) that Obama's electoral apparatus embodies it.

Organizing and Writing

Alinsky often denigrated academics and traditional scholars. "The word 'academic,'" he wrote, "is a synonym for irrelevant."[8] In an interview, he complained about "all the horse manure" the scholars he knew "were handing out about poverty and slums."[9] It is important to understand, however, that he actually came to organizing equipped with the best academic training available at the time. In graduate school at the University of Chicago he worked with the most brilliant scholars of urban poverty in the nation, conducting ethnographic studies of youth gangs, the Capone gang, the justice system, and more. He even wrote articles for academic journals. In Back of the Yards, his vision of community organizing emerged out of a synthesis of an eclectic academic background, key components of the social theory developed by the Chicago School of sociology, his extensive practical experience working in poor communities, and the strategies and tactics of union organizers. He did not hold in contempt all scholarship, then—just most of it. He hated bad scholarship—that is, scholarship that was not rooted in the realities of the people it purported to understand and describe, and glossed "over the misery and the despair."[10] In the ten-day workshops on organizing he led, mostly for clergy and potential organizer recruits, an extensive reading list—with the books on sale at a back table—was among the handouts, with some of the readings required of attendees.

In fact, Alinsky himself often breezily quoted from Heraclites, Plato, Montesquieu, Jefferson, Madison, Tocqueville, and others, and certainly from the Bible—both Old and New Testaments. Reading widely across philosophy, theology, political science, sociology, and other areas, he drew on the best for his training workshops and books. He ran reading groups with local priests and encouraged those he worked with to read broadly as well. One early Alinsky organizer, Lester Hunt, fondly remembers weekly book discussions at a local restaurant where he, Alinsky, and von Hoffman grappled with writings ranging from the sociology of Wirth to the Bible, to Thucydides's Greek histories, to *Alice in Wonderland*, and tried to relate them to organizing.[11] In addition to founding a tradition of community organizing, then, Alinsky modeled a particular kind of thinker and actor—someone who was continuously learning from the world and from what the best writers of his time (and before) could tell him.

Always evaluate after you act, he told organizers. "You, young man," he accused an unreflective activist of the 1960s, "are a pile of undigested actions."[12] It is no surprise, then, that the best of the organizers who came after him kept writing and thinking as they were acting. "What did we learn?" "How can we do this better?" "What are we missing, here?" In the pages that follow, you will find some of the best organizers of a generation engaged in this creative work, exploring what organizing can and should mean for their time.

Uncertainty and Practice

The best writing in a particular tradition often comes at the beginning, or during moments of change and uncertainty. After the initial aspects of any vision are developed, the thinking that follows has a tendency to become procedural; it often degrades into a kind of dogmatism. "This is the way we do things," many organizing manuals say. Those coming after a pathbreaking thinker generally try to clarify what the master was really trying to say, summarizing things down into neat concepts and diagrams. And, in fact, it makes sense that this will happen. "Okay," practitioners often say, "all that complexity may be interesting, but I need to know what to do on Monday morning."

Alinsky himself struggled against this kind of simplification—against efforts to collapse the challenges of organizing down into some simple model or set of tips and tricks. In his second organizing book, *Rules for Radicals*, he included fewer actual examples because he had found that organizers would run into a problem and, instead of coming up with their own solution by responding to the particular demands of their own unique situation, they would riffle through the pages of *Reveille for Radicals* and look for one of Alinsky's tricks. He probably shouldn't have bothered—some might say that this second guide suffers in comparison to the first, lacking some of the vitality of *Reveille*'s stories. The simplification came anyway. Perhaps it is inevitable.

In a recent book reminiscing about his time with Alinsky, von Hoffman complains about this tendency toward dogma in organizing. In a discussion about former vice presidential candidate Sarah Palin, von Hoffman writes that "Saul's understanding of the community organizing business was almost as nebulous as Palin's. For Saul organizing varied in method, shape and scope depending on the times and the circumstances."[13] Speaking of today's standard model of community organizing, von Hoffman says, "I doubt that Alinsky would have much use for it in the changed society we live in. The least doctrinaire of men, he would in all likelihood be tinkering with new ways to realize the old goal of democratic self-rule."[14]

White Men

The Alinsky organizing tradition of the period covered by this book has been critiqued for the dominance of white men. To some extent this is simply a fact of history—Alinsky didn't hire women, and all the major organizers he hired were white. As we note in the section on Heather Booth, the attitudes of Alinsky and some of his lieutenants toward women were sexist. This began to change in the 1970s, however, and by the 1980s the number of women organizers was rising rapidly. The issue with respect to organizers and leaders of color is somewhat more nuanced. Alinsky's groups did hire key organizers of color, most notably Squire Lance, Bob Squires, and Leon Finney at TWO. More importantly, as Alinsky was drawn into African American neighborhoods, African Americans became major leaders of his organizations. These included important figures like Minister Florence of FIGHT and Rev. Arthur Brazier of TWO. In fact, Alinsky seriously considered supporting Brazier in a run for Congress. Further, Alinsky sought partnerships with black-led organizations such as the Southern Christian Leadership Conference and SNCC. However, they didn't come into being.

This book reflects the reality of the tradition during this period. At the same time, however, we include the work of influential leaders of color and that of prominent women leaders and organizers like Cincotta and Huerta. We also discuss the efforts of Booth to make organizing a more productive and welcoming space for women.

A Brief Overview of the Book

The sections of this book each contain chapters related to a particular organizer or historical moment in organizing. Overall, we seek to present this tradition of organizing as an ongoing dialogue and debate.

This introductory chapter is followed by a chapter on the core concepts of organizing in the Alinsky tradition. Also included in this first part is an overview essay, "What Is an Organizer?" (1973) by Richard Rothstein. Part II starts by introducing Nicholas von Hoffman, one of Alinsky's early colleagues and a close friend for the rest of his life. Von Hoffman played a central role in creating one of Alinsky's most important organizations, The Woodlawn Organization (TWO); we devote a chapter to TWO, including excerpts from documents and statements by key TWO leaders. This is followed by an edited version of a memo written mostly by von Hoffman and Hunt, providing a series of answers (1959) to a group of religious leaders who were questioning the IAF approach. The section ends with a classic essay by von Hoffman, "Finding and Making Leaders" (1963), which is still read by organizers today. In this text, von Hoffman describes how organizers should approach the challenge of identifying and developing leaders in impoverished areas.

Moving from Alinsky's home base in Chicago to California, Section B introduces Ross and colleagues like Chavez, Huerta, and Padilla. The centerpiece of this section is Chapter 8, which draws together excerpts from transcripts of 1960 CSO and 1975 UFW trainings to demonstrate how Ross introduced leaders to the house-meeting approach to organizing. This is followed by an essay by Miller on Chavez and his efforts to develop an association and then a union of farmworkers. The section concludes with a chapter that provides excerpts from texts by others who worked with Chavez, Ross, Huerta, and Padilla.

Section C shifts to the work of Gaudette, another colleague of Alinsky. An extensive chapter gives an overview of Gaudette's vision, drawing on a life history interview and interviews with those who worked with him. This is followed by a chapter on Shel Trapp and Gale Cincotta. Trapp, a colleague of Gaudette, fine-tuned and refined a block club approach to organizing, and Cincotta was the key leader who worked with Trapp. A chapter by Stan Holt is titled "What Every Community Organization Should Know about Community Development" (1975). The section concludes with an interview with John Baumann, who helped create PICO in California after working with Gaudette in Chicago.

The next two sections bring us back to the IAF and its post-Alinsky activities. Section D focuses on Dick Harmon and reprints a still widely read piece on organizing and education, "Making an Offer We Can't Refuse" (1973). Section E looks more broadly at the work done under the leadership of the first post-Alinsky IAF director, Ed Chambers, and includes a range of documents. As we elaborate elsewhere, Chambers led the transformation of an IAF that operated out of Alinsky's briefcase, as it were, into a major network of more than fifty organizations in the United States and a growing number elsewhere in the world, with dozens of talented organizers. He was, in the best sense, an "organization man." "Organizing for Family and Congregation" (1978) first laid out the IAF's post-Alinsky vision in a comprehensive way. Other chapters include a 1993 interview with Ernesto Cortes, a 1995 speech on organizing and confrontation by Johnny Ray Youngblood, and a 1990 manifesto by IAF organizers.

In Part III, we turn to two figures who drew on but also diverged from Alinsky in different ways. Section A looks at the work of Heather Booth, which combined aspects of Alinsky's approach to organizing with insights from the social movements of the time—especially the women's movement. The key document in this section is chapter 1 of *Direct Action Organizing: A Handbook for Women* (1974). The first version of the Midwest Academy organizing manual, *Direct Action Organizing* explicitly addressed ways to integrate the women's movement and women into organizing.

Section B turns to Wade Rathke, who created ACORN after working in the Massachusetts Welfare Rights Organization (MWRO). Rathke's mentor in the MWRO was Bill Pastreich, who had learned from Ross in a Syracuse University–sponsored organizing effort and stayed connected with him afterwards. Pastreich drew on aspects of Ross's organizing in the MWRO, and with Rhoda Linton developed what became known as the Boston Model. As the welfare rights organizing movement began to decline, Rathke went to Arkansas to create something new, which became ACORN. It focused on organizing individuals by knocking on doors one by one. We reprint "ACORN Community Organizing Model" (1973), an early document written by Rathke that lays out his understanding of how ACORN organizing should proceed.

We wrap up with concluding statements that look back over the entire book, point to recurring themes and issues, and muse about what these writings have to teach us today about organizing.

Note that many of the documents have been abridged because of space limitations. We use ellipses to indicate text removed from written documents, but given the number of necessary edits, we have not employed them for text deleted from or moved within previously unpublished interviews.

Notes

1. T. George Harris, *The Professional Activist: A Conversation with Ghetto Organizer Saul Alinsky* (Tucson, AZ: Educational Research Group, 1969), cassette tape.
2. Saul Alinsky, interview by Eric Norden, *Playboy* 19, no. 3 (1972); republished as "Empowering People, Not Elites: Interview with Saul Alinsky," *Progress Report*, October 23, 2003–September 4, 2004, *www.progress.org*.
3. *The Democratic Promise: Saul Alinsky and His Legacy*, produced by Bob Hercules and Bruce Orenstein (Chicago: Media Process Educational Films, 1999), DVD.
4. Sanford D. Horwitt, *Let Them Call Me Rebel: Saul Alinsky—His Life and Legacy* (New York: Vintage, 1992).
5. Horwitt, *Rebel*, 488.
6. See, for example, INCITE! Women of Color Against Violence, *The Revolution Will Not Be Funded: Beyond the Non-Profit Industrial Complex* (Cambridge, MA: South End Press, 2007).
7. Our argument is about associational life, and very different from conservative assertions that the existence of welfare encouraged dependency.
8. Saul Alinsky, "Introduction to the Vintage Edition," in *Reveille for Radicals* (New York: Vintage, 1969), ix.
9. Alinsky, interview by Norden.
10. Ibid.
11. Lester Hunt, interview by Aaron Schutz, March 14, 2013.
12. *Democratic Promise*.
13. Nicholas von Hoffman, *Radical: A Portrait of Saul Alinsky* (New York: Nation Books, 2010), 22.
14. Ibid., 30.

2

Saul Alinsky and His Core Concepts

■

MIKE MILLER

Controversy accompanied Saul Alinsky wherever he went, and he thrived on it. Indeed, he cultivated it. What follows is both my experience of Saul—stories I possess because I was there, he told me about it, or someone close to him told me about it—and an introduction to his core concepts.[1] This chapter begins with introduction to Alinsky, the person, and how he did his work. I knew him from 1960 until the time of his death, and worked for him from 1966 through the first half of 1967. The chapter then turns to a discussion of the core concepts that oriented Alinsky's work.

An Idealist and a Child of His Times

Alinsky became a man during the Great Depression of the 1930s, and was swept up in its social movements. Most importantly, the Congress of Industrial Organizations (CIO) was successfully organizing unskilled workers in the country's major industries.

Opposition to the growth of fascism in Europe was growing. Support for racial equality and other causes began to simmer. His understanding of how the world worked, and how to change it, was born of these experiences along with his doctoral sociological studies at the University of Chicago and his experiences as a researcher and criminal sociologist with juvenile delinquency and crime.

An important participant in the social change efforts of the time was the organized political left, particularly the Communist Party. He encountered and worked with Communists, socialists, capitalists, small "d" democrats, and religionists who didn't identify with these categories but thought of justice in theological and moral terms. And he worked with people who didn't have a label, but just wanted to do the right thing. In their different ways, they believed that we all are our brother's keeper, have an obligation to work for the common good, or are members of the working class and have to stand in solidarity with one another.

Saul Alinsky was both a person of ideas and of action. Both were guided by a passion for justice, so before looking at his core ideas, I'd like to give the reader an appreciation of who he was.

Msgr. John "Jack" Egan was a leading Catholic apostle of democracy and social and economic justice who was a close associate of Alinsky's. At Alinsky's Chicago memorial service, Egan said, "As a very young man, Saul Alinsky imposed upon himself the obligation of caring—for the poor, the dispossessed, the disenfranchised, those discriminated against. . . ."

Egan once asked him, "Why?"

"I can't stand to see people get pushed around" was the simple answer.

"What stands out in my mind when I think of Saul," Egan continued, "is his integrity, his fidelity. Throughout all his life and all his work, he believed in people. . . . He was faithful to that belief in season and out of season."

Imagining Alinsky facing the Lord, Egan had God saying to Saul, "You saw me despised and you treated me with dignity. You saw me powerless to secure a job and decent housing, and you helped me organize with my brothers and sisters to secure my rights as a human being and as a citizen; you saw me still enslaved, and you lifted my eyes to freedom and self-determination. You saw me being pushed around, and you cared constantly."[2]

Those who saw Saul Alinsky as a cynic are simply wrong.

Back of the Yards and the Pre-World War II Period

In Back of the Yards, the slum neighborhood adjoining the Chicago stockyards, Alinsky launched his life as a community organizer. Here I want to focus attention on five people: Bishop Bernard James Sheil, Joe Meegan, Herb March, Marshall Field III, and John L. Lewis.

In the broader Chicago context, the most important person was Sheil, who became an auxiliary bishop of the Chicago archdiocese in 1928. An outspoken advocate of social justice and supporter of organized labor, he put his money where his mouth was. Told by a Catholic banker in Chicago that he would never become an archbishop if he spoke at a labor rally to be addressed by John L. Lewis, head of the CIO, he spoke. Sheil served under Archbishop George William Mundelein, himself committed to the union movement. Mundelein said:

> The trouble with us [the Church] in the past has been that we were too often allied or drawn into an alliance with the wrong side. Selfish employers of labor have flattered the Church by calling it the great conservative force, and then called upon it to act as a police force while they paid but a pittance of wage to those who work for them. I hope that day has gone by. Our place is beside the workingman. They are our people, they build our churches, our priests come from their sons.[3]

The Chicago archdiocese was one of the most liberal in the United States.

In the Back of the Yards neighborhood, Joe Meegan was everything that Alinsky wasn't: locally rooted (supervisor of recreation at Davis Park); Irish, Catholic, and well-connected in the church. (Alinsky met Sheil through Meegan's monsignor brother). Meegan's horizon was circumscribed by Back of the Yards—for fifty years he was executive director of the Back of the Yards Neighborhood Council.[4] Alinsky, on the other hand, didn't live in Back of the Yards, and he was a nonpracticing Jew who wanted to work in a neighborhood rife with anti-Semitism. Before connecting with Meegan, Alinsky had few ties to the Catholic Church.

During this time, there was a union organizing effort in the neighborhood's huge slaughterhouses and packinghouses. The key person Alinsky met there was Herb March, who was also an open member of the Communist Party. Like many radicals of his day, to become an organizer March had dropped out of college and become a blue-collar worker. He won his fellow workers' respect for his courage (he was almost assassinated during the union's organizing drive), his intelligence, and his consistent commitment to them. The United Packinghouse Workers of America (UPWA)—the union that emerged from the organizing committee and for which March worked full time in an elected position—was one of the most committed to racial equality of the industrial unions, all of which were publicly opposed to segregation and discrimination.

Marshall Field III was an heir to the Marshall Field department store fortune, a major publisher (including of the *Chicago Sun-Times*), an investment banker, a race-horse owner, a philanthropist, and a founding member of the board of directors of Alinsky's Industrial Areas Foundation (IAF). It was his financial contribution to the IAF that launched the organization, and it was central to Alinsky's effort to spread his work across the country.

John L. Lewis led the 1930s organization of industrial workers in the United States. Nothing in our nation's history since has equaled the people power of those unions. They were part of a social movement that engaged in massive mobilizations of the disenfranchised; at the same time, they were powerful organizations whose leaders negotiated with chief executive officers of major corporations, the president of the United States, and thousands of other politicians. John L. Lewis was one of Alinsky's major teachers.

When automobile workers staged an occupation of a major General Motors (GM) plant, Chevrolet #4 at Flint, Michigan, the liberal governor of the state threatened to use the National Guard to eject the workers. Lewis confronted him. In his peroration, which contrasted justice with law and order, he reminded the governor that both the governor's father and grandfather were Irish revolutionaries. Lewis said that he would stand in front of his union men, telling the governor that "when you order your troops to fire, mine will be the first breast that those bullets will strike. And as my body falls from that window to the ground, you listen to the voice of your grandfather as he whispers in your ear, 'Frank, are you sure you are doing the right thing?'"[5]

The order to vacate was not issued. The next day, GM capitulated. The sit-downers won. In his biography of Lewis, Alinsky wrote, "When the agreement was reached,

General Motors' John Thomas Smith said, 'Well, Mr. Lewis, you beat us, but I'm not going to forget it. I just want to tell you that one of these days we'll come back and give you the kind of whipping that you and your people will never forget.'"[6]

Alinsky concluded that an agreement is only as good as your power to enforce it.

Democratic People Power

Around 1970, GM began giving the United Auto Workers (UAW) that whipping; it continues today. Detroit's recent bankruptcy makes vivid two lessons: first, the conflict between the haves and the have-nots is a continuing struggle. If you fail to recognize that, and go to sleep after winning some concessions, you will win battles but lose the war. Since the pattern of organizational life seems to be that every generation has to make its own revolution, I hope this book will contribute to a new generation non-violently doing just that.

The second lesson is more difficult to learn, and even more difficult to implement: people power is not simply about winning campaigns; it is about changing the relations of power—which means in the case of the present plutocracy that really governs the United States, ways must be found to break it up, regulate it, or expropriate it. We must spread the ownership of the corporate institutions it now governs to some combination of consumers, workers, communities, government, and a much wider base of investors than those who now control things. We need not have a formulaic idea of what that will look like. But we should be talking about the need for alternatives, and what they *might* look like.

Alinsky had a fairly easy-to-grasp set of core ideas. Their simplicity makes them attractive. They are simple, but not easy to implement.

Putting the Pieces Together on the Ground: Alinsky and Meegan

I don't know the sequence of how Alinsky got Meegan, March, and Sheil to form the unlikely alliance that led to the Back of the Yards Neighborhood Council.

With Meegan, the conversation would have been something like this (to be clear, I'm making this up. I was two years old when this happened!):

ALINSKY: Joe, you've been telling me about the horrible conditions that you're seeing here in Back of the Yards. I've got an idea to do something about them. You interested?
MEEGAN: Of course!

[*Alinsky then would have outlined with Meegan the prospect of an organization that brought together all the organizations, small and large, of the people living in Back of the*

Yards—the most important of them being the Catholic parishes of the neighborhood, and their pastors.]

MEEGAN: You can't do that, Saul, they all hate each other.

ALINSKY: I know that, but they all seem to trust you.

MEEGAN: So what am I going to say to them? They know their people are hurting. But they're more consumed by their hatred of one another than by the suffering of their members. They all have food pantries, clothes closets, and other handout programs. They think they're doing enough.

ALINSKY: That might all be true, but they also know that they're losing their people to the union, which they think is a Communist outfit. They preach against it every Sunday, and on Monday another parishioner joins the union. We can give them a vehicle in which the church has its own voice to address these issues.

MEEGAN: How are we going to get these conservatives to become liberals?

ALINSKY: They're not. This is where your brother comes in. Let's meet with him, and get him to introduce me to Bishop Sheil. With Sheil on our side, we'll get the cardinal. With the two of them behind us, the pastors can't openly oppose us. And once we get inside the parishes, we can build up support that will push the pastors to come on board—or have to deal with a lot of anger from their own people.

Oh, and by the way, we need to ask the PWOC [Packinghouse Workers Organizing Committee] to be part of this as well.

MEEGAN: What are you saying, Saul? They've got an open Commie as their key guy here!

ALINSKY: I know. But Sheil admires John L. Lewis and the CIO. I know Lewis from volunteering with the coal miners' union [which Lewis headed]; I've interviewed him on several occasions. If the PWOC is good enough for Lewis, it will be good enough for Sheil.

Here's another thing: if the Catholic Church in Back of the Yards doesn't get on board to do something about poverty here, the church is going to end up losing its people to the Communists. And you can't do anything serious about poverty if you limit yourself to neighborhood organizing. Unionizing the slaughterhouses where most of their people work is a key piece in this struggle.

By the way, I've been talking with Herb March, the Communist organizer over there at PWOC. Here's what he said to me: "The Catholics aren't going to support us. They're hand-and-glove in bed with the meatpackers. Hell, Saul, these fat cats are in their Gold Coast parishes, give major bucks to their charities, are trustees at their universities—you name it."[7]

MEEGAN: He said that? We'll see about that. This archdiocese takes the social encyclicals seriously.[8] Yeah, Saul, let's see my brother and see if we can pull this thing off.

Putting the Pieces Together: Alinsky and March

While this conversation was taking place (more elaborately than I've imagined it), Alinsky would also have been talking with March. I met Herb March and his wife in the late 1980s after he had retired as a union organizer and leader. While he had left the Communist Party, he had not abandoned any of his beliefs in unions, democracy, or the necessity for basic change in the United States for social and economic justice. I also corresponded with his son in the course of putting this book together. Both father and son described a close and warm relationship between March and Alinsky.

Another imagined conversation:

ALINSKY: Herb, you've been telling me about the impasse in the battle with the meatpackers, and how worried you are that the strike might fail. Do you think the possibilities for victory would be increased if you could have support from the Catholic parishes in Back of the Yards?

MARCH: Does two plus two equal four? Of course it would, Saul. But you and I know that these old reactionary pastors aren't going to do a damn thing to support the union. Either they come from the old country themselves, or their parents do, and they're all tied into the anti-Communism of the churches of Eastern Europe.[9]

Plus, I'm tired of their bullshit. I'm a democrat—small "d" version—and I respect the people who work in the industry. They know that. I've earned their trust. I don't have to listen to this anti-Communist crap.

I know for a fact that they preach against the union in their homilies; our members complain about it. And they argue with their wives about it. I'm their favorite target! You're not going to get them to be in the same room with me, Saul.[10]

ALINSKY: Yeah, I know all that. But let's say I could get the Catholics to agree to meet with you and your organizing committee. If I can do that, I want to know that you and your committee will be on your best behavior. No airing of history; no complaints about their homilies. Will you agree to that?

MARCH: Nothing ventured, nothing gained. Why not? Sure, Saul, go ahead. You're a clever guy, Saul, but I don't think you can pull this off.[11]

One week later:

ALINSKY: Well, Herb, they want to meet. And you know what I discovered? Some of them admire you. They think you're a decent guy.

(In *Reveille for Radicals*, Alinsky proudly admits to making up small lies in the service of big justice. In his workshops, he frequently noted that the Declaration of Independence didn't list all the things King George had done for the colonies. "You know," and here I paraphrase, "there's also lying by omission. If the writers of the Declaration had listed all the things the British had done for the colonists, do you think they would have laid down their plows, left their farms, kissed their wives or girlfriends good-bye, and enlisted in Washington's army?")[12]

With both Meegan and March, Alinsky used a combination of flattery and persuasion, appealing to personal and organizational self-interest, deeply held values, and the confidence in him he had cultivated. For Bishop Sheil, Alinsky provided a way for the bishop and cardinal to put their commitment to the church's social and economic justice teachings "on the ground" and to develop a vehicle for progressive social action in Back of the Yards in which they were equals with the secular left.

The idea Alinsky projected of the churches, the union, and everybody else working together for the common good in a new organization was appealing because the projected neighborhood council was separate from the union but included it. If the church was merely supporting the union, it would be a Johnny-come-lately to an organization already led by left-wingers, including an open member of the Communist Party.

With these three people, and his preexisting relationship with the CIO's John L. Lewis, Alinsky accomplished the central objectives at the beginning of one of his organizing projects—establishing legitimacy in the community that is targeted for organizing, and getting a broad base of initial support within that community for the idea of a mass organization.

The Back of the Yards Neighborhood Council (BYNC) did support the strike, and its support was important to the winning of union recognition and a contract with the employers. The BYNC also won relief jobs, free school meals for children, health care, and much more. Its breadth of support forced the Chicago political machine to negotiate with it.

It was after the nationally renowned success of the BYNC that Alinsky met Marshall Field III, a multimillionaire.[13] Field had a liberal political bent. His newspapers' editorial policies reflected this. Field's funding allowed Alinsky to spread the work he had started in Back of the Yards to other parts of the country. Field provided a core budget for the IAF so Alinsky could travel and agitate for the formation of local projects elsewhere—in these early years for the most part in the Midwest—particularly where there was a combination of a favorable Catholic diocese and a local or organizing presence of the packinghouse workers union.

Fast Forward to the 1960s

By the 1960s, Alinsky was deeply involved with mainline Protestant denominations as well as with Catholic dioceses across the country. He lectured in public forums and at major colleges and seminaries, and led ten-day community organizing workshops for clergy and lay leaders. The workshops were typically organized by some combination of inner-city clergy leaders and denominational staff and executives responsible for urban work and/or social and economic justice ministry. Typically, they had at least the tacit approval of their denomination's equivalent of a Catholic bishop (though none had quite as much authority). By the mid-1960s, almost all the major American mainline Protestant denominations had made commitments to legitimize and fund Alinsky's approach to community organizing.

The next section of this book features The Woodlawn Organization (TWO), the first African American organization that Alinsky put together. Here I turn to the second—FIGHT in Rochester.

Rochester, New York

In Rochester, New York, Rev. Herbert D. White served as the director of the Board of Urban Ministry for eight Protestant denominations that were members of the Council of Churches. He got their agreement to invite Alinsky to Rochester in the wake of 1964 riots in the black community. These were mostly white denominations, however, even though most of them had some presence in the black community.

The invitation initially didn't sit well with the historically black churches. One of their key pastors was Minister Franklin Florence, of the Church of Christ. Florence, an associate of Malcolm X, a militant, and in important respects a black nationalist, was initially suspicious of Alinsky.

Rochester's major news media met Alinsky at the airport upon his arrival. Asked what he was going to do there, he replied that he didn't know if the IAF was coming to Rochester (this was his first time in town). He then characterized Rochester as "Smugtown, USA"; Eastman Kodak was the city's dominant corporation and largest employer, and Alinsky described the relationship of Kodak and Rochester as similar to the plantation relationships of slaveowners and blacks in the Deep South. The media were outraged. Alinsky was bombarded with attacks. He responded with ridicule, one of his favorite devices, and said, "As far as I know the only thing Kodak has done on the race issue in America is to introduce color film."[14]

Why did Alinsky do this? Did he simply enjoy insulting the establishment? No doubt! But there was more to it than that. Within days, Florence was having second thoughts: "If the white power structure hates this guy so much, maybe he has something to offer us." He checked Alinsky out with Malcolm X, who told him, "Alinsky is the best organizer in the United States."[15] Why was a black nationalist seeming to endorse Alinsky, an avowed integrationist? Because in Chicago's Woodlawn neighborhood, Alinsky had put together a black power organization before the term "black power" was a slogan. Indeed, TWO's slogan was "self-determination through community power."

Alinsky's attack on Rochester's white power structure combined agitation with provocation. As he goaded the enemy, the principle at work was "my enemy's enemy may be my friend." Florence proceeded on that basis, deciding to welcome Alinsky's organization.

That wasn't all. White and Alinsky cultivated Catholic support as well. White introduced Alinsky to Fr. P. David Finks. Already committed to civil rights, Finks initially didn't know if he supported Alinsky. He had been dismissed as chaplain of the Motherhouse of the Rochester Sisters of Mercy because of his liberal theology, and assigned to an inner-city parish. The dismissal and reassignment "had a profound effect on him and his future."[16] Coincidence and accident played a role: Fulton J. Sheen became Rochester's bishop and appointed Finks vicar of urban ministry—a position from which he worked closely with White, Alinsky, and FIGHT. White developed a relationship of trust with Finks, which is what opened the door to the meeting with Alinsky.

Finks and White established the ecumenical Joint Office of Urban Ministry, which was designed to "help urban and suburban communities organize around economic and political issues which affected them."[17] Finks subsequently played a national role in winning Catholic support for Alinsky, and later wrote a biography of Alinsky. In a letter to the Ford Foundation, Finks stated, "He had a crucial effect on my life and way of doing things."[18]

Kansas City, Missouri

Another example of what Alinsky called "organizational jiujitsu" comes from my own experience. The Kansas City organizing project had similar origins to Rochester's. Presbyterian minister Ken Waterman and a key Catholic diocesan priest staff member (whose name I no longer remember) were the initial supporters of an IAF organizing project. A white pastor of an inner-city, predominantly black church, Rev. Waterman already had relationships with many black ministers and was able to enlist them in the effort. But an important black clergyman was a holdout: Rev. John W. Williams was pastor of the large St. Stephen's (American) Baptist Church, highly respected in both the black and white communities of Kansas City, and a leader in the National and World Councils of Churches. Without Williams's participation, a black community organizing effort would not be as strong.

A group of black and white inner-city pastors worked for months to develop a broad-based invitation, but Alinsky told them, "I'm not coming to Kansas City unless Rev. Williams is part of the invitation." Deeply disappointed, they asked him, "What can we do?" Alinsky conspired with them; the outcome was a delegation of black clergymen visiting Williams and asking him to have an individual meeting with Alinsky.

What Alinsky realized was that Williams's stature in the black community had not been sufficiently recognized in the original invitation process; in a word, he had been bypassed—if not literally, then substantively. Now Williams was being offered a private meeting with Alinsky at which the two of them would get to know each other. Alinsky would respond to questions Williams might have, and, most importantly, there would be implicit acknowledgment of Williams's importance in Kansas City's African American community. As a result of that meeting, a deal was struck: Williams endorsed the project, and one of his assistant pastors, Rev. Solon Fox, was nominated by the preconvention nominating committee to be the new organization's treasurer—a sign of the trust the organization had in Williams and St. Stephens. I learned of the deal when I was briefed on Kansas City before going to work there to direct what by then was the Council for United Action (CUA).

There was another side to the Williams lesson. Faced with a broad-based delegation of fellow black clergy, he would have been hard-pressed to say no. Holding an internationally known clergyman accountable to the larger black community was an application of the general democratic principles that were central to Alinsky's thinking.[19] In historically African American congregations, especially Baptist ones, the pastor is a star figure. But he is also vulnerable to dismissal if he angers the congregation, especially key leaders. As a result, black pastors learn how to build protections around themselves while seeking roles that will enhance their reputation with their congregants. It was important to be aware of this balancing act when seeking to hold these leaders more accountable to their own constituencies.

While I was in Kansas City, we put together a jobs campaign similar to Rev. Jesse Jackson's Operation PUSH (People United to Serve Humanity) in Chicago. There were no lay people on the committee, which met at 10:00 a.m. on a weekday at St. Stephen's Church—a time when many potential lay members would be at work. There was one exception. A black caucus at the General Motors Fisher Body assembly plant was a member of CUA, and a number of its members worked the swing shift, which would have made it possible for them to come to a morning meeting. I tried to get them to simply show up at one of the meetings, knowing that the clergy wouldn't have asked them to leave, and they probably would soon have found themselves welcome. My IAF supervisor and mentor, Ed Chambers, pushed me to make it happen, but I was unable to get the black caucus members to do it, despite the fact that one of the major reasons for the existence of their own organization was to create greater accountability within the UAW and end discriminatory practices within it. However, this is an example of the IAF's efforts to go beyond simply organizing existing leaders.

Another key lesson I learned in Kansas City: the black churches, especially the historically black denominations, were deeply suspicious of the Catholics. They viewed Catholic schools and their recruitment of black inner-city students as a Trojan horse opening the door for Catholic churches to "raid" the black congregations' member families. But by the time I got there, the associate pastor of a Catholic inner-city parish was the chairman of CUA's all-important Jobs and Employment Committee. The experience of working together had diminished black mistrust of the Catholics.

Core Concepts

I now turn to the central ideas that guided what Alinsky did. I call him a radical democrat. At times he called himself a radical, and he sometimes used the term "populist." He also had a streak of conservatism in his appreciation for local traditions and values.

Values

Alinsky's work was rooted in two intellectual/theoretical/moral sources. First, the small "d" democratic tradition: this philosophy, which goes back to Jeffersonian and Athenian democracy, postulated the righteousness and wisdom of "the people" governing themselves, and their capacity—*given the right conditions*—to do so.[20] The second source was the moral, social, economic justice teachings of Judaism and Christianity. As other immigrant groups with different religious beliefs became part of these community organizations, parallel teachings from Muslims and Buddhists became part of the organizing values framework.

Alinsky thought that given the opportunity, most people would do the wise and moral thing most of the time. They would do the moral thing because as active citizens they would recognize and respect the rights of others and their responsibility toward them, and because groups whose rights they might violate also had the power to defend themselves. (Checks and balances were essential; Alinsky did not have a rosy, uncritical view of human nature.) And, if and when they did something unwise (from a policy point of view), they would be able to correct it in the course of their ongoing processes of self-government.

He saw his work as creating the opportunity for self-government. At their core, the organizations he built were vehicles for the expression of democratic citizenship. He believed that without such vehicles, people were susceptible to demagogues, the pursuit of the narrowest and most parochial interests, and to other ills that afflict and undermine democracy.

He also was deeply appreciative of local traditions and values. He immersed himself in them when he organized. He thought the only way to communicate with people was within their experience, and you couldn't do that if you didn't learn how they thought or talked, or the stories they told.

The Vision

According to Alinsky, a democratic society is one in which people participate in voluntary associations that give voice to their values and interests. Together, these associations constitute civil society. These groups, which include religious, labor, identity, interest, and other organizations, are participatory in character and funded by their members (via tithing, collections, dues, raffles, annual dinners, events, etc.).

This participation and funding from the bottom up ensures that the groups are expressive of the values and interests of the members, and that leaders will be accountable to members.

Life in a democratic society is a continuing process of negotiation among groups over what constitutes the common good. Public policies come out of a process of discussion, discernment, deliberation, debate, negotiation, and compromise within one's own group and between groups that have relatively equal power. To Alinsky, the central feature of a democratic society is a vibrant civil society with relative equality of power among groups that represent different interests and constituencies. Without this equality, the forms of democracy might exist (such as free elections and competing political parties), but the substance won't—as in the present concentration of real power in the American plutocracy.

While Alinsky's ideal was this democratic pluralism, he understood that it was not American reality. On the contrary, it was in order to realize the ideal that present concentrations of wealth and power had to be challenged, and divisions among the American people—particularly that of race and ethnicity—had to be overcome. People who shared his values had to learn how to operate effectively in the real world—or as many organizers think of it, the world as it *is* as distinct from the world as we would like it to be.

Strategies of the Powerful

The major obstacle to justice and righteousness prevailing in the United States is the way power is organized. "Power," Alinsky said, "gravitates to two poles: organized money and organized people." Where there is a concentration of unaccountable power the core conditions of the democratic ideal are violated, whether the power is in the hands of a political machine boss in a local precinct, a gang-ridden neighborhood, an employer whose workers lack an effective union, a landlord whose tenants lack effective voice, or a multinational corporation that moves jobs to cheap labor markets where there aren't effective unions in order to maximize profit.

Unaccountable power seeks to maintain and extend itself because that is how it assures the privileges of power. These privileges are both financial (income and wealth) and social (status and prestige). Alinsky was fond of quoting Lord Acton: "Power tends to corrupt. And absolute power tends to corrupt absolutely."[21]

A major characteristic of American society is the concentration of unaccountable power in the hands of a very few. At the national level, these few are principally to be found in American financial and corporate institutions and in key political positions in the federal government. Local patterns vary, but if you follow the money you will soon find them out.

Effectively challenging the unaccountable concentration of power, wherever it may be found, requires organizing people to use their capacity for collective political, economic, and social action to reclaim power that is, in democratic theory, rightfully theirs. But this apparently obvious response to the corruption of power is more easily said than done.

Incumbent power uses a variety of strategies and tactics to preserve its privileges and prerogatives. At one end of the spectrum are cultural/ideological strategies, whose function is to convince people that the way things are is the way they ought to be, and indeed must be, and that tampering in any basic way with the status quo will only make things worse.

At the other end is repression, including violence.

In between are a variety of tools to undermine or co-opt any person or group that might challenge the status quo.

Incumbent power typically begins by ignoring any protest that comes "from below." Efforts to weaken and destroy an organizing effort are likely to follow, including the use of various "divide and conquer" approaches. Co-optation—through appointments, grants, jobs, and advisory bodies with no power—is a favorite. At various times in American history, the police (ranging from the FBI to local cops to privately hired security forces) infiltrated and sought to disrupt organizations. Paid goons beat up organizers. African American history in the United States is filled with examples of leaders and activists being murdered by both agents of the government and private parties.

However, incumbent power is not monolithic. Within it are conflicts and divisions that make it possible for effective "people power" to itself use "divide and conquer." Careful power analyses by people power organizations seek to identify and take advantage of these weaknesses in their adversaries.

Powerlessness and Overcoming It

The experience and reality of powerlessness is democracy's great weakness. When participation doesn't translate into results, when voting results in politicians who promise x and do y, when folk wisdom says, "You can't fight the powers that be," or "Money is what talks," or "You can't beat city hall," democracy is in danger. The challenge is to overcome this sense of powerlessness. But powerlessness isn't something you can talk people out of. People have to *experience* their way out of it. Thus:

- The experience used to engage a person has to happen now, not off in the distance.
- The sought-after result has to be specific so that the skeptical listener can picture the outcome. For example, the goal has to be not "good schools" but x, y, and z results at the local elementary school attended by someone's seven-year-old.
- The victory must be achieved in a fairly short amount of time—especially in the initial stages of organizing, when skepticism and doubt are the constantly lurking enemies of participation.

The initial issues undertaken by a people power organization have to meet Alinsky's criteria of "immediate, specific, and winnable." A problem is turned into an issue when it becomes a proposal to someone with the power to do something about it. If she or he says yes, you've got a win; if she or he says no, you've got a fight that you can win.

Personalize the opposition. Only *individuals* within institutions, or owners like landlords, can decide to change policies, practices, and structures. Further, only *individuals* can react to a proposal for change, not buildings or street corners. Carefully research who the appropriate target is, and then freeze it, and either get an agreement or polarize the situation so you can engage in battle. When a reasonable proposal is presented and rejected, or when a decision-maker refuses to meet with the people, the people's response is anger. Anger is an emotion that can lead to positive action.

All *powerful* organizing is rooted *locally*—whether in a factory, a religious congregation, a neighborhood, or in a particular interest or identity group. That's where people regularly see each other, and where they can share stories of frustration and hopes, and begin new relationships or deepen ones that already exist. They can gather face-to-face to create a new organization or revitalize an existing one. From a solid base "at the bottom," delegates can represent organized people on regional, state, and national bodies, or on a large campaign committee, encompassing diverse constituencies and interests.

Recognize at the outset that while conflict is essential, so is compromise. People power demonstrates to a decision-maker that you can adversely affect his or her interests. These interests vary according to the target, and might be profits, votes, stability, or reputation, or a combination of them. Having demonstrated your power, however, it's time to negotiate an agreement. And if the agreement is going to be implemented in good faith, you need to leave room for your adversary to save face.

Continuing organization is essential to evaluate and monitor progress. An unenforced or inadequately enforced agreement isn't worth the piece of paper it's written on. Further, with continued victories the organization should grow—both in numbers and in the competence and self-confidence of its leaders. As people power increases, more significant proposals that get at broader injustices can be made. The cycle of conflict and compromise is a continuing one.

Mass-Based Organization

Small "d" democratic and highly participatory mass-based organizations are the tools with which the vast majority of the people can claim the power that is rightfully theirs. To ensure widespread participation, Alinsky and the IAF's organizing efforts shared some important features.

Most important, the organization was internally democratic and highly participatory. At annual meetings (called "conventions" or "congresses"), delegates adopted and subsequently revised a constitution and bylaws, approved policies and priorities, and elected officers to govern the organization between conventions. A monthly or quarterly delegate assembly served as the interim voice of the membership between annual meetings. A weekly meeting of a large elected leadership body guided the organization between delegate meetings. In weekly committee meetings organized around different interests expressed in the organization—including bad schools, poor housing, cheating merchants, un- and underemployment, neighborhood crime, police harassment and brutality, and more—people gathered to formulate proposals for action. These committees reported to, and sometimes required approval by, between-convention leadership bodies.

The internal democracy of the organization taught people to negotiate with one another as they sought to arrive at a common program they could all live with—something I call a "lowest significant common denominator" program—one that includes something important for everyone, but nothing that deeply offends anyone either. This internal democracy included election of the organizational leadership to guide them down the path to realize their program.

The organizations were built on local values and traditions, within the context of the larger umbrella of the American democratic tradition. Being rooted in local life and tradition ensured that the organization spoke for the majority of the people of the constituency in which it was organized. The broader commitment to American democracy expanded the horizon of local leaders.

The organizations were both multi-issue and multi-constituency. These are two sides of the same coin. In order to fully express the concerns and interests of a community, an organization had to encompass in its membership the various constituencies of the community—i.e., different religious, ethnic, interest, age and other groupings. But for these differing constituencies to invest themselves fully in the organization, it had to be multi-issue. The young parents whose child is about to enter elementary school have different priorities and interests than the retired couple whose children no longer live in the area. The presently employed packinghouse worker has different priorities and interests than an unemployed laborer. The small business owner has different concerns than those of a welfare recipient.

The multi-strategy character and tactics of Alinsky's work is what is most known about him. By careful analysis of the vulnerable points of adversaries, a people power organization can discover weaknesses it can exploit. The threat of denial of a substantial number of votes might affect a politician but be irrelevant to a business that, on the other hand, might be very vulnerable to a boycott. A public bureaucracy might feel a threat to its annual appropriation if large numbers of citizens publicly show their anger at its lack of responsiveness.

But it is not adversaries as abstract entities that are the focus of action. Rather, actual individuals with the power to make decisions are targeted for action. Institutions are not faceless entities. There are within them decision-makers who can respond to proposals made by a people power organization. Thus it is not only the general contours of incumbent power that must be understood, but the very specific details of individuals in positions of authority. Careful power structure analyses are required if the people power organization is to be effective.

The people power organization is highly partisan about its values and interests. At the same time, it is not affiliated with, nor does it formally endorse, a political party. If it is successful, it gets politicians to adopt its program rather than the other way around. In order to make their weight felt in the political arena, people power organizations developed a variety of means to let the electorate know where candidates stood on a given organization's program or the priorities within it. Targeted voter education, accompanied by massive voter registration and get-out-the-vote efforts, demonstrated people power at the polls. In numerous instances, this approach made a measurable difference in electoral outcomes.

The early Alinsky organizations, except for the Community Service Organization (for reasons elsewhere discussed in this book), took the form of an "organization of organizations" ("O of O") that included long-standing and widely known churches, nationality groups, small business or merchant associations, unions, athletic, social, fraternal and sororal associations, mutual aid societies, and others. But it also included newly organized "from scratch" groups, like block clubs, tenant unions, unemployed groups, parent groups, and others. The objective was to have the full range of interests in a community reflected in the organizational composition of a foundational meeting by the time it took place. This assured the legitimacy and representativeness of the organization that emerged. Alinsky called these "mass-based" organizations. The current, generally used term is "broad-based."

The Creative Use of Conflict Tactics

The thing that most people think of when they think of Alinsky is his tactical imagination. This imagination was harnessed to the broader goals, vision, and values I've thus far described. Many groups claim to be using Alinsky's tactics, but it is important to examine whether the tactic is simply to get into the news media, or whether there are actual organization-building results embedded in its use.

Alinsky thought that the best ally of the powerless was the hypocrisy and arrogance of the powerful. They had to be goaded by the action of a people power organization into reacting. "The action," he said, "is in the reaction." Richard Harmon's "Making an Offer We Can't Refuse" (see Chapter 16) provides a step-by-step description of how a people's organization goads the opposition to react and makes use of that reaction.

Alinsky didn't believe in the "educational value" of losing campaigns. For people with cumulative experiences of defeat, the lesson of not winning is that you were right in your initial understanding of being powerless and a fool to get suckered into this new organization.

The Primacy of "Self-Interest"

Alinsky used self-interest to move people to participate in a mass-based organization. Self-interest was a motivational tool to engage people in organizing. He understood self-interest in both personal and institutional terms. His Back of the Yards experience made clear to him its power for moving people to do things they would not otherwise have done. He harnessed self-interest to work for the common good.

The leaders he approached had self-interest in the performance of their roles, expanding their base, winning things for their people, and looking good among their peers. Alinsky used flattery to tap this source of motivation.

They had institutional interests as well. A prime example of Alinsky's understanding: he once told a group of ministers, "Don't talk to a pastor about his Christian obligation. If you do, he'll thank you for your visit and tell his secretary, 'Next time that guy calls, tell him I'm not available.'" But if you can tell the pastor of a church with declining members how his participation in a mass organization might help him revive his membership, then he'll open his ears . . . and later his church treasury . . . to membership.

Self-interest properly understood is placing oneself among others. It is thus distinguished from selfishness, which views the self as isolated from, and to the exclusion of, others. Self-interest is also distinguished from selflessness, which is to think of others to the exclusion of self. That was for saints.

Self-interest is also key to getting previously antagonistic groups of people to work with one another. It is, as Alinsky said, "the low road to morality." People, he observed, often do the right thing for the wrong reason. But once doing the right thing, they change. In the stories told in this book, the reader will find dramatic examples of deeply prejudiced white ethnic homeowners ending up in mutually respectful alliances with blacks because they were persuaded that only in those alliances could they win something they wanted. Contact and respect soon led to relationships, and prejudices dissolved as people became people to one another. And as new relationships formed across historic lines of division, and as a new understanding of the common good came with the creation of a people's organization national movement, there would emerge a notion of self-interest properly understood—the enlightened self-interest found in Alexis de Tocqueville's *Democracy in America*, an important influence on Alinsky's thinking.

Alinsky's observations and experiences told him that simple appeals to virtue were nice for seminars and coffee shop conversations, but unlikely to move real social forces in the world. Similarly, correct analyses of the nature of the system might make for great debates in the pages of radical books and journals, but if they are unrelated to the possibilities of where an organization may go, that is where they are likely to remain.

The Key Role of the Outside Organizer

Alinsky thought that the leadership, energy, talent, and wisdom to build people power lay in the community itself. "Apathy" was a misnomer. I've come to think of it this way: "apathy" is the label put on people who won't come to your meeting. Rather, Alinsky thought people didn't want to bang their heads against a stone wall.

Generations, if not centuries, of divide and conquer have led to serious divisions "among the people." Overcoming these was the task of the outside organizer. Since local people were typically fighting over scarce resources, there was a basis for the continuing antagonism that ran through and between the neighborhoods Alinsky and his early associates sought to organize. In Back of the Yards, for example, it was common among various ethnic parish priests to barely speak with one another, and then only on those occasions where the archdiocese required them to do so.

Parallel divisions existed within the packinghouses where Back of the Yards residents worked. For example, the "killing floor"—the most dangerous and onerous place to work—was for blacks.

To overcome the misnamed "apathy" and the internal antagonisms required an outsider who had the self-confidence and skills to bring together these heretofore nonparticipating (and therefore powerless) and antagonistic groups. The advantage of the outsider (and they were all men in Alinsky's days) was that, not being a part of any one of the groups or identities within a large neighborhood, he could be a part of them all. Because he was a stranger to all of them, he could stand outside each of their perspectives. Because he possessed great empathy and imagination, he was able to stand inside the shoes of each.

Alinsky categorized the vast majority of Americans as "the have-nots," "have-a-little-want-mores," and the middle class. In his later years, the organizing task writ large was to develop organizations that could bring these divided groups into value- and self-interest–based relationships with one another.

Alinsky's organizers used everything from personal flattery to talk of broader self-interests to entice leaders of different groups to negotiate with one another, even with their histories of refusing to have anything to do with the others. "You scratch my back, and I'll scratch yours" kinds of deals would be struck over items that one group cared a lot about but which were of little or no concern to the others. The combined power of the several groups would make possible the realization of the particular interests of each.

Once these conversations had taken place, and particularly after initial victories had been won on relatively small things, a different kind of self-interest could be lifted up—one that affected all the groups, such as alleviating unemployment or promoting unionization (major priorities during the Depression era, when Alinsky began his work). Self-interest provided the initial stickiness to hold people together in a common organization, but human relationships and the capacity for empathy that grew with them would then take over. The broad democratic ideals to which they all paid lip service would take on a reality that would make adherence to them part of the worldview of the participants in a people power organizing movement. While Alinsky clearly thought that racism and democracy were incompatible, his organizing mind sought ways to bring blacks, browns, and whites together on practical matters of self-interest rather than preaching or lecturing about the immorality or antidemocratic character of prejudice and discrimination.

Where possible, mass organization boundary lines encompassed diverse constituencies. But where that wasn't possible, Alinsky hoped that parallel organizing efforts in adjacent or nearby areas would enable subsequent alliances in which new relationships could be forged, with the end result of past antagonisms being overcome.

The organizer's job was this: to assist local people to form and sustain a people power organization; that was simple but not easy. His tools were four: empathic listening, challenging (or agitating), thinking through, and training.

His attentive ear to the concerns of people provided the organizer with the agenda for the formation of the organization. "You organize with your ears, not your mouth," Alinsky was fond of saying. His empathic way of listening helped him earn the trust of the people with whom he was meeting.

Having heard what people cared about, it was then the task of the organizer to challenge (or agitate) them to act on their own concerns. Alinsky's "rub raw the wounds of resentment" was a phrase that aroused the dander of power-structure holders and their apologists, who accused Alinsky of being a troublemaker. (It disturbed liberals as well.) He reveled in the accusation. Alinsky thought that all people developed a rationalization both for what they were doing and what they were not doing. The rationalization for not acting had to be broken by the organizer before people would take the first steps toward building an organization.

The organizer also needed a believable idea of what could be done to change things. Storytelling was a favored form of doing this. When local leaders would, in effect, say to the organizer, "All right, wise guy, let's say I agree to participate—what the hell are we going to do to get what we want?" the organizer had to have a ready-at-hand story—often embellished, tailored, and modified to fit the local circumstance—that described how a similar group of people in a similar situation had been able to accomplish a similar objective by doing x. As time went on, Alinsky and his associates would lead workshops in which a growing number of available stories, based on a growing number of people power victories, could be told.

Finally, the organizer trained people in the specific skills associated with building the organization. These included:

- research—both on proposed solutions to problems and on power structures
- conducting effective meetings
- dealing with media and external allies
- negotiating—first with one another to arrive at the lowest significant common denominator program, and then with adversaries to bring about change in the world
- defining and carrying out action campaigns when good faith negotiations didn't take place—these might be in the political, social, or economic arenas and could include public shaming, boycotts, massive nonviolent disruption of business as usual, or making a difference in election outcomes

- fundraising
- evaluating actions and planning next steps
- reflecting on the meaning of what was being done—i.e., connecting action to deeply held beliefs of the people
- developing internal education by creating a story that placed their organization in the historic context of democratic struggles between the haves and the have-nots
- celebrating new heroes—the leaders and members of the people power organization who were themselves now history makers.

In Alinsky's day, the teaching was typically informal; today it is formalized in workshops led by various organizing centers for their affiliated groups.

The objective of the outside organizer was to form an organization that could do without him by the end of a three-year period (Alinsky's IAF was typically funded for three years for such projects). The outside organizer would hire two or three local people to be his field staff, training one of them to become the staff director who took over when he left. He would also develop the capacity within the organization to raise an annual budget to pay the two or three organizers from a combination of significant organizational dues and fundraising mechanisms (such as raffles, ad books, and festivals).

But how was the outside organizer to gain acceptance on the "organizing turf"? (His very existence was, Alinsky knew, in some ways an insult to the community. His presence raised the question, "Why can't we do it ourselves?")

He could implant himself in it and spend years earning the trust and confidence of local people. Indeed, many radicals did that—both in workplaces and neighborhoods. And many of them became effective organizers on that turf, even though they were initially strangers to it. Those organizers who took this approach usually got a job at the place they hoped to organize, where the organizational form would be a union, or they had to get a paying job to do the work they really wanted to do, which was to organize the neighborhood.

The full-time organizer required something more. Alinsky's "sponsor committee" solution had two parts. The first was to form the committee with esteemed people who collectively had access to funding—typically from religious bodies that supported action for justice in the world and from a handful of foundations that were similarly committed.

The sponsor committee also had to have the respect of the local community that was targeted for the organizing work. This second part made possible a broad-based invitation to Alinsky's IAF from organizations and individuals within the targeted community saying they wanted the IAF's organizing assistance. Thus, when the outside organizer arrived, he had a good answer to the question, "Who sent you?" which would ideally lead to "Well, if _____ sent you, then I'll listen to what you've got to say."

The Outside Organizer and Local Leaders

"A leader," Alinsky said, "is a person with a following." The only place where there aren't local leaders is in a high-transiency hotel, or the most atomized places. Alinsky's early work as a criminologist, his education in Chicago School sociology at the University of Chicago, his observation of the Capone gang, and his work as an organizer in Back of the Yards all taught him that there were local leaders to be found in every constituency, including the poorest of neighborhoods. It was through them and their perhaps relatively small followings that the professional outside organizer worked.

If the pastor of, say, a two-thousand-family Catholic church was its titular leader, it remained to be seen if he was the de facto leader. If he was, he would know and have strong relationships with dozens of both formal and informal leaders in his parish. The formal ones headed the numerous groups, clubs, committees, and societies within the church. The informal ones were people who simply commanded respect; they might have no official title, but others would turn to them for advice on issues facing their families, the parish, or the neighborhood. On a block, a neighborhood leader would be someone to whom others on the block similarly turned for advice on matters affecting them where they lived. In a school, it would be a parent to whom other parents looked for advice on school matters.

Leaders of leaders were people to whom leaders of more than one group would turn. Typically, they were pastors or heads of organizations. A mass-based organization created more such leaders—i.e., people able to speak for the entire community.

At the other end of the spectrum of leadership, a potential leader was someone with an interest in developing a following, or who might become interested. An organizer would create relational tasks that would challenge someone like this and test whether she or he indeed had the capacity to lead. For example, could the person convene a group of neighbors in a house meeting?

Beyond an Ideology of Scarcity

In fact, any neighborhood targeted for mass organization is already organized. That is, there are patterns of relationships between leaders and followers. Thus, the real task for the outside organizer is to break apart the existing pattern and assist local leaders to build in its place a new one—"reorganizing the casbah" is how Alinsky organizer Nicholas von Hoffman described it.[22]

At the center of the present pattern is the ideology of scarcity: "I've got to get and keep for 'my people'; our greatest enemy in getting and keeping for ourselves is those people right next door who are competing to get the same thing." This view has to be replaced with an ideology of sufficiency—a sufficiency that can be realized only if we "unite and fight," and recognize/realize that our enemy is not the people next door but those who make decisions in the institutions that have the resources our people need for a decent life.

This ideology cannot be simply preached. It must be seen and learned in the course of action, which begins in relatively narrow self-interests but broadens as relationships of mutual support are forged and a common identity emerges. Conflict tactics externalize the enemy and teach where the resources to solve community problems really lie. The very nature of conflict cements unity among those engaged in the battle; it creates a "them and us." The organizer makes use of this dynamic, while at the same time recognizing that she or he has to teach the art of compromise when it is time to negotiate. In contrast to those who believe in violent, transformational revolution, this approach understands transformation to be possible, nonviolent, and negotiable—at least in formally democratic societies.[23]

Popular Education

Alinsky was interested in educating people, but not in the usual meaning of "education," which tends to be telling people about how the world works, how it might be better, and how they ought to think. Organizing stripped away the masks of unaccountable power. As people power organizations sought the real decision-makers in the institutions where the important decisions about their lives were being made, they would learn the difference between pluralism as ideology and pluralism as reality. One of the reasons Alinsky wanted to keep electoral politics at arm's length from people power organizations is that he thought it far more efficacious to negotiate directly with corporate power than to rely on politicians as the in-between brokers between the people and money power. But that didn't mean he was against politicians or, in carefully defined circumstances, electoral participation.

Alinsky would initially polarize a conflict between "the people" and "money," and then go into the political arena with the question to politicians, "Whose side are you on?" Some politicians would identify with a people power organization if the organization demonstrated it had strong voter support. They would benefit in an election from this identification.

Second, organizing created "teachable moments," as it demonstrated the resistance of the status quo to proposals for greater justice. Among everyday people, it is often thought, "If only the people at the top knew what was going on at the bottom, they would do things differently." The educational reason for meeting with real decision-makers and making well-thought-out proposals to them was to expose to leaders and members of the people power organization that the obstacle to justice wasn't ignorance or misinformation. Similarly, the obstacle wasn't incompetence, because the specific proposals made offered means for their implementation. What every organizer who did this work theoretically believed at the outset, and quickly learned on the ground, was that everyday people, often with not a great deal of formal education, quickly mastered vast amounts of factual detail and policy acumen when this knowledge was related to something they thought they might actually accomplish for themselves, their families, their neighbors, and their communities. They made competent proposals to policy-makers. Organizers were a resource on whom leaders could draw, not providers of handed-down "from the top" solutions.

If neither ignorance nor incompetence were to blame, then could it be that these policy-makers had different interests, and that the task of people power was to either change those interests or to change the system within which they were embedded? These problems of political, economic, or social justice would not be solved until the people understood that the self-interests of incumbent power holders had to be sufficiently challenged for them to negotiate with people power organizations. (I will later deal with the question of what is put on the table in those negotiations.)

Third, education extended to "conflicts among the people." If you initially got into a relationship with people whom you thought of as "the other" because you had to borrow their power in order to realize your own aims, you might have seen it as a necessary evil. But in the course of so doing, if people shared their frustrations, hopes, and dreams in the storytelling moments that would have been a part of building relationships, there would then have been cognitive dissonance—a gap between stereotypes held and the reality being experienced. That was another kind of teachable moment. It was an opening, for example, to this question: "Whose interests are being served by the prejudiced attitude you had toward _____ (women, blacks, gays, whomever) in the past?"

But note: this approach was contingent upon the organization creating the possibility of relationships among people who had previously been antagonistic toward one another. And that contingency was based on a further one: that there were organizers at work on the ground capable of doing this kind of adult citizenship education, which used the everyday experience of people in the world as the curriculum for making "democracy" more than a word.

The organizer was an educator, "but a special kind of educator, one who did his education within the experience of the people with whom he was working." That's how Alinsky described it.

The Democratic Promise

The big lesson for me in all this is that Alinsky's confidence in everyday people was well placed. "Given the opportunity," he said, "most people will make the right decisions most of the time." I saw it happen. I saw prejudices based on race, ethnicity and national status, religion, gender and gender orientation, ideology, neighborhood, and other reasons diminish and evaporate over time as diverse people worked together. The experiences of working and winning together make a deep impression on participants.

I saw people who never imagined themselves as civic leaders learn the citizenship skills of research and public policy discussion, negotiation with both the powers-that-be and with one another, compromise, dealing with the news media, lobbying, conducting nonviolent action campaigns, and much more. These, and more, are the lessons taught in this book.

Alinsky was a radical democrat. He saw a vital civil society as the essential under-pinning of democracy. He had a bold vision for an egalitarian, highly participatory, and free society. This equality applied to all dimensions of life: discrimination based on one identity or another violated the democratic premise. But so did vast inequalities of income and wealth. He saw corporate economic power and its increasing ownership of the political system as the enemy. The vast incomes of today's CEOs and other elites would have repulsed him. At the end of his life, he identified the have-nots, have-a-little-want-mores, the insecure middle class, and segments of the economically secure but morally disturbed upper-middle class as the constituency that had to be united in order to realize the democratic vision. This constituency had to be unified and organized if it was to act powerfully on the major issues of the day. The agency that would express that unity and power was the mass-based (or "broad-based") organization whose character is described above, and the alliances of such organizations that would be required to challenge increasingly concentrated elite power. The agent who would build such organizations was the professional organizer who understood his or her role as assisting people to build power, not aggrandizing power for himself or herself.

Notes

1. Where not otherwise indicated, my anecdotes about Alinsky and my quotations of his words are from these observations and conversations.
2. John Egan, "Saul David Alinsky, 1909–1972: A Memorial," copy in possession of author.
3. George William Mundelein, "Religion: Catholics for Labor," *Time Magazine*, June 2, 1941, 65.
4. Keenan Heise, "Joe Meegan, Back of Yards Council Co-founder," *Chicago Tribune*, July 9, 1994, *articles.chicagotribune.com*.
5. Quoted in Saul Alinsky, *John L. Lewis: An Unauthorized Biography* (New York: Vintage, 1949), 145.
6. Alinsky, *John L. Lewis*, 146.
7. The Gold Coast is an expensive Chicago neighborhood.
8. In *Rerum Novarum: Rights and Duties of Capital and Labor* (Vatican City: Libreria Editrice Vaticana, 1891; *www.vatican.va*), Pope Leo XIII initiated the church's involvement with unions and, more broadly, causes of social and economic justice.
9. The major ethnic groups in the neighborhood were Polish, Lithuanian, Slovak, and a scattering of other Eastern Europeans—all from countries adjoining the Soviet Union, and all with Catholic churches that were deeply anti-Communist.
10. In fact, this last line ("You're not going to get them to be in the same room with me, Saul") is one that March used at the time—at least that's what he says in the film documentary on Alinsky that was nationally aired by PBS (*The Democratic Promise: Saul Alinsky and His Legacy*, produced by Bob Hercules and Bruce Orenstein [Chicago: Media Process Educational Films, 1999], DVD).
11. "You're a clever guy, Saul, but I don't think you can pull this off" is from *The Democratic Promise*.
12. Paraphrased from *Democratic Promise*.

13. After World War II, the BYNC became a segregationist community organization, preventing racial minorities, particularly African Americans, from purchasing homes in the neighborhood. Alinsky critics used this fact as a basis for criticizing his work. My own commitment to racial equality made me deeply interested in the question, and I spent time investigating it, and came to these conclusions: (1) Indeed, the BYNC did block black purchase of homes in the neighborhood. Alinsky later said he might have to organize against the BYNC. (2) Alinsky supported a citywide quota system that would have required of all Chicago's neighborhoods that they integrate. He was roundly condemned by many for his approach. He noted that without the dispersal of African Americans throughout the city, residential integration would be impossible. He said integration characterized the time between the move-in of the first blacks, and the move-out of the last whites. History proved him right. (3) The combination of block-busting, redlining, intentional arson, and other acts by private property owners, along with city complicity by selective withdrawal of public services, planning and zoning, was then, and remains today, almost impossible to overcome—despite anti-redlining legislation. (4) I spoke at some length with Herb and Jane March. Herb was the open member of the Communist Party who was a leader in the packinghouse workers union; his wife, Jane, was active in the neighborhood. They were deeply committed to challenging prejudice and discrimination, and the packinghouse workers union was among the best in the CIO on this issue. Initially in our conversation they disagreed with each other on whether Alinsky could have done more to address racism. But by the end of their conversation with each other—with me intently listening—they agreed that the BYNC could not have overcome the forces promoting racism no matter what it might have tried. There had been changes in the demography of the packinghouse industry (whites could move out into other industries while blacks couldn't because of discrimination in hiring); there was a high degree of residential segregation in Chicago; there were the deeply prejudiced views of the white ethnics who lived in Back of the Yards; and the reality was that no neighborhood (except perhaps the upper-middle-class Hyde Park, which adjoined the University of Chicago) had been able to stabilize as an integrated neighborhood. (5) Alinsky's critics said a more explicit antiracist ideological position could have made a difference. Herb and Jane were explicit in their position on race, as was the union. But they didn't think "taking positions" would have made a difference. Indeed, the BYNC Constitution was explicit about race: "This organization is founded for the purpose of uniting all the organizations within the community known as the Back of the Yards, in order to promote the welfare of all residents of that community regardless of their race, color or creed, so that they may all have the opportunity to find health, happiness, and security through the democratic way of life" (quoted from Saul D. Alinsky, "Community Analysis and Organization," *Clinical Sociology Review* 2, no. 1 (1984): 28; reprinted from an article originally published in 1941). Neither Alinsky nor his critics successfully challenged the deep racism that existed in the country or that exists today.

14. Saul Alinsky, interview by Eric Norden, *Playboy* 19, no. 3 (1972); republished as "Empowering People, Not Elites: Interview with Saul Alinsky," *Progress Report*, October 23, 2003–September 4, 2004, *www.progress.org*.

15. *Democratic Promise.*

16. University of Rochester Libraries, Introduction to P. David Finks manuscript collection, Department of Rare Books, Special Collections, and Preservation, River Campus Libraries, University of Rochester, accessed August 8, 2013, *www.lib.rochester.edu*.

17. Quoted in ibid.

18. Quoted in ibid.

19. Creating clergy accountability was one of the things that Alinsky's community organizers

did. In San Antonio, Catholic parishioners insisted on meeting with the clergy assignment committee to ensure that a new pastor would be favorable to their membership in Communities Organized for Progress and Services (COPS), the IAF organization there. The bishop, an old friend of Alinsky's, told the story with a twinkle in his eye, and added in jest, "Had I known they were going to be doing that kind of thing, I might not have invited you here, Saul" (Alinsky, conversation with Miller, late 1960s).

20. There are three general understandings of what "political democracy" means. "Elite democracy" limits citizenship to voting. Elites represent the citizens and negotiate differences among them, which results in public policy. "Throw the bums out" is the major tool citizens have to redress their grievances. "Strong democracy" proposes more participatory procedures and structures within government—e.g., advisory committees, "people's budgeting," local government, and other official governmental bodies that engage citizens. "Civil society democracy" emphasizes the importance of voluntary associations outside the formal · structures of government, and argues that without a vibrant and strong civil society, money and the self-perpetuation of elites will be the controlling factors in government. There is an elaborate political science and political sociology literature on these schools of thought. Alinsky belongs in the last.

21. Lord Acton, "Letter to Bishop Mandell Creighton," April 5, 1887, in *Historical Essays and Studies*, edited by J. N. Figgis and R. V. Laurence (London: Macmillan, 1907).

22. See Nicholas von Hoffman, "Reorganization in the Casbah," *Social Progress* 52, no. 6: 33–44.

23. The discussion here omits any reference to mutual aid—e.g., addressing problems by developing alternative institutions like co-ops or credit unions. This subject is addressed later in this book.

3

What Is an Organizer? (1973)

■

RICHARD ROTHSTEIN

Editors' preface: Written in 1973, this is one of a number of essays that have become fairly widely known in the organizing field. It has been used in classes and given to many new organizers to help them understand their role. When asked about the history of the piece, Rothstein responded that "you are asking me to remember something from nearly forty years ago. All I can tell you is that I wrote it at the request of Heather Booth," who was then director "of the Midwest Academy, which "used it as part of its training curriculum."[1] See Part III, Section A, for more on Booth and Midwest Academy during this time.

Organizers Organize Organizations

A romantic mystique surrounds the notion of "organizer" because *conventional descriptions* of organizations never include the organizer's role. According to the conventional description (which most of us have grown to accept) organizations have members who decide broad policy; leaders who guide the group in a fashion responsible to members' instructions; and staff who carry out the mechanical work of the organization, accountable to the leaders.

This conventional description is dangerous. It does not prepare us for the fact that few organizations ever work this way. Unprepared for the reality of organizations, we have a tendency to blame organizational leadership for failure to fulfill the conventional model. The conventional description is static, while most organizations are dynamic, in a process of constant change and growth. Those who are most concerned with pushing the organization's growth, who have the greatest vision about how to get from here to there and who patiently try to organize that vision—those are the organizers. Sometimes unacknowledged, organizers are present in every organization that is growing. If the conventional description is fully believed, it becomes necessary for the organization to hide its organizers, pretending they don't exist. One consequence is that the very notion of organizer, which should be an everyday fact in the life of

---

"What Is an Organizer" was originally published by the Midwest Academy (Chicago). It is reprinted here by permission of the author.

an organization, becomes mystified. A more serious consequence is that when organizers are hidden, the open functions of teaching, counseling, confidence-building,
modeling, guiding (all the functions of organizing) become the hidden functions of
manipulation. An organization can hold organizers accountable and can offer constructive criticism of the organizer's function only if the organizer's function is publicly
defined and approved.

The conventional description implies a "bottom-up" view of organizational
structure and democracy. It implies that organizations come into being spontaneously at the bottom (mass-membership) level, and then create representative levels
of leadership. This conventional description is such a cliché in our political culture
that it may shock you to hear that no organization ever has or ever will function that
way. In fact, organizations grow mostly in a "top-down" manner: organizers (hidden
or publicly acknowledged) not only find and train leaders but they mobilize, inspire
and educate members. Since no action organization's leadership can be effective
without a mobilized and active membership, the organizer always places top priority on increasing the involvement of the rank and file. In this sense, the role of
the organizer is to create and increase democracy (rank and file participation and
direction) in an organization, for the strength of an action organization increases
with the participation of its rank and file.

In short, *organizers organize organizations*. Organizations are not made, fully
formed.

The Conventional Description
of a "Finished Democratic Organization"

The conventional model of a finished democratic organization has members, leaders,
and staff. The members debate and decide policies and actions. The leaders propose
those policies and actions to the membership. The members elect leaders whose proposals are most often sensible, who speak well in public on behalf of the organization,
and who are trusted to make interim decisions on policy between membership meetings. When leaders in a finished democratic organization lose rapport with members
and no longer make the interim decisions members would want, these leaders are
defeated for re-election and replaced by those who know what policy initiatives members would approve.

While members and leaders, in democratic interaction, make policy, staff ad-
ministers policy. In this way, the limited time and energy of the membership and
leadership is reserved for the most important deliberations, while the necessary day to
day work which makes the organization possible is delegated to staff. Administration
means keeping the organization going along policy lines decided upon by members
and leaders. This includes everything from making coffee and arranging meeting
halls to sending out newsletters and writing leaflets. Not all staff work is mechanical
(though most mechanical work is staff work), but all staff work takes place within the

boundaries of democratic decided policy—at least in the conventional description of a "finished democratic organization."

None of you has ever been in an organization like this, however, and most likely none of you ever will. This organizational model was dreamed up without real human beings in mind, but it is an "ideal type" toward which "organizers" push real organizations.

Real Organization Members Come with Everyday Lives to Lead, with Limited Time, with Normal Prejudices and Personal Needs

The members of real organizations have marriages or affairs, jobs and children; and problems with each. They may join an organization because, in the long run it *might* alleviate some of those problems, but in the meantime those problems occupy most of their time and energy. In real organizations, leaders are not just those with best policy and action proposals (although that helps), but often those who are more willing and able than most to ignore their everyday lives. (Only when conditions get so hopeless that people can't alleviate their everyday problems will most ordinary people ignore those problems and throw themselves into organizations *en masse*—and things haven't been that bad in 40 years.)

Consequently, real organization members never have the time or energy to think carefully about all the issues and actions their leaders contemplate. In real organizations, democratic debate is only partly a process whereby members instruct leaders; it is also a process whereby leaders get members to agree to proposals those members haven't fully developed. Not only are leaders more experienced in thinking about such proposals, leaders are also those prepared to spend more of their time thinking about organizational problems and proposals. This fact alone makes it likely that trusted leaders will influence members more than members will influence leaders. And the more active, flexible and powerful an organization is, the more complex and frequent will decisions be—and the less will members be able to invest the time and energy required for full participation in decision making. (The deader a group, the more democratic it can be: the once a month bridge club is the perfect democratic form.)

All people are equal in the eyes of God, but real people are unequal in every other respect. This is another difficulty with the model of a "finished democratic organization." Those with more organizational and political experience can understand issues more quickly and easily. Those with better judgment, more insight, greater empathy, charisma or articulation tend to be listened to. But so are those who are more intimidating, have more status and polish. And in various cases, people are listened to more because they are white, black, male, female, sexy, tough, rich, poor, Catholic, Jewish, Protestant, celibate, or prolific. In real organizations, decisions are based only partly on what is said in meetings; and partly on what isn't said—the status and influence hierarchies which members bring to any group. (The more homogeneous a group, the easier it is to organize democracy within it.)

Action organizations bring together people with common problems and grievances to fight for common solutions. But real people seldom define their problems in the same way at the same time, even when, to an outsider, they seem to be in similar straits. The actions of real organizations only partly address the problems members feel are common; and partly members articulate a problem because their organization is working on it. Moreover, real people rarely join real organizations only to work on the "organization's" goals. They join also because organizations are fun, because friends are in it or they want to make friends, because they seek recognition, power, creativity or an escape from boredom. (Groups which attract only those with a shared commitment to a well-defined cause have no members.)

Effective Political Activists Are Not Born, They are Made (Out of Real People) by Organizers

Real-world organizations not only have members, leaders and staff; they also have organizers (acknowledged or not) whose function is to increase the active participation of members and to create the conditions in which strong new leaders emerge. For an action organization's strength grows with the extent of its members' participation. An action organization's creativity and flexibility grows with the growth of its leadership ranks and the self-confidence of its leaders. Such growth rarely happens "spontaneously." Empathizing with the pressures on members' everyday lives, with their aspirations and prejudices as well, the organizer develops relationships and structures which make real-world organizations more active, participatory, rational, strong and democratic.

Organizers develop leaders; they spot people with a capacity for growth and create structures and incentives enabling them to think and act in ways they never before dared. An organizer creates situations where less experienced members are better able to debate the most essential organizational problems. So organizers remind members of meetings, prepare agendas, define alternatives, simplify issues.

An organizer is a teacher, understanding that people become leaders step by step, assimilating experience at every stage before moving on. An organizer plans these steps so that members can learn for themselves the lessons others have learned before.

An Organizer Views Activity Not Only for What It Accomplishes, but for What It Teaches Apprentice Leaders

Oppressive social structures are maintained in part because authorities masquerade as benevolent, define inequalities as too complex for resolution, and hide real conflicts of interest in a fairy tale of paternal benevolence. An organizer, therefore, seeks out confrontations and conflict; for the organizer understands that only in conflict situations do issues become clear with real interests no longer camouflaged; only in conflict situations does the rhetoric of the powerful lie exposed and the mobilization of a movement become possible. Yet the organizer is also aware that all conflict is partially premature; that in the polarization that ensues some members and potential members will be frightened, choosing the side of authority against their "true" interests. And in the need for instant decisions in crises, participation in decision making is narrowed. Yet here new leadership is also tested.

An organizer learns to view each organizational activity not only for what it accomplishes but what it teaches. Organizations need adversity; the reactionary interests of those in power are best exposed when they resist popular movements making reasonable and humane demands. Yet adversity also discourages, by showing that the organizations' path may lead to defeat. Organizations, even more, need victories—concessions wrung from administrators and officials. Such victories encourage members and leaders, preparing the way for greater targets. Yet small victories can also lead a group to underestimate the forces against it; easy victories can distract members from fundamental issues to symptoms. The organizer uses ambiguous victories as well as defeats, to educate, to train, to encourage.

Organizers know that the line between manipulation and honesty is very thin. No organizers play all their cards at the beginning of a conversation or relationship; yet honesty is an important value for organizers. Teaching the truth about people's own power to transform their lives (like teaching anything) is a gradual, one-step-at-a-time process. It compounds, piece by piece, a little self-confidence, some political understanding, observing a model, learning from a mistake, a little more self-confidence, redefining an identity, and so on, until an activist, ready to lead and struggle, is made.

Finally, organizers know that most people learn best by doing. Since most people have never experienced a successful action organization, they've never learned how to run one. So organizers begin by running an organization on behalf of its potential leaders and members. Some leaders are asked to share responsibility for decisions already made—and are better prepared to make those decisions in the future. All serve as apprentices to the organizer, practicing the leadership skills they will later use. The most important judgment an organizer makes is that of any master craftsman: at what point are apprentices ready to learn more from their own mistakes than from the successes of others.

Organizers are Necessary for Organization: Organizations are Necessary for Social Change

Organizers are present in every organization that is changing, growing, involving new members. But they are not always acknowledged. In some organizations, the leaders play organizing roles: those leaders create their constituencies at the same time [as] they respond to them.

In other organizations, staff play organizing roles. These staffers are involved in creating and training the very leadership from whom staff claim to take orders.

In all organizations, some more experienced members are *organizing* other less experienced members.

Just as people frequently lead without a formally elected leadership position; just as many members pitch in on mechanical work without being part of the formal staff; so do some people not formally designated "organizers" play organizing roles—guiding, teaching, encouraging the less experienced. What is argued here is not that all those playing this role must be given the title "Organizer"—but only that *organizing* is as crucial an organizational function as *leading, staffing,* or *participating.*

In a healthy organization, each of these functions is publicly acknowledged, never kept hidden. Only then can suspicion of manipulation and the resulting organizational rancor be avoided. For the formal organizer, it is particularly important to avoid the fiction that organizing and administrative staff are indistinguishable—the fiction that the organizing staff merely takes orders from the leadership it is training. This fiction becomes particularly dangerous when organizers themselves come to believe it—and are forced to hide (i.e., manipulate) their own necessary techniques of leadership development.

Spontaneous militancy is rare in social life. When it happens, a spontaneous movement, a mass unplanned uprising, is very powerful. It is also very short-lived. Spontaneity is the process whereby people suddenly put aside their everyday concerns and devote more time and energy to political affairs than they did before, *or will later.*

Many of you remember the spontaneous campus uprisings against the invasion of Cambodia in 1970. These unorganized, unplanned rebellions which spread almost instantaneously across the country represented the height of the anti-war movement's influence. Yet within a very few months, the spontaneous rebels were more apathetic than they had been for five years.

To build a lasting political force on any issue requires not spontaneity, but organization. It requires a slow process of leadership development. It requires the multiplication of leaders with a long term perspective, with the ability to plan strategy and the skill of marshaling forces at the right time in the right place. The people who painstakingly create these organizations and leaders at a time when most people attend to the problems of everyday life—these are the organizers without whom no movement can win.

Notes

1.   Richard Rothstein, personal communication to Aaron Schutz, May 13, 2013.

PART II

ALINSKY'S COLLEAGUES

Section A
Nicholas von Hoffman: The Woodlawn Organization and the Civil Rights Movement in the North

4

An Introduction to Nicholas von Hoffman

■

AARON SCHUTZ

In 1953, Saul Alinsky hired Nicholas von Hoffman. Even though, ten years later, von Hoffman decided to leave the Industrial Areas Foundation (IAF) to become a writer, it is generally acknowledged that von Hoffman became closer to Alinsky than any other member of his coterie of organizers. In fact, Alinsky had hoped that von Hoffman would eventually take over the IAF, and their relationship remained strong even after von Hoffman left.

Von Hoffman came to Alinsky's attention when he and some friends, including Lester Hunt (who also ended up working for Alinsky), were trying "to organize a self-defense group of some kind" for the impoverished Puerto Rican immigrants flooding into their neighborhood. Two priests they worked with, John Egan and John O'Grady, were also friends with Alinsky and decided that von Hoffman could benefit from a chat with the organizer. At the meeting, von Hoffman told stories about what they were doing, including running a "social first responders service, trying and failing to get people jobs, saving [people] from landlords" and "extricating them from the police."[1]

"It's a bucket of shit," Alinsky declared.[2] And the discussion went downhill from there. Von Hoffman started accusing Alinsky of being a "has-been" who had "sold out," while Alinsky "chastised von Hoffman and his friends for their irresponsibility" and lack of coherent strategy. Egan recalled that "there was shouting and yelling" and that "waiters thought there was going to be a fistfight."[3]

A few weeks later, Alinsky called von Hoffman and offered him a job—on the condition that he get a haircut and buy a suit.

Von Hoffman started off doing "research" for Alinsky, who ordered him to "go out to the Near West Side" of Chicago and "find out what was going on." Alinsky's only other instructions were that he wanted a weekly written report and that, as von Hoffman remembered it, "under no circumstances was I to call him, turn up at the office, or in any other fashion make my existence on the globe known to him." So von Hoffman took to the streets, talking to people, digging up information, and generally trying to figure out "what was going on."[4]

After a while, von Hoffman began to understand some of what he had been doing wrong in his work with the Puerto Ricans. He blundered "into a home truth about organizing: Good organizers don't organize. They get other people to do it."[5] He and his friends, he now understood, had created an organization that was run and owned by outsiders instead of people from inside the community.

Von Hoffman remembers these months as "the most interesting months of my life." He stated, "I learned more . . . than I ever learned in my life. . . . It was day after day of going out and finding out about other people and other things, taking it home, putting it down, thinking about it, trying to make sense out of it."[6] He described the experience of an organizer entering a new community this way:

> It is a very strange thing. You go somewhere, and you know nobody . . . and you've got to organize it into something that it's never been before. . . . You don't have much going for you. You don't have prestige, you don't have muscle, you've got no money to give away. All you have are . . . your wits, charm, and whatever you can put together. So you had better form a very accurate picture of what's going on, and you had better not bring in too many a priori maps [because] if you do, you're just not going to get anywhere.[7]

"The finding-out part," von Hoffman concluded, "is where the magic [of organizing] is."[8]

Von Hoffman worked with Alinsky for ten years, until 1963, on a range of different projects. He became Alinsky's primary on-the-ground organizer, his go-between with the hierarchy of the Catholic Church in Chicago, and, as Tom Gaudette remembers, a kind of researcher without portfolio, exploring different efforts springing up across the city and looking for potential organizers.[9] Von Hoffman served as lead organizer for The (originally "Temporary") Woodlawn Organization (TWO), Alinsky's first effort to organize an African American neighborhood, which launched him into the civil rights movement. In this section, we focus on TWO as a case study of the way Alinsky approached organizing.

The Genesis and Development of TWO

In 1960, the University of Chicago announced that it planned to essentially annex part of the African American neighborhood of Woodlawn, creating a buffer between itself and the "ghetto." Two Presbyterian ministers—Ulysses Blakeley, who was black, and Charles Leber, who was white—approached Alinsky about the possibility of organizing in Woodlawn against this effort. Initially, after conducting some research in the area, von Hoffman concluded that organizing in Woodlawn was a dubious proposition. He had found that West Woodlawn was fairly stable: it was a "middle-class neighborhood" for an African American community of the time "in fairly good condition," and it was "a *community*," with congregations and block clubs.[10] East Woodlawn, in contrast, was "a classic example of a disorganized big-city slum. Anyone who claims to have anything remotely resembling a representative organization in East Woodlawn is either a liar or a fool."[11] But he and Alinsky eventually decided to proceed.

For the Woodlawn effort, von Hoffman hired the IAF's first black organizer, Bob Squires, and drew in some volunteers, including Dick Harmon, who eventually became a key IAF organizer, and a black student, Jeff Williams, who worked with the black churches.[12] They split up the neighborhood and walked the streets until, as Squires put it, "I knew every son of a bitch in [my] area. I knew every bookie, every whore, every policy runner, every cop, every bartender, waitress, store owner, restaurant owner."[13] In his biography of Alinsky, Sanford D. Horwitt describes how, as the men "made their rounds, they listened to what people told them about problems in the neighborhood, looked for leaders . . . , and agitated." At the end of each day they dictated reports onto "dictabelts" for Alinsky and met together to talk over what they had learned.[14]

Arthur Brazier, the black pastor of a small Pentecostal church in the area, joined Blakeley and Leber as a leader in the effort. Horwitt notes that Brazier was "a perfect example of Alinsky's theory that the best potential natural leaders in a community were often unknown beyond their immediate circle of followers."[15] A powerful speaker and a thoughtful leader, Brazier quickly became the public "face" and eventually president of TWO.

Because of the focus on congregation-based organizing today, it may surprise some readers that an extensive network of block and building clubs was an essential part of TWO. Von Hoffman remembers that they "were able to do things like work the equivalent of telephone trees in all of these houses, apartment houses, many of which had been subdivided and subdivided. Sometimes using the building manager, sometimes using that dynamic woman, you know, on the fifth floor." They kept these groups engaged by "always thinking of activities. Fundraisers. Parties. Something going on to keep people goosed. You know, it had to be one thing or another. You had to do that."[16] In the IAF archives there are long lists of block and building clubs that were a part of TWO.

It was because of this wider participation in the neighborhood, von Hoffman remembers, that even without a visible picket line TWO was "able to organize" a school boycott

> so completely. When the day came to close the school, we had placards that
> said TWO School Strike, or something like that, in the windows of almost

every apartment house there, on the streets. And not a single picket in front of
the school. Nothing. Just nobody showed up. I was just so delighted with it, I
remember, because it was a real tour de force to do something like that. Not a
single picket. Nothing, you know. The authority had nowhere to turn.[17]

TWO's first action came before an actual organization had even taken form. Von
Hoffman got a tip that the University of Chicago was going downtown to ask for an
ordinance that would allow it to get urban-renewal funds for building on a vacant lot
it owned. While this was only tenuously linked to the larger issue, Alinsky and von
Hoffman saw it as an opportunity to transform a "simple real estate transaction into
a moral issue," by painting "the university with the tar of sinister motivations." While
they managed to get only about fifty people to the meeting, in a city unused to seeing
so many black faces this seemed like hundreds to startled officials. The headline in the
Sun-Times the next day was "Uproar Stalls U of C Plan OK," and the decision was
postponed.[18] The nascent organizing effort had won its first small victory—critical for
convincing those sitting on the sidelines that there was a good reason to join.

To rally local residents and build up a sense of power in the neighborhood, TWO
continued with a series of different campaigns. For example, they "organized squads
of shoppers to investigate" merchants suspected of short-weighting sales, the squads
bringing their own scales with them to check.[19] Always the pragmatist, Alinsky was
careful to make sure these little campaigns didn't get too big for the capacity of his
organization to handle. He constantly examined how much power he thought TWO
had and how "winnable" an effort seemed to be, pulling the plug—often over von
Hoffman's objections—when a campaign threatened to go too far. It might later be
undertaken, but this wasn't the time.

An unexpected event, however, pushed Alinsky and von Hoffman to move beyond
their usual cautious effort to build power and relationships slowly. Von Hoffman was
asked to coordinate an appearance by some of the Freedom Riders who had ridden
buses into the South to test federal laws barring segregation in interstate transportation. Some of the riders had been beaten by mobs, one bus had been burned, and
federal marshals had been called out to protect them, generating enormous media
attention. Although von Hoffman didn't think there would be much attendance, the
meeting was held.

But the riders were greeted not by a mostly empty room, but by hundreds of interested attendees who spilled out into the street, requiring loudspeakers to be set up
outside.

After a long phone conversation, late into the night, Alinsky and von Hoffman
decided that it was a "moment of the whirlwind." They were "no longer organizing but
guiding a social movement."[20]

After this conversation, they stopped looking "only or primarily for 'specific, immediate, and realizable' issues."[21] Instead, they organized their own "freedom ride" to

city hall. After only a couple of weeks of planning, 46 buses carrying more than 2,500 African Americans headed to city hall to register to vote. Led by a convertible filled with TWO leaders and organizers, including religious figures in full regalia and a bus full of nuns (in Chicago, Alinsky believed, "you couldn't be too Catholic"), they faced down a phalanx of police. "Hey, what are you going to do," von Hoffman shouted, "machine-gun the nuns?" It ended up being "the largest single voter-registration event ever" in Chicago, fundamentally altering the city's view of its black residents and its attitude toward Woodlawn.[22]

Other successful campaigns were undertaken. Over this time, the conflict with the University of Chicago continued, with the university trying to avoid either negotiating with TWO or recognizing it as the legitimate voice of the neighborhood. But the many different rules and reports and laws that governed the urban-renewal effort made it difficult to ram a plan through the bureaucracy. As von Hoffman noted, "this was just an open gearbox asking for sand to be thrown into it." At every stage, TWO was there to cause delays. The issue remained "in a holding pattern."[23] The key leader of TWO by this time was Rev. Brazier. With Brazier at the helm, the organization held a convention to take "Temporary" out of its name. They managed to secure the attendance of two prominent participants: Rev. Ralph Abernathy, a colleague of Dr. Martin Luther King, provided a visible link to the movement in the South, and the attendance of Mayor Richard A. Daley demonstrated recognition by the power structure of the city of a force with which it had to deal. While some radicals at the time were appalled that a black community organization would invite Daley to address their founding convention, they missed Alinsky's core strategic understanding that only Daley could grant the kind of recognition they needed in Chicago.

Von Hoffman would not make it to the end of the IAF's work with TWO. Facing total exhaustion, he finally told Alinsky he needed to move on and pursue his dream of becoming a writer. Alinsky brought Ed Chambers over from the IAF's Organization for the Southwest Community to take over. According to Horwitt, "Morale was so bad among TWO leaders at that point that Art Brazier, among others, was on the verge of quitting."[24] Chambers conducted a "housecleaning" of von Hoffman loyalists, including Bob Squires, and, with Alinsky's support, instituted a more disciplined, less movement-oriented operation.[25]

For a number of years after von Hoffman left, and even after the IAF ceased to be formally involved with the organization, TWO engaged in a range of creative efforts, including an eventually aborted collaboration with major youth gangs on a youth job-training program that led to direct conflict with the city and national administrations. TWO still exists at this writing, but like many formerly radical organizations, seems to have become absorbed in the administration of various programs and projects rather than remaining on the cutting edge of institutional change.

Some argue that, having won recognition, TWO is now merely administering programs, and that in the face of continuing poverty and racism this is a sellout. Others believe, given the Chicago power pattern and the absence of significant allies, TWO is doing the best it can to defend and advance the interests of Woodlawn's people. That debate about Alinsky and his work continues to this day.

Von Hoffman after TWO

Von Hoffman would go on to be a reporter for the *Chicago Daily News*, a commentator on CBS's *60 Minutes*, and a controversial columnist for the *Washington Post*. Often willing to say what others thought but did not have the courage to utter, he was fired from *60 Minutes* for calling Nixon "a dead mouse on America's kitchen floor."[26]

In part because he left organizing behind, what von Hoffman did not do, unlike some of the other organizers discussed in this book, is develop his own branch of the organizing tree. He clearly would not have wanted to in any case. In fact, in his recent book about Alinsky, *Radical*, he disparages those who would try to collapse the complex, context-driven activity of organizing into some more discrete, established process for action.

Von Hoffman's work is important not only because of his own experience and insight, but also because of his unique connection to Alinsky. Both Horwitt and von Hoffman himself describe an almost father-and-son relationship between the two, and *Radical* is really something of a love letter across the years to his long-lost mentor. In his essays, interviews, and in *Radical* we can hear one of the clearest echoes of Alinsky's vision in the words of someone who knew him perhaps best as an organizer.

For von Hoffman, Alinsky was "the least doctrinaire of men," someone "amused by his own inconsistencies," and a pragmatist who was able to "turn on a dime" and to "jettison long-held, old ways of organizing" when circumstances warranted. Von Hoffman's Alinsky was a man who, "toward the end of his life . . . had decided that society had changed so much that new patterns of organization would have to be invented."[27] For von Hoffman, the organizing approaches dominant today in the post-Alinsky IAF, the remnants of ACORN, and in other groups discussed in this volume are "akin but not closely akin" to what Alinsky "thought of as community organizing."[28] Von Hoffman worries that organizers have forgotten that organizing must be constantly reinvented on the ground amid the struggle for power.

In my 2013 interview with him, von Hoffman spoke about the limits of preset visions of how one should organize:

> When you are on the ground somewhere, be it Milwaukee or Tulsa, [a preset model] isn't going to get you very far. Because everything depends upon your ability to observe. It's the most important thing that you can do. You have to have an amazing set of eyes and ears. Good organizers always do. And that means, far from going to someplace with a model, you really go with an absolute tabula rasa. With nothing. You just want all these bits of pollen and things to fall on your sticky plate, however they will. Then you can study them and see if you can make

sense out of them. But if you have something in the back of your mind already, you will not see things, or you will not hear things. And also you will think you see things and think you hear things that aren't there.[29]

Of course, his point is not that you go completely empty. You don't forget history or different organizing approaches or your own past experiences. What you don't do, however, is go in thinking you either know who the leaders are or what the issues are, or what specific approaches are likely to work. Too many current organizers, von Hoffman believes, have forgotten this basic truth.

When asked what he thought about the current IAF approach to congregation-based organizing, von Hoffman remembered that when he and Alinsky started TWO they "were looking for a formula that would work for that time, [for] organizing in lower class, black—well, we called them 'ghettos' then. And we had a formula. And we knew that it was something that would work for a while. And then it wouldn't work anymore, because, first of all if you were at all successful you would destroy the basis on which the formula was constructed. And so forth. But times change." He noted that many organizers, including many of those who took over the IAF after Alinsky, "are not really very imaginative." They "get a formula" and "they just hold onto it. [And] of course, as time goes on they get a bigger and bigger vested interest in doing it that way. This is how we build Fords. And you just have to recognize that."[30]

When asked about what others have written about Alinsky's own rigidity—that he rejected "movement" approaches, or that he completely opposed engaging in political action—von Hoffman disagreed with this idea. He referred to Alinsky's willingness in TWO to throw their whole plan out the window when they realized after the Freedom Riders' event that they were in the "whirlwind." And he noted that they were often involved in political issues at TWO, although he felt that some of the specifics were still too sensitive to talk about. Von Hoffman also noted, as have others, that Alinsky wanted Brazier to run for Congress, but backed off from pushing the idea because von Hoffman didn't want to quit his job as a reporter to run the campaign. When asked whether Alinsky was opposed to political action, von Hoffman notes, firmly, that "Saul never was. No, no, he was never that way. Never, never, never."[31]

The Essays in This Section

Mike Miller and I have chosen a range of selections that together provide a picture of Alinsky and von Hoffman's vision of organizing and of the context of TWO. The next chapter draws together excerpts from two key essays by Blakeley and Leber describing the emergence of TWO as a force in Chicago. Excerpts from a 1966 speech by then-president Lynward Stevenson give a sense of how TWO represented itself during a high point in the power of TWO. The chapter concludes with text from Brazier's retrospective book on his experience in TWO.

Chapter 6 reproduces a document that was written to answer concerns by a range of religious leaders at the beginning of TWO. In it, von Hoffman, Hunt, and Alinsky try to describe their approach to organizing to a somewhat skeptical audience.

The section concludes with von Hoffman's "Finding and Making Leaders," an essay that became justifiably famous among organizers. Since its writing, it has been distributed among organizers and leaders from a range of traditions.

Notes

1. Nicholas von Hoffman, *Radical: A Portrait of Saul Alinsky* (New York: Nation Books, 2010), 2–3.
2. Ibid., 5.
3. Sanford D. Horwitt, *Let Them Call Me Rebel: Saul Alinsky—His Life and Legacy* (New York: Vintage, 1992), 273–74.
4. Von Hoffman, *Radical*, 6–7.
5. Ibid., 2.
6. Horwitt, *Rebel*, 275–76.
7. Ibid., 397.
8. Von Hoffman, *Radical*, 10.
9. Tom Gaudette, oral history interview by an unknown interviewer, May 10–15, 1990, Thomas A. Gaudette Papers, series 3, box 1, folders 1–4, Special Collections, William H. Hannon Library, Loyola Marymount University, Los Angeles, CA.
10. In the days before black suburbs and the breakout from Chicago's ghetto into adjoining neighborhoods, a "middle-class neighborhood" might have included everyone from black lawyers and doctors to just-making-it but steadily employed private sector workers—ranging from union members getting good pay to people only marginally above poverty—to postal workers and other public employees. Evidence of the presence of higher-paid working-class African Americans living in Woodlawn is in the early community power structure analysis that identified auto, packinghouse, and steelworker unions as having a presence in the neighborhood.
11. Nicholas von Hoffman, memorandum to Saul Alinsky, October 14, 1958, 3, Industrial Areas Foundation records, box 27, folder 459, Special Collections and University Archives, University of Illinois at Chicago.
12. Horwitt, *Rebel*, 398.
13. Quoted in ibid.
14. Ibid., 398–99.
15. Ibid., 417.
16. Nicholas von Hoffman, interview by Aaron Schutz, January 18, 2013.
17. Ibid.
18. Horwitt, *Rebel*, 393.
19. Ibid., 399.
20. Ibid., 401.
21. Ibid.
22. Ibid., 403.
23. Ibid., 411, 414.
24. Ibid., 438.
25. Ibid.

26. The incident is discussed in *Q&A with Nicholas von Hoffman*, interview by Brian Lamb, August 24, 2010, C-SPAN; transcript by Morningside Partners available at *Q&A Podcasts*, September 12, 2010, *www.q-and-a.org*.

27. Von Hoffman, *Radical*, 30, 183, 180–81.

28. Von Hoffman, interview by Schutz.

29. Ibid.

30. Ibid.

31. Ibid. In her dissertation, "Democracy in Action: Community Organizing in Chicago, 1960–1968" (Ohio University, 2001), Renee A. LaFleur writes that after the idea of running Brazier for Congress fell through, "Alinsky . . . pushed TWO to support Abner Mikva against the incumbent and machine loyalist Barrett O'Hara" (241–42). She cites Horwitt in *Let Them Call Me Rebel* on this point. Although Horwitt does not state that Alinsky personally "pushed" TWO to do this, he does imply that Alinsky was involved, noting that "Alinsky was furious" about TWO's failure to win the campaign for Mikva. "Alinsky, even without von Hoffman and Brazier, thought that a Mikva victory, made possible by TWO's political muscle, could have been a springboard to bigger things on the South Side" (514–15).

5

The Woodlawn Organization
Assorted Essays (1961–1969)

■

VARIOUS AUTHORS

TWO is certainly the most unusual, and perhaps the most significant, exercise in community organization now occurring in the US. A district supposedly incapable of any response but apathy or chaos is cultivating hundreds of leaders, insisting on initiative, grasping for responsibility, and rejecting absentee decisions as a solution for its enormous problems.

—Jane Jacobs, 1962[1]

Introduction

The decade between 1954 and 1964 was a period of great hope, optimism and, in retrospect, naïveté about what it would take to end racial discrimination in the United States. What is mostly remembered is fire hoses aimed at young black kids in Birmingham, the March on Washington, and the phrase "I have a dream" from Martin Luther King's speech there.

But in the North, blatant and subtle segregation and discrimination—in housing, education, employment, and other major areas of public life—characterized America's major urban centers. Urban renewal and freeways demolished black (and other usually poor) neighborhoods. Redlining and block-busting—both to be further described in this book—created turmoil as neighborhoods turned from white to black in a matter of months. The civil rights movement grew in the North as well. But it did not blossom as it did in the South. While nonviolent direct action won some battles, it left vast problem areas untouched. It was in these untouched areas, involving powerful institutions—banks, insurance companies, universities, developers, major corporations, and others—that Saul Alinsky's emphasis on people power made sense. This was the context in which major decision-makers and decision-making bodies in American Catholicism and mainline Protestantism agreed that the help of Saul Alinsky was needed to break down the barriers of racism. Their involvement represented a major break from how they had discussed race in the past. By and large, that had been

---

This chapter was edited by Mike Miller.

a discussion within their own largely white congregations. Turning to Alinsky, they decided to fund black communities so they could have the power to be equal—indeed leading—participants in this discussion. As Aaron Schutz indicates in his introduction to Nicholas von Hoffman, The Woodlawn Organization was Alinsky's first foray into these troubled waters.

From "The Great Debate in Chicago" (1961)

—Ulysses B. Blakeley and Charles T. Leber Jr.

Blakeley and Leber, the black and white co-pastors of Woodlawn's First Presbyterian Church, were prime movers of the effort to bring Saul Alinsky into Woodlawn. This essay was published early in the life of TWO in Presbyterian Life *as the church struggled with internal conflict over involvement in organizing.*

Churchmen—lay and clergy, Protestant and Roman Catholic—are embroiled in the "great debate" going on in Chicago these days. . . . The debate centers around the most basic problems of contemporary American life: segregation and integration, legitimate political and social action, the part of the Christian Church in the community, and the obligations of municipal and Federal government in the urban era. The eventual outcome is hidden in the future. Yet wise heads agree that the debate is not only necessary, but good for democracy in Chicago.

The fuse was ignited in a section of Chicago called Woodlawn.

Woodlawn, situated just south of the city's famed University of Chicago, is a mostly Negro area of about eighty thousand predominantly working-class inhabitants. . . . The last ten years of Woodlawn have been largely a failure. Innumerable civic groups (on paper chiefly) have come and gone, but the situation has remained the same. Everybody has tried to do something to prevent a slide into slum. Businessmen have agitated; social workers have held conferences. . . . We clergymen have worn out the seats of several good pairs of trousers while attending an uncountable number of meetings held to "do something about Woodlawn. . . ."

So it was that some of us Woodlawn clergymen, our joints stiff from sitting at meetings that led only to more meetings, got it into our heads to visit Saul David Alinsky. Four of us Woodlawn clergymen—the two authors of this report, another Protestant minister, and a Roman Catholic priest—took the plunge.

If you are familiar with Saul Alinsky's name, you will know why we say we "took the plunge." Alinsky is Chicago's patron saint of lost causes and impossible situations. And, like any good, reliable, miracle-working saint, he performs more than his share of wonders. But he is no benign father-figure; far from it. No one in the city is as detested or as loved, as cursed or blessed, as feared or respected. . . .

Blakeley and Leber's "The Great Debate in Chicago" was originally published in *Presbyterian Life*, June 15, 1961, 35–38. The selection here is reprinted by permission of *Presbyterian Life*.

Some few of the Woodlawn pastors declared that they would never have anything to do with him, that he was an evil man. The rest of us, after much researching, debate, thought, and prayer, decided that we would invite him to come into our community and help us organize ourselves. When all of us—clergymen, business leaders, and civic leaders—came to the decision, it made us a little nervous; it seemed a bit like inviting Hurricane Donna in to tidy up the living room. . . .

The Industrial Areas Foundation people came quietly into the community. They asked questions, had discussions, and discovered places and people that we who have lived in Woodlawn for years did not imagine existed. Some of us ministers found ourselves being escorted to meet pool hall proprietors, janitors, distracted looking women on relief, stern retired mailmen. These individuals, we were informed, were community leaders. It was hard to believe. Most of them had little education; they spoke peculiar English, and their areas of greatest knowledge had nothing to do with traditional organizations.

How could such people be leaders, we asked Alinsky's men? Because each of them, the Industrial Areas Foundation representatives explained, had a larger or smaller following, a greater or smaller number of people who listened to what they said, who usually did what these "leaders" suggested. And the first proposal that came from these people seemed shocking. They said the retail stores were cheating the people, short-weighing the merchandise, making people sign sales contracts to pay for clothes and appliances at exorbitant interest rates, and selling second-hand items as new.

These actual leaders wanted to do something about it. They wanted to put on a campaign, and they did. Calling it the "Square Deal Campaign," they had a parade. It was a strange parade, without drum majorettes, or music, or floats; just a long line, a thousand strong, of men and women, white and Negro, English-speaking and Spanish-speaking, carrying signs of protest, chanting and singing.

Some of the clergymen and businessmen took alarm. That man Alinsky was helping the people in Woodlawn build themselves an organization, but it seemed to have a wild and dangerous streak about it. Imagine marching and chanting down the streets of Chicago. Some churchmen, ministers and laymen, began to ask, is this the business of a Church? Won't it divide people? Won't it stir up animosities? These declared that they would have no connection with such goings on. The old recognized spokesmen went to the powerful neighbor to the north, the University of Chicago, to complain. The University's undergraduate newspaper announced that the organization was a hate group, sponsored by the Roman Catholic Church. Hadn't the Chicago Catholic Church given the Industrial Areas Foundation a fifty-thousand-dollar grant? . . . In the last fifty years, how often had the Church stayed within closed doors when the people marched? . . . It seemed dangerous . . . but that seemed nothing compared to the danger of letting the marchers pass us by.

The Square Deal Campaign has resulted in a novel thing, a board of arbitration made up equally of merchants and consumers to hear and settle all complaints.

The marching, instead of leading to riot, led to order and a better way of doing business.

New storms were in the making. Our Pastors' Alliance, composed of Protestant ministers and Roman Catholic priests, was attacked from various sides, the Roman Catholics as archplotters, and we as amiable dupes and simpletons. . . . Recently one of Chicago's leading Protestant figures said, "I've never known so many men whom I respect as persons of integrity to disagree among each other so thoroughly and completely."

The many questions as to the part a church is to play in community and city life, the kind of social and political life we want, and how we should get it, are being debated. . . .

Decisions are being made in Chicago as they should be made in a democracy, consciously and after true deliberation.

From "Woodlawn Begins to Flex Its Muscles" (1962)

—Ulysses B. Blakeley and Charles T. Leber Jr.

After a year of hard work The Woodlawn Organization in Chicago has demonstrated that something can be done [about the major issues facing Woodlawn]. . . .

On Saturday morning, August 26, 1961, [two thousand members of TWO were aboard] forty-five rented buses. . . . [They] formed a cavalcade headed for downtown . . . in order to register en masse to vote.

For Chicago the date marked the beginning of a major, mass-membership, Negro civic organization. For the civil-rights movement it marked the appearance in the Midwest of the new spirit of Southern Negroes. For the economic and political interests which have prospered by exploitation of Negroes it marked the beginning of a serious challenge. For the churches it marked a new ministry and a new life in places where faith itself seemed doomed to die and where the churches had almost disappeared from the urban scene.

TWO is permeated with a Christian outlook, but it bears little resemblance to the calm and ordered Christianity of our suburbs. In Woodlawn the Church of Christ lives and grows in the same world that Elijah Muhammad and the Black Muslims do. In Woodlawn black supremacy is preached, and anti-Christianity is openly and militantly proclaimed. When Christianity is castigated on the streets as a faith foisted upon Negroes to hold them in subjection, there are some people who listen and believe; there are more who listen and ponder—how different from communities in which Christianity is accepted as casually as the air. In Woodlawn Christianity must

Blakeley and Leber's "Woodlawn Begins to Flex Its Muscles" was originally published in *Presbyterian Life*, September 15, 1962, 12–15, 41–42. The selection here is reprinted by permission of *Presbyterian Life*.

maintain a lively and constant contact with the struggles of that community to achieve justice and hope for all its residents, or die. . . .

Slumlords Exposed

TWO, which has grown to be a federation of more than one hundred and twenty church and civic groups, voted to do something about absentee "slumlords. . . ." A bank vice-president looked up from his desk one morning to see standing in front of him forty TWO members led by a minister and a priest. They explained that they wanted to know when the bank was going to repair an overcrowded, run-down apartment building in which tenants were paying a hundred and twenty dollars a month for three-room apartments. . . .

A sit-in, the committee told the banker, would take place in his bank until the slum building was repaired or the owner's name was divulged. . . . [The banker asked for a twenty-four-hour delay.]

The next morning at nine o'clock, the bank called to say that it had resigned the trust and made public the long-hidden name of the building's true owner. What years of litigation by city officials had not been able to produce, the people of Woodlawn had obtained for themselves in twenty-four hours. . . .

The TWO housing committee is led by a Lutheran layman. It has grown to over two hundred active members and has gone after dozens of bad buildings. In dealing with some slumlords, who have purchased immunity from the law and have lost all sense of shame, these methods of public exposure are the only effective way of getting results. . . .

Shoulder-to-Shoulder Cooperation

Saul Alinsky . . . began to work with the people of the Woodlawn area in establishing a truly democratic organization. From the very beginning clergymen and laymen from the Roman Catholic and Protestant churches in the area have been active workers and supporters of the organization. And from the very beginning, critics from both religious groups have attacked the arrangement and sought to destroy it. . . .

Woodlawn church people and the great numbers who have no church connections are intensely concerned about housing, jobs, schools, and the other issues which hold minority groups back. Racial prejudice is as hard on Negro Catholics as it is on Negro Protestants. Shoulder-to-shoulder action against a common injustice has taught mutual respect. Ministers and priests are working together now. . . .

The Band Played "Old Black Joe"

By last fall the people in TWO had gained the confidence needed to face up to larger questions than those affecting their community alone. The first and biggest problem was education. Chicago's public schools are tragically segregated . . . indescribably overcrowded and understaffed. . . . Led by the clergy, TWO joined the campaign to bring the truth about Chicago schools to the attention of the city and the nation. . . .

School officials, instead of trying to correct the injustices, refused to budge. The Woodlawn pastors decided it was time to bring the issues home to the principal apologist for the school board (its president), a steel-company vice-president. Eighteen ministers called on him personally in the executive suite atop the company's brand-new skyscraper. . . .

School officials began to make a few token concessions. To dramatize the tragic overcrowding of Negro schools, while classrooms in white schools remained vacant, TWO organized "truth squads," composed of mothers and led by clergymen, to visit white schools with empty classrooms. . . .

[*TWO was also beginning a long fight with the University of Chicago against urban renewal (noting it was often called "Negro removal"). Among other actions, TWO hired its own urban planner and began an unusual democratic process of planning, actually meeting with and listening to the voices of community members.*]

Dangerous Relevance

TWO, with its slogan of "self-determination" was bringing surprise to Christian pastors as well as politicians, slumlords, educators, and city planners. Many of us clergymen had approached TWO with the idea that such a broadly representative action organization was necessary but that our people were not ready for it. It was quite a shock to find so many laymen who confided their fears that it was the clergy who would never be ready.

A Baptist minister reported that shortly after his church had voted to join TWO, a very influential layman who had been limiting his church activities to sending a weekly contribution by mail suddenly began turning up in person. When asked why he returned, he said, "Now that you've put Christianity back on a seven-day week, I have to do more than support this church with money." . . .

The image of the Presbyterian Church is being changed in Woodlawn, within the congregation, and in a small way within the city. The Church has become involved in a militant program of change. Bearing a Christian witness against flagrant injustice often means fighting against powerful interests. It is not a safe occupation. What is more, Christian witnesses are often held responsible for what they have seen and for Whom they testify. This is true for the Christians of Woodlawn, as it is for the new South today, and as it was for the Christians described in the Book of Acts. A Biblical faith in Jesus Christ leads us to believe that in our part of his mission such a dangerous path is ultimately the safest.

From "The State of the Community" (1966)

—Lynward Stevenson

Rev. Stevenson, the African American pastor of the Parkway Garden Christian Church, wrote this address during a high point in the power of TWO.

Mr. Chairman, delegates, and alternates to this great convention—I come to you tonight at the end of two years as president of The Woodlawn Organization—the highest office this community can offer.

Not many men have been placed in the path of history by so many people.

Most Negro leaders are hand-picked by rich white men, rich white politicians, for example, who use them as black Quimbos and Sambos to crack the whip.

In The Woodlawn Organization, the leaders are elected by the people themselves.

TWO has been in existence for more than five years now. A friend said to me recently, if TWO stays alive for two more years, the professors will have to rewrite all the textbooks on community organization. . . .

I cannot describe to you what it means to negotiate with people like [Sargent] Shriver and Richard Daley and not be alone. For when the president of The Woodlawn Organization goes anywhere to bargain, he has a collective leadership beside him and huge numbers of people behind him. He goes into battle with a real weapon—the weapon of the poor—their numbers. What does it mean to a man to have that kind of support? It means that he and those that support him are free men in every sense of the word. . . .

That power has produced major victories since our last Convention. . . .

The politicians in Chicago—of both parties—must get one thing clear. The Negroes of Greater Woodlawn are not going to march automatically to the polls and pull just one lever. We are going to pull lots of levers. We are going to pull levers ONLY for the men who respond to what we want. For we are not black robots, or animals in the zoo that always do the same thing behind our bars. . . .

City Hall says that the Chicago poverty program has employed some 6,000 people. Then City Hall asks, isn't that representation of the poor? It most certainly is not. Putting a man on a payroll is not the same, as asking him to help make high-level decisions. In fact, it can be just the opposite, because very often—as the Chicago machine makes clear—people on payrolls have to keep their mouths shut to keep the jobs. . . .

Since before the Mayflower there have been flunkies. . . . Those house Negroes kept telling their white plantation masters that we weren't ready to learn to read

Stevenson's "The State of the Community" was originally published in the *Woodlawn Observer*, April 28, 1966, 2–3.

and write, or we weren't ready to live with our families. Then they kept telling their masters that we weren't ready to be freed from our chains. Then they said we weren't ready to vote, we weren't ready to fight alongside white soldiers. They said we weren't ready to eat in white restaurants, or go to school with white students. They still say that, and they still say that we aren't ready to move in with the good white folks, in their neighborhoods. And they still tell their white bosses that we poor black folks aren't ready to run our own communities.

Well, I've got news for Brooks and the white establishment that he fronts for.[2] It's he and his bosses that aren't ready yet. They aren't ready to believe in democracy and self-determination. They aren't ready to look at Negroes as adults. Greater Woodlawn is ready, brother Denton—we've been ready for five years. But poor Denton—He's just the latest version of the house Negro who thinks he's better than the man out in the fields. Poor old Denton—he's just not ready for 1966. As a matter of fact, he may not be ready for 1865. . . .

We who are here tonight have a tremendous responsibility to those people all over the nation who dream that the poor people can organize their own communities and change the future for themselves and their children. Our friends are praying that we continue to win—and our enemies are praying that we fail. The only way TWO can carry out that responsibility is to build our strength—keep solid what we have, and increase our numbers.

For we are in the center of American history right now. We have been challenged over the past five years to do this job, and that challenge will remain before us for the next twenty years. There must be no letup, because TWO must set the example to America and Chicago that democracy CAN work, and that poor people can take part in the decisions of their city and their community.

At the close of my two years as your president, I came to say this:

You have made me proud to be a part of The Woodlawn Organization. You have made me proud to be a member of the Greater Woodlawn Community. You have made me proud—more than I can say—to be a Negro. And, finally, you have made me proud to be a man.

From *Black Self-Determination: The Story of The Woodlawn Organization* (1969)

—*Arthur M. Brazier*

An African American pastor of a small black congregation, Rev. Brazier was heavily recruited by von Hoffman but initially wary of participation in TWO. As a result, he agreed

Brazier's *Black Self-Determination: The Story of The Woodlawn Organization* was published by Eerdmans (Grand Rapids, MI) in 1969. The selections reprinted here are from pages 18–21 and 142–43.

to be spokesperson but not president of the first incarnation of the organization. Soon taking on the role of president, he became one of TWO's most important leaders. Alinsky was so impressed with Brazier that he later considered urging him to run for Congress. This brief section is taken from Brazier's book Black Self-Determination: The Story of The Woodlawn Organization. *Because the detail from that book is difficult to reproduce here, we recommend that readers seek it out themselves.*

To build up their own communities black Americans must acquire power. The need is not for slogans and rhetoric, but for mass-based organizations that can develop the kind of power necessary within the black community to change the domination of white power structures that continue to exploit black people. . . .

When powerless people begin to demand power and self-determination they generate within themselves a real sense of dignity that demands respect. Where there is no respect, there is no real understanding and no love. Love is a word that is bandied about a good deal today. When people begin to respect each other as human beings, then and only then is there opportunity for love to develop. This is the relationship between power and love. Power brings about the conditions whereby respect and dignity can be obtained so that love can grow out of that respect and that dignity. . . .

The loss of dignity is, in reality, the loss of that which God has given man in the first place. Man is a self-determining creature. This is a part of what the Scriptures mean by saying he is made in the image of God. . . . Freedom today means that people of color must turn their backs on even the most benevolent paternalism and make their own way. Only then will they be a self-determining people. . . .

There are two sources of power in the body politic of this country: money and people. The ghetto has no money; but it has people, and people are more important than money. So in the ghetto there is power, raw power—plenty of people. Unorganized power, however, goes nowhere. This is not to imply that there has been no organization in the black ghetto. It has come, however, from the outside for the self-interest of others rather than for the self-interest of black people. A community with people organized from within provides the route from powerlessness to power. This route was followed by The Woodlawn Organization. . . .

Simply making an emotional speech denouncing "Whitey" is not a strategy. Announcing plans to go back to Africa is not a strategy. Telling people not to participate in politics, not to vote in a particular election, is not really a strategy. I, as one man, will not attempt to play God and tell black people what the strategy should be. From now on, any strategy that we pursue should represent the opinions, thoughts, insights and experiences of a large number of black people, not just a few who happen to hold office at the top. We must discontinue the nationwide practice of allowing a few people to set national black policy off the top of their heads. We must stop basing our programs on ad hoc decisions that respond only to some crisis of the moment.

From this moment on, we must understand that we are in a war against extinction. Call it a struggle against genocide and suicide if you will, but do not understate the plight of the black man. We are in trouble, and because of its long history of racist habits, this whole nation is in trouble. We of TWO cannot solve the problems of the nation, but we can set an example of black people in a disadvantaged community asserting their humanity with solidarity.

We really have no alternative. Either we establish community power or we shall forever remain at the mercy of poverty, poor housing, inadequate education, and joblessness. . . .

We must unite. We must consolidate; we must get our minds, our souls, our bodies, our money, and our energies together.

Notes

1. Jane Jacobs, "Chicago's Woodlawn," *Architectural Forum*, May 1962, 123.
2. Denton J. Brooks Jr. was the director of the Chicago Committee on Urban Opportunity, Chicago's official poverty program.

6
Questions and Answers (1959)

■

**SAUL ALINSKY, NICHOLAS VON HOFFMAN,
AND LESTER HUNT**

Editors' preface: In early 1959, Alinsky met with key Woodlawn pastors and major Chicago and national religious leaders—Lutheran, Presbyterian, and Catholic—to discuss a possible organizing project. In response to written questions posed to him prior to the meeting, he submitted a document that is excerpted below. These questions reflect deep concerns about Alinsky's approach (especially on the part of some of the Lutherans, one of whom framed most of them), and the answers should be understood at least in part as attempts to sell the IAF approach to organizing to an at least somewhat hostile audience. While the document was originally presented under his byline, Alinsky constructed it mostly by combining text from memos written by two of his organizers, Nicholas von Hoffman and Lester Hunt, with a small amount of his own. More than half a century later, Hunt was somewhat critical of the style of his youthful writing, which "I often find arrogant." He went on to note, however, that overall, "I think it is a pretty good exposition and description of the philosophy and practice of the IAF. Most of what it says the IAF did is, in general, true."[1] Von Hoffman generally agreed.[2] Because of the length of the original document, we have abridged it significantly.

1. What specifically do you propose to do, and how? . . .

We propose to select and train a special staff in the principles and practices of the Industrial Areas Foundation's procedures. . . . Simultaneously, the Industrial Areas Foundation would carry on an intensive research program collecting all data on this particular community, data ranging from formal statistical descriptive materials on various facets of community life to masses of informal information concerning individuals, institutions, the relationships between various individuals and institutions, the hierarchy of power interests. . . . [We would examine] the general power patterns of organization in the community, [develop] an understanding of the combination of forces necessary to effect sufficient citizen participation that would have the power for

---

The original document is in Industrial Areas Foundation records, box 27, folder 459, Special Collections and University Archives, University of Illinois at Chicago. It is published here by permission of Nicholas von Hoffman and Lester Hunt.

constructive changes in the life of the community, and [conduct] an analysis of the character of the probable opposition.

The proposed program would in general be a ferreting out of the common desire and common needs of the representative groups of the community. These common desires and common needs would be the basis for a series of common agreements which would be in fact the local program of the people of the community.

This would include the stimulation of the desires and even more importantly the demonstration to the organizations and peoples of the community that there is a way, through organization, where they can effectively come to grips with their problems and be able to deal with them in a significant fashion. One of the major reasons for apathy is the feeling that even if the local institutions and citizenry got excited and very much concerned about their problems that there really was not much use in becoming concerned since they could see no way out. . . .

In Woodlawn the Protestant and Catholic churches have the opportunity to set up a demonstration of national significance as to what these religious institutions can do in the face of this common situation. The issue facing the Protestant and Catholic churches in this kind of a changed-over community is clear: either they close up shop and move or else they stay and join hands in becoming spearheads in a total community effort to meet the problems plaguing the new residents. . . .

4. Where has your approach been shown to be effective in organizing a community like Woodlawn? Have you ever organized a community like Woodlawn?
We have never organized a community like Woodlawn. Neither has any other organization. We have never organized a community similar to any community which we have organized. . . . There are no communities that are "like" each other.

If the question were rephrased to read, "Has our approach been effective in organizing communities which have characteristics such as a high mobility, a preponderant minority group, housing conditions similar to Woodlawn, a paucity of effective public services such as police protection, health services, etc.," then our response would be in the affirmative. . . .

10. What kinds of checks and balances will be in effect to protect the initial church underwriting of this work (What kinds of guarantees do the churches have that they are not bringing a "monster" into existence?)
Nothing that has ever been undertaken in the history of mankind that has been worthwhile has not involved a certain risk. The entire democratic process and the idea of a popular electorate involved such a risk, but we assume this risk on the basis of a faith in the democratic way of life. . . .

"Monsters" have a way of being born and growing up in a vacuum of indifference and apathy and not in a community of healthy active participation.

The kind of personnel which is employed for the development of this kind of an organization . . . would be a substantial argument against this possibility.

11. What is your basic philosophy today about organizing people in a community—especially in reply to the accusations made that your organizing purposes and/or tactics are not in accordance with sound moral principles?

. . . . The character of the many outstanding national leaders of the highest moral stature such as Jacques Maritain explicitly answers this question. The character of our Board of Trustees, the nation-wide praise from the religious press, titular leaders of major religious institutions, and from all quarters of American life could never have come about if the Industrial Areas Foundation had been involved in activities "not in accordance with sound moral principles." . . .

As to the issue of the basic philosophy of the Industrial Areas Foundation. . . . All we do is contingent on the wishes of the people who are forming a new organization. The Industrial Areas Foundation only exercises a control to the extent of refusing to lend aid or encouragement to groups and individuals whose true purpose is contrary to the letter or spirit of the nation's laws. . . .

[We are not] indifferent to moral questions. Quite the contrary. That is why we believe every person and every institution must realize his own moral responsibilities, and we trust that our work has frequently helped many to do exactly that. . . .

In the last analysis the people themselves decide on the tactics they use. Actually we cannot organize a community. The community does it itself. . . . We have as much and the same kind of relationship to organizational tactics as the midwife has to the birth of a baby. It is the community, and above all its leaders, its ministers, its social and economic leaders[,] who decide what the tactics are to be. It is their responsibility to do nothing they will ever be ashamed of having a part in. . . .

14. What kind of people does the Industrial Areas Foundation hire? How are they picked? How are they trained? What do they do?

. . . . Regardless of whether we are talking about political, labor, community or any other kind of mass organization we find that the people who have been most successful at this sort of work are unanimous in their contention that the ability to organize cannot be transferred from one person to another by any known academic curriculum, even with the superficial accessory of "field work." . . .

[A key] distinction . . . is the ancient one between art and science. Science is frigidly analytic and impartial. . . . The reasoning in art is illogical, paradoxical, and intuitive. The reasoning in art . . . is grounded in acute observation, in an understanding and a memory of all experience which culminates in a method of approach that is not analytic, but rather synthetic. The kind of person we look for must be able to deal rationally with the irrationalities of life.

It is for these reasons that we cannot speak of an organizer being . . . a "professional." Our organizers, and we might add they are good organizers, may be professional in the sense that they are paid to do what they do; but in no other sense. When they are very good at their jobs we cannot refer to them as professionals, but perhaps we could use the description that certain sports reserve for their outstanding performers when we say that such and such a man is "an old pro." . . .

We are looking for someone who not only has intelligence and the personality to use it, but also emotional stamina. We search for people who are able to control themselves without repressing themselves, are able to assert themselves without gratifying themselves, who are able, in form, to put their personalities to one side in order to get the work accomplished.

We ask our people to work sixteen and eighteen hours a day; we ask them to work without days off for rather long stretches of time, and we ask them to work very hard while they are on the job. It stands to reason that you cannot pay any individual enough money to compensate for such dismally poor working conditions. Nevertheless no one can work as hard as we expect our people to work on occasion without their doing it for a reason. Before hiring anyone for our staff we inquire very minutely into the reasons why he is willing to engage himself in such an arduous job. We are looking for people who will do this kind of work and bear up under the sacrifices that go with it because they believe in what they are doing. Further, we are also looking for moral capacity. . . . After all we cannot forget that a trained and skilled organizer is potentially a great weapon for good or for evil. We must be sure that the people whom we form into skilled and effective organizers are people with values commensurate with their organizational abilities. . . .

If a man or a woman has these qualities, we know we can, in the course of a few years, turn him into a top-notch organizer of the sort who will make a profound contribution. . . .

How they are trained?

Since our people are hired on merit and ability, in training we are merely asking them to do what they are capable of doing. . . . Our major training job is to turn [their] hot anger into a cold, bridled anger so that they know what they are doing, why they are doing it, and the relationship of their specific act . . . to a general plan of action. . . .

In organizational work no substitute exists for teaching people but allowing them to do the work and learn by making mistakes. This is the basis of our staff training. . . . Naturally we do not leave [new organizers] alone, but attempt to train them by setting up what we might call a dialogue between the experience they are having and the mass experience of the Foundation. By constantly discussing, by bringing up analogous situations, by asking our staff people to look at the organizational problems in front of them from various angles, we set in motion a mental discipline that allows our people to teach themselves. Perhaps in no other form of organization does the Socratic cliché, "Know Thyself," so quickly cease to be an old bromide and become the foundation for one's personal and working life as it does in organizational work. . . .

[*The document mentions education in "the arts, philosophy, the intellectual disciplines" for those who come without such a background.*]

The method of training is Socratic, but before this can be done the right kind of atmosphere must be created. It is essential that the staff person feel free enough and secure enough that he can think and speak with complete candor and fearlessness. Otherwise, rather than real learning taking place, the staff person is essentially accepting passively those ideas which he thinks will be most pleasing to whoever is supervising him. This freedom and security, however, cannot be played at. It must be real. It cannot be a "gimmick" which is carried out because it is considered the newest way of teaching staff. . . .

Each staff person is required to keep a daily diary. This serves the twofold purpose of keeping a record of what he is doing day by day and giving him a method to reflect on the things that have happened during that day. [*This daily diary was sent to Alinsky for critique and suggestions.*]

Staff meetings are held almost daily at first and frequently from then on. At each staff meeting a series of questions about what has been going on is raised and a series of problems to which answers must be found posed. The staff person is required to reflect on what he has been doing and to extract the essential principles and ideas out of it. The staff person learns to become critical of what he is doing himself and to question it continually. There is no expert with expert answers to be appealed to and a staff member must develop his own critical faculties. . . .

Each staff member is responsible to work out his own plan of procedure, but it is always discussed thoroughly in a staff meeting before it is carried out. No aspect of the plan is left un-attacked and unquestioned and no appeals to "authorities or experts" can replace adequate reasons for or against an idea. Each situation is examined from several points of view. One question which is always asked to any proposal which a staff member may make is the following one. "Let us assume that your plan will work out exactly as you hope it will without any flaws, although we know that no plan ever works out 100% perfectly, what have you got then?" Unless you can see that you will have some good and worthwhile results, the idea is discarded. Another point of view which is always raised is to examine the positives and negatives of every situation and even of the project itself rigorously. If a plan or a situation has more positives than negatives and the positives are worth spending some time on then one can proceed intelligently. No staff member ever goes into a situation without a full realization of exactly what he is doing and what the positives and negatives are. . . . A healthy and continuous skepticism is developed, not unadorned with a good deal of humor and fun, about every idea and everything which is done, and no concept is so sacred that it cannot be ruthlessly scrutinized.

What they do?
The first job of a staff person, whether he is a native of a community or not, is to familiarize himself with every aspect of the community. [He must learn who actually runs the community, and how.] It is not unusual to find that the person who really

controls a certain organization is not the president at all, but one member or a group of members who may not even hold any office. . . .

What are the issues which are most important and what are the things which the people in the community want changed or something done about? . . . People like to talk about themselves and when they talk about what they think of their community they are really talking about themselves. Also, when they find that the organizers do not have a preconceived program to sell them, they become intensely interested in their own problems. It is this which must be done next, finding out what the issues and problems which are important to the people in the community are. This is not always easy to do. . . . It is the organizer's job to build enough confidence and trust with the people that he is interviewing so that they will be willing to talk openly and frankly with him and then to be able to question in such a way that the vague and general issues are made more specific. It does no good to say that politics is corrupt. One must get down to exactly who is corrupt and what corrupt actions is he guilty of. It is at this point that something can be done.

It is not true, however, that just because people know what some of the problems in their community are that they will do anything about them. As a matter of fact, we are more correct to assume that they won't do anything about them. It has always been somebody else's job. It is at this point that the organizer becomes an agitator, very much like a union organizer in an unorganized factory. Until people realize that it is THEY who must do something about their own problem, and that it is only they who can be trusted to do the right thing, and until they realize that only if they organize enough power in their community that something can be done about these things, nothing will get done. It is the organizer's job to get people to realize these things and, in spite of what the pessimists may say, it can be done.

When these things have been accomplished, and this may take many months, it is time to start building an organization. As a matter of fact the people will start demanding that an organization be created. . . . When enough organizations are re-cruited so that the organization is truly representative, a Community Congress is called to work out a constitution and elect officers.

It should be pointed out that no policy decisions have been made up to this point. This is not an organization to do certain specific things. It is an organization which will now decide what it wants to do. The organizer has only insisted on two things up to this point: The organization must be democratic. It must represent most of the interests, no matter how small, of the community. . . .

Notes

1. Lester Hunt, interview by Aaron Schutz, March 14, 2013.
2. Nicholas von Hoffman, interview by Aaron Schutz, August 11, 2012.

7
Finding and Making Leaders (1963)

∎

NICHOLAS VON HOFFMAN

Editors' preface: According to von Hoffman, this essay was written for the second Students for a Democratic Society conference in 1963. As he tells it, no one actually showed up to his talk, but he left some mimeographed copies around, and apparently people read it. As von Hoffman notes, "I don't know how this thing managed to find a life for itself, but it has never died."[1] In fact, as Richard Luecke put it, the piece "became a near-canonic text" in the 1960s and 1970s "on how to enter a community and make your way to the indigenous persons who really call the shots."[2]

Leaders are found by organizing, and leaders are developed through organization. The statement is so self-evident and so simple-minded that it is usually uttered only to be assented to and forgotten.

Instead of acting on the assumptions implicit in the observation, we begin the great hunt for the 'natural leader," "the indigenous leader"; he is the great organizational nugget, whom we could find by panning for him if we only knew what the hell he looked like, and how he differed from the silt washed into our tin.

It's worth noting that practically everybody is looking for him. The civil rights movement, big business, big social work, church organizations. Everybody finds it handy to blame their problems on expressions like the "dearth of leadership," the "problem we're having finding leaders," etc.

He does not exist. If he were there—that wondrous all-purpose leader that every organizer dreams about in his moments of exasperation with and anger at his would-be constituency, you would not be necessary. The all-purpose indigenous leader with the sharp tactical mind of Lenin, the forensic abilities of Demosthenes or F.D.R., and the general loveableness of your mother would have long since asserted himself.

The quest for the natural leaders—the quest as it is actually carried on—is like the quest for the natural man. There is no natural man; there is no natural leader. The

---

Since 1963, "Finding and Making Leaders" has been reprinted and copied in different places. This particular version was published by the Southern Student Organizing Committee (n.d.); we have silently corrected a handful of typographical errors within the original. It is reprinted here by permission of Nicholas von Hoffman.

ideas are important because they remind us in any group of men some can come to live by certain ethics and some can become leaders—given the occasion.

I am hammering at this point because I have seen so many ardent young people run into communities, zoom around frantically for eight or ten months, and then say they can't find indigenous leadership. Now when it is put to them in so many words that this is what they are doing, they deny it. Nevertheless, it is obvious that they are acting on notions of leadership that are wholly unrealistic.

Let's try and see why. Bear in mind, I am now speaking of the lower class Negro ghetto. In the main the same observations would hold for any community, but in white areas there are certain differences in application.

The first objective in the ghetto is building an organization that wields power. That is in marked contrast to the flash-flood demonstration kind of thing that northern big shots quickly get blasé about. An organization that wields power as opposed to the kind that throws an intermittent stink-bomb, must be big, must be broad, must be quasi-institutionalized.

The kinds of leadership it must have to operate successfully are the kinds that cannot exist in the community because no one or almost no one in the community has had the chance to gain any experience with big organizations. Most of the communities' people will not even have been in the army. The few that have will have served in such a low echelon that they will not have had the opportunity to acquire a sense or a feel for the big organization, how it is put together, how it stays together, and what you have to do to run it.

A few people in the community may work for a large corporation or the government but here again they are cut off from gaining experience with the big organization. For another few the church may begin to supply the experience, but most people aren't church members or are very passively so, and most churches aren't very big, and most big churches are not very organizationally run.

The long and short of it is we are speaking of people whose organizations are mostly small, and consequently, whose leaders are schooled in techniques which work for small groups, but seldom for large ones. If they had the large enduring organizations they would have the leaders to run them, and you would be superfluous.

However, it is also true that every community has a few naturals, that is a few people who are by accident of life experience, an exceptional intelligence and some other qualities can begin to move to the forefront almost as soon as the first organizational beginnings are under way. But who are they? How do you find them, and how do you make sure they actually do begin to assume the major roles they are capable of? It would be so much easier if we could spot these people in advance—unfortunately that is impossible. At the beginning of organization, you are the leader—natural or otherwise—because at least theoretically you know more about what you are doing— building an organization—than anyone else around. If any of these three conditions doesn't hold, by-the-by, get out and give the job over to somebody else.

Recognize the fact that the organizer who comes into the community for the first time is internally in a precarious position, he is afraid—or at least he should be if he has got any brains which he doesn't want beaten out.

He is afraid because he doesn't know the people, and we are all vaguely afraid of people we don't know. If he is white and he going to work in a Negro community he is doubly afraid. If he is a middle class Negro, he is afraid too, for similar but not quite identical reasons.

He is afraid because he is the bearer of a new idea. Mankind does not cotton to new ideas in general, but especially not to the new ideas that organizers bring. This is so because they may mean trouble and because the organizer's mere presence in the community is a tacit insult. The organizer, merely by his presence, is saying in effect to the people, "you are so dumb that you need me to think your way out of this mess you are in." Don't kid yourself about this. I shouldn't have to remind you here—who have actually organized—of this reaction. (Nor I might add, does blaming the white man or the status quo or anything else absolve the organizer of the sin.)

The organizer is also afraid because a failure is a crushing blow to his ego or his self-respect. Even a bad organizer puts a tremendous part of himself on the line when he goes into a community. In his own eyes, he is being tried as a person, in a huge test of his own worth. To fail is to be adjudged a capon, a sexless, impotent thing by one's self, or so I always found it.

These fears work on most organizers to make them very susceptible to thinking that people they meet in the community who are sympathetic are the people to listen to and work with. I can't count the number of times I have wandered into communities to find the people who were supposed to be building a mass organization mucking around with pious, middle class clergymen or teenagers.

Or, of course, there is the organizer who sees the weakness in himself, and over-compensates by finding a bunch of social outcasts, usually winos, addicts, or semi-criminal types, the kind that talk a good fight but lack the self-discipline to make hard-core organizational material. This kind of organizer may also be playing to a gallery of middle-class friends (often white) who will be mightily impressed by his acquaintance in the demi-monde. It's nice to have one's outside friends think you are "in," but the question is, in what?

For the organizer who gets beyond acting as a reaction to himself—in my experience, few do—plucking out "natural leaders" by dint of casual observation and conversation is very chancy. I recall having picked a number of these on-first-sight-gems, and I also recall spending months kicking myself for having done so.

The guy who is indeed the natural small group leader may turn out to be the guy who gets hopelessly and permanently confused by committees or simply by having to keep in mind that now instead of dealing with ten old faithfuls in the block club he's got to worry about what 400 people think. The guy you met at the barber shop, who seemed so articulate and understanding, may turn out at second meeting to be a dogmatist of the first order or a flannel-mouthed idiot. The guy with the big line about how "it's about time the black man showed these "m-f's'" can turn out to be one great chicken, or what can be worse yet, a lazy bum who only comes to meetings to make long theatrical monologues.

Those of you who may recognize your own experiences in some of these words will say, "Don't tell us what won't work, tell us what will."

To you I repeat, leaders are found by organizing and leaders are developed through organizations. So let's discuss organizing and organization.

But before we get to that, I want to set down two of the observations I have made where leadership has developed. They are: the leaders in the third month of an organization's life are seldom the leaders in the third year; a few leaders, ourselves included, are really all-purpose; and the best organizations create a "collective leadership."

Why should so few of the leaders in an organization's infancy be around as it grows and maturity?

The first leadership is usually the closest leadership at hand. It is selected usually in the enthusiasm of the first campaign, because it is available. You don't have a choice and you have to go with what you've got.

It may be a rent strike, a school demonstration, or what have you. Reverend So-and-So says he'll be the spokesman, and you want him because he's a clergyman and you figure he'll cut more ice because he's respectable. Maybe it's Mrs. Jones, because she's the only one of the tenants who shows signs of being able to speak out in front of a judge. Or, perhaps, it's So-and-So else because he has a reputation (with you anyhow) as a regular freedom fighter.

Note that all these people were picked on the basis of what they could do in a one-shot affair. And the beginning of every viable organization smacks of being a one-shot affair, for the simple reason that theorists who fiddle around waiting and delaying until they've got a full blown across-the-board organizational program set are never ready to commence swinging into action.

But you will notice, too, that the reasons for your picking the first leaders (and you know it's you who pick them) say nothing about how they will wear over a period of time. That respectable clergyman can turn out to be a timid jerk; the lady who was good at sounding off in front of the judge may be good for nothing else, and that big freedom fighter can look like a vain egomaniac living off the deed done many years ago.

The lesson I draw from this is that at the beginning keep the organization very loose, spread the responsibilities and the conspicuous places around. This permits you and the new membership, which you are supposed to be recruiting, to judge the talent, and it keeps things sufficiently porous so that new talent isn't blocked off. Nothing is more absurd than an organization that's six months old, without a dime in the treasury and a membership that can fit in a Volkswagen, having a cemented-in, piggy leadership. Vested interests are only tolerable when they are protecting something of value, not fancy organizational charts, letterheads and research programs.

Don't laugh. This kind of thing is a clear and present danger. Vain men frequently prefer to be members of obscure executive committees where they can spend years expounding doctrine. It is safer and easier than the realities of making and using power.

Men with the most to lose or men with the most to give in talent, money and experience are often not the first to join an organization. They will never join if they see there is no room for them in the top leadership.

Why should some of the most talented people hang back? One reason, of course, is that they want to check you and the incipient organization out. If they are worth having, they won't be the kind who must be on a guaranteed winner, but also, by the same token, they don't want any part of a born loser.

A big northern city is not like the south. In one sense the people are all in the same boat thanks to skin pigmentation, but not quite. People can and do make a variety of deals with life. In the North there are a lot of Negroes who may have cause to think that they have more to lose than to gain by signing on with you. They will be those who fear loss of jobs, prestige, business or such—and many will fall into that category. But there will also be those who think they can make a better deal by joining with somebody or something else, and those who just may not think what you're driving at is worth it OR that you can deliver goods.

The varieties of reactions have to be tackled in a variety of ways, but all the people who fall into these groupings—your potential second generation of leaders—must not be driven away gratuitously. They must not be allowed to dismiss the organization out of hand at the very beginning.

Yet in fact many organizations are killed off by their organizers even before they get close to a second leadership generation. It is pure charity of course, to speak of such preliminary groupings as organizations at all. Most of these endeavors never grow to look like much more than an aborted six-month fetus. They have been murdered by their own parents, the organizers who were supposed to give them life.

In the case of young organizers, their youth is enough to do it. People may admire youth, they may praise, they may believe that youth is showing the way in which age should follow, but they are very, very reluctant to trust youth with anything of immediate value. Youth is not an insuperable handicap, I rush to add. I have known top-notch organizers in their twenties.

The good ones know, however, that they must pick up more in the way of membership than the people with the least to lose, the people who are willing to put themselves under guidance to unreliable appearing strangers. Beware of the groups led by a couple of college students, composed of a membership of teenagers, ministers without serious institutional responsibilities and a few desperate mothers, driven to trying anything to get their kids into a decent school. Anyone who has been around knows the type of enterprise I am talking about. Yet such is the look of the organizational endeavor which has failed to bud a second generation of leadership; it is also the characteristic profile of the collegiate organizer's botched job. It is as recognizable as the insulated, desiccated organizational product put out by the professional social worker.

At the risk of sounding like mother, may I say that impressions do count. I'll mention clothes. It is one thing to wear overalls in Mississippi where many of the people actually do wear them—it is another to wear them as an occasional stunt in a big northern city. But to indulge in peculiarities of dress and speech simply makes you look like faddists. I apologize for saying this to those of you who know better, but those will also know it has to be said. Faddism makes you look like a horse's ass. White middle class girls from Des Moines, to be extreme about it, did not grow up referring to males as "cats," and when they do it on the south side of Chicago they sound either patronizing or idiotic—take your pick.

Nothing is so reassuring as a person who acts like himself. If you don't know who you are, stay out of organizing until you do and are willing to accept yourself as yourself. When you do, you will find that other people will.

Next, may I urge you to drop as much of your excess ideological baggage as you can outside the place where you are organizing. You are building a power group, a mass organization to serve a particular constituency, one that has certain paramount demands to be met. The demands are remote from "peace" or from any number of other, perhaps laudable, but irrelevant interests.

In other words, don't act like cultists. If you are a vegetarian, keep it to yourself, hide it, because there are a certain number of butchers in the community and you want them in the organization too.

This work demands self-discipline in every way. It means you either get your rest or hide the fact that you haven't because people who arrive at sixes and sevens and announce they haven't slept for 26 consecutive hours give the impression of being unstable. It also means that you recognize that you have no private life, or put differently, you do not offend against the public morals of the community. Why? Not because the morals are necessarily correct, but because organizers who do not seem to be observing them alienate potential members for no good reason.

Some people may read what I have just said and think, "Ah ha! White man's conventional middle class values—ethnocentrism, etc., etc." To which I reply, these are the public values held by substantial portions of the people you hope to organize.

Whether they practice them is as beside the point as whether middle-class whites do. The cultist will say that there can be no surrender and that freedom of the individual is involved. Perhaps it is, but he who wastes time debating such abstractions, or, worse, insists on making it clear by his behavior that he believes otherwise is enjoying a luxury that is organizationally ruinous.

As organizers, apostolic vegetarians can only organize and inspire confidence among other vegetarians.

The best organizers have single-track minds. They care only for building the organization. When they alienate a potential member, they do so out of organizational need, not out of the egotism of irrelevant personal values. The best organizers stifle their tastes, their opinions, their private obsessions.

Now at least we have taken a few preliminary precautions to prevent killing off the leadership before it even arrives and we can turn back to the question of finding and developing it.

From what I have seen, most of the organizational life in the ghetto is the small group, usually no bigger than the number of people that make up an extended circle of acquaintance. This usually figures out to twenty-five or less and rarely more than fifty. Numbers that get larger than that have to be held together by different, written, systems of bookkeeping and communication.

Two conclusions can be drawn from this: (1) Building a mass organization in the ghetto is the tedious job of stringing beads on a necklace, and (2) self-evidently, most of the available indigenous leadership will only be practiced in the arts of the small organization.

I have in mind the block club, the local janitors' association, the multitudinous sororities, the choirs, the teenage groupings, the local political and business associations, the perennial members of the local pool tournament. I am sure you can name many more. Every one of these groupings has some kind of leadership. So the quest for leadership is abruptly over. There is, for practical purposes, no other leadership to be found, because there exist no vehicles for leadership to drive.

What this boils down to, then, is your discontent with what leadership can do—namely, lead the groupings you find in the community. Your dissatisfaction with the leadership has real enough basis in fact. It is a narrow leadership mostly interested in what concerns the small group; it has little save only the most conventional understanding of the great issues which brought you into the community in the first place.

Great issues absorb the interest either of small highly specialized groups, as for instance many a chapter of SANE or CORE or NAACP, or of a great organization. The small group can make mischief and propagandize in a diffuse way, but power, power is the property of the big organization. All this you know, for it again is what brings you to the community.

At every turn, the leadership is unsuited for your purposes. And so it will remain, changing only as the big organization emerges. The same holds true for the leadership you "find," that is, people who enter the organization without a following, but create one in and by means of the organization. The character of leadership, to put it in other words, is determined by the character of the organization that trains it and which it leads. The making of an organization and the making of leadership are inseparable.

The proposition is not presented to you as a new great truth. It is no more than another 'application of the ancient observation that a man finds both his limits and his growth in his own personal experience. I have the temerity to advance this old bromide yet one more time, because it is often ignored. The fact that you are still thinking of leadership as an isolated category, one meriting its own workshop, shows how far people are from treating the leadership question as integral to the making of an organization.

This said, we can now spend some time talking about organizing as it fits into leadership.

The organizer's first job is to organize, not right wrongs, not avenge injustice, not to win the battle for freedom. That is the task of people who will accomplish it through the organization if it ever gets built. When things are looked at through the glass of organizational calculation, they assume new shapes.

A couple of examples may help to explain my meaning:

1. When the cops pick up a whore, shake her down, and beat up her pimp, they have done wrong. Both the whore and pimp have rights, which have been grossly violated, but a thinking organizer may wonder how good an idea it is to commit his new group to their defense. What will the public at large say? More important, what will the different segments of the community say?

   The caballeros on the street hustling will love you, but what about the solid family types? Should the solid family types be taught the relativity of all human values, and will they consent to learn? Six months from now, will the caballeros think enough of the organization to support it by coming to one meeting, by contributing one dollar?
2. Rent strikes. They are very popular now, but as with leadership, they are seen as something that is good to do merely if you can do them. However, as anybody who has ever run one can tell you, they gobble up an organizer's time—which should be a valued asset—and may produce very few organizational dividends.

How might an organizer look at a rent strike proposition? (I am spinning this example out to illustrate the mentality, which we might call organizational calculation.)

Of course he looks at the building. He does this for two reasons—the first is defensive; he wants to make sure the tenants aren't lying to him. Who doesn't think his landlord is a louse? Nothing is worse than getting into a fight in which the enemy can publicly prove your facts are wrong—note I said publicly prove.

The second reason he looks is to see how the building will photograph and will strike the eye of the often not very sympathetic press. I recall once having an argument with a photographer from the *Saturday Evening Post* as to whether a dead rodent in a slum building was a rat or a mouse. In short, the rats should look like rats.

If it still appears that a strike is feasible, he must ask what it will do for the organization. I will list a few possible things it might do, again by way of illustrating the organizational mentality.

1. If the political climate is right and you know local government is with you, it may provide a quickie victory—something every organization needs on occasion.
2. It can be a device to show people via face-to-face confrontation that a big important white man like a slum landlord can be humiliated and beaten.
3. It may be a way to force a municipal government to begin rigorous enforcement of minimal housing standards.

4. It may be useful in building up general organizational cohesion. I recall one rent strike during which the landlord retaliated by such tactics as failing to buy coal for the building. The organization responded in its turn by taking a portion of the sequestered rents to buy coal. The coal truck was decorated with appropriate signs; the gentlemen from the teamsters union who customarily drove the truck was replaced by several local leaders in the cab, while other people from the organization surrounded it as it paraded around the neighborhood before finally coming to its destination. Humor, color, the relish of a small triumph and greater organizational solidity came out of this little episode.

5. The strike may also be a useful method for organizing the people in the immediate locals around the building in question. Unless you have all of officialdom on your side, a rent strike is liable to be a protracted contest of nasty little surprises which each side springs on the other. The landlord's surprises are usually legal ones, bailiffs, court orders, etc. If the whole area is mobilized and organized into a big warning system, the landlord can't pull off much.

But if the fight is really you and a few tenants verses the landlord in the midst of an indifferent populace, you are likely to invest hundreds of hours of time keeping the tenants' morale up, with little to show for it but some publicity.

There are other reasons, good organizational reasons, for having rent strikes, but the point to bear in mind is having some reason other than the pure injustice of it all. It is, of course, very hard for an organizer to know when he has a valid reason for doing something, and when he is conning himself.

By nature most organizers are optimists—they have to be or they wouldn't be doing what they do. Optimists tend to be credulous. They get so fascinated by the putative advantages of a proposed line of action that they never seriously examine either its drawbacks, or—and this is just as important—how they might be better spending their time.

I found in my own experience that my ego was incessantly trying to sabotage my judgment. For instance, I would argue in favor of striking a slum on the basis of organizational advantage without ever realizing that actually I was in a rage over the conditions the people in the building were living in. A good organizer cannot afford to vent his anger, any more than he can use his position to push miscellaneously irrelevant pet social beliefs.

The ego works in other ways to deform the organizer's powers of judgment. Promising young organizers are prone to come up with clever ideas—and in their pride of invention, or in the egotism of mischief-making, to attempt to carry them out in circumstances that are neither propitious nor even apropos.

The calculating organizer is forever suspicious of himself, forever mistrusting his analysis of the situation and his plan of action. He is always asking himself questions like, "What am I doing? Why am I doing it? If I succeed in doing what I am trying to do, will we really have gained anything worth gaining?" However, the organizer with a calculating mentality shall assuredly fail if he is trying to do the undoable.

What is an attainable organization in the working class ghetto? It is an organization of perhaps two percent of the people. Those who talk about organizing "all the people" or "the masses" or "the great majority of the people" are talking unrealizable balderdash.

In the first place, it cannot be done. The only way all the people or most of the people can be organized is by drafting them into the army. On the rare occasions when large percentages of a population are directly "participating" in the affairs of the community, they are probably having a riot. But this form of mass participation—I use the word that is fashionable—hardly gains much. Moreover, if you stop and reflect a second, you will see that any non-governmental organization comprising huge portions of the population would be so completely unwieldy that it couldn't ever achieve anything.

The purpose of organizations is, I remind you, at least in this discussion, power. As a practical matter, the organizing of two percent of a population is more than sufficient for the purpose of power. This you know from the history of modern revolutions—or if you look around, from the composition of the most effective present-day political machines. Indeed, even two percent of a population actively in an organization is an immensely formidable number. With two percent of a district's population closely organized, the organization should have an unbreakable control over things.

When the problem is viewed this way, it becomes more manageable intellectually and actually. To begin with, it now becomes possible to see where are the plausible places to start organizing and to sort out what elements in the community demand organizational attention and which are purely optional, to be courted provided the occasion arises and you have the time.

An organization needs three things: (1) A network of people spread out and in position to reach and mobilize the inert majority; (2) Continuity; and (3) Money.

The majority of small groups in the ghetto districts I am familiar with turn out to be potentially strongest in one of these three qualities. Thus a block club adds a good deal to the mobilization network, has some money potential, but is usually quite low in supplying continuity. The same can be said of the sorority or the poolroom gang, while a business group scores higher on the money and may bolster an organizations' continuity.

Obviously, what is needed is the right mix of groupings to make up the sinews of organization. Sometimes this is accomplished by finding what the textbooks call the most common denominator. But the catch is, the most common denominator evokes the least general interest. Everybody is against juvenile delinquency, but who cares enough about it to do anything? An issue which lines a whole community up on one side is most often so innocuous as to be organizationally useless.

There is an exception to this, and that is the outrage, the atrocity, the bad slum fire, rat-bites-child, bombing the Sunday school. However, such crises are of limited organizational value. The shock and anger they cause are soon dissipated. Furthermore, they are of much greater value to an existing organization than they are to building an organization.

Where an organization exists, the emotion the momentary crisis causes to be released can be harnessed to well-thought-out political maneuvers and demonstrations; it can also be exploited for money raising and recruiting in sections of the district where you are organizationally weak. But where there is no organization, there is no way to capitalize on the opportunity. There may be a few indignation meetings, or even a riot, and then all collapses back into its previous shape.

The foregoing should suggest that the right balance of network, continuity, and money is engendered by an organizational program containing a balance or mix of goals or would-be pay-offs (which organizationally is all that a goal is) for the various groupings you need to recruit. For homeowners the program may be defense against venal building inspectors, for the unemployed it may be pressure on some well-known local firm that discriminates, for the church group or local civil rights sentiment, it may be some sort of an assault on the local educational system. Hence, it has been said that organizing of this nature is, at least in part, building up a community-wide set of interlocking log-rolling agreements: "You scratch my back and I'll scratch yours, but if we don't combine, nobody's back'll get scratched."

Purists may find such a procedure intolerable. For example, you don't put pressure on the white small store past a certain point—even if he can hire an extra Negro clerk. The reason is you need his money, which you will get if he fears you, but not if he hates you. You will also get his money, I hasten to add, if the organization's program includes objectives that are worth something to him. Purists will find many, many of the things the individuals and groups which you are courting want, to be picayune. Yet these "picayune" wants are the stuff of which organizations are built. They are the things that must of necessity most occupy people and which move people to action as great abstractions seldom do. Moreover, it is by meeting thorough organizational conquest the picayune demands that the great issues are made immediate and divested of their abstract distance. The mother learns about segregated education by fighting for schoolbooks for her child, the home-owner struggling with urban renewal learns about the society's huge engine of residential segregation by battling to save his property—the people learn these lessons and the most important lesson about how the world that bears down on them actually functions. However, the organizer is there to draw the lesson, to make the experience valuable, to lead on into the next and larger round in this match which will only be won by those adaptable enough to use victorious methods.

The organizer who merely sees the people's day-to-day problems as the proof that oppression demeans men, and not as the change to be exploited, lacks the patience, the ingenuity, and the opportunism that makes success. The I-can't-be-bothered-with-that attitude is self-important and the organizer who is mostly concerned with "big issues" will never meet success outside the debate room.

Again, I am speaking of the ability to see the calculation and act with calculation. It is not easy, particularly once you have sensitized yourself to the importance of little favors, little worries, little preoccupations, to know which are the organizationally useful ones and which are heart-rending but profitless. I remember a newly founded organization that was offered several thousand dollars' worth of Christmas baskets by a group of terrified local businessmen hoping to placate the popular wrath. First we battled with the local sufferers-for humanity about putting whisky in the baskets. They wanted the money spent on extras for the children. After that we argued over who should get the baskets. They wanted to give them to the needy! The organizers wanted to give them to the strategic, the flat janitors and other key people whom it is good to have obligated to the organization.

If I may I would like to advert to the stringing of beads on the necklace one more time. The beads, it turns out, are not all of one shape and color. They are a variety, and as you pick them out and string them, the necklace will have a correspondingly different pattern.

The bead analogy holds with leadership also. Too many money beads—that is organizations brought in primarily for the dough they can contribute—and you will find yourself with a lot of money, but a soggy, conservative leadership. Too little money, too many youth groups, and you will get an organization that's always broke, that's short on continuity, and always undertaking more than its organizational base can carry out.

A big organization demands a variety of leadership talents. Money-raising leadership, oratorical leadership, tactical leadership, leadership for routine, leadership that can measure community sentiment, that knows when to move and when to stay put. The different kinds of groups that come into your organization train up their natural leaders with greater skills in one area than in another. You need them all, and for that reason, I spoke earlier about collective leadership. It is just unrealistic to expect a big organization to produce more than a few all-purpose leaders who can perform most of the various leadership tasks exceptionally well.

When you do find the all-purpose leader, you would do well to beware of him. More often than not his domination leads to organizational despotism. And it is nice to think that social change can be more than the replacement of undesirable despots with more commodious ones. I confess, though, this may not be the lesson which history teaches.

I have an addendum. It concerns the use of white organizers, and I bring it up because it is obvious to you and to me that the growth of Black Nationalist sentiment has put a lot of them on the hot seat.

Like it or not, white men have their uses. Organizationally, an astute pretty white boy with an Ivy League manner can run circles around anybody else in certain kinds of highly proper middle-class situations. White organizers can be useful in dampening the often destructive battle for prominence that has wrecked many a promising Negro endeavor. Remember, your white organizer has no political future in the ghetto, therefore, he can be used as neutral absorbent material for out of control ambitions which are emitting dangerous rays. The white organizer sometimes can be a reassurance when making deals with outside white groups—and I hope there is no one here in such a retarded political babyhood as to think such deals are not necessary.

On the other hand, it grates in this time of rising independence to see the old dependence on whites—to see the old razzamatazz of whites leading Negroes. But for the good organizer, this should be no problem because the good organizer should never—or virtually never—make a public speech, never get his name in the paper, never enjoy any formal authority in the organization. The big deal organizer who becomes a figure in his own right was never serious about developing leadership. He is the man who always meant to be the leader himself; when this type asks how do we find an indigenous leadership, you can translate his words to mean, "How do I get myself a personal following?"

The good organizer is the self-effacing mentor who judges his work a success when he can leave the organization without even being missed. He is rare, rarer than first-rate leadership, but he exists and he comes in a variety of colors and he can work in almost any situation.

Notes

1. Nicholas von Hoffman, interview by Aaron Schutz, August 11, 2012.
2. Richard Luecke, "Saul Alinsky: *Homo Ludens* for Urban Democracy," *Christian Century*, November 15, 1989, 1050; available at Claremont School of Theology, *Religion-Online*, *www.religion-online.org*.

8

Fred Ross and the House-Meeting Approach

■

VARIOUS AUTHORS

The house meeting is such a great tool because it is the best way of doing a very, very thorough, systematic job in a blazing way. Every organizer becomes a social arsonist, able to set people on fire in a milieu that invites the best possible exchange between the organizer and those present.

—Fred Ross[1]

Introduction

During the depths of the 1930s Great Depression, Fred Ross Sr. got his start as an organizer when he served as an administrator in a New Deal Farm Security Administration (FSA) camp.[2] Meeting individually and in small groups with migrant workers living in the farm labor camp, he earned their trust and friendship. The organization he built became a school for democracy for the residents and an effective voice on some of their issues.

During World War II, Ross sought justice for Japanese Americans who were forcibly relocated from their homes and communities. After the war, he began what would become the focus of his life's work—organizing low-to-moderate-income Mexican Americans in California—by organizing Civic Unity Leagues in the Citrus Belt. He then became involved with the Community Service Organization (CSO), and subsequently with Cesar Chavez and California's farmworkers (the latter effort included work with more diverse groups).

In 1949, Ross met Edward Roybal, a Mexican American leader in the barrio of East Los Angeles who had just lost a close election for city council. Roybal wanted

This chapter was edited by Aaron Schutz. Introduction by Aaron Schutz and Mike Miller. The excerpts from the UFW and CSO training workshops are published here by permission of Fred Ross Jr.

more than to win an election; when Ross encountered him, the nascent CSO (which Roybal was involved with) was where "real people" were at. Its members included "workers from foundries and garment factories, short-order cooks and young students" who were "interested in rooting out the injustices" in their community.[3]

Alinsky found out about Ross from University of Chicago professor Louis Wirth and hired him as an organizer for the Industrial Areas Foundation. When Alinsky failed to get Ross to go to Butte, Montana, to organize copper miners, he raised funds to support Ross's work in California with Mexican Americans, and Ross went into Los Angeles.

In an early 1960s conversation, Alinsky said to Miller that he didn't have enough time to talk with Ross about the "organization of organizations" approach, in which groups (rather than individuals) joined, paid dues and served as the formal members of the people power organization. Ross disputed this version of the history. In an early 1960s conversation on the road from San Francisco to Alinsky's summer home in Carmel, California, he told Miller that Alinsky had agreed that it would be impossible to reach the Mexican American population through the formal participation of the institution to which it owed its primary allegiance—the Catholic Church—because Archbishop James Francis McIntyre, prelate of the Los Angeles archdiocese, was an archconservative and wouldn't allow parishes to be part of such an organization. On the local level, however, Ross did seek relationships with priests and nuns and asked them for local contacts.

Also, during a 1975 training session, Ross explained to participants that he had decided that the organization of organizations approach was a bad idea before he met Alinsky.[4] It is impossible to know whether this was an after-the-fact rationalization or whether his disagreement with Alinsky went beyond the particulars of the Los Angeles situation.

Here's the essence of Ross's "house meeting" approach: First, find local leaders or potential leaders and have one-on-one meetings to learn their issues and concerns. Gain their trust, and demonstrate to them you have something to offer. Sometimes organizers met such people through referrals by trusted third parties; sometimes they just met potential recruits "on the street." Ross's organizers used scripted stories of past successes to make an impression and build a sense of hope. Their key aim was to convince the people to hold "house meetings" to which they would invite five to ten people they knew.

As described below in the quotes from training meetings, Ross developed a detailed set of guidelines to get organizers to make sure the hosts actually invited people and followed up to ensure invitees were attending. The actual meeting opened with a clear and rehearsed statement that became increasingly detailed in the farmworker organizing years: "Why organize?" Organizers were taught to run the meeting with a tight agenda and attention to detail (no alcohol, chairs in a circle, etc.), using stories to demonstrate that collective action can work.

Plenty of time was given for people to ask questions, allowing the "story" to morph into a "discussion" so that the organizer knew where the attendees were coming from and ensuring that they understood the "pitch." Then organizers would use the momentum built over the course of the meeting to move skeptics, sweeping them up in the enthusiasm. The chief goal was to recruit additional potential hosts for additional meetings to make the organizing spread. Every new house meeting replicated the first one.

In a five-week to two-month drive, organizers could keep the attention of those who attended the first meetings, building momentum for a founding chapter meeting to elect officers and adopt an action program. This was an extremely high-intensity effort that sometimes featured multiple house meetings every day, combined with follow-ups with hosts and potential leaders and more.

As Ross refined his method, he also became increasingly persuaded that it was *the* way to do things. Years later, when he was supervising Syracuse University graduate students in fieldwork placements, there was a revolt against his demand for precision. "We want to experiment," one of the students told him. "As Picasso said to a young artist," Ross replied, "'learn how to render, then you can experiment.'"[5]

After the CSO was firmly established in East Los Angeles, Ross moved north to a second major barrio in California, East San Jose. There Cesar Chavez was recommended to him as a potential key leader. Although Chavez was initially suspicious of an outside Anglo coming into the community, he soon became an active leader in the CSO, then a volunteer organizer, then a paid organizer, and finally the CSO's executive director. Subsequently, Ross met Dolores Huerta, and then Gilbert Padilla. Along with Chavez, they became the core staff of the CSO, traveling up and down the state, developing and sustaining chapters. They ultimately maintained more than thirty chapters across the state with only a few full-time organizers.

Throughout California, in the barrios of small agricultural towns and urban centers, the CSO used individual complaints with cheating merchants, government agencies, or others as vehicles to organize people, and took on larger issues, such as urban renewal, police brutality, and discrimination in the distribution of benefits by various government agencies. A CSO hallmark was voter education, voter registration, and get-out-the-vote (GOTV) campaigns in which CSO members became deputy registrars, getting thousands of new voters. As politicians soon learned, CSO chapter voting drives made a difference.

While CSO didn't endorse candidates, it did let its members and supporters know where they stood on key issues; it was a distinction without a difference in outcome, but one that allowed CSO to be officially nonpartisan. The CSO's voting power culminated in the 1958 election of Edmund G. "Pat" Brown (father of a later governor) as governor of California. Reliable sources attribute to the CSO the registration of half a million Mexican American voters—voters who overwhelmingly supported Brown.[6] The CSO also achieved many other victories, including a range of legislation supporting farmworkers and others.

Later, the CSO institutionalized much of its individual service work—representing aggrieved individuals with various public bureaucracies or private exploiters, and providing social service programs—in its "service centers."

As readers will see below, Ross's mature approach to training organizers combined three basic tools: a set of practical guidelines for organizers; stories about how the approach had worked and how other approaches had failed; and extensive practice sessions where they role-played the different components of the approach and critiqued each other's performances. By 1975, Ross was also videotaping people's presentations so that they could watch and critique themselves. Note that while Ross did extensive work with people in these workshops, like other organizers he believed most of the important training and learning happened in the field.[7]

Except where noted, the rest of this chapter is in Ross's own voice, transcribed from audio recordings of two trainings—in 1960 and 1975—that can be found at the Farmworker Movement Documentation Project website (*farmworkermovement.com*).

Why House Meetings?[8]

The thing you can do at a house meeting that can't be done [otherwise] is that the organizer can feel the people out. And the people can feel the organizer out. By the end of the meeting, they know something about each other. They've got something going between them if the organizer has done a good job. When they go away from that house meeting, they know the story themselves, pretty well, because they've asked questions and you've really had a chance to explain it to them.

Naturally they're not going to keep all of it in their heads, but they'll keep an awful lot more than they had [before]. They'll be able to tell other people better. It helps to start this rippling out. And you've been able to sink those points into the people so that they can pass them on, pass the truth instead of gossip.

Something else [that] happens at a house meeting that doesn't happen anyplace else is the help you get from the other people who are there. It's the pressure from [some attendees] on people who are resisting you. [If you have formed a relationship with the host and/or others in the house meeting,] you can usually count on getting some help from somebody at that house meeting in convincing others who are resisting you.

[*Why small meetings, not big ones?*] In a big meeting not very many people talk. What happens if [people] don't ask questions? What's going to happen when [they] leave the meeting and [they] go out and start telling people what happened at the meeting? All they're going to be doing is spreading a lot of misinformation.

[*Ross figured this out after one large meeting when*] a few [people] were hanging around and talking. And so they started asking me questions. From the questions they were asking it was just as though each one had been to a different meeting. They each had different ideas about what I had said. So I realized that I had gone about that in the wrong way. I wasn't getting the message across.

On What's Wrong with "Organizations of Organizations"[9]

Ignacio Lopez used to run a newspaper called *El Espectador* out in the citrus belt in Pomona. And he said, "No, Fred. You're just doing it all wrong. To organize another organization is to be a failure. We don't need any more organizations. We've got too many organizations already that don't do anything. What we need to do is to bring them all together."

So, wow, I thought, "Gee, that sounds pretty good. It's a shortcut. And you don't have to go out and get the people. You just go to these various organizations where the people are already organized and you bring them all together and you pull a rabbit out of a hat and you've got an organization." So I did that. And we got, oh, about the same number of people. And we started to register the voters. And about two weeks later, on the weekend, which was when they could come out and help the most, well, none of them showed up.

Well, that happened to be the Cinco de Mayo. They were on the parade that day. In other words all the workers went on the parade and there wasn't any voter registration done.

And that taught me that we don't want to organize by means of other organizations. You can't count on them when you need them.

Some people have the idea that they can take a shortcut and find people inside of organizations. [But] the shortcut turns out to be a detour. And the people they try to get through organizations to become part of, say, a poor people's union don't turn out to be very good, because most of their loyalty is already given to another organization. Nine-tenths of that loyalty [is owed] to another organization, and we want to get 1000 percent of the poor people in our organizations with us.

Finding People to Host a House Meeting[10]

Once the house-meeting drive gets going, new house-meeting hosts are found in the meetings. But when an organizer first comes into a new area, he or she needs to locate people to hold the first meetings. They look for people who could serve as potential leaders, locating them either through contacts with respected people in the neighborhood (priests, nuns, small business owners, unions, etc.) or simply by knocking on doors. In either case, Ross repeatedly emphasized, it was important to make a direct and personal contact.

[Don't make your pitch on the phone. If] you call somebody up, you think you are taking a shortcut. This is really fundamental. You think you're going to be able to call somebody up and save a lot of time by saying, "Look, I'm calling you because I want you to hold a house meeting. And this is what we want to talk about. So will you please do it?" And this person likes you, probably, and says, "Okay, I'll do it."

Well, then [at least] two things can happen. After they've hung up they get [to] thinking, "Gee, I have some people to call. What am I going to tell them? Gee, I better figure that one out before I do any phoning." So the hours go by and the days go by and they don't ever get around to phoning, because they don't know what to tell the people and they're afraid to call. Or else they do call. So they pick up the phone and get somebody on the phone and say, "Hey Joe, somebody from the farmworkers just called up and they want to come over and tell us about the program. So can you come on over on Friday night?" The person on the other end says, "What are they going to talk about?" "Well, I don't know. About the program." "Well, what?" "Well, I don't know. Come on come over and find out." [*Laugh.*] "Well, hell. I've been working as a farmworker as long as you have. Why do I need to come over and find out more about it? I already know." That's one of the reasons—you can't get the right information to them over the phone.

The other thing is, you can't do it with the kind of enthusiasm that you need to get them souped up to the point where they want to do it.

[Finally,] you can't make friends over the phone. But you can begin to make friends when you go over to somebody's house and spend forty-five minutes or an hour talking about [the organization].

Getting People to Attend House Meetings

[*On reminding people:*] You just can't hardly remind [hosts] enough. Many of them aren't used to inviting people over for a house meeting. It's outside of their experience. So in order to make sure that it comes off you have to be especially careful. You've got to remind them [more than once].

[*Ross doesn't take excuses from trainees for low turnout. So when his audience at the training gives excuses, he challenges them.*] [If a house meeting doesn't happen, it is because those hosts] weren't sold. We kid ourselves into thinking we did [a good job], but when we are really, really truthful with ourselves we know we didn't sell them well enough.

But very often an organizer refuses to take that blame, and projects the blame onto the person. "Ahh, well, they're just no good. I should have realized when I talked to them. You can't count on them. They let me down." Well, actually, who let who down? You let them down. You let yourself down.

In order to guard against cancellation on the day of the meeting, [it's a good idea] for each one of you to go out to that [host's] house and make a second personal visit. You can talk to them and find out what they're doing, if there's anything they need to know. Just keep after them. Not only that, but you have got a shot at getting to know them a little bit better. Cementing the friendship that you've got going just a little better after you've been with them another time.

At the House Meeting

Most of this section is taken from the 1960 CSO training. As a result, it focuses on the vote and on civic power, in contrast to the National Farm Workers Association (NFWA) training, which focused more on the issue of farmworkers in particular—although the vote and civic power were always on Ross's mind. As we note below, the CSO meetings were also less scripted and more open to the issues attendees brought with them to the meeting. While Ross emphasizes the responsibility of the organizer for whether a house meeting is successful, strong attendance at a meeting was also a key test of the leadership potential of the host.

You start out with a low-key introduction, just telling them why you're there. And then you get into the problems. And then they interrupt you, and then you take it from there. You're talking power right away. "You haven't been able to get any of these things done because you haven't got any power. There's no power in numbers here, you see, to put the pressure on the people who can really [give you what you want]."

Wait till you think everybody's there [before] you start. [People will still dribble in, so] go back and fill them in, or else they don't know what the hell you're talking about. And you've lost them. You do that very quickly, or otherwise the rest of the people get bored. This is about patience.[11]

The more they talk about their problems, the more they're selling themselves on the need to get an organization. They're proving to each other how valuable it is. In other words, what you're doing is building an army out there to fight the opposition. We're not building a little group to go down and get reconciled with each other and not get anything done. We're building an army to go down and confront the opposition with power. Power on that side, and power on this side.

There's that big decision-making table down there in the county, or the city, wherever it happens to be, where all the decisions have been made for all these years about the people who live out there [in the poorer areas]. Only those people out there never had a chance to sit down at that table and fill that vacant chair. What we are pushing for and organizing for is to get enough power so that the poor people can sit down there and decide not only what is going to be done in their community, but what's going to be done in all the rich communities, in the middle income communities, and all the rest of them. There isn't any representation from the poor to do that right now. And that's what's wrong in this country.

[*Ross's key pitch during the CSO era was on "the power of the vote."*] There are neighborhoods where the people don't have very much money, but where the registration is high and they're getting improvements made just because they've got the power of the vote behind them.

[*The bigger picture:*] Leading up to the last climax in the house meeting after you've gotten all through with voter registration, you say, "We're not only organizing here!" You say, "You folks are not going to be alone in this. We're organizing all over, in all the low-income areas. [We're] getting together and building their power in numbers [*pounds on the table*] registering all the voters. And some day, probably at the end of this year, we'll all come together in one big organization. And then we'll really have the power. Because all of us will be working together. We'll be putting all of our power of numbers together. We'll be putting all of our power of votes together.

This is going to be a part of a big *movement* that is going to sweep through this state. And this helps a lot, when they know they're not going to be out there all alone.[12]

At the house meeting itself you have one friend there, and that's the host or the hostess. But you're going to be trying to get other people to do things. You're going to try to get all of them to hold house meetings, all of them to become active in the [organization's] activities. So it's very important, from the time you reach that house meeting, to be watching for the person that seems to be the most interested. And then, when you get to the point of going into the hustle at the end, when you're after people, call on that person first. When you're trying to get a house meeting, "Well, how about you?" Well, that's the one you've been watching. [It's important to ask someone you're pretty sure is going to say "yes"; that way you get a positive ball rolling, not a negative one.][13]

[*Ross returns to the responsibility of the organizer. Successful house meetings are the test:*] You gotta rouse these people in the house meeting [to have their own house meetings], or else they won't react. If they don't hold house meetings, you'll know you've got to go back and perfect your approach and perfect the pitches you're making to them. [*A key to the "pitch" was reading the audience and giving the right story and the right intensity for* this *particular group. Ross did this when he recruited Chavez. He saw that his initial meeting wasn't going well, and then told the story of the CSO's victory over police brutality, knowing that some of Chavez's friends would be interested in it. This turned the meeting around.*][14]

[*The house meeting ends with informal socializing, which also provides another chance to get people to host house meetings.*] Then the café and pan dulce [*sweets*] comes in. It relaxes you and gets everyone relaxed, and you can talk and make friends. And plus you get this extra shot at the people that didn't agree. The organizer should become very mobile at that point and move around and talk to these various people who refused for some reason or another to help. And likely as not, here and there, you're going to be able to win somebody else. And that's what you're there for.[15]

[*Responding to naysayers and critics:*] If somebody insults you, let 'em have it! They'll respect you for it. If somebody takes a crack at you, crack right back at 'em. Don't be afraid, because you are liable to hurt somebody's feelings or something. If somebody gives it to you, give it right back to 'em.

If they slap you and give you a dirty dig and you just take it, they lose respect. And anybody else that knows about it loses respect for you too. You're not reacting the way you should. You've gotta be a human being when you're out there.[16]

The House Meeting Post-CSO

At the 1975 UFW training, Ross read parts of a letter from Chavez, written in 1962 right after Chavez left the CSO to start his farmworker association, in which Chavez described how he was tailoring his presentation to fit his farmworker audience. In the letter, Chavez laid out how he was developing his extended "pitch" to farmworkers—selling them on the association while educating them about their own history.

[Chavez] says, "You might be interested to know that the whole approach [to the house meeting] has changed somewhat since the beginning. This is what I tell the workers when we get together. [*Chavez thanks people for coming and emphasizes he is not trying to form a union, but is not against unions.* Then I tell] them that that this is a movement, *un movimiento*, and that we're trying to find a solution to the problem[s] faced by farmworkers. Here I throw in a little bit [of] the history about how agriculture developed in California." See, the same thing that we're going to be doing. "And then [I] start to mention to them how the Chinese were the first farmworkers [to be brought] in large numbers in California. And then I briefly trace the other groups that they brought to California to assure the growers will always have more than enough workers on hand. Here I ask them to keep in mind how there has always been more workers than work in California, and say that this has been our biggest problem. I trace the various groups until we come to the *braceros* [temporary workers brought in from Mexico]." And the next thing is, he goes into the various attempts of the farmworkers to organize to improve their condition and what happened and why it happened. And then he talks to them about legislation. "The history has been that those who never see a potato grow are the ones who are always trying to help the workers by saying that you deserve so much per hour. That always those trying to help never even care to know who the workers are." And then he talks about the strikes and unions. "I then tell them how the workers have been getting together to form their own committees in many towns in the valley." He says that, "I don't know how far they'll go when the association is formed, if it ever is, especially when the dues matter is brought up." [He worried] about the dues but brought it up anyway. "So far the meetings I think are interesting and the response of those present seems very good. The valley-wide meeting will be held in Fresno, the date has been set for September 30th." See, he was building up toward that first meeting. This, you see, was written August the 7th, and he'd been organizing since April, and he'd been changing his approach around until he finally hit on the very best approach, and that's the one he used from that time on.

Finding People Willing to Become Staff[17]

This section is from Ross's 1975 farmworkers' union training, and it is important to remember that when he talks about "staff," he is referring to people who were each paid around $5 a week plus expenses.

You've got to get staff. You can depend on [volunteers] off and on. The union isn't first for them, they're just helping. Even if it looks like they are going to be helping every day something comes up in the family and they're just not there. They're just doing it in addition to the other thing.

But if you have somebody that you can take on as staff, why you can just increase the effectiveness of the thing by double. And if you can get three or four of them, well you know what, how important that is.

If you resist bringing people in to work with you, you're killing yourself. You're killing your own program. And it's going to show up right away because other people in other offices are going to go zooming ahead, because they've been able to find up more staff and they're out just tearing through the community like gangbusters. And here you are with no staff and you're way back here and these other guys are way up here.

Power and Do-Gooders[18]

Some people say that, well, you don't have to build power to get these things. There are all kinds of things these people can get without having to have any power. Well, the only way that this comes about is when some do-gooder comes in and hands it to them. You know how that makes people feel. And this is what's been going on for all these years. Along about Christmas time. And then during the year some little ladies aid society is going to bring out the old, dirty clothing full of holes. And all this to help the poor people out there. And that's about the worst thing you could ever get into.

[This kind of "charity" is counterproductive to building power.] They feel unhappy when they have to take these things. They need them, so they take them. But it still makes them feel bad to take them. And they hate the people that give to them, usually. So if you're the one that gives them to them, well, they'll start hating you. And that's not what you're trying to do.

Helping Individuals[19]

From time to time the organizer himself is going to have to go with [a] family to the welfare office, to the agency, whoever it is that's causing the problem, and help win that little case [because you can't wait until the next organization meeting]. You're trying to keep that to an absolute minimum because if you don't it slows down your organizing. You can't be holding house meetings and taking people down to the welfare, social security, worker's compensation, all that.

But if an emergency comes up, you have to do it. You gotta prove that you mean business on this. And this is a good way. Because if you win the case down there, that woman's gonna tell other people, "Gee, this is a good organization. You know what happened yesterday?" And that woman will probably hold several house meetings because of what you did to help her get her problem solved.

Follow the System We Gave You[20]

Let's put it this way: Fred and Cesar are here because they have tried a system. They don't talk from the ivory tower of a university, nor do they sit behind a table and tell people what to do. These boys have been in here you see. They've been doing it for all these years. And this has worked. This is not a thing that you take or leave. This is a thing that I am—I hate to use the word, but I don't know what else to do—this is a method that I am sincerely hoping—as a matter of fact I'm insisting—that you try. Now at this point maybe it looks like something else[, some other approach,] might be better. But I'm saying give this a try. I can't be too strong on this. This is a system that we're going to try. I know there may be other ways of doing things. But this is the way it's going to be done because this is a program that has been tried and it has accomplished the things that we want it to accomplish. You can't leave out any one thing. You do the steps as it's been stated.

Problems with Organizing the Middle Class

—Aaron Schutz

According to Bill Pastreich, one of the students in the above-mentioned Syracuse University class, Ross "said that in Community Service Organization, what happened was that as they became more respectable and local politicians responded they got more middle-class people involved. And the middle-class people were more verbal, more used to running meetings, and therefore would control the meetings."[21]

There were benefits for those who became leaders in the CSO: appointments to political and state bureaucratic posts, grants for new nonprofits, recognition, and other perks, along with real and substantial changes in the barrios of California. Ross told this story in the 1975 training about why Chavez left the CSO:

> [Chavez] was made the national director of the CSO, and for the next year and a half or two years he tried to convince the leadership of the CSO to move further and further into the field of farm labor. And actually to convert itself into a labor union, [though] he wasn't talking to them in those terms. But they knew what was in his mind. And they were willing to help get things like the state disability insurance passed and other legislation. [They were] willing to work on a legislative basis, but they weren't willing to go any further than that. Mainly because the people in power in the CSO by that time were sort of the, well, the middle-class people among the Mexican Americans. They were skilled workers, they were small business people, lawyers, doctors, teachers, and so forth. The rank and file of the organization was made up primarily—all through the [Central] valley at least—of farmworkers. But the leaders, the great leaders, were these other people, and they were afraid to give Cesar what he was after. And so in March of 1962 he resigned [and started what became the UFW].[22]

The co-option of the CSO by more privileged members is a story that has been repeated across the history of social justice efforts since World War II, assisted by the emergence of the professionalization of poverty work described by Alinsky as "political pornography."[23]

Conclusion

—Mike Miller

I think during most of his life Fred epitomized Alinsky's picture of the selfless organizer. Note that this selflessness was a function of his superb sense of self and self-confidence in what he did. He had no need to be a celebrity, to be in the news media, or to hang out with "influentials." No single person in the history of the development of professional organizers trained or influenced more of them than Fred. As Aaron and I indicate elsewhere in this book, there is a clear, if not direct, line between Fred and ACORN, and ACORN was the school for many organizers who went to work for unions. The farmworker boycott was the school for a second group of labor organizers. In addition, the world of "community-based nonprofits" (which I don't think of as part of organizing) is populated by many people who got their first experience working with marginalized people within this Fred Ross "school."

After having thought about this for many years, I am saddened by one part of the Fred Ross legacy. Even after lots of thought, I remain ambivalent about another. Finally, I think there were parts missing in the best of his work. Let me try to summarize each of these reactions, starting with the last.

The CSO was a stunning success. With a very small organizing staff, it put Mexican Americans on the political map in California. People who owe their first taste of civic and political life to the CSO went on to play leadership roles in labor, politics, civic life, government, and the religious world. When I went to a 2012 reunion of the CSO in California, numerous Chicano leaders could not speak of their CSO formative years without tears in their eyes—and everyone there knew the feeling that provoked those tears.

Since 2013, there has been an effort to get President Obama to award Fred Ross the Presidential Medal of Freedom. It is an award he surely deserves. But to me there is even a more important accolade that has already been bestowed: people who were bitter rivals, who in some cases to this day do not speak with one another, are unanimous in their endorsement of Fred for this national honor. What could be a greater testament to his talent at bringing diverse strands of militancy and moderation together?

The CSO, however, was not without weaknesses. Its strong emphasis on the political world (voter education, registration, and get-out-the-vote) meant that it didn't master—though it sometimes used—mass, nonviolent, disruptive direct action. And its direct membership form required constant rebuilding by its organizing staff. It did not master the boycott as a powerful tool for the liberation of oppressed communities. These were missing elements that could have contributed to an even more powerful CSO.

I am ambivalent about Fred's training of organizers. That there are so many people who proudly call themselves organizers who may not otherwise have been exposed to the work is the huge positive. That their experience was limited to the mobilizing work of the boycott rather than building units of power in marginalized communities—as Fred had earlier done in the CSO—has contributed to the present staff-intensive character of many unions, and to the view that members are "troops" to be turned out, volunteers to be given tasks, and picketers to be given signs, rather than cocreators of a social movement deeply rooted in democratic values. Organized labor in the United States will continue to shrink in its influence and power until it makes members owners of their unions rather than insurance policyholders in them.

As we pointed out above, Ross's direct membership approach diverges radically from Alinsky's usual "organization of organizations" approach. There are several parts of Ross's discussion that confirm his lack of connection with Alinsky. First, Alinsky thought that a new dynamic was created within existing associations that became part of a mass-based organization. This dynamic thrust new people into organizational life, and created new possibilities for leaders to emerge. It also changed some already-existing leaders. Second, Alinsky thought that there were large issues that required a united community in order to tackle them—and that a united community was expressed in the "organization of organizations" he was interested in creating. Third, Alinsky's organizing incorporated both already existing and newly created organizations—many block clubs, tenant associations, and other types of organizations were created during an IAF organizing drive patterned on Alinsky's early work in Chicago. Ross's understanding of Alinsky's "organization of organizations" isn't really accurate. The reader can read his understanding of them above, and then contrast that with the character of TWO and von Hoffman's understanding of what he was building in Chicago's Woodlawn.

Finally, I am saddened by Fred's ultimate unwillingness (described in the next chapter) to hold Cesar Chavez's feet to the fire of democratic accountability within his own union. In the CSO, Fred saw part of his role as holding top leadership accountable to members. In the UFW, when faced with that question, he succumbed to his loyalty to Cesar Chavez. But that only proves that he was human.

Notes

1.　Quoted in Ellie M. Cohen and Fred Ross, *The Ross Housemeeting Method: A Brief History* (Oakland, CA: Institute for Effective Action, 1985), 4, Fred Ross Papers, box 16, folder 29, Special Collections and University Archives, Stanford University Libraries, California.
2.　The FSA was a program to benefit poor rural farmers. In the Deep South, it provided land for black rural workers who had been totally dependent on plantation owners; in California,

it provided decent housing for migratory workers who had been dependent on agribusiness for their housing. Southern Dixiecrats and northern agribusiness teamed up to undermine and defeat FSA, but it and the New Deal work that preceded it accomplished a great deal.

3. Sanford D. Horwitt, *Let Them Call Me Rebel: Saul Alinsky—His Life and Legacy* (New York: Vintage, 1992), 228–29.

4. Fred Ross, UFW training in California, 1975; audio files available at UC San Diego Library, *Farmworker Movement Documentation Project, farmworkermovement.com.*

5. Ross, conversation with Miller.

6. E.g., Herman Gallegos, cited in Jorge Nicolás Leal, "The Post-Electoral Hopes of the Southern California Viva Kennedy Clubs, 1960–1963" (master's thesis, California State University, Northridge, 2011).

7. For more on Ross and his work, see Gabriel Thompson's forthcoming book, *America's Social Arsonist* (University of California Press).

8. Fred Ross, UFW training.

9. This section from Ross, UFW training.

10. Fred Ross, CSO training in Arizona, 1960, audio files available at UC San Diego Library, *Farmworker Movement Documentation Project, farmworkermovement.com.*

11. On the other hand, Ross was a bear on details, and had no patience to spare for organizers who failed to observe them. For example, he didn't tolerate people being late. A favorite tactic of his was to lock the door of a room exactly at the beginning of a training session and leave those who were late to stew outside for a while until finally letting them in and using their tardiness to teach about discipline. Another was his insistence on completing an assigned number of individual and house meetings within a designated period of time.

12. The previous eight paragraphs are from Ross, CSO training.

13. This paragraph is from Ross, UFW training.

14. The previous two paragraphs are from Ross, CSO training.

15. This paragraph is from Ross, UFW training.

16. The previous three paragraphs are from Ross, CSO training.

17. Ross, UFW training.

18. Ross, CSO training.

19. Ibid.

20. Ibid.

21. Bill Pastreich, interview by Aaron Schutz, January 17, 2012.

22. Ross, UFW training.

23. Saul D. Alinsky, "The War on Poverty—Political Pornography," *Journal of Social Issues* 21, no. 1 (1965): 41–47.

9

Cesar Chavez and the Fate of Farmworker Organizing

■

MIKE MILLER

They come and they go, good organizers and would-be organizers. But one thing they all have in common is that all of them have failed and will fail.
—Mexican American farmworker to Cesar Chavez[1]

No one associated with Saul Alinsky was as well known as Cesar Chavez; indeed, it is likely that by the mid-1970s more people knew his name than Alinsky's. Catholic bishops, heads of various mainline Protestant denominations, rabbis from the Conservative, Orthodox, and Reform Jewish traditions, and an occasional imam gave him their blessings. Presidential candidate Robert F. Kennedy broke bread with him when Chavez ended one of his fasts. Chavez was a man of deep Catholic faith, and he rooted his thinking about organizing in his faith. With only an eighth-grade education, he read widely and was deeply knowledgeable of the Catholic social encyclicals.

When the farmworkers' union called their boycott of grapes (to be followed by head lettuce and Gallo wine boycotts), a cadre of mobilizers fanned out across the country and into Canada, focusing on densely populated metropolitan areas where they sought to persuade consumers to honor their boycotts. Their points of entry were supportive congregations and union locals. They enlisted congregation and union local members who, along with people from minority communities, middle-class liberals and student activists, became the nucleus of boycott efforts.

Crusty George Meany, head of the American Federation of Labor/Congress of Industrial Organizations (AFL-CIO), and one of labor's more conservative leaders, gave Chavez "no-strings" money to organize and granted a direct charter with the promise of becoming a new international within the federation rather than a division of some other union that might claim the jurisdiction. Meany's continuing rival, Walter Reuther, head of the United Auto Workers of America (UAW), supported Chavez. And Paul Schrade, the UAW's western director, about as politically left as anyone in mainstream labor at that time worked closely with him. The left-wing independent West Coast International Longshore & Warehouse Union (ILWU) was also an early supporter of Chavez and, at some risk to its members' livelihoods, refused to load or unload boycotted produce onto ships. (To do so violated the longshoremen's contract with the stevedoring companies.) Internationally, boycotts were honored in ports around the world. Almost no American union failed to support the farmworkers' cause.

Jerry Brown, in his first time around as California's governor, successfully got the state legislature to adopt the best labor relations legislation in the country—a bill designed to bring farmworkers into collective bargaining. Cesar Chavez reciprocated that support by making some of his most talented organizers, including Marshall Ganz (who later put what he'd learned at the disposal of Barack Obama's successful 2008 presidential campaign), available to Brown for his presidential run. Brown's surprising success in eastern primaries was due to the importation of the farmworkers' union's mobilizing tactics there (see the previous chapter on Fred Ross and the house-meeting approach). Brown was not alone among politicians in wanting to be associated with Chavez and the farm workers' cause. Mayors, city councils, boards of supervisors, state legislatures, and members of Congress all wanted that connection.

Though initially skeptical about its odds for success, Saul Alinsky publicly supported the cause as well, showing up to testify at California farm labor hearings called by then-senator Robert Kennedy. He told me that Chavez was embarking on an impossible mission; no one had successfully organized farmworkers. He said this publicly as well; it was "like fighting on a constantly disintegrating bed of sand."[2]

When Chavez did, in fact, succeed, Alinsky told me his Monday-morning-quarterbacking version of why: liberals in the country had nothing else to do. The black movement had thrown them out and repudiated their support. Here was a cause that was as compelling and dramatic as Martin Luther King's demonstrations in Birmingham or March on Washington. The white northern student movement was similarly isolated from the black cause, and the anti-Vietnam war movement lacked the concrete victories that were to be seen in support work for the farmworkers. Students flocked to Delano, California, the union's initial home, and enlisted in the hundreds as full-time boycott workers, and in the tens of thousands as boycott supporters. Here was a "movement"—something generally viewed critically by Alinsky—that was succeeding. And before it all happened, Chavez had the vision to see that it might.

Origins: The Break from the CSO and the Early National Farm Workers Association (NFWA)

Chavez left the CSO in 1962, he said, because its board refused to make organizing farmworkers a major program of the organization, and because the organization was becoming too middle-class. It is what his closest former CSO associates—Dolores Huerta and Gil Padilla—said as well.

He moved to the "shoestring" farmworker communities in an extended area surrounding Delano, stretching from Arvin in the south to Stockton in the north. These small towns, farm labor camps, and unincorporated areas were home to families who were able to live year-round in them because of the close-by, almost-year-round availability of farm labor work.

A benefit of organizing in table grapes in and near Delano was the presence of an enclave of Chicano farmworkers there, and the absence of *braceros*—the imported Mexican workers who were vulnerable to deportation in the event of a strike. Further, Chavez's wife, Helen, had many farmworker relatives in these communities. The problem of legitimizing "outside organizers" was solved with these familial connections, Chavez's reputation from CSO and CSO-related connections, and Chavez's own background as a farmworker.

But he liked to approach "cold contacts" as well, and he'd talk with people on the street, at work, while they were shopping, in their homes, and anyplace else—except in a bar. He said, "I'd rather work in a community where no one knows me and I haven't pre-judged anyone out of the picture. That way everyone is a potential member."[3]

The initial funding problem was solved by Chavez's Spartan lifestyle, combined with the financial support that Fred Ross Sr. developed through his own network of Quaker, radical, and liberal sources in California. Chavez conducted an intensive organizing drive over a widespread portion of the San Joaquin Valley that culminated in the fall founding meeting of the National Farm Workers Association (NFWA).

Chavez was not simply talking union. It is important to recognize that his initial organizing plan was built around (1) mutual aid and (2) advocacy and service work with farmworkers, drawing from his experience with CSO service centers.

The former included a credit union; group burial insurance; a group purchase plan to buy auto tires, batteries, and other supplies (farmworkers drove many miles from their homes to worksites in the general area); and other mutual support. The second included representation of and service to farmworkers and their families in their dealings with various government and private decision-makers, including cheating merchants, landlords, and administrators in public agencies like immigration, public health, welfare, police, and schools. Initially, Chavez himself might accompany a farmworker to deal with someone responsible for an injustice. But the next time around, this farmworker would accompany another. Soon there would be delegations or groups of farmworkers tackling more recalcitrant issues. The beneficiaries were the members of what was deliberately called an "association," not a "union."

Chavez insisted that people join the NFWA, and dues were significant—adjusted for 2013 inflation, they were about $30 a month. As he put it in an oft-cited 1966 interview:

We started with [the principle that] no matter how poor the people, they had
a responsibility to help the union. If they had two dollars for food, they had to

give one dollar to the union. Otherwise, they would never get out of the trap of poverty. . . . The statement "They're so poor they can't afford to contribute to the group" is a great cop-out. You don't organize people by being afraid of them—you never have; you never will. You can be afraid of them in a variety of ways. But one of the main ways is to patronize them. You know the attitude: Blacks or browns or farmworkers are so poor that they can't afford to [pay for] their own group.[4]

Dues weren't the only investment. Farmworkers fed Chavez and his small group of initial organizers in their homes; he would sometimes sleep at the home of a family he visited; others gave him gas money.

The organizers worked for sacrificial wages; later on, the standard weekly pay for all organizers in the union was $5.00. In true guerrilla fashion, they lived as fish in the sea of farm workers—with this important exception: Chavez was committed to nonviolence. A careful student of Gandhi, he insisted that the farmworker struggle had to be a nonviolent one.

There was a great deal of farmworker skepticism about unions. They had come and gone over the years, leaving a trail of unfulfilled promises behind them, including workers who had been fired and blacklisted for union activity, evicted from grower-controlled housing, and physically beaten by local law enforcement personnel or strikebreakers. In the most violent confrontations, workers had lost their lives.

What workers did learn was that in the brief peak harvest periods when their labor was most in demand they could stage slowdowns or mini-strikes and win concessions, including higher pay. But no permanent union had been built. More within the experience of the workers were promises made, promises broken, and the disappearance of the union and its organizers when it became clear that no quick union recognition would be won, contracts signed, or "dues check-offs" (automatic dues deduction from paychecks) obtained.

A Union in the Community

The NFWA strategy applied Fred Ross/CSO lessons to farmworkers. Using the full range of his existing relationships, and talking with "cold contacts," Chavez conducted his door-to-door and house-meeting organizing drive. He acknowledged that wages, hours, benefits, and working conditions (including such indignities as no cold drinking water or toilets in the fields) had to be addressed because they were the root cause of farmworker poverty, and that the competition of legal and undocumented immigrant farmworkers also required attention because they were more fearful of employer and government sanctions (the legal farmworkers in this case being those in the *bracero* program). But he quickly added that the farmworkers had to be strategic in how they confronted both agribusiness and the elaborate governmental apparatus of legislation, subsidies, regulation, and services that supported it. When asked, "Can we win?" he replied, "There is nothing we can't do if we have enough people." The organizer's question was always foremost: how do we organize enough people?

According to Chavez interviewer Wendy Goepel, by the time of the major Delano strike of 1965, the NFWA had "local leaders and local groups in 67 different areas in eight [San Joaquin Valley] counties."[5] Chavez had visited thousands of farmworkers and their families, and held hundreds, if not thousands, of small house meetings with them; action had been taken on hundreds of local issues, and numerous members had benefited directly from NFWA services and advocacy.

Chavez knew that to organize people required victories along the way. The combination of mutual aid, advocacy, and service was one part of that. Another was a carefully targeted strike of rose grafters that won a wage increase, though not a contract. Additionally, in the face of an effective strike, a small grape grower granted a wage hike to his workers. Throughout the Valley, wages increased just because organizing was taking place—growers wanted to head off a union before it could take root.

A rent strike supported by the California Migrant Ministry (CMM) demonstrated the power of organizing as well. Had Chavez had his way, there would have been numerous carefully targeted nonviolent direct action efforts to show how farmworker power could work before any major confrontation in an entire industry.

In this period, Chavez recruited the nucleus of people who built both the NFWA and the UFW with him: Fred Ross, Dolores Huerta, and Gil Padilla, all of whom came from the earlier CSO experience, and Rev. Jim Drake, who was initially on the CMM staff but subsequently became a full-time United Farm Workers of America staffer. Further, Chavez had the full support of the Migrant Ministry and its staff—both on the ground with farmworkers, and as an advocate throughout the religious communities of the world.

A Union Begins: From Strike to Boycott

But the NFWA didn't control the timetable for organizing agricultural workers in California. Filipino farmworkers themselves struck in 1965. The AFL-CIO had a stepchild organizing effort called the Agricultural Workers Organizing Committee (AWOC). Its strategy was to organize the migrant stream of mostly single Filipino men who moved with the crops. AWOC supported the strike; the NFWA's members called it "a Filipino strike," and told Chavez they wanted to support it. He called a membership meeting to discuss the matter, and himself urged strike support—even though it was not at a time of his and the NFWA's choosing. Soon there was a joint committee between the two organizations, and then an official organizing committee—the United Farm Workers Organizing Committee (UFWOC).

Thus was born what became the most famous of strikes of the second half of the twentieth century—the "strike in the grapes"—and the organization that led it, the United Farm Workers of America (UFW), AFL-CIO. When the strike showed signs that it would not be sufficient to win the struggle, the farmworkers shifted their strategy to a boycott. (I was cocoordinator of the first, and successful, farmworkers' union boycott of Schenley Liquors.) There followed more boycotting of grapes, a head lettuce boycott aimed at Salinas Valley, and a boycott of Gallo wines, plus so-called secondary boycotts of stores that refused to discontinue carrying boycotted products. For most union workers secondary boycotts were illegal. But in the 1930s Dixiecrat racists and northern agribusiness interests had blocked efforts to include farmworkers in the National Labor Relations Act, thus exempting them from later-adopted secondary boycott prohibitions!

The boycotts brought many of the growers to their knees, and were instrumental in winning state legislation that led to multiple union collective bargaining election victories. Soon tens of thousands of farmworkers were covered by union contracts.

Reliance on the boycott, however, presented a different set of problems. By its very nature, organizing the boycott was not organizing people around their own concerns in their own communities. It was an appeal to conscience—a request that others act in behalf of someone else. In the 1960s and 1970s, such an appeal could, and did, gain traction. But it did not build a strong union rooted among farmworkers. Nor did it build strong community organizations in the places where it was successful. It built campaigns led by cadres of activists who set up boycott operations outside grocery (and liquor) stores; disrupted grower shipping operations; descended upon political bodies to win passage of endorsing resolutions for the farmworker cause; circulated petitions that drew the signatures of tens of thousands of people; and otherwise made the farmworker cause the most widely supported U.S. struggle for economic justice of the 1960s and 1970s.

These activists built a community among themselves, but not the kind of deeply rooted in place, faith, or work community that is envisaged by community organizing. As the principal school for union organizers of the latter part of the twentieth century, both the positives and negatives of this experience were translated into subsequent union organizing throughout the United States, as former farmworkers' union organizers went on to unions like the Service Employees International Union (SEIU), the United Food and Commercial Workers International Union (UFCW), the Hotel Employees and Restaurant Employees Union (HERE), the Amalgamated Clothing and Textile Workers Union (ACTWU), and others.

Furthermore, despite the UFW's successes, all was not well. The 1982 election of George Deukmejian as California's governor changed the union-friendly state labor board that administered farmworker elections into a grower-friendly agency. Not one successful election was held after Deukmejian transformed the board. Problems in the UFW had existed before this: contracts were not enforced, or were enforced badly, leaving a bitter taste for many farmworkers; in the grape industry, the union lost elections it had won the first time around. Within the union, divisions that were nascent at its peak of power and influence became more prominent. Internal purges eliminated from the staff many talented and dedicated organizers, while others quietly resigned in protest. The boycott became the principal strategic weapon of the union;

on-the-ground organizing of farmworkers at workplaces was shunted to the sidelines. Power increasingly was concentrated in the hands of Cesar Chavez, who brooked no internal opposition "from below"—i.e., from among farmworkers—and vigorously worked to defeat leaders whose views were different from his own. Even the union's proclaimed nonviolence was compromised, though not explicitly.

Some Alinsky Principles and Their Application by Ross and Chavez

There is now an extensive, controversy-filled historiography of UFW and its antecedents that ranges from earlier books that romanticized the union to later, sharply critical analyses. A farmworkers' union website (*farmworkersmovement.com*) contains elaborate discussions of the issues faced by the union, and how they were handled. I cannot attempt to summarize those views here. And the debate continues as new books appear. Instead, I want first to draw some distinctions and lessons from the Alinsky tradition, and its application by Cesar Chavez, and then use the CSO-NFWA-UFW developments to illustrate Alinsky's national impact.

The Role of the Organizer

Alinsky's classic organizer was a behind the scenes, sociological stranger to the constituency in which he (and in those days his organizers were all men) worked. This outsider was typically comfortably middle- or even upper-class in social origin. (At the same time, Alinsky stressed that as the opportunity arose, people from within the working class would arise to assume these roles themselves. Chavez himself illustrated the principle.)

This background afforded the organizer the education, experience, and perspective to see a bigger picture than that typically seen by local leaders struggling to survive. The organizer could be an "integrated schizophrenic," polarizing the fight in battle while at the same time recognizing that there would necessarily be a time to sit at a table and compromise.[6] He could stand in the shoes of many, including adversaries, and engage in disciplined analysis of strengths and weaknesses of all.

By moving on after a few years, organizers avoided the steps often taken by other reformers to institutionalize their own positions, often becoming impervious to new voices that might want to take the organization in a different direction or have a different leadership. Alinsky frequently noted in his lectures and workshops how, once themselves in power, revolutionaries as different as Sam Adams, Robespierre, and Stalin opposed subsequent voices who sought to carry the initial revolution's aims forward. His point was not that these men were hypocrites; rather, it was that the world looks different once you are in power, and that checks on power are always needed.

In the CSO, Fred Ross played the outside organizer role almost to perfection. He told me of an instance when the CSO executive board was going to adopt a course that contradicted earlier-adopted membership policy. He told the board they couldn't do that; they responded that they were going to; he said he'd take the matter to the membership; they said, "But you work for us." "No," he replied, "I work for the membership." Chavez learned that as Ross's prime organizer pupil.

In the NFWA and the UFW, however, Cesar Chavez became a leader/organizer. He explicitly said he wanted voice and vote on the organization's board. He served as the major public spokesperson for the organizations. He shaped the board by his influence in the nominating process. He, or people directly accountable to him, controlled and allocated staff resources.

Even in Alinsky's vision, the organizer role can lend itself to abuse. In this book's section on the IAF, for example, Arnie Graf describes how he resisted Ed Chambers's efforts to unilaterally make decisions about the Milwaukee organization Graf was working for. Instead, Graf took the issues to the local leadership. The power of the organizer exists even when she or he follows all Alinsky's strictures. The key organizer concerns are not typically about issues or program, however. Rather, organizers worry about organizational, not issue, questions (although issues must be consistent with core values).

In the UFW, Ross was approached by one of the union's most talented leaders, who appealed to him to challenge Chavez's abuses of power. "I've been with Cesar too long to do that now," was Ross's reply—a 100 percent turn from an earlier parallel circumstance.

Alinsky once said to me something like, "When you're organizing people who don't spend much of their lives in discussion about strategic alternatives, they want to know what you think." This contradicts the idea of the organizer "thinking things through" with people. Resolving the contradiction is part of the organizing art; role-playing is an important tool to do it. In my own work, there were times when I presented a conclusion, but then role-played the opposite point of view. I looked for a way to engage leaders in a "thinking through" process. People are used to thinking in moral terms (i.e., something's right or wrong), and they're used to thinking in policy terms (i.e., something's good or bad policy). But they're not used to thinking in power terms, and that is one of the most important things an organizer teaches.

The tension between trust in an organizer or leader and developing the capacity of new or secondary leaders to "think organizationally" is unintentionally captured by something Dolores Huerta said. On the one hand, she said that the UFW is "Chavez's union. . . . The workers have complete faith in Cesar." On the other, she said, "The farm workers' respect for leadership extends down to the level of the . . . ranch committees [whose leaders] are elected." Are the ranch committee leaders supposed to ask Cesar what to think and do, or are they supposed to consult with their members and, on matters having to do with their ranch, draw their own conclusions, and on matters affecting the whole union engage in discussion and debate with others? Building a democratic organization requires the latter. Building a Cesar Chavez organization requires something else. When Chavez was confronted with the question of how ranch committee full-time representatives were to be chosen—by the members or by Chavez—his choice was the latter. In itself, that might not have been a concern. But it was part of a pattern, symbolized by the absence of "locals." Everything was run from union headquarters. No organization better illustrates the dangers of things being run from the center than the UFW.

Organizational Structure

Elsewhere in this book, Aaron Schutz and I discuss the controversy over "direct membership" versus "organization of organizations" (O of O) structures; it is a controversy that can obscure as much as it clarifies. Effective organizing requires the identification of real leaders (i.e., people with a following), and potential leaders (i.e., people who can develop a following). There is no people power without this.

If we stretch our imaginations, we can make up an Alinsky-shaped scenario for organizing farmworker communities, even assuming that no church was going to be a member. In Alinsky's organizing plan, there would be farmworker community organizations with multi-issue agendas as broad as the interests of those communities, and membership that extended beyond farmworkers to others living in those communities—though, of course, farmworker interests would have been primary. (Note: drawing boundary lines—i.e., defining the constituency—is a key organizer interest.)

Like the NFWA's agenda, their interests would not have been limited to the workplace; at the same time, figuring out how to create workplace power would have been high on Alinsky's priority list.

The basic units of membership would have included the following types of organizations:

- extended families or other groupings that would have come together in house meetings and would then be given a name and a minimum of structure
- work crews that were often semi-permanent groupings (sometimes led by people distrusted by the workers and beholden to growers, in which case they wouldn't have joined, but in other cases headed by respected members of an extended family or home town group)
- soccer and other athletic teams and "mutualistas"—various mutual aid groups, small business associations, and town-of-origin clubs (many recent immigrants who came from the same small town in Mexico held loyalties to it and to family members who remained there)

There would have been multiple opportunities for face-to-face work together on issue, cultural, social, mutual aid, and other activities. And there would have been some intermediary-level structure at the level of neighborhood, town, or county that stood between the very local and the state or national picture. Similarly, once contracts had been negotiated with employers there would have been some democratic structure at workplaces.

Within the few friendly congregations that might have been identified (grower influence generally precluded this possibility), leaders or potential leaders with neighborhood issues would be sought; they might develop a block club or tenant association, or they might directly join a committee of the O of O and find roles in it that provided deep meaning for them. The O of O's organizing staff would also directly organize other new groups that would become O of O member units.

The earlier CSO organizers did not ignore existing formal leadership structures. Rather, they met with their leaders, sought support from them, and asked them for contacts. They used the endorsement for legitimacy when they entered new terrain. Ross and Chavez's close associate and fellow organizer Gil Padilla describes this process: "My method of starting a new chapter—let's take Mendoza [a small rural town]—was this: First, visit all the religious leaders—not just the Catholic bishop, but all of them. Ask them for the names of people who are trying to improve the community. Then go see those people; tell them the religious leader who gave me their name."[7]

Vision and Ideology

Local units of power have a tendency toward parochialism. Leaders of local units tend to view the world through the lens of their local experience and the day-to-day demands it places upon them. There is typically a tension between what they see and do and what a big picture calls for. Alinsky thought that if you could get people together across historic lines of division—be they religion, country of origin, race or ethnicity, class, place, ideology, age, interest, or whatever—you could bridge these conflicts. If the organizing was rooted in the values of Judeo-Christian teachings and the American democratic tradition, and if it paid attention to issues that required solution at a state or national level, then broader people power organizations would emerge to challenge the concentrations of wealth and power that undermined democracy.

But Alinsky didn't think you could get to his vision by simply preaching these values. One of his phrases was "the low road to morality"—he thought you had to make creative use of personal and institutional self-interests to build people power. In his organizing work he sought to build structures that could at some point address the "big issues." One could say that he was a conservative radical . . . or a radical conservative, as well as a populist and democrat.

Alinsky didn't want to go "outside the experience" of the people he was organizing. If you did that, he said, you would lose them. Thus when challenged by the student Left over organizing black people so they could simply obtain "bourgeois, bankrupt, materialistic, values," he wryly observed that in the black community what people wanted were precisely those bourgeois, materialistic values.[8]

This book deals elsewhere with Alinsky's failure to accomplish his vision (see Chapter 2), but here I want to contrast Alinsky with Chavez. Chavez's initial statement of vision was consistent with Alinsky's. He alluded to it: "One day we can use the force that we have to help correct a lot of things that are wrong in this society. But that is for the future."[9]

But after that, Chavez went into new terrain. It included a sacrificial and communal lifestyle for the organization's staff, and a cooperative organization of the economy. Both of these ideas were largely "outside the experience" of the farmworker communities in which he was working, particularly the more assimilated Mexican American communities. (Recent migrants might have had exposure to cooperatives at home, or been part of revolutionary political organizations.) Further, his deep Catholicism made Chavez vigorously anti-Communist, no matter what kind of Communist you happened to be. In purges within the union, the charge of "Communist" was leveled at people whose loyalty to the union had not previously been questioned, who were not members of political parties that imposed "democratic centralism" (party discipline) upon them or who, if they were, would have responded to those parties in the same way that Herb March responded to the Communist Party during Alinsky's Back of the Yards organizing days.[10]

As the pressures to become a "real union"—one with an agenda relatively limited to wages, hours, benefits and working conditions—increased, Chavez used his power to resist them. But it increasingly became a bureaucratic resistance—one imposed from central authority rather than one argued for in countless democratic forums created in "locals" that might have been the constituent pieces of the union. Perhaps Chavez was fearful of the co-optation he observed in the rest of the American labor movement. But his solution to that problem caused even greater problems, and ultimately undermined whatever his vision might have been.

Alinsky's Impact

Alinsky's direct impact is clearly seen in the CSO. He initially hired Fred Ross, raised the money for the CSO, and supported hiring Cesar Chavez, Dolores Huerta, and Gil Padilla. He connected the CSO with the United Packinghouse Workers of America in Oxnard, where the first effort to organize farmworkers took place. While Ross developed his own house-meeting approach to organizing, the deeper principles of community organizing were similar to Alinsky's, and the conversations between them enriched organizational development in the CSO. All this was transferred to the NFWA and the UFW.

Alinsky's impact on American Protestantism also played a key role in the development of the union. Rev. Doug Still, the director of the CMM, moved it toward community organizing, with support from sponsoring church bodies; this direction expanded with his successor, Rev. Wayne C. Hartmire. As early as 1957, the CMM connected with the CSO. Alinsky, in quarterly intensive seminars, and Ross and Chavez, in on-the-ground experience, were all involved in training CMM staff.[11] Rev. Jim Drake, who became national coordinator of the union's boycott operation until he left to pursue organizing work with black Mississippi woodworkers, was among them. Drake went on to join the IAF staff, and became an important IAF organizer working in Texas, the South Bronx, and Boston.

Throughout the country, Catholic and Protestant churchmen and churchwomen, many of them influenced by Alinsky's work with their local, regional, and national structures, were central to the boycott's success in their respective cities and metropolitan areas. I elsewhere elaborate upon Alinsky's influence on American (and worldwide) Christendom (see Chapter 28).

No U.S. struggle for social and economic justice makes Alinsky's role clearer than that of the CSO, the NFWA, and the UFW. While he disagreed with the direct membership approach, it was more important to him to support these organizations than to abandon them, including through fundraising, consulting, and training. While there were important departures from his core strategic principles, there was the ultimately more important goal of justice to be served, and he had confidence that the people with whom he was working were committed to that, and that they were effective organizers. In the confrontation with agribusiness, California's most powerful industry, the CMM effectively demonstrated, as perhaps only the FIGHT versus Kodak battle did in the urban scene (see Chapter 2), that Alinsky's influence had transformed the American church from charity (direct service) and advocacy (speaking truth to power)—however important at any time either of these might be—to a willingness to speak truth with people power to status quo power.

Notes

1. Susan Ferriss and Ricardo Sandoval, *The Fight in the Fields: Cesar Chavez and the Farmworkers Movement* (New York: Harcourt Brace, 1997), 66.
2. Saul Alinsky, quoted in Randy Shaw, *Beyond the Fields: Cesar Chavez, the UFW, and the Struggle for Justice in the 21st Century* (Berkeley: University of California Press, 2008), 16.
3. Cesar Chavez, "A Union in the Community c. 1969," 13, available at UC San Diego Library, *Farmworker Movement Documentation Project, farmworkermovement.com.*
4. Cesar Chavez, "Cesar Chavez on Money and Organizing, October 4, 1971," in *The Words of Cesar Chavez*, edited by Richard J. Jensen and John C. Hammerback (College Station: Texas A&M University Press, 2002), 66.
5. Wendy Goepel, "Viva La Causa," *Farm Labor* 1, no. 5 (1964): 26.
6. Where not documented otherwise, the quotes of Alinsky, Ross, and other leaders in this chapter are from my conversations with them and their associates during my years of working as a community organizer.
7. Gil Padilla, interview with Mike Miller, April 23, 2013.

8. Saul Alinsky, *Conversations on Revolution* (Kansas City, MO: National Catholic Reporter, 1967), 10.

9. Cesar Chavez, "An Organizer's Tale," in *An Organizer's Tale: Speeches*, edited by Ilan Stavans (New York: Penguin, 2008), 25.

10. Mike Miller, "Putting 'Isms' in Their Place: A Review Essay," *Social Policy*, Spring 2012. My comment on March is also informed by my interviews and correspondence with Herb March and his son Richard March. (See the discussion of March in Chapter 2.)

11. Sidney D. Smith, *The Grapes of Conflict* (Pasadena, CA: Hope Publishing House, 1987).

10

Dolores Huerta and Gil Padilla

■

VARIOUS AUTHORS

She's like a character on *Star Trek*. She doesn't really need sleep or food.
— Juanita Chávez, daughter of Dolores Huerta[1]

Organizing is the hardest thing in the world.
— Gil Padilla[2]

Editors' preface: Many organizers and leaders beyond Cesar Chavez worked to make the Community Service Organization (CSO) and the United Farm Workers of America (UFW) what they became. This chapter addresses two of the most important: Dolores Huerta and Gil Padilla.

Dolores Huerta

I n the 1950s, Dolores Huerta met Fred Ross at a CSO house meeting in Stockton, California. In her mid-twenties, Huerta was from a middle-class background, the holder of an associate's degree, and already a mother with children, and she was looking for a way to do real social justice work. At first, she was suspicious of his ideas. She remembers that she thought he was a Communist, and that she "went to the FBI and had him checked out."[3] What won her over was that he showed he could actually get things done. In a story about Huerta written by Ross, Huerta remembers that Ross called "a big, city-wide meeting of all the people [he'd] met at the house meetings. . . . Well, I couldn't imagine more than 20 or 30 people there, because I'd never seen that at any Mexican Club business meeting in my life. So, when I came to St. Mary's Hall that night and it was jammed, and I saw people I hadn't even heard of for years, I knew right then that something really big had come to Stockton."[4] Later, Huerta said, "I always thank the day that I met Fred. I always hated injustice and I always wanted to do something to change things. Fred opened a door for me. He changed my whole life. If it weren't for Fred, I'd probably just be in some stupid suburb somewhere."[5]

This chapter was edited by Aaron Schutz.

She worked for a number of years with the Stockton CSO, many of them as the chapter secretary, participating and often driving different campaigns on voter registration, illegal hiring practices, urban renewal, and more. This chapter includes a text written by Ross that gives a sense of her personality and her work there. Eventually, the CSO hired Huerta as its lobbyist under the direction of Cesar Chavez, who by then was the CSO's executive director. In the early 1960s, she became legendary in Sacramento "as a forceful and articulate communicator and advocate."[6] She successfully lobbied for fifteen bills and administrative changes, including "old age pensions, a higher minimum wage for field workers, and aid to dependent children of unemployed agricultural workers."[7]

In 1962, when the CSO rejected Cesar Chavez's proposal to form a farmworkers' association, Chavez quit to do it on his own. Huerta stayed on at the CSO to maintain a paycheck while working almost full time as well for the fledgling National Farm Workers Association (NFWA). (For more detail on the NFWA, see Chapter 9). Finally, it became clear that she could not successfully juggle both jobs. She was, in her words, "terminated" by the CSO in 1964. After that, she survived on "temporary translation assignments, . . . teaching, and even a backbreaking stint in the onion harvest, in addition to her work for the NFWA."[8] Then and later on she was supported by donations, as well as limited child support from the fathers of her children. The most challenging times came when Chavez convinced her to move to Delano to work with him, which meant leaving a teaching position and her Stockton support system. She once noted, "You don't think about how to do it. I always say that if you start to think about all of the things that you have to prepare to do, it's not going to happen. You just have to get out there and do it and then play catch up."[9]

Huerta became the vice president of the association and then the union, and was widely viewed as the second in command. In the early days, both she and Chavez organized, holding house meetings late into the night. And she was well known as a leader on the picket lines. But her most important contributions were likely as negotiator with employers, lobbyist in the halls of state, and key leader of the boycott on the East Coast, starting in New York City. Chavez had a great deal of respect for Huerta. They often argued about strategy—for example, she gave greater weight to lobbying than he—but in the end Chavez had the last word.

She was sometimes attacked for her refusal to fulfill the role of "mother" as framed for her by Mexican culture and the 1950s, and she struggled to get male farmworkers to take her seriously as an organizer. When Margaret Rose interviewed her, "she recounted incidents when meetings, attended primarily by men, were abruptly canceled when she arrived at the appointed hour."[10] At one point, she apparently resorted to using her husband at the time (before they divorced) as a front "man" while she actually did all the work and made the decisions as organizer.[11]

Huerta frequently struggled to find child care for her growing family, often leaving her children with family, supporters, and friends. In "Woman of the Year," Julie Felner reports that Huerta's children "grew up on the picket lines" and that, according to one daughter, "the union always came first."[12] That daughter, Lori Huerta, also remembered being told "that the sacrifices that I make today will help hundreds of farm worker children in the future. How can you argue with something like that?"[13] Dolores Huerta would later reflect that

> the kids have never gone hungry. We've had some rough times. . . . It's made them understand what hardship is, and this is good because you can't really relate to suffering unless you've had a little bit of it yourself. . . .
>
> Sometimes I think it's bad for people to shelter their kids too much. Giving kids clothes and food is one thing . . . but it's much more important to teach them that other people besides themselves are important, and that the best thing they can do with their lives is to use it in the service of other people. So my kids know that the way we live is poor, materially speaking, but it's rich in a lot of other ways. They get to meet a lot of people and their experiences are varied.[14]

Although her union work in the 1970s coincided with the emergence of the women's movement, Huerta didn't really see herself as a feminist until later on, although she always pushed the importance of women's participation. "For years," Rose writes, Huerta "had dismissed the women's movement as a middle-class phenomenon."[15] But working in New York City as director of the boycott there gave her an opportunity to engage with local feminist supporters, and she began to voice more concerns about sexism in the union.

Here are excerpts from documents that give a sense of Huerta's work with the CSO and with the union.

From "Woman in Motion" (n.d.)

—Fred Ross

The following text is from a manuscript Ross wrote about Huerta's early work in the CSO in Stockton. It gives a taste of Ross's writing and of how he saw Huerta in the years before she was hired as one of the few staff members in the organization. This segment is about an effort to annex an impoverished area called Goat Flats to Stockton. Ross and Huerta discuss how they can learn more about the plan, and then attend a CSO executive committee meeting about the issue. The other key player is "Joe," then president of the CSO in Stockton.

"Hey! I've got it!" [Dolores said.] . . . "How about having the Planners come to our Meet your Councilman Candidates' Meeting? Then, after we get through putting the

---

The quotations from Fred Ross's "Woman in Motion" are published here by permission of Fred Ross Jr.

Candidates on the spot . . . , we can work the Planners over a little. How about that, Mr. Ross? . . . I could start calling right now."

"Slow down, Dolores," I laughed, "This all has to go before the Executive Board first, you know."

"Oh," her hand hit her mouth, "that's right. Well anyway, we can have Joe call a special meeting of the Board tonight right after registration. We don't have much time. . . ."

"Good idea," I pulled into the curb in front of the Ritz Hotel just as the bells of St. Mary's bonged out twice. . . .

"Don't bother calling me," she hopped out of the car. . . . "I'll be ready."

"And don't forget to call Joe, uh?"

"Don't worry," she nodded nervously, "I'll get right on it."

And driving off I got the feeling she would, too. That I could just put that one out of my mind completely and concentrate on the business of the moment.

Which, as I learned that night, is a luxury you can never afford around Dolores. . . . Oh, it wasn't that she forgot to call Joe; the point was *when* she called him. She was right on his tail the second he usually got home from work; but he wasn't in. Well, normally, when you want the President's O.K. . . . , you just keep calling until you reach him. Not Dolores. Once she's got that phone in her hand she just can't stop until she'd called the whole Board and told them about the meeting. . . . As Joe told me later, by the time she gets around to Joe again, he already knew. One of the other Board members . . . had told him. . . .

But Joe took that in good spirit, and, figuring she hadn't done anything worth worrying about, I relaxed too. . . .

At the end of the board meeting, however, Ross learned that he'd figured wrong:

"Well," Joe let out that timid, boyish chuckle, "looks like we've loaded our Secretary here with a lot of work. Let's see, Dolores," he glanced at the points he'd written down during the meeting, "we've got to . . . write to the ACLU, invite the Candidates and the Planners to our next Membership Meeting. Golly! Dolores, you're gonna be pretty busy tomorrow."

"Oh no I'm not," she smiled, her face a study of child-like innocence, "It's all done."

Well, the thing was so preposterous that there's a full fifteen seconds of silent horror, before we all bore on her at once. But, of course, as she explained when calm was restored, she'd only done it to speed things up a little since, after all, those were the only logical steps we could have taken. Weren't they?

For a moment, Joe bowed his head, as if to dismiss the painful topic. When he looked up a sick smile twitched his lips. "Well," he cleared his throat, ". . . I guess we better start figuring what we're gonna tell em, [h]uh?" He shot a hard look at Dolores, "Unless Dolores has already taken care of that part, too. . . ."

Later, parked in front of the Ritz, in the glow of the Row's pink neons, I tried to straighten her out. You know—the democratic process, the organizational value of group-planning, the demoralizing affect when one of them "jumps the gun," the works. And through it all, she sat there, quiet as a kitten, in a corner of the car. When I'd finished she gave a low sigh.

"I know I'm wrong in doing what I did," she said, "and I really don't know why I did it. Unless I was afraid the other Officers might get scared and back away from this thing. And that, maybe," she laughed, "if I got them into it a little ways they wouldn't be able to; it'd be too late."

"But why should you think that?" I wanted to know. "None of them had ever been put to the test, really, until tonight."

"That's *why*," she shot it out. "They're all so green, you know. . . . You saw how they hesitated at first tonight."

"Well, but you're kind of green too," I reminded her.

"Oh, sure," she chirped, "and I'm kinda scared, too. . . . But, you know Mr. Ross, it's a funny thing; even though I've got this scared feeling, at the same time I wish the meeting was gonna be right now. . . ."

"Look, Dolores . . . , *take it easy*. Give the rest of the guys a chance, too, [h]uh?"

"Oh, I will," she jumped out of the car smiling. "I learned my lesson."[16]

From "The Eternal Soldadera" (1999)

—James Rainey

When the great grape strike of 1965 began, it was Huerta who marched up and down the picket lines, rallying the men and keeping them out of the fields. When the growers formed a bloody anti-UFW alliance with the Teamsters union, it was Huerta who flew to Miami Beach and camped for a week outside Jimmy Hoffa's suite, pleading—futilely, as it turned out—with the Teamsters boss to back down.[17]

Before the union's first walkout—at the Mount Arbor Rose Co. in McFarland— she led a final unity meeting for nearly 100 workers. Huerta held out a cross and had the mostly Catholic workers place their hands on it. They had to swear they would stick together.

Not trusting providence alone, she was up before dawn the next day, patrolling in front of the workers' homes. When one group of men appeared as if it might break ranks, Huerta rolled her car in front of their driveway. She hid the keys and would not move. (The strike eventually led to a pay raise, although not a permanent contract.)

When the first proud grape grower finally buckled in 1966, Huerta negotiated the contract—the first in the state's history between a corporation and a union led by nonwhite workers. Then she went to San Francisco and learned from longshoremen how to run her union's first hiring hall.

Huerta framed every fight as part of a larger class struggle. Some of the growers seemed as pained at being depicted as greedy oppressors as they did at granting wage increases. They called Huerta "the dragon lady."

Three decades have not softened the view of one old foe, a Central Valley farmer, who said: "You don't get anything from Dolores Huerta unless you fight for it and you earn it. . . .[18] She is vindictive and carries a certain amount of resentment." . . .

"Dolores had a gift for making you believe in yourself," [former farm worker Eliseo] Medina says. "She has an ability to inspire you and urge you to do things you could not think were possible. She is one of those life-changers."[19] . . .

Chavez once summed up his right hand quite simply: "Totally fearless, both mentally and physically."[20]

From "Reflections on the UFW Experience" (1985)

—Dolores Huerta

Today, the farm workers refer to the United Farm Workers as "La Union de Chavez," Chavez's union. I am the first vice-president of the union. In a difficult situation the workers trust me because they know that whatever I represent is what Cesar is thinking. The workers have complete faith in Cesar.

In our American educational system, students, as early as in high school, are warned to be wary of the man on the white horse, the demagogue, the false leader. But working people and poor people do not have that problem. They recognize genuine leadership, and they are willing to follow whomever they consider their leader. It is a simple kind of faith. They want leadership, and to them leaders are people who are responsible, who are willing to take risks, who will be out in front fighting for them.[21]

Gil Padilla

—Mike Miller

Gil Padilla was an organizer before he met Fred Ross and Cesar Chavez, and he was a key organizer with both—initially in the CSO, then in the NFWA and UFW. All of Padilla's words in this section are taken from my interview with him in 2013, when he was eighty-five.

Padilla and his eight brothers all served in the U.S. military. He says that after they came "back home, we were treated like shit. That's the motivation for what I did." It was CSO leader Pete Garcia, a natural organizer who never worked full time as one, who introduced him to Chavez and Ross—who "taught me that all Anglos aren't ass-holes." Padilla continues: "From Pete, I learned how to listen, how to talk with people, how to fight. He would have been a great organizer, but his wife kept him from going full time. By the time I met Fred, we were figuring things out together. But I learned things from him too."

With Ross, Padilla developed as an organizer: "Fred didn't tell us what to do. He asked questions. He wanted to know how he could help. He offered low-key suggestions. He told stories from the experiences of other CSO chapters. He pushed local people to act; he always worked with local people to help them. He never spoke at conventions or big public meetings. I began to appreciate him."

Padilla's first major chapter organizing was Stockton. "I loved CSO," is how Padilla describes the relationship. In June 1963, after Chavez's resignation from the CSO, Ross visited Padilla: "There's a vacuum without Cesar. CSO is dying. Come to work with me, and let's revitalize the organization."

They divided the state in half, with Padilla taking Southern California, and Ross the north. Ross and Padilla would go into a chapter with an invitation from the board to be there:

> Fred and I would regularly meet. We'd compare notes, talk about what was working and what wasn't. We'd analyze a problem, then come up with a way to deal with it. We'd talk about everything—issues, personalities, strategies. My method of starting a new chapter—let's take Mendoza—was this: First visit all the religious leaders—not just the Catholic bishop, but all of them. Ask them for the names of people who are trying to improve the community. Go see those people; tell them the religious leader who gave me their name. Ask them to have a house meeting; ask them for other people who might have a house meeting. At the house meetings, ask people to hold a house meeting. If someone says, "I don't know anyone," ask them, "What about your compadre? Your neighbor? Etc." I would explain how a chapter works, electing a board of directors, adopting an action program. Then I'd work with the board to teach them to lead the organization. I wanted to give people a sense of their rights, their power, how they could use the vote to make the politicians afraid of them instead of them being afraid of the politician. "They work for you; you pay their salaries." Sometimes I would lead an action so people could see how it's done; then they had to do it. A big lesson I tried to teach was to ignore gossip.

The Poverty Program and its millions of dollars is what ruined CSO. First, there were a bunch of Poverty Program rip-offs. People who had degrees got hired because they could write proposals, not the people who knew anything about poverty because they'd lived it, or because they'd worked with poor people. So CSO people said, "That's awful. Let's take over and make these programs work for people." But then they got caught up in the money. The CSO people started becoming consultants, paid executive directors or some other paid position, starting nonprofits, getting grants. The chapters started dying. Keeping a chapter going was hard work; it took a lot of time. These were mostly men who were the leaders, and they had jobs and families. When I asked Fred Ross for an example of how the Poverty Program money was destroying CSO chapters, he replied, "People want to be paid to go to a board meeting. When I ask them where they got that idea, they say, 'The Poverty Program pays people to go to board meetings.'"

Padilla worked with Ross in the CSO for four years. A big thing he learned was to be focused and disciplined. He then went to the farmworkers and started working as one of Chavez's key organizers.

Leaving the UFW

From its mid-1960s birth into the 1970s, the UFW was widely supported and rarely criticized, though heated debate surrounded many of the issues it faced. Organizers and activists ranging from liberal to radical were drawn to its cause and the drama surrounding it. Cesar Chavez was an idol, and his organizing genius, modest personality, and charisma widely acclaimed.

But the union fell on hard times. No doubt a very large part of its difficulties was the result of grower intransigence, disruptive activities by the Teamsters, a more conservative political climate and, in particular, the election of an antiunion governor in California. These "external" factors are part of the environment any organizer and people power organization must face. Organizations that are able to adapt and remain united are able to survive, fighting defensive battles until they and their allies can turn the tide toward better times.

That is not what happened in the UFW. Many observers believe that Cesar Chavez became increasingly isolated from the farmworker base of the union. Purges within the union led to the dismissal of some of its most talented people, and resignations from many more. (I address some of these incidents in Chapter 9.)[22] Below, in what must have been as painful an experience as can be imagined, Padilla gives his version of the implosion of the UFW.

In October 1975, Chavez moved the UFW staff to La Paz; Padilla was part of the staff, serving as secretary/treasurer. He says, "During our time at La Paz, we became part of the 'community' of UFW staff. One of the significant changes in early 1977 was that of the involvement that Cesar had with Synanon and the introduction of 'the game.'"

Synanon was a self-help drug addiction and alcohol treatment center; the game was a method used by groups like Synanon to work with their residents. A person would be assigned to be in the middle of a circle of other residents, and be assaulted with criticism about his or her behavior. Then, after being broken down, the person would be built back up by the group. In the UFW, staff were trained to participate in the game and it was sometimes used as a method of reprimand.

Padilla recalls that

this use of the game caused internal controversy and many loyal volunteers, including some of our attorneys, left the union. Cesar felt that these were disloyal people and did not acknowledge that this method was destructive.

Cesar voiced many times to me that he felt there were people in the union who were out to destroy the union and working against us. I recall one evening in La Paz when we were walking to our homes, he told me that our union was "full of Communists who came to destroy the union." Cesar also told me that he knew who it was who had brought in these people. He said it was Nick Jones. Nick [and his wife, Virginia] had been with the union since the early days and were very dedicated and committed. Thereafter many volunteers were purged as a way of "cleaning house" of people who were thought to be "suspicious" or disloyal to the union. Many volunteers left the union during this time.

In October 1980, I spoke with some of the board members and Cesar about concerns I was hearing from the workers in Coachella and Salinas Valleys. Cesar refused to acknowledge that there were problems. I brought these issues up at our October board meeting, voiced my concern over the philosophical change in direction that Cesar was taking.

The following day, we had a meeting of the credit union, of which I was president. Before the meeting started, Dolores wanted to speak. [She] told me that I should resign because I was talking to other board members about the direction that Cesar was taking the union. Dolores made vicious—and unfounded—allegations against me. Dolores made this vicious attack with Cesar's blessing—he sat quietly, did not intervene, and said nothing.

I was extremely upset and disturbed that my loyalty to the union was questioned and challenged. The next morning, I called Cesar and told him that I would honor his request and I would resign. All he said was "OK." I wrote my letter of resignation, saying that I was resigning for personal reasons, because I did not want to hurt the union.

I never spoke with Cesar again.

Notes

1. Quoted in Julie Felner, "Woman of the Year: Dolores Huerta, for a Lifetime of Labor Championing the Rights of Farmworkers," in *A Dolores Huerta Reader*, edited by Mario T. Garcia (Albuquerque: University of New Mexico Press, 2008), 135. Originally published in *Ms. Magazine*, January-February 1998.
2. Gilbert Padilla, interview by Mike Miller, April 23, 2013.
3. Dolores Huerta, "Dolores Huerta Talks about Republicans, César Chávez, Children, and Her Home Town," in Garcia, *Dolores Huerta Reader*, 28. Originally published in *La Voz del Pueblo*, January 25, 1973.
4. Quoted in Fred Ross, "Woman in Motion" (unpublished manuscript, n.d.), 25, Fred Ross

Papers, box 21, folder 7, Special Collections and University Archives, Stanford University Libraries, California).

5. Huerta, "Republicans," 165.
6. Margaret Rose, "Dolores Huerta: The United Farm Workers Union," in Garcia, *Dolores Huerta Reader*, 12. Originally published in *The Human Tradition in American Labor History*, edited by Eric Arnesen (Wilmington, DE: SR Books, 2004), 211–29.
7. Richard Griswold del Castillo and Richard A. Garcia, "Coleadership: The Strength of Dolores Huerta," in Garcia, *Dolores Huerta Reader*, 45. Originally published in *Cesar Chavez: A Triumph of Spirit*, by Richard Griswold del Castillo and Richard A. Garcia (Oklahoma City: University of Oklahoma Press, 1997), 59–75.
8. Rose, "Huerta," 13.
9. Vincent Harding, "Interview with Dolores Huerta: Early Family Influences," in Garcia, *Dolores Huerta Reader*, 181. Originally published in the Veterans of Hope Project, n.d., *www.veteransofhope.org*.
10. Rose, "Huerta," 14.
11. See del Castillo and Garcia, "Coleadership."
12. Felner, "Woman of the Year," 135–36.
13. Quoted as Lori de Leon in ibid., 36; slightly altered in response to e-mail information from Lori Huerta, February 7, 2014.
14. Huerta, "Republicans," 167–68.
15. Rose, "Huerta," 17–18.
16. Ross, "Woman in Motion," 32–36.
17. Hoffa was president of the Teamsters at that time.
18. Ellipses in the original.
19. Medina was a farmworker when he met Huerta. He later became a leader of the UFW and the Service Employees International Union.
20. James Rainey, "The Eternal Soldadera," in Garcia, *Dolores Huerta Reader*, 146–47. Originally published in the *Los Angeles Times*, August 15, 1999.
21. Dolores Huerta, "Reflections on the UFW Experience," Center for the Study of Democratic Institutions, July/August 1985, 3, available at UC San Diego Library, *Farmworker Movement Documentation Project, farmworkermovement.com*.
22. Readers interested in pursuing these issues should visit the official UFW website, *www.ufw.org*, and the independent farmworker documentation project website, *farmworkermovement.com*.

11

Tom Gaudette
An Oral History

■

VARIOUS SPEAKERS

Introduction

Tom Gaudette was one of the most important of the core group of organizers who worked with Alinsky. Yet, outside the organizing world, he is probably the least well known among them. Like Ross, Gaudette came to Alinsky with extensive organizing experience under his belt from Chatham, his neighborhood in Chicago, and through activities with the Christian Family Movement. Alinsky provided him with a more coherent understanding of ideas of power and a broader vision of what organizing could accomplish. As an Alinsky staffer, Gaudette created Chicago's Northwest Community Organization (NCO), which ultimately became one of the most impressive organizations in the early Industrial Areas Foundation (IAF). One of its major accomplishments under Gaudette was to take over an enormous urban renewal project, substituting its own plan for the design of what became the Noble Square project. NCO also created and spun off different community development organizations.

In 1966, Gaudette refused to move to Kansas City, Missouri, to direct the IAF's project there—breaking Alinsky's "have gun, will travel" rule for organizers. After this, Alinsky and Gaudette went in different directions. Gaudette left NCO and the IAF and went south in the city of Chicago to create Organization for a Better Austin (OBA), where he and Shel Trapp developed an approach to block club–based organizing to deal with the limited strength of churches in areas that were quickly shifting in racial composition. In OBA, Gaudette, Trapp, Gale Cincotta, Stan Holt, and other organizers and leaders fought against "panic peddling" efforts by real estate agents to scare whites cheaply out of their homes and then sell these same homes at a higher price to incoming blacks. We discuss OBA in more detail in Chapter 12.

This chapter was edited by Aaron Schutz. Selections from the interview of Tom Gaudette appear by permission of John Gaudette.

Gaudette trained a large number of organizers who went on to create organizations and networks across the country. As we describe in later chapters, Trapp and Cincotta went on to create NPA and NTIC, and John Baumann went to California and with his associates eventually created PICO. Gaudette also worked with Gregory Galluzzo, who later was the key person in the creation of the Gamaliel Foundation, and with Herb White, who ended up organizing in South Korea, the Philippines (Manila), and India (Mumbai).

As I discuss below, in his later years Gaudette became somewhat estranged from the networks he had helped create. But he kept working individually with organizers around the nation, his family's house becoming a kind of Grand Central Station for visiting organizers. In 1972 he called himself the Mid-America Institute. He traveled widely—he was away from home two weeks out of every month—and, back in Chicago, he was constantly on the phone or sitting with organizers in his living room. He loved working one-on-one with organizers, "reacting" to what others said and acting as what his son John describes as a "ring coach." He worked tirelessly to bring organizers across the country to work together and learn from each other.

What follows is largely drawn from a life-history interview found in his archives that was conducted by an unknown interviewer in 1990.[1] The text has been rearranged for clarity, and I have supplemented it with text from interviews with others who worked with him and articles about the efforts in which he engaged. Also, for space and clarity reasons, I have removed the names of most of the many people Gaudette frequently refers to in the interview—indicative of his constant focus while organizing on relationships with particular individuals.

Early Years

In the interview, Gaudette describes being raised in an Irish neighborhood:

> I grew up in Medford, Massachusetts. I had two sisters that were nuns, a brother, a priest. My dad worked for the Boston-Maine railroad. So when I was growing up I visited convents and churches in that atmosphere. In my neighborhood, the place was loaded with church people.
>
> Mom was always making me go out and do community stuff. Get over there and cut the grass. Or go see Mrs. Healey, she needs her kitchen washed. Or run over here with the food [for] my dad and my brother.
>
> Mom taught me things about community and church which I still insist [are] important. There cannot be a church without community. There can't be a community without a church.[2]
>
> And Mom drilled that into us all. We went to church when anybody was in trouble, whatever. I don't know whether she used these as excuses just to get us to

go, or if it was for real. If there was a birth, then we went to church. If there was a
death, we went to church. The community. She always had us for every day, a list
of things that needed to be done: sweep the floor, or cut the grass, or so forth. And
then the people in trouble. Me and my brothers [needed to be of] service to the
[poor], whether it was food or so on. And that was drilled in you as a little kid.

My dad was [in a railroad] brotherhood, and my brother was the big man
in the plumbers union. So I spent a lot of time going around [union] halls as a
young kid before the Second World War. Bringing the food to the picket lines
and so forth.

He learned a lot from his brother, but saw the danger of his brother's anger:

That's why a lot of the stuff Alinsky brought up I understood, because I went
through it. Wild crazy anger is nothing but violence. And Alinsky said we got to
have anger, but it's got to be directed and controlled.

And then the war came along and I didn't want to go in but I was the youngest
of the street gang. Everybody went to the Air Force. So I went along with them
and I'm the one who got accepted and became a [bomber] pilot.

He flew forty missions in the war, at one point crash-landing in Yugoslavia and
hiking out. Then he returned to Massachusetts: "I came back and went to Boston
College. In my parish there was nothing going on. So a bunch of the [guys] started a
glee club. We had, I think, a group of about 250 people just like ourselves who had
nothing to do and we used to put on concerts all over the campuses, all over New
England. And we developed a whole bunch of friends which we called the Mulford
Club."

In the summer, he went south to Mississippi, where one of his brothers was serving
as a Josephite priest in an African American parish. It "took me into that world of
the challenge and the joy of working with people. It was a ball. We had a great time
in Mississippi. I used to work with his high school students. He [and the kids] built
a high school. And [he] worked with these kids about jobs. Where the hell are they
going to work?" Gaudette worked with his brother to get a major employer in the city
to hire blacks.

In 1953, Gaudette married Kay, a woman from Chicago:

It was the most logical thing to me to get involved with people, doing things,
whether it was sports or whatever, in the community. I love community, just the
concept. So when I get married, I came to Chicago, began to work at the Admiral
Corporation [where] I had a lot of freedom. Kay pried open up that whole thing,
the Chicago-style community. Don't tell her I said this, [but she] motivated me.
She was the one who gave me all the motivation.

Her mother [challenged me]—she was a son of a [pause]. "This city [is in] trouble, and it is our fault. And what the hell are you going to do about it? We can't keep turning our back and blaming somebody else." I said, "I'm doing fine. I've got to raise a family. I am working at Admiral." "No you don't. You are the young person. And it is your job to do."

You talk about getting beat up by a theology. She was marvelous! Fearless! That whole family, her side of the family, which came from Ireland, were the writers, the journalists, the politicians. That was the atmosphere. So when you're there, it's coming at you like this: politics, do it! It's your job. Responsibility. I loved it! See that's why I challenge people. I think a lot of people want to do something.

I was a simple man [who] painted the gutters, which I never paint now. Came home every night at 5:30, had kids, and so forth. And if people think that's the total thing in life, and that's what the churches taught you, what a fucking waste of time to get born! You know, clean gutters and the grass is cut, and all this nice stuff.

Kay and I came out of that experience [believing] that one of us has to go out and extend himself into the community. But we go as a family, not as an individual.

So I logically got into the community of Chatham [in Chicago] and organizing, which led into others.

The Christian Family Movement

In the interview, Gaudette also describes his involvement with the Christian Family Movement (CFM):

One day a doorbell rang and a guy named Father Larry Kelly from St. Rayfield's parish came in and talked us into joining. I just became a dog. I just loved it. Every night we'd meet and we'd argue. And shit let's do it.

What [CFM] did was prepare you to get involved in the community. When I got involved in [the] Chatham [Community Council], it wasn't the community organization, it was the community.

It wasn't all of the jargon that we got today. It was where I *lived*. The streets were dirty, I got to clean them. Whatever.

Our CFM grew big. And that group became, if you want, a community. We'd be up at CFM at a Tuesday night meeting at 1 and 2 o'clock in the morning and arguing like a son of a bitch about what we're going to do. We all had big families, black and white. It was great. It was every night of the week. I mean we were over here helping this one, that was part of the game, you know, help.

I find that we've been blessed with that. People that are generous, happy, able to contribute, and come into your life, and so forth, and they just stimulate the hell out of you. It wasn't just sitting down saying, this is my thought, or this is the way I see life. It's reacting to people. Which I think is the key to organizing. When they react to you, you react to them. That's what it's about. If it's done right, that's what makes it fun. Christ.

Because of its importance to Gaudette's story, it seems important to lay out some key characteristics of CFM. The CFM manual explained that

> if even one family is oppressed by circumstances—moral, economic or social. . . . then Christians must be concerned. CFM is a practical way for couples to become aware of the community. All the members bring to a meeting information based on personal observations. Then by discussion they judge the situation in the light of Christian teaching. The last step of the method is for the group to decide on some practical and attainable action . . . to improve the situation they have been observing.

Or, more simply, to "observe, judge, act."

According to historian Jeffrey Burns, the "independence" of many lay CFM members "made them a challenge for many pastors and bishops."[3] A mostly middle-class, suburban, Catholic organization, it peaked at around fifty thousand couples in the 1960s and faded in the 1970s. CFM participants grappled with the big issues of their time in their meetings and yearly conferences—civil rights, world peace, economics, politics, international relations. Most CFM efforts were relatively small: Have lunch with a black co-worker. Bring international students into your home. Bring food to the needy. As the movement developed, more involved efforts emerged: voter registration, a medical services program, a vocational counseling service, international mission work, support for refugees, and more. Many members ran for office. Some groups, like Gaudette's, "became involved in neighborhood improvement associations."[4] While the level of community organizing Gaudette and his co-CFM members engaged in was unusual, it reflected the wider aims of the movement in spirit.

Gaudette recounts how, in Chatham,

> we had one of the biggest CFMs in the city. Because I'd go out and I'd get you in that damn thing or break your leg! And then [when] all [the] blacks started to move in, we went after them. That's when I started to learn how to ring doorbells.
>
> [The Chatham-Avalon Park Community Council] was my first "community organization" meeting that I remember.
>
> I never knew what the hell the meetings were for. So when I used to have a meeting, everybody's going to know why they're there. I used to *over*compensate by informing people why they're there. Because I remember I used to sit there. You see most of my experience of organizing is through my negative experience. Because I was one of the people in the last row, I was one of the people who was insignificant. [And I] never knew what the hell was going on.

And I says, this is stupid. What the hell? Why don't we go out and ring the doorbells and ask the neighbors what they think about whatever's going on, what they think the big problems are? We were up until 1 or 2 in the morning. As soon as we got inside, they realized we were neighbors. "Yeah, come on in. Here have a drink." And some of them never even heard of the council.

And that was the first experience I had. So we decided to take this thing over and see if we could turn it around and make it work. We literally took it over. And we used to have more fun. And we began to form clubs. Joe [Valis, the president,] was a genius at organizing. So we divided the [community into seven] areas. And we'd have a meeting in each area in which people would be elected. We would have three of them elected to the board of the council, which was a great strategy.

They also began to have meetings for each individual block, "and we found that damn thing worked." This taught him how to draw together the different self-interests of people from all the different areas: "I mean, we could easily get eight or nine thousand people out, without really much effort."[5]

When there was a problem in the school his kids went to, Gaudette "got the parents together. I think we got the principal fired. And the street gangs [were starting up]. So we organized some of the biggest guys you ever seen to take care of them."

In addition, Gaudette and his neighbors fought "panic peddling" by real estate agents, foreshadowing work he would later do in OBA. They also managed to vote the entire area "dry" to eliminate the taverns:

As a result, you began to get people coming in from all over to observe what was happening. Because Mayor Daley gave us an award. [And there were other awards.]

As this began to happen, I began to find myself going to meetings, going to churches, going to city council. And I was still working at Admiral Corporation. I had a job. So when I had to go down to city council, you know, I took off work. And some of these politicians started to go after my job. So the old man called me up and he said, "Sit down." He was the Chairman of the Board. "What is this all about? Love, love it! How can you get some of the other sons of bitches in this company to do something about this city? That's what you should be doing. Don't you worry about a thing, you're protected. And anytime you want to take off to do this stuff." And Kay, of course, the true believer. Just support, support, support. And by the way she had kids coming out her, boy did she ever. And you know, it was just marvelous.

When you are organizing you could use these contacts. That's how you knew what the hell was going on. Good people would tell you what's going on. And that's what [Ed] Chambers and Nick [von Hoffman] and that [Industrial Areas Foundation (IAF)] crowd never had. They never had that real context, social context in Chicago.[6]

Integrating the Churches in Cabrini-Green

When Gaudette was introduced to Jack Egan at a meeting, he found himself enjoying the priest's style: "He was so friendly and so interesting and so funny. And at the moment it was exactly what I needed. I wasn't aware of his experience with Alinsky, until [later]. I was beginning to get a reputation in Chicago as the president of the Chatham Council, and he would come to meetings or we'd get together. I says [to Egan], let me work for you. I'll work for you for nothing."

In 1956, Cardinal Albert Meyer "was asking about what's going on" at the parishes around the Cabrini-Green housing project. According to Gaudette, "Jack said, why don't you check it out? [We had] Cardinal Meyer come in. And he went and visited the pastors. And then he [asked me], 'What's going on?' I said, 'Blacks are not being served.' I said, 'They can't get in the [churches].' They were like tokens, you know—sweep the streets."

Gaudette accompanied Meyer on a Saturday night visit one of the priests. He remembers the archbishop saying, "Father, this is Cardinal Meyer, and we just checked out your two parishes. They are just a disgrace to this diocese." Meyer stated, "I want these two churches. Sell them to me or give them to me, I don't care." According to Gaudette, the priest was "this great Father Victor. Great guy, great guy. And [he] said, 'I'm embarrassed,'" and asked to work on solving the problem himself. Gaudette continues:

> And again, Kay would say, "This is what we're supposed to be doing. Let's do something." So we took over that and [Egan] said, "What do we do?" I said, "Jack, here's a chance where I can show you the lay people in Chicago. The greatest people I've ever met in my life. The clergy are great, but the lay people . . ." I said, "Jack, God damn it, give us a chance. Let's try it. And if they don't, they don't."
>
> So we call up the president of [the CFM]. He came over, and we started drinking. And we had more fun. We said, "What are we gonna do?" [*rubbing hands together*] Within three weeks we have five hundred couples. And immediately, the organizing mind. I said, "All right, we're gonna break up into teams, we break up by parish."
>
> And we began to divide the whole damn place [the housing project] up into sections, the high-rise, the low-rise, and so forth. And that thing got outta hand. I mean, it just got bigger and bigger.
>
> So we cleaned out the bottom of one of the rectories, made a gym out of it. We had carpenters, you know all the skills that were sitting around. We took this other place, made it a reading room. We formed a team on jobs and they began to train people. It was alive! And the cardinal come in and said, "This is the greatest privilege of my life to be the cardinal here." It was great. I said, "Jack, we cannot let this stop. We got enough public housing in this city [to keep this project going for a long time]."

The Catholic Church, however, shut the parish integration project down, for reasons that Gaudette is not clear about.

The Northwest Community Organization (NCO)

Gaudette's work in Chicago had not gone unnoticed:

> Saul came along in '61 and called me. I knew about him, I heard him talk, [but that was all]. So he asked me to come down in October 1961 for the famous meeting in which he bribed me into quitting my job. And it was just the way our relationship was. Now that I think about it, nobody else had a relation like that [with him].
>
> "Tom, what I want you to do is the very thing that you're doing in Chatham." I said, "How do you know?" He said, "Well, Nick [von Hoffman] works for me." I didn't know that.
>
> Alinsky asked me to come in and be interviewed. So I went to the office and I said, "I'm not that interested but let's talk about it."

An exchange then occurred between Alinsky and Gaudette that concluded with Alinsky saying: "You're too old. I was looking for a much younger person who really gives a shit about people." Gaudette's fate was sealed:

> And I'm still working. That did it. "Pick up the phone and quit your job." I did it. [Laughs] I figured, you damn fool, why'd you quit your job?
>
> But [Alinsky] does the opposite, he thinks the opposite. And it was intriguing that he could set me up, because in those days I thought I was pretty good. Nobody could upset me. But he knew how to do it. He heard about me. You know, he just baited you enough to get you angry. That damn thing, anger.
>
> And I went home and talked to Kay. And still to this day, she denies it, [but] she knew about it, I swear to God. Because she had that sneaky smile on her face. I said, "What do I do?" She says, "You want to do it? Do it. I'll take care of the kids, you go out and let's go out and get something going." Because she knew I loved it.
>
> So I went back, and Alinsky says, "Well, Egan got me this place up there. I don't know that much about it. There's twenty-two Catholic parishes. I want you to go teach the people what you learned in Chatham. Go in and check it out and see what the problems are. Let me know if I can help you." I swear to God, that was my training. That was it.

A 1964 article about Gaudette and the NCO reports otherwise, however:

> Gaudette's first assignment consisted of reading passages from or about Moses, St, Paul, Lenin, Robespierre, John Adams and Tom Pendergast, the Missouri machine

boss who made Harry Truman famous. Alinsky would call Gaudette into his office and, with the air conditioner wheezing away, discuss organizational tactics as used by Moses in the Israelite trek through the desert and the principle of self-interest as applied by Tom Pendergast. After four months' training, which included work in other IAF projects, Gaudette seemed ready to organize a section of northwest Chicago. "Begin with guerrilla tactics," Alinsky told Gaudette. "[But] your job is to organize an army, not to score victories."[7]

Gaudette recalls that, as he began the campaign, "Twenty-two Catholic churches put [up] about $108,000. And it was just logical to tie the church, the community, the words, the language, the theology, if that's the word. I don't give a fuck. But what I had to do was learn the people. If I am working in a Polish church, I better know something about Poland."

And from this, the Northwest Community Organization (NCO) was formed. Gaudette speaks of how his relationship with Saul evolved:

> Saul was my inspiration. I think Saul came to me at a time in my life when I needed some. Because I was so tired of Chatham. And living in that situation, at that age with a lot of kids, a big family.
>
> I had to write a memo every night. He would react to the memo.[8]
>
> I had an office downtown, but I hated it. I wouldn't go down there. I used to say I worked out of the back of my car. And I would work it out. And then I began to realize what he was doing. He was baiting, he was teasing, he was—that style of his—so I said, I can outdo him.
>
> So I never called him. I purposefully was, "You're gonna crawl," and I never called. Because in those days he began to travel. So you'd get calls: "This is Alinsky from LA" or something like this. "Do you still work for me? I mean, you're getting your paycheck, aren't you? Do you mind if I ask you what the hell's going on out there?" And I'd just say "Everything's fine," hang up. Drove him buggy. And I was determined to get him angry. And I got him angry.
>
> I made Saul come to the staff meetings. And he loved it. He used to come once a week. And I knew he was going to play games, so we had a strategy. One day we wouldn't be there, we'd lock the office. And we'd be sitting across the street. And he'd be banging away, nobody there. Another day I packed the place, I'd bring the whole board in, whole clergy. They wouldn't open their mouth, and Alinsky'd walk in. You know, he's waiting, "Something you want?" We'd just drive him nuts. And it just stimulated him and he loved it.

Organizing at NCO

Bud Kanitz was another Chicago resident and organizer. He provides a look at the original NCO:

The organizing was done by what we call civic organizations—"civics." Every four-square-block area became a civic area that also coordinated closely with a Catholic parish [that was within it], and organizing was actually done within those areas. The meetings were typically held in the basement of [a] Catholic church in that area.

Each organizer was assigned to just go out in the neighborhood and just talk to people. What are the problems in the neighborhood? It was definitely an outreach kind of thing which the organizer would do. I mean, a lot of the church-based organizing, I don't think they emphasize the community organizer getting out and doing it as much as getting people in the church to do it, getting volunteers like that. So we were all very poorly paid organizers, but that was what we would do. We can go out in the hood and talk to the people and find out what's bugging them and that would be the way of getting them involved in the neighborhood group and also developing new leadership.[9]

While leadership was developed in this way, there was no effort to build and sustain block-by-block clubs as Trapp would later do in OBA. Rather, it was the "civic" that was the focus of organizing attention. Sometimes a connection with a key person in the neighborhood was made through church connections—referred, for example, by a priest. Other times, this person was encountered by door-knocking. Door-knocking organizers would identify themselves with the local parish to give them legitimacy in the neighborhood.

Kanitz also supplies a look at the organization's governance:

NCO held an annual congress. The congress was made up of representatives from all of the member organizations which included the civic groups of course but also included lots of other disparate groups: business groups, or Caballeros de San Juan, credit union, or [whatever]. There were like 150 or 200 groups that were members of NCO. They would send people as delegates to the annual NCO congress and that was typically four hundred to five hundred people.[10]

At that time there was a slate of board members that was put forward by the nominations committee. And the delegates would elect the board of directors for the next year. And there were resolutions [on issues] that were presented to the whole congress. So that basically served as the priorities for the next year in terms of organizing.[11]

The Noble Division Project at NCO

NCO engaged in a major fight against a city-proposed urban renewal project that would have leveled eight acres around Holy Trinity Church and built thirty-eight-story high-rises that Gaudette characterized as "rich, rich rich." The organization enlisted a prestigious Chicago architecture firm to assist it in developing an alternative plan. Gaudette recalls, "I said I want the best of everything. Who's the best?"

Their plan was rejected by the planning commission in favor of one designed by a Texas company. "And we said, 'Who the hell are they?'" It appeared NCO had been defeated. But Gaudette soon learned from Alinsky what to do next:

> Saul came to the organization and he says, "Can I ask you something? Where the hell is this goddamn money coming from?" "Oh, ah, Washington." He says, "You know anybody in Washington?" "Well yeah, yeah, we know . . ." I can't remember who it was. And he says, "What's your name? Mary? You got a phone in this god-damn office?" "Yeah." "Can you get some tickets to fly there? What's the matter, you afraid of Washington?" And he took that leadership and just turned 'em around like that,

They flew to Washington, DC, met a high-ranking HUD representative, and created leverage for a meeting with Mayor Daley.

> And I kept saying, "Now why the hell didn't I think of it?" That was [Saul's] genius. You could never box him in. Because you get boxed in. "What do you do next? You know what's your strategy? You went after the mayor, you went after . . ." and so forth. You couldn't break that stranglehold. But he figured [it] out, as he always does. I didn't.
>
> And I swear to God, within a week we got a call from Mayor Daley's office. "Oh, this is Mayor Daley's office. The mayor would be very honored if you would come down and meet with him. We'd like to talk about your housing plan." We went down, the mayor said, "I like this plan. I don't know what happened before. And I think you'll get better consideration the next time you go up before the planning commission. Father, is that all right? I'm sorry to take up your time." And that's how we got that Noble Division development of 514 units [designed by the firm we'd selected].
>
> We used to have public meetings on the street. The architect would come out on the street and meet with the people. Everybody had their chance to talk to him. And they would design this stuff. The architects loved it. They said, "These people are great!" And we developed that plan and that was approved. And you can go see it now. And we built into there a plaza, just like Europe. We have stands for art fairs, or any kind of celebration. So it was a great plan. It was really a good plan. We, we went all over that neighborhood [to the Polish, Irish, and Latino low-income sections] to make sure we got approval.

After NCO

Gaudette left NCO in 1966 to create what became Organization for a Better Austin (OBA). Alinsky had asked him to direct the IAF's new Kansas City project.[12] Gaudette didn't want to leave Chicago. Alinsky demanded of his organizers that they be available to move as the work required. This led to a parting of the ways, with each moving in different directions, but Gaudette maintained his deep respect and affection for Alinsky till the end of his life. According to Gaudette, Alinsky even talked about bringing him back in as director of one or another aspect of IAF at different times. Gaudette's son John believes that disagreements between his father and Alinsky also grew over what Gaudette saw as Alinsky's effort to "go big." Gaudette had concerns about increasing distance between larger efforts and the people on the street. This became a continuing theme for Gaudette in the years to come.

As we noted in our preface, relationships between Gaudette and NPA and PICO, the networks created by his protégés, went through periods of strain. In the case of NPA, Gaudette was only distantly involved, if at all, in its developments.

John Gaudette reflects on these relationships:

> My dad was loved by Baumann and PICO. They gave my dad the proper respect and tied his legacy to the history of PICO.[13] [But] he was [also] the bull in the room. He wouldn't let you go past until he was done defending his position. I think my dad [felt that] if the question[er] gets repetitive, then one of us needs to get out of the way. Part of it was just kind of seeing, this is not where I'm going.
>
> If you look at my dad's legacy, he's not liked so much by the institutions, but he's loved by the individual organizers. Which is exactly where my dad wanted to be. Because my dad always said, "Kill the organization every ten years. Kill it! If you don't kill it, you're owed to it." If you don't kill the organization, then you're worried about: How do we keep the board going? How do we find new money? How do we perpetuate our existence? Which is exactly what we fight in organizing.[14]

In what follows, we seek to give a sense of Gaudette's vision of organizing and his concerns with the shift among organizing networks toward what they perceived as a "new" approach to organizing. This approach emphasized reaching deeply within institutional members, particularly churches, and focusing on relationships rather than going from issue to issue.

On the topic of training and the independence of organizers, Gaudette stated:

> I never considered myself a teacher. I call myself a trainer. A teacher's one that talks for three hours and is the expert. I'm not an expert. You and I will have a conversation. You'll tell me something, teaching me. I'll help you with something. That's the way I work. I've never been that comfortable getting up in front of a group of people, although I've done it. My lectures used to take fifteen minutes. I'd say, you got any questions? Saul and I were very similar that way.

Mike Miller tells this story about Gaudette's ability to get to the heart of an organizing problem:

I was at his house in Chicago, and he was having a conversation with an organizer who told an elaborate story about a situation in which the organization was trying to get from point *a* to point *b* and was stalled in the process. Gaudette listened carefully for what seemed an interminable length of time. Finally, the organizer stopped talking. Gaudette paused, and then asked, "What's his [the target's] self-interest?" The details of the story had so enmeshed the organizer that he'd lost sight of how to move in the situation—which Gaudette clearly saw, and raised with one brief question.

Gaudette was not interesting in lecturing in organizing courses:

What the hell do you talk [about] after a month? I remember Saul at Loyola, after two weeks. Ran out of things to say.

Saul's style was to react, which is the style I've often used. Rather than, "Here's the package," which is the way it's going today. And this was a great freedom [for organizers]. In other words, you go out and screw it up and whatever you do, but he would react and give you some advice, and that style. That was the training. In the conversations, some of these things occurred—the words: power, balance of power, and that kind of stuff. But it wasn't that formal. Saul said, organizing cannot be taught. You've got to go out from your own experience and find out what needs to be done. But the principles of organizing, I give up. And when I watch it today and see how academic it is—it's almost like computer training.

PICO organizer Stephanie Gut remembers Gaudette's emphasis on experience:

I was going into one of my first formal neighborhood meetings. And [Gaudette] said, "You know what you're going to do?" And I said, "Well, I talked to Scott [Reed]." "What do you mean, you talked to Scott?" "I talked to Scott, the director." "You don't listen to a goddamned thing he says! You're out there in the neighborhood. You think for yourself. You know people better than anybody else. What do *you* think?" It was that sense of, "You know something. You're out there and you're important, and what you bring is precious and don't ever forget it."[15]

On the topic of "How big is too big?" Gaudette said:

I have always struggled with the question of how far and how big you can get [with organizations]. Because [of] the key that we talk about, one-to-one. The personal. When you get too big, can you still do it? You know, when they have a convention of ten thousand people [in PICO] and an organizer sitting there. Oh, my Jesus, did they have name tags? I hope they have a lot of restrooms.[16]

But when you go before a big body, all you want is approval for something that has already been decided. Now I'm just the opposite. I love the floor fights, the debates. If it's important, I love that. They say, well, all that's done in committee. Okay. That's the difference. I love the regular folks that get up on their feet in front of everybody and participate.[17]

John Gaudette, who eventually became an organizer with PICO, adds:

His concern was that the institution becomes so big that the leaders are less significant. He's okay with PICO, he's okay with organizing, but he was worried about when you start worrying about the organization.

[This] was the tension for PICO. We've reached the level of power and we can't keep fighting for stop signs. We can't keep fighting for a cop on the corner. We have to go bigger. My dad would say, "That's fine, that's great. But talk to me about how you are going to keep building power. Talk to me about Mrs. Johnson on the corner. How you're going to keep her involved?" The more you go away from your community the less you're developing leaders, you're stuck with the same leaders. And that was the tension.[18]

The Shift to Church-Based Organizing

When John Baumann and his colleagues started PICO in California, they began with the kind of neighborhood-focused organizing they had learned from Gaudette and Shel Trapp at OBA. Although Trapp drew on churches, he focused on block club organizing (see Chapter 12). Over time, Baumann and his PICO colleagues became convinced about the effectiveness of the "church-based model." The shift took root when PICO connected with Jose Carrasco, who had worked as an organizer in IAF's Los Angeles project and in the PACT (People Acting in Community Together) project in San Jose.

John Gaudette reports that PICO still wanted church members to get out into the neighborhood around the churches. He notes that "for the Catholic Church, this was easier to do, as the parish was mostly the surrounding community."[19] This wasn't the case with most Protestant churches. "The challenge was connecting the members of the church with what was happening in the community. The tension focused on 'who are you organizing' the church or the community? PICO wanted the church members to build a relationship with the surrounding community to fight together over a common concern. This means shared power, not the rich helping the poor. This was a constant tension."[20] Over time, organizers themselves seem to have increasingly focused on the church itself as an institution and using the church to mobilize the community. Where laity didn't engage in "outreach" in a way that organizers would, it didn't happen.

Tom Gaudette saw dangers in this shift. While he had used churches as a base from which to engage the community in NCO and later in OBA, the focus was on the community in the entire neighborhood, not on the churches as institutions. He seems to have worried, at least in part, that focusing on the internal workings of churches—becoming experts on these institutional issues—combined with the fact that it is easier to organize people inside a church than to go out and knock on doors, might end up reducing the importance of the neighborhood as the key site for organizing. "The temptation," as John notes, "is to work with the church's existing leadership and never work in the surrounding community."[21] Congregation-based organizing might become an alternative to neighborhood organizing, not a different way to relate to the neighborhood that PICO thought had the potential to be both less staff (organizer) intensive, and that got lay people to connect with non-church member neighbors.

John Gaudette adds:

> On one level he understood that [PICO was] succeeding and that they were worth investing [in]. And he was very happy, and impressed. You know, talk about, "I couldn't imagine bringing ten thousand people together at a big level to do what you guys are doing on education." His concern was that we were limited to just church. So if you are going to do institutional organizing, that's fine, but why get locked into a model? I mean the only real model is: what's the role of the leaders? Are they defining the issue and are they figuring out the solutions? What information do they control and what solution can they define?
>
> My dad always worries about the laziness of an organizer. So if you're just with the pastor, you're just with the [lay] council, you're just with the leadership of the various associations of the church, what do you really represent? You can get comfortable just there. And then again you're not only institutionalized, but you're institutionalized within the church. The tension was always, "What the fuck are you doing? Get out in the neighborhood and talk to people. That's where all the answers are." That's why he would go in and push everything off of Baumann's desk and give him the finger and tell him to get the fuck out of the office [when Baumann was working for him]. "Listen, don't sit here. You're not here sitting around coming up with the answers. You should be out there with your leaders."
>
> If you get stuck in the institution of the church, that's an energy suck, because you've got to deal with their institutions, their knowledge, their prejudices, and all that stuff. So there's plusses and minuses to the church. I think it was more a cautionary tale of: why not take small business organizing? Or ethnic-based organizing? Or whatever. These were all limitations on something that fights not to be limited. Why are you leaving the other structures behind? So if you're going to [be] church-based, does that mean you're not going to do local neighborhood organization?
>
> A good organization is going to keep moving because it's alive. There's laughing, there's crying, there's stories, there's new folks coming in, there's food, there's folks getting to know each other, that was the organization.[22]

In what PICO then called its "model" (Baumann now prefers "approach"), a "local organizing committee" (LOC) was the internal mechanism within a church that was to link the church to the larger community organization, link the church's members to its mission in society, and connect the church to its neighbors. Some LOCs accomplished all these tasks; others didn't.

Relational Organizing

Gaudette also struggled with his protégés' emphasis on relationship-building, and about the numbers they talked about:

"We had a meeting last night at the church, eight hundred people." I'm sitting there saying, "What did you accomplish? You know, what are the issues?" They don't talk that way. "No, no, Tom, see, that's the old style. That's the Alinsky style. We don't work on issues anymore. We work on building relationships. Then you get on the issues." I said, "Okay. Now you've got 'em, you've been at it for many years, now you got 'em. What are you going to work on?"

They are doing stuff in drugs. They get two thousand people on the drug thing. What are they doing? We [would] get the police to take over the vacant building and either get the owner to fix it up and kick those people out or we'll demolish the building. Hell, I could do that in a neighborhood. Because I'm an organizer, and when you talk to me in terms of two and three and four thousand people, I have to address a strategy that encompasses that kind of power. I've never had that kind of power. But yet we were able to get many things done.

So when you talk in terms of that, they say, "No, you're missing the point. Those are relationship experiences, which affect their family and their churchgoing, and so forth." I say, "Don't get me in to the church thing again, because I'll be glad to discuss that with you. What good does it do to go to church every day if you're not out there doing something. What the hell do you mean by grace? What is grace? Do you eat it? What do you do with grace?"

I can't disagree with building relationships. Hell, that's what we did. If we had to mobilize people that's what we did. I have no difficulty working with the churches. But the churches to me were the means to get out in the community. Because, to me, church *is* community. I don't understand how you can say church is over here and community is over here. I don't understand. It's a contradiction.

My whole point was, if people are happy, if people have a sense of community where we work together on whatever the common problems are, and get them resolved, we have a support system built in, we support each other.

I don't know what the hell the rest of it's all about. It's a mystery. And I read as much of this stuff as I can find to understand it. And the language is fine. Relationships and power and yackety yack. Hell, okay. But the point is at the end of the year what did you do? And if you're trying to tell me that good schools aren't important and people aren't able to walk down the streets secure, and so forth and so forth. Then I don't understand what you're about.

I say, "Do it to me. You interview me" [for a relational meeting]. And you don't talk issues? No, you're building a relationship. And you can build a relationship in twenty minutes? Son of a gun! I must be too Irish. God. But it takes me longer than that to brush my teeth. Oh, no, and you've got to do a thousand, and so. A thousand? After about five interviews a day I'm ready to commit suicide.

I have sat in people's kitchen drinking coffee that'll come out your pores, maybe all morning, and when you've got intimacy, [asked] "Tell me what you think is the most serious problem?" Baby, if you've done a good job and get them going, you think they're gonna stop because you're [not] ready to wait? Saul used to say, when you ask people questions they're going to vomit up this stuff they've had inside them for the last many years. And he said, what you do is put it in a package and give it back and say, is that what you mean? "Hang on, my time is up?" I've never been good at that.

They like to hold back on the anger, passion as I call it. And this is the difficulty.

But at the same time they're getting masses of people, they are doing that thing and so forth and so on, so what can I say. I still worry about *the* community. I'm not in the business of saving the church. *The* community. I was able to take people from a church experience and *logically* communicate it into the community so they, logically, every night when they got home from work would be up talking to the non-church people, ringing the doorbells.

Piety and Profanity

To appreciate this story, you first have to know—as this chapter on him amply demonstrates—that Tom Gaudette was a devout, respected, recognized, and cele-brated Roman Catholic lay leader. He also used profanity with sometimes reckless abandon to make a point—usually one having to do with his anger at injustice in the world.

In the early 1970s, sponsored by the World Council of Churches, Gaudette went to India to lead workshops on Alinsky-tradition community organizing. He was leading a workshop in Calcutta with an organization of lepers who worked closely with Mother Teresa. The organization needed more space for its activities. The diocese had empty space, but the group had been unable to get its use. Gaudette applied an Alinsky organizing axiom: if you push a negative far enough you will find a positive within it.

He painted a scenario: "Imagine you doing a sit-in at the Chancery. What's the first thing they're going to want to do?" As he told the story, you could see the grins spreading on the faces of the workshop participants as they pictured the consternation their presence would create. "They'd want to get us out," they correctly replied. They then began plotting the action, enjoying every minute of it. The leader of the group said, "One thing we have to do before we implement this. We have to seek Mother

Teresa's approval." They agreed to resume their planning the next day, after they discussed the plan with her.

The next morning, the people came into the workshop room with downcast looks on their faces. "What's up?" Gaudette asked. "Mother Teresa said we can't do the action." "Why?" Gaudette inquired. "Because it is undignified," was the reply. "What do we do now, Mr. Gaudette?"

After a moment of silence, Gaudette said, "The first thing you have to do is get rid of that fucking saint."[23]

Gaudette's style also shines through in his answer to the question "Why organize?"

> These are the people. And there's the people that's hurting, whoever it is. And it seems to me if you don't know those people, and see them, it's rhetoric. It's a farce. That's the way we used to work with the church. How can you see it out there, and not react?
>
> I remember when I was in Seoul, Korea, with the Jesuits, sitting there drinking a martini at 4 o'clock in the afternoon. We were smoking cigars.
>
> "Tom, why are you here?"
>
> I said, "See that family out there?" Korean family, begging out in the middle of the street, all sitting on the ground. I said, "See that? That's why I'm here. And the other reason is because you don't give a God damn about that. That's my feeling. And if I ever come back, I'll get you."
>
> "Oh, well, I mean, there's always things in the world."
>
> "Look at you in this castle and look at them."
>
> Shit. That was clear.

Notes

1. All the text from Tom Gaudette in this chapter is from an oral history interview by an unknown interviewer, May 10–15, 1990, Thomas A. Gaudette Papers, series 3, box 1, folders 1–4, Special Collections, William H. Hannon Library, Loyola Marymount University, Los Angeles, CA. Note that because the conversation on the tape is difficult to hear at points, small portions of the text are approximations.
2. Gaudette believed two interrelated things: first, that the church could not isolate itself from its surrounding community. It had to be deeply engaged with it. At the same time, the church *itself* had to be a community. That is, it had to be a body of deeply related people, not simply a gathering that occurred when people showed up at Mass on Sunday morning, and for weddings, funerals, and other occasions.
3. Jeffrey M. Burns, *Disturbing the Peace: A History of the Catholic Family Movement, 1949–1974* (Notre Dame, IN: University of Notre Dame Press, 1999), 5.
4. Burns, *Disturbing the Peace*, 57–58.
5. This is an extraordinarily high turnout for a voluntary neighborhood association even in the best of circumstances.
6. Gaudette was immersed in community from the start because he was that kind of person.

But other IAF organizers immersed themselves in a different way—as outsiders who carefully listened to the hundreds of insiders with whom they spoke.

7. Hillel Black, "This Is War," *Saturday Evening Post*, January 1964, 2.

8. This was the core of Alinsky's "training" of organizers, as reported by von Hoffman and others: write detailed reports to Alinsky and get his reactions to them. It is consistent with Miller's later experience in Kansas City, when he directed Alinsky's project there under Ed Chambers's supervision: write or dictate a report, and receive detailed feedback on it.

9. Bud Kanitz, interview by Aaron Schutz, January 6, 2013.

10. Miller: These are delegates, whereas a later described mass meeting of 10,000 is a mass meeting attended by any member of a member organization who wants to attend, not a delegated body in which representatives are selected proportional to the number of members in an organization—for example, 15 delegates for an organization with 150 members.

11. Ibid.

12. A year later, Mike Miller became staff director of that project.

13. John Gaudette, e-mail to Aaron Schutz, September 13, 2013.

14. John Gaudette, interview by Aaron Schutz, March 9, 2013.

15. Stephanie Gut, on a panel celebrating Tom Gaudette, Applegate, California, July 1997, cassette tape, provided to author by John Gaudette.

16. Annual conventions that adopted a "platform" (stands on issues), elected leaders, and adopted or modified a constitution and bylaws were part of Alinsky's earlier organizing procedure. A well-attended convention put the organization on the map and gave legitimacy to its elected leadership and subsequent action on issues. Gaudette's conventions were often characterized by "floor fights" on controversial matters, with caucusing during the meetings and compromises hammered out in adjacent small meeting rooms. In more recent practice, conventions have turned into mass meetings that are a show of strength, but largely scripted and without internal tension. Gaudette is commenting on this difference.

17. Miller recalls the contrast in San Francisco between his organizing in the Mission Coalition Organization (MCO)—where committees had resolved most conflicts before the annual convention—and the organizing work that Gaudette-tradition organizers Larry Gordon and Jim Dickson did in Communities of the Outer Mission (COMO). COMO's "congress" was filled with debate and caucuses right on the floor of the meeting, illustrating the distinction Gaudette makes above.

18. John Gaudette, interview.

19. Ibid.

20. John Gaudette, e-mail to Schutz.

21. John Gaudette, interview.

22. Ibid.

23. Mike Miller wrote this section in consultation with John Gaudette.

12

Shel Trapp and Gale Cincotta

■

VARIOUS AUTHORS

Introduction

S tarting in 1967, and continuing until Gale Cincotta's death in 2001, Shel Trapp and Cincotta worked together as organizer and leader. They met in the Austin neighborhood of Chicago as part of Organization for a Better Austin (OBA), where Tom Gaudette had hired Trapp in 1966 as an organizer and where Cincotta eventually became president. After Trapp left OBA and became the director of Northwest Community Organization (NCO), Trapp and Cincotta collaborated to build the West Side Coalition, which was officially formed by NCO, OBA, and Our Lady of the Angels Catholic Parish. Together, in 1972, Trapp and Cincotta held the first national housing conference on what would eventually be called "redlining" by banks and savings and loans (as well as insurers and others who engaged in parallel practices). This was the practice of not lending, or charging substantially higher rates, to entire neighborhoods, typically resulting in racial turnover.

Soon after the conference came the creation of National People's Action (NPA) and the Neighborhood Training and Information Center (NTIC); for convenience, I refer to them collectively as NPA.[1] NPA worked to form a national coalition of groups to fight for federal legislation, first on housing and then around other issues. They also created the Metropolitan Area Housing Alliance (MAHA), a coalition of NPA organizations in Chicago and then Illinois. In 1974, they won city and state regulations mandating mortgage loan disclosure and outlawing redlining. Nationally, NPA led the charge for the passage of the Home Mortgage Disclosure Act (HMDA) in 1975, which Cincotta and Trapp helped draft, and the federal Community Reinvestment Act (CRA) in 1977.

This chapter includes writings by and interviews with Trapp about his organizing approach and philosophy. It concludes with selections from documents telling the story of Cincotta's life. It focuses more on Trapp because he was the organizer in the pair.

This chapter is indebted to Michael Westgate and Ann Vick-Westgate, who collected a wide range of information for their book, *Gale Force: Gale Cincotta—The Battle for Disclosure and Community Reinvestment*. In Trapp's case, this chapter generally emphasizes Chicago-based organizing efforts prior to his work with NPA; the later work of NPA is referred to more generally in the Cincotta section. For more on Trapp,

---

This chapter was edited by Aaron Schutz.

see his book *Dynamics of Organizing: Building Power by Developing the Human Spirit*, as well as his other writings (some available online).[2]

How Redlining Worked

"Redlining" is the name for a process that hurt white ethnic neighborhoods and made African Americans pay dearly for the opportunity to move into previously all-white neighborhoods. Here's the basic outline of how it worked.

(1) Lenders and insurers would either stop doing their business or charge substantially higher rates in a white lower-middle-income/working-class neighborhood. When asked "Why?" the response would be, "The neighborhood is deteriorating."

(2) City agencies would diminish the level of public services so that the quality of life in the neighborhood did, in fact, decline.

(3) "Block-buster" or "panic-peddler" realtors would tell white homeowners, "Sell now before the blacks move in and your house loses a lot of its value." Realtors would purchase at below the previous market rate and then sell to blacks at a much higher price. On both transactions they earned commissions and often participated in the profits. (Sometimes the block-busters were themselves black.)

(4) The presence of the newly moved-in African American households would confirm what the block-buster had been saying to the white homeowners. Soon there would be panic as home prices plummeted.

(5) A self-fulfilling prophesy was created by this often deliberate and conscious conspiracy of public and private parties.

(6) Redlining continued to hurt African Americans who moved into the neighborhood. Among other issues, they had greater difficulty obtaining home improvement loans and paid higher interest rates on them when they did get them.[3]

Within redlined neighborhoods, it was difficult to obtain a standard loan, so borrowers had to turn to FHA (government) guaranteed mortgages. These mortgages came with additional fees, and the federal guarantees encouraged predatory lending, as Trapp explains below.

Shel Trapp

From "Here Comes Trouble" (1995)

—Mike Ervin

Trapp is a chain smoker of Marlboro Light 100s, a hard drinker who tosses around expletives like a man in prison. He can be as warm, patient and approachable as a

Mike Ervin's "Here Comes Trouble: Shel Trapp Teaches People How to Fight City Hall—and Win" originally appeared in the *Chicago Tribune*, February 17, 1995, and is available at *articles.chicagotribune.com*.

growling marine drill sergeant, especially in battlefield situations where he has no tolerance for nonsense and timidity. Shel Trapp is not a hugger.

But he takes the pain of others very personally. That may have contributed to his leaving the Methodist ministry and moving into the activist trenches. In 1965, while leading his own Chicago congregation, he went to Alabama from Chicago with other ministers and congregation members, both black and white. Their simple mission was to try to enter a segregated church together. Trapp was among those who served a week in jail for the attempt, the only time in his career he's been arrested.

When he returned to Chicago, Trapp says his church superior told him, "'Shel, if you keep doing these kinds of things, you're never going to get a suburban church.' I thought if that was the symbol of success in the church, it was time to part company."

At OBA: Developing a Block Club Approach (2003)

—From an interview by Michael Westgate and Ann Vick-Westgate[4]

One of Trapp's contributions to organizing was a particular approach to "block club" organizing. As Trapp notes below, this began as a pragmatic response to the specific conditions he faced in his territory of OBA. In OBA, Trapp had the South Side, which was quickly shifting from white to black residents, while Stan Holt had the North Side, which was at the time still made up of mainly stable white neighborhoods. On the North Side, then, following the approach Gaudette had earlier used in NCO, Holt grounded his neighborhood work more in the churches, which were still strong in the areas where racial turnover had not yet happened.

The turnover in the South Side, however, meant that in many areas the institutions were not strong enough to support an organization. African Americans were not members of these churches. So Trapp and Gaudette needed to come up with a different approach.

SHEL TRAPP: I started in organizing in [Austin] in 1966. . . . First [Gaudette] put me up north in the all-white area. [But] then he couldn't get anything going in the south area where blacks were moving in.

ANN VICK-WESTGATE: Was the block club then something you came up with as an organizing [tool]?

TRAPP: Well, historically in the black community there's been block clubs. Gaudette had never dealt with that because at NCO [it] was a very [white], ethnic, big ethnic community.[5] So I got into the block club mode because people, as I'd knock on their doors, were saying, "Well, gee, there's no block club here." First time I heard that [I said], "Well, what's that?" "Well, you form an organization . . ." "Okay. So then we'll start a block club." . . .

Excerpts from Michael Westgate and Ann Vick-Westgate's interview of Shel Trapp are published here by permission of Kathy Trapp and Michael Westgate. Selections from *Gale Force* are reprinted here by permission of Michael Westgate.

Each block club was each block facing you. . . . The way Chicago's laid out on a grid, every four blocks there's a major thoroughfare. So from like Cicero to Laramie would be a street club, and then Cicero to Laramie, Madison to the Expressway was what I called a civic. And all of those layers would meet once a month. So I had like probably fifty [block club] meetings a month. And usually about three to four [street] clubs a month. And I had two civics that I ran, with all the block clubs and street clubs structured underneath. . . . So I had over a hundred meetings a month. So every night there were four or five block club meetings. And then once a month the street club meeting would also meet. And once a month the civics would meet and the civics would deal with bigger issues.

[The block clubs] usually start around one bad building or a pothole, something very small. As soon as that's done, it usually becomes a social club.[6] And I didn't want to deal with that, so then I formed street clubs so we could keep dealing with issues. And I formed the civics so we could deal with issues that covered the whole area, whether it was crime, bad buildings, panic peddling, whatever.

Gaudette [told the groups that brought him in,] "[I] guarantee you we'll give you an organization that represents the community." And at that first convention they shit bricks when they saw 50 percent of the people here are black. They went ape shit. Gaudette said, "That's what I promised you. It represents the community."

We did a very good job of slowing panic peddling down.

VICK-WESTGATE: How did you do that?

TRAPP: Confrontation. We declared law in Austin that a realtor could not solicit. And we said it often enough that people really started to believe it was the law. And so people would set up a realtor: "I want to sell my house. Could you come out and take a look at it?" And we'd have 20–30 people in the basement. And after the guy had looked 'round, "Oh, let's go to the basement." He'd come down there and we'd [say], "Get the fuck out of here." And surround him so he couldn't get up the stairs. Sometimes I was a little nervous that we were going to get assault charges. It got pretty testy.

Other things people would do would [be] to call and say, "Could you come out and appraise my house?" And the guy would come out and we'd have folks hiding behind trees and bushes throw eggs and tomatoes at him. And then every Friday night we had a "For Sale" sign stripping, and we'd go through the community and tear down "For Sale" signs. And so it slowed it down. We knew we weren't going to stop it, but we wanted to slow it down.

Anyway to be against that was walking a fine line, because that's what white communities had always done. So very quickly I got some [African Americans] into it. And so we had a good balance whenever we picketed a realtor or went to a realtor's home. Both sides were getting screwed. That was our battle cry: "Look. Whites aren't the enemy. Blacks aren't the enemy. The realtor is the enemy."

And so basically we wiped out panic peddling in South Austin. People still sold. But we were able to slow that down enough that I could build block clubs so that people would know each other. 'Cause that's what tears the community down, when there's no network. So we were able to quickly rebuild a network of all black from the all-white network on the blocks and throughout the community.[7]

"Blacks aren't the enemy. Whites aren't the enemy. It's the slum landlord. It's the city or it's the School Board of Education, panic peddlers." And as blacks and whites started to fight together, they suddenly [learned to work together, even if they didn't like each other].

Trapp tells the Westgates a vivid story of conversion: a white racist leader sees that blacks are fighting for the same things he is and exclaims, "God damn, those nigger . . . [I mean] black people . . . want the same thing as I do." Trapp argued that "preaching doesn't do it," and that "people change themselves" based on new experiences.

Ed Shurna on the Block Club Approach at OBA (2013)

—From an interview by Aaron Schutz[8]

AARON SCHUTZ: So how did you organize block clubs in OBA?

ED SHURNA: I would go and knock on every door on the block [in my assigned area]. And I would say, "I'm with St. Catherine of Siena Church, and I'm knocking on doors to find out if there are any problems in the community." And we'd start conversations on the front porch. And then somebody would bring up an issue: "Curbs are falling apart, and I blew two tires while I was trying to park my car, and the city never cares about this neighborhood." So I knock on the door next door and I used this same rap, "Hi, I'm Ed Shurna. And I was just talking to your neighbor, and he was complaining about the damn curbs that are cutting up his tires. And we were talking to see if there's an interest in people getting together to see if they could do something about this." And then I'd go to the next door. And maybe by then I'd have identified some woman who was willing to walk with me and knock on the doors so that I'd get more credibility. [So] that I wasn't just some outsider. It's the neighbor down the block and I.

And after I had knocked on as many doors as I could, I would ask three or four people that seemed the most interested if we could get together and talk with their neighbors about what we might do about the curbs, or what we might do about the abandoned building on the corner, and we would have a small planning meeting. Trapp would say [that] you shouldn't have more than two planning meetings before you do an action, otherwise people are just masturbating or something. And so I knew when I had a planning meeting I had a plan for a bigger meeting where we can invite the whole block out, and then we'd have a strategy from that [bigger] meeting. We wanted to get the city department of sanitation, or the city police, or the building owner on the corner to come out to that meeting. So the building process was pretty simple that way.

And then Shel would say, "Okay, now that you've done it on ten blocks, can you pull two people from each block together to talk about what we as a bigger community might do?" They don't all come, but maybe you get five or six people and you're building relationships.

And then they decide on a bigger meeting because they need more power to go after bigger issues.

The goal was always to have some action step at the end of a meeting. It wasn't just a discussion. It was not a meeting for the sake of a meeting. It could be a research piece. But Trapp was big on attacking enemies. So he wanted you to move from research fast to having a target. Because nobody organizes better than a good enemy. The best organizer is an asshole [*laughs*]. It's somebody that antagonized everybody.

[Over time,] you constantly went back and met with what you started to consider your core leaders. And you got to a point that you would have a monthly meeting with a core of people from several blocks, because you were trying to build a bigger core group. Trapp's idea was [that] we don't want to stay on the block, we want to get together all of South Austin. So if we could pull a core group in each one of these different quadrants—quadrant thirteen, quadrant fourteen—then we could create that kind of infrastructure which would allow us to produce a couple hundred people. And they would have had practice doing it very locally in their own block club, and they'd have gained experience in how to go after somebody at the multi-block level [where up to 250 people would turn out in a real show of power].

SCHUTZ: How stable was the leadership and membership?

SHURNA: [The buildings were more transient than the houses, and there was a mix of homeowners and renters.] You had to constantly [*laugh*] reorganize the buildings [and blocks] you had organized in the year before. And the key leaders in the organization, all the key leaders were homeowners, when I think of it. The homeowners you could count on being there. It was a fluid situation. And also it was a changing area. There was a lot of change going on in general. The old white homeowners that might have gotten involved in the beginning were moving out. We probably had fifteen, eighteen organizers, and your turf could be relatively small. So your job really was in that probably eight-block by eight-block area, you kept continuously trying to go back through and renew.

OBA had a reputation for having exciting meetings. So sometimes people liked to come out because it was more interesting than television. They knew if they came to a meeting with the school board or a landlord it was not going to be boring.

Issue organizing was the way Trapp built structure. He didn't build structure first [as in institutional organizing] and then fit the issue into it. It was the other way around.

[Don Elmer, who worked with Trapp at NCO, described a very similar process of organizing.[9] *The block clubs in NCO seem to have been less formal than in OBA and were less stable, because NCO lacked the tradition of block club organization in the black community. Interviews with others who worked with Trapp at NCO indicate that some of his organizers there didn't use block clubs at all for organizing—a sign of Trapp's flexibility about the approach to use in a particular circumstance.]*[10]

Targeting Redlining

—Aaron Schutz

In 1970, Trapp left OBA and "became director at NCO, which was the organization Gaudette had started."[11] He and Cincotta "kept working together. 'Cause when I went to NCO, I discovered we had some of the same problems that they had over at OBA. 'Cause we were just starting, when I left OBA, to nibble around the edges of [the FHA]."

At NCO, Trapp continued his approach to block club organizing. The discovery of the practice of redlining particular neighborhoods for the denial of loans was a step-by-step process. A homeowner or small businessperson would be denied a loan. He or she would tell the story to a friend who had or knew of a similar story. The story would be repeated in meetings where others had heard similar stories. This led to meetings with lenders who admitted they wouldn't lend to racially changing neighborhoods.

NCO's first engagement with this issue came when two different members showed up at the office to report that they couldn't get a loan. In his interview with the Westgates, Trapp recounted what happened next:

A group of leaders and I] go over and have an appointment [with the bank]. Italian guy tells his story; Puerto Rican guy tells his story. All very low key. Just what is this problem? Bank president—I could have kissed the son of a bitch—said, "Well, of course we don't make loans in this neighborhood. Haven't you looked around? It's a slum!" I thought, "Oh, I love you." [Laughter]. . . .

Suddenly this very low-key meeting erupted, people screaming and hollering. That goes on for ten–fifteen minutes. We storm out and go back to NCO offices.

"What are we gonna do?" "What are we gonna do?" "We're gonna kill that guy!"
So then nobody knows what the hell to do. "Let's picket!" NCO's famous for
pickets. We had a very tough, powerful organization. "Alright."

So the next Saturday we show up with about a hundred and fifty pickets. We're
outside, and people going in and out of the bank [said], "It's great somebody's
doing something." "Man this is marvelous!" And several squad cars and a paddy
wagon. I think we might even [have] had some press.

And people had a great time. . . .

Go back home. No reaction out of the bank. And that was before we'd learned
about storming in and taking over. "Okay. We're going to go back next Saturday."
We go back next Saturday and we've got about sixty to seventy people. And people
went, "Oh, that's great. Keep it up." They're going in and out. "These are bad
guys." Go back home. . . .

Another strategy was needed. At a meeting, a woman said, "Well, why don't we
have a bank-in?"

I said, "Well, Josephine, some folks here might not be familiar with that." I
didn't say, "Including me." [Laughter] "Why don't you explain that to us."

She turns to the blacks and Hispanics and says, "Well, you people are doing it
all the time! You're sitting in here, laying in there. . . ."

So the next Saturday we had the first ever bank-in. Basically I think they had
five teller windows. We had about five people lined up to go to each teller window
and they'd come up and say, "I want to put a dollar in my savings account." That's
when you still had a passbook. And the teller would ring it up. "Oh, I'm sorry. I
meant I want to take a dollar out of my account." The teller had to go back and do
it. The next person would come up, "I want a dollar worth of pennies but I don't
trust your rolls. Count 'em out for me." "Well, lady, our rolls are perfectly . . ."
"No. Count 'em out. I don't trust 'em. I was cheated here once last week. No.
Count 'em out." Teller would count a hundred pennies. The person would go to
the back of the line, come back up . . .

Things got to the point where NCO members were actually throwing their change on
the floor. The commotion finally drew the bank president out of his office. He asked,
"What's going on? Who's in charge?" and eventually "What do you want?"

The protestors replied, "We want a meeting with you this afternoon and your board
of directors at two o'clock." The president agreed to this. Trapp remembered stopping
the action, returning to the NCO office, and thinking, "What the hell are the demands?
We don't have any damn demands! We just want to talk about this thing."

At the meeting, the bank agreed to four million first mortgages, four million small
business loans, and a thousand-dollar donation to NCO. According to Trapp, "We
actually brought the check back with us to the office. And that was it. We had a big
party and thought, 'Okay. That's terrific. The issue's all over.' No monitoring committee. Nothing. I'm clueless if one loan ever went out."[12]

NCO's leaders were an inspiration to other people, who came to them to learn how to try for similar results. Trapp recalls that NCO's approach to organizing "just kind of spread that way." The West Side Coalition was formed shortly after the bank-in, with leadership from NCO, OBA, and Our Lady of the Angels. Trapp described to the Westgates how this led to the 1972 housing conference:

> Gale would roll in with black leaders. I'd come with Italian, Polish, Hispanic, and occasionally a black. We had a very small black area in NCO. Then all these white guys who just hated blacks and Hispanics. And [organizer] Al Velto just laughed, "My guys really hate those meetings. But as they say, 'We need them niggers.'" And so we formed this very tough coalition and started fighting.
>
> And from then we went to start fighting FHA, and that was pretty much how we came to the first national conference. We won several concessions from the regional office.
>
> I remember this fight had been going on probably a year with [the local FHA director], and he called Gale and me in and said, "Look. I agree with everything you're asking for, but I can't do anything more. You want anything more out of me, you got to go to Washington and change national policy." So Gale and I went back, "Holy shit! What are we going to do?"
>
> So Gale and I went [to a conference put on by Jack Egan at Notre Dame] and we're at this thing and still stewing, "What the hell can we do with this thing, that FHA can't do any more for us?" So sessions end. I got a bottle of Jack Daniels; she got a bottle of vodka. We go up to one of our rooms. We were sitting there drinking and talking about this, and one of us said, "Well, let's have a national conference!"
>
> So that's where the idea for the first national conference was born.

The term "redlining" was invented after a meeting at Bell Federal Savings and Loan, thanks to a "big map on the wall, red line around basically the black and Hispanic community." The bank president explained that everything inside the red line was the bank's FHA loan area, and that everything outside would be approved only for conventional loans]. So Trapp and his colleagues "coined the term 'redlining,' meaning you'd only get an FHA mortgage inside that area."

Trapp stated that the problem with the FHA program—specifically after President Lyndon Baines Johnson extended it "to black and racially changing communities in the cities" in 1968—was that it had opened "the flood gates of fraud." He explained why:[13]

> The first several years of a mortgage the borrower basically pays off interest, with very little coming off the principal owed. So if you foreclosed on the family, the government reimbursed the mortgage broker most of the amount of the original loan. Lenders walked off with several thousand dollars of interest and the chance to sell the home again. We actually had a mortgage broker tell us at a public meeting,

"A good loan is one that we can foreclose on in the first five years. That's where we make our money. . . ." Real estate agents and mortgage bankers teamed up to trick folks into buying homes they couldn't afford.[14]

Trapp noted that "another common scam" was for realtors to sell a "lemon home"— i.e., one with many undisclosed, expensive problems.[15]

FHA loans came with additional fees and requirements. As Trapp and his colleagues worked on the issue, a pattern emerged:

> Increasingly we saw the connection between bad FHA loans and the lack of an
> alternative. The abandoned buildings resulting from FHA were a big problem,
> but the lack of conventional, non-FHA loans, was in many ways the flip side of
> the same problem. If neighborhood borrowers had non-FHA options available to
> them, the problems of the scandal-laden program would not have been so disas-
> trous. Plus, people who preferred to use conventional financing might not have
> been steered away from the neighborhood in the first place.[16]

Out of the national conference, NPA was formed, and they started working on a statewide and national level. Trapp went on the road to build, strengthen, and recruit local organizations to be part of NPA.

> When I went on the road I always told groups, "I work for you. I'm here to
> deal with dog shit, dogs, pigeon shit. I don't care what the issue is; I'll work on
> that." And before I'd leave I'd say, "You know, have you heard about this thing,
> redlining?" And start trying to plant some seeds. In a month or two, I'd come back
> there. Usually after about the third trip somebody else was saying, "Gee, the banks
> don't seem to be doing much." Suddenly I had a CRA fight going. I didn't go in
> preaching it. Work on what you got first. People learned to trust me and under-
> stand, "Hey, he does know one or two things about organizing, and how to win."[17]
> I was on the road 20–25 days a month, all out. And I was not dealing with
> NTIC issues. We started a group in Denver on stray dogs. That's how that organi-
> zation got started. Those were the kind of issues I dealt with.[18]

In an undated interview with Elmer, Trapp summed up his view of NPA:

> I always saw NPA like Daley sees the machine in Chicago; the machine is a myth,
> it's all built on local precincts. I always thought NPA is a myth: it doesn't exist.
> It's built on what real power is out there that we have helped build. That's why
> it was so important for me to be on the road and other of our staff to be on the
> road to keep those local power bases strong, working on whatever the hell they
> wanted to work on so that they would be available when [we] needed them at a
> national level.[19]

More research needs to be done on NPA: How did the different organizations work together? To what extent were individual organizations able to maintain strength over time? What were the specific strategies that Trapp used to organize in different areas? There isn't time or space to answer those questions in this volume, but they deserve investigation. Mike Miller, for instance, questions the actual "strength over time" of a lot of the local affiliates of NPA.

On Organizing

—Shel Trapp

Before moving on to the section on Cincotta, which provides more information on NPA and its national fights over housing, I include a few more excerpts from Trapp's writings and discussions on organizing. See also "Dynamics of Organizing" and "Basics of Organizing," both available online at tenant.net.

BELIEF IN THE PEOPLE

A . . . major tenet in the myth of the organizer is his belief in and respect for people. This belief and respect is expressed in many ways. It is first exhibited when he enters the arena in which he is organizing. He samples as many opinions and ideas as possible from every economic, educational and ethnic strata of his arena. He does not judge the person who presents him with a concept contrary to his own, but accepts it as part of the mosaic that he is called upon to build. It is further exhibited in the selection of the issues to be worked on by the people. When a staff charges into the office saying, "I've got a great new issue," the lead organizer's immediate response is, "Did you check it out with people?" Once it has been determined by the people what issues will be worked on, then the organizer's job is to express his belief in and respect for people by . . . [assisting them or working with them] to set the timetable, the tactics and the goals. He may lay out alternatives, but in the end it is the people who make the decision on what course of action is to be taken.

At this point, all kinds of rhetorical questions are thrown out. "How far do you let people go? Would you organize for segregation? Doesn't the organizer have a moral right to take a personal stand on issues?" On and on. Once the organizer has analyzed the arena in which he intends to organize, and, if he accepts that arena, then the myth by which he lives dictates that he is bound to respect the decisions of those people within the arena. For from his experience he has seen that when people are given the opportunity in a democratic arena to wrestle with their lives and the life of the community, the way in which people look at themselves and others changes, horizons broaden, self-interest expands beyond myself to my community and my city. He has

Selections from Shel Trapp's publications ("Dynamics of Organizing," 1976; *Blessed Be the Fighters,* 1986; and *Dynamics of Organizing,* 2003) are reprinted here by permission of Kathy Trapp.

seen homeowners fight for the right of the tenant; he has seen tenants fight for an issue that only benefits homeowners. He has seen people lose a day of work to fight for issues that will not directly affect them.[20]

ON ORGANIZING MODELS

"*The old models just don't work anymore.*" The model is not the important thing, the important thing is that an organization is being built and the people are winning. We often get locked into the same kinds of pointless debates when discussions occur about what is the best type of organizing. In some conversations, you get the feeling that if you do not adhere to a particular organizing model, you are at best outdated, and at worst a carrier of a social disease.

I've always found it fascinating that very seldom, if ever, in these discussions are people mentioned. These discussions are quite similar to those about ideology, in that they are carried on in a vacuum that does not exist in the real world.

Every local organization that we have assisted in getting started has developed in a different manner and ends up looking a little different. Yet in each case the organizations have gained local victories and developed local leadership. That is the important thing, not what model was used.

I remember Saul Alinsky once saying, "There is only one rule in organizing, and that is that there are no rules." He would find all the discussion about models pretty amusing, perhaps pathetic, given all the human need waiting to be organized.[21]

[*Despite this apparent embrace of an ecumenical approach to organizing, Trapp was well known for dismissing "church-based organizing" because, as he said at one point, members lacked the "desire to engage in confrontation. They think by being nice you win."[22] (Drew Astolfi reports that Trapp, in 1994, encouraged him to leave the IAF, saying that "church based organizing sucks. It doesn't do anything.")[23] Trapp directed NCO, which drew from and was largely funded by churches (although his organizers spent most of their time out in the community knocking on doors); he used churches where possible when he organized in OBA, and he brought a large Catholic church (Our Lady of the Angels) in as one-third of the West Side Coalition, with OBA and NCO as the other two-thirds. Nonetheless, he remained rooted in and generally seems to have stayed focused on the issue-based, usually block club-based approach to organizing that he had started with in OBA, continued in different form in NCO, and often promoted in his later work in NPA. If someone was organizing people on the street, Trapp was open to whatever form that would take, but his default mechanism was the block club approach.*]

ON DIGNITY

You're not supposed to talk about [this]. The myth of the organizer is [that he's] the toughest son of a bitch in the valley, and it feels all touchy feely if you talk about people's development. But that is to me a big part of [organizing]. Really talking about a human being changing and developing.

And that is not to say the organizer does that at all. All of that is in the individual already. All the organizer does is build the arena in which the person can participate, in which they discover who they are. There's a gold mine in everybody. The organizer didn't put the gold there, didn't discover the gold, the person's got to discover that gold for themselves. Because the only way a person changes is when they discover [it] in themselves and they change themselves. See, I tried changing people for seven years as a minister. Nobody ever fucking changed from one of my sermons, I can guarantee you that. But the number of people I've seen change dramatically. . . .

The dignity [is] ingrained, not taught. Like we would talk about an instinct in an animal. I think the dignity is an instinct that the Great Spirit put into each one of us. And institutions I think are designed to kill that instinct or suppress it. Because if the individual starts to find dignity in themselves, why do I need the institution? The job of the organizer is to build an arena or create experiences where individuals get a chance to have that revealed to them for maybe the first time in their lives.

You don't change people by telling them. They've got to do that on their own. But you can provide the arena.

What organizers [and] leaders have taught me is the dignity of the human animal that's there. If you don't have that understanding, I don't see how the hell you can be an organizer.[24]

WHO IS SHEL TRAPP?

I'm not sure who I really am. [*Laugh.*] I'm Shel Trapp. My mother called me Sheldon. . . . I believe that the Great Spirit gave us all the gift of life and the chance to be a hell of a lot better than we think we can be. And the reason we are put here is not only for ourselves to grow but to somehow be a catalyst, the fuse, whatever the right word is, to help other people grow and to reach their potential and beyond their potential. I think that's the Great Spirit's purpose for each one of us. I don't know what else to say.[25]

TRAPP AND CINCOTTA

When Ann Vick-Westgate asked Trapp, "What was your relationship with Gale?" he replied, "Love-hate," and described an incident that took place before an NPA conference, in the presence of recently hired colleagues.[26]

Gale and I had some disagreement. I am clueless about what it was over. We're just screaming and screaming with the staff all around. . . . Just on and on and on. Usually those things just came to a loggerhead, and we just went and sat down at our desks. . . .

And the next morning we're in, "Hi, Gale." "Hi, Trapp." You know, we'd go on like nothing had ever happened. And the staff couldn't fathom that. It just was the way we worked.

I spent a lot of time on the road [after the development of NPA], selling the issues, making the issues make sense to local groups. So that they could see why they should buy in, so that I could provide a power base behind Gale. When we got to negotiations, very seldom did I ever go into those. That was her arena.[27] In the early days we did some role-playing but she was so good. I just stopped that.

Gale Cincotta

—From writings by NTIC, Anne Witte Garland,
Christopher Hayes, Gale Cincotta, and Liz Enochs

In the general parlance of organizing-speak, Trapp took on the role of "organizer" in the relationship, and Cincotta played more of a role of "leader." This meant that Trapp dealt with the nuts and bolts of organization building and maintenance, while Cincotta focused on policy questions and negotiating with targets. Trapp was in the background, and Cincotta was the public spokesperson and face of the organization. They spent time together thinking through how each of them played out their respective roles.

As documented in the endnotes, the text in this section comes from a range of different pieces.

Growing up Greek in a large family in the culturally diverse Austin community on Chicago's West Side colored Ms. Cincotta's experiences. Meeting and serving neighbors in the restaurant her father ran and living with her extended family in one building were early experiences of family and community. Later she had six sons of her own. Her husband ran a gas station.[28]

When the neighborhood began to change and other white families started moving out, Gale didn't want to leave. . . . "But I learned that if I stayed, I had better get involved, because otherwise, for starters, my kids wouldn't learn anything."

Gale's first fight . . . was for better schools. The resources Gale employed were drawn from the main experience she had had up to that point—managing a family. "A lot of what's called 'research' is really just common sense," she says. . . . "I don't have a college education, but I've figured out a budget, I've paid a mortgage. . . . You look at the board of education. They have just so much money; if they put all that money in one area they don't have it to put in another. . . ."

She discovered proof of . . . discrimination by going to the board of education and attending hearings and poring through school board records. . . . She took the information to the school principal and local aldermen. These officials ("people I thought were supposed to take care of things for me") refused to recognize the problem, and dismissed Gale as a troublemaker. . . .

So Gale got together more and more of her neighbors who had children in the school and started to advocate change. . . . Gradually their active presence brought about some improvements. . . . All along, though, Gale found that she and her friends had to watch officials carefully. . . . [At one point, after they thought they had an agreement about where to place a new school,] the parents discovered that builders were planning to raze a hundred homes for the school site. Gale and the others got officials to . . . agree to build the school on [several] acres of vacant land a few blocks away.[29]

Eventually she crossed paths with Trapp [who was working with OBA]. . . . He still remembers their first encounter, in the basement of Mandell Methodist Church. "I was pretty nervous about this powerful person. So I go up and say, 'I'm Shel Trapp,' and she says, 'Well, who are you with?' and I say, 'It's a new organization that's just starting but doesn't have a name yet.' And she slaps her head and says 'Oh Christ, not another one!'"[30]

Gale was the first woman to be elected president of any Alinsky-style organization in the country, and men in the organization placed bets against the chances of her winning. "Up until then," she says, "it was always the women who did the work, and the men who got elected. And even when I ran, although I was obviously qualified, people in the organization made a point of saying, 'Do you want a man or a woman for president?'—not who was smart, who could do the job, or whatever."

Gale infused a different kind of life into the organizing, says one woman who worked with OBA. . . . "She had a different style from many of the men organizers at the time. She wasn't caught up in the mystique that many of the men were caught up in. For them, organizing was almost a romantic thing. For her it wasn't; it was a practical need." . . .

"Gale has encouraged more women to get involved," says another organizer.[31]

After Trapp moved to NCO, Cincotta and Trapp continued working together, creating the West Side Coalition and then holding the housing conference out of which MAHA and NPA were created. Later, Gale remembered the conference this way:

> The theme of the 1972 conference was "We have met the enemy, and it's not us!" Powerful institutions were doing their very best to set blacks, whites, and Hispanics against one another, to pit the young against the old, to force different neighborhoods to compete instead of cooperate. They wanted us to fight one another for the scraps from the table, so that we wouldn't be looking while they feasted themselves with the wealth they got by draining resources out of our neighborhoods. They wanted to divide and conquer us, but we decided to unite and fight back.[32]

Ms. Cincotta spearheaded efforts to organize against redlining. She testified before Sen. William Proxmire numerous times throughout the 1970s in support of what became the Home Mortgage Disclosure Act, passed in 1975 and [the] Community Reinvestment Act, passed in 1977. "This disclosure bill," Proxmire said in 1976, "would never have become a law but for the research and local organizing activity undertaken by NPA." . . .

At protests, Ms. Cincotta would alternately schmooze and threaten her targets, until they conceded the meetings she demanded. Shel Trapp . . . described

Ms. Cincotta's ability to "run rings around a target's mind." When those meetings finally happened, though, her intelligence and grasp of the issues, as well as that of other neighborhood leaders, typically impressed the most hardened banker.[33]

That talent, he says, explains why Cincotta was eulogized by the same institutions— Harris Bank, Fannie Mae, American Banker—that she'd centered in her crosshairs. "The enemy realizes that we're not idiots. We're not just out there screaming. While we're out there screaming, we're also gonna bring some answers to their problems that can make them look good."[34]

Former HUD Secretary Jack Kemp once called her during a Washington, D.C., activists' meeting with a personal request. . . . Kemp had heard about Cincotta's strategy of bringing hundreds of activists to camp out in front of officials' homes until they agreed to a meeting, said Trapp.

Kemp asked Cincotta to stay away from his house the following day because he would be hosting a reception for his two soon-to-be-married daughters. But Cincotta didn't back off, according to Trapp. "She said, 'Maybe you should set out 1,000 more plates,'" he recalled. That was enough. Kemp agreed to meet with Cincotta and 20 of the group's other leaders two days later, Trapp said. "After that, he really got some good reforms through," said Trapp.[35]

Although NPA started with housing, it shifted over time to other issues, including energy and insurance redlining.

[An NPA] staff organizer says, "One important thing that Gale brings to this work is that, to the people we work with, she's one of them, rather than someone who has a college background, and has done all these glorious things and then comes back to talk to people about what they should do. She's really one of the folks. She helps keep staff honest about what people are really interested in. When we come up with ideas, she'll say, "Will our people really give a damn about that?" . . .

"Gale acts as a spokesperson," says a friend who has watched her work. "But a good thing about Gale is the way she develops leadership in other people, too. She recognizes others' contributions, and always acknowledges them."[36]

Reflecting on her work with NPA, Cincotta stated that "I think the most important thing to me is seeing the changes in people." Having to "deal with bigger issues made us see that we could really do something. . . . That's exciting to me."[37]

Like Trapp, Cincotta understood the importance of supporting local organizations to maintain power on the national level. In a 1985 column in NPA's Disclosure magazine, she wrote:

NPA's strength lies in the fact that while we pursue national issue agendas, we also support the diverse local issue agendas. . . .

- We bring the organizations which are addressing their neighborhood issues on a local level together so that we can all unite and fight for solutions to neighborhood problems on a national level.
- We bring the leaders and organizers from these local organizations together so everyone can share strategies, ideas and victory stories. By doing so, we reinforce each other's commitment to organizing and fighting for our neighborhoods.[38]

She elaborated on the same theme two years later:

Sometimes we start talking and making theories about organizing, but we have to remember to bring things down to earth and look at the block clubs and other local efforts that are where organizing's life blood really comes from. What's more, the problems we face at the local level, on our street or in our building, are ultimately the driving force behind the organizing we do on a grander scale. . . .

It's this strength that makes us such a force to be reckoned with when we hit a bigger target. . . . These local battles make us strong. This is the reality of organizing. This is where the leadership [is] developed, learn[s] the ropes and first stand[s] up to fight, and this is who the issues are won for. . . .

It's a two-way street. The big victories that we do win on a national level—like the Home Mortgage Disclosure Act and the Community Reinvestment Act—only have meaning back at home. CRA would mean nothing if local groups didn't use it. Communities use CRA to make banks put the people's money back into the neighborhoods. . . . This is how we keep our grassroots healthy and growing; we have to get together and hone our skills. Big corporations have their expensive think tanks; we don't have the same big bucks, but we have to share our ideas. . . .

Local organizing is like maintenance. Some may complain it's not exciting. No it's not always glamorous, but the need for it never goes away. You don't stop washing your floor because after five years of washing it doesn't need doing anymore; just because you fixed your roof once, doesn't mean it'll never need another repair. . . .

The problems we face at the local level, on our street or in our building, are ultimately the driving force behind the organizing we do on a grander scale, be it state-wide coalitions or the whole NPA network descending on Washington, DC, to straighten out our issues on a national level. We tackle the federal government to win victories in our communities, to make things better on our street. Whatever level we fight on, the payoff is for people at the local level.[39]

Gale obviously loves what she does. "I'm stubborn; maybe I'm naïve, but I operate on the idea that things are going to happen, that if you work hard enough and get enough people behind you, you're going to win." And "'winning,' according to Gale is getting to a point 'where people really have a say in their lives, where *they* call the shots.'"[40]

The evening before her death, from her hospital bed, Ms. Cincotta told NTIC's new executive director Joe Mariano to "get the crooks."[41]

Notes

1. NTIC was the technical training 501(c)(3) organization. NPA was a 501(c)(4) lobbying organization.
2. *Dynamics of Organizing: Building Power by Developing the Human Spirit* (Chicago: National Training and Information Center, 2003; available from NPA). Note that this publication is different from the similarly titled "Dynamics of Organizing" (1976), another document Trapp wrote for NTIC, which is available online at *tenant.net*.
3. See Louis Lee Woods II, "The Federal Home Loan Bank Board, Redlining, and the National Proliferation of Racial Lending Discrimination, 1921–1950," *Journal of Urban History* 38, no. 6 (2012): 1036–59; and Gregory D. Squires, "Community Reinvestment: An Emerging Social Movement," in *From Redlining to Reinvestment*, edited by Gregory D. Squires (Philadelphia: Temple University Press, 1992), 1–37. Thanks to Michael Westgate for his comments on the introduction.
4. Shel Trapp, interview by Michael Westgate and Ann Vick-Westgate, 2003, "Consolidated_ Interviews.pdf" file, Collection on Gale Cincotta, Special Collections and Archives, DePaul University Libraries, Chicago. Sections of this interview were later used in Michael Westgate with Ann Vick-Westgate, *Gale Force: Gale Cincotta—The Battles for Disclosure and Community Reinvestment* (Cambridge, MA: Harvard Book Store, 2011). Sections of the part of the interview quoted here appeared in *Gale Force*, 80–81.
5. Gaudette notes in Chapter 11, however, that they did use block clubs when he was president of the Chatham-Avalon Park Community Council.
6. Organizers like Shurna and Elmer remember constantly going back to reinvigorate these block clubs for action. Organizing activity on the block club level maintained the base for the leaders at the higher levels to draw on and provided a stream of new leaders as well.
7. "Network," in this context, is another word for relationships. Trapp and his organizers used issues to build and strengthen relationships that are the base of networks, and these are what can be used to build power.
8. Ed Shurna, interview by Aaron Schutz, January 24, 2013.
9. Don Elmer, interview by Aaron Schutz, December 18, 2012.
10. For example, Bruce Gotschall, interview by Aaron Schutz, September 24, 2013, and Roger Hayes, interview by Aaron Schutz, October 4, 2013.
11. All the quotations in this section are from Trapp, interview by Westgate and Vick-Westgate; portions of this section of the interview appear in Westgate with Vick-Westgate, *Gale Force*, 42–45.
12. The lack of follow-up was a violation of one of Alinsky's organizing principles: "An agreement is only as good as your ability to enforce it." Trapp later laughed about this, noting that it was an indicator of how unprepared NCO's leaders were at that point.
13. Before 1968, "FHA insurance often was isolated to new residential developments on the edges of metropolitan areas that were considered safer investments, not to inner city neighborhoods. This stripped the inner city of many of their middle class inhabitants, thus hastening the decay of inner city neighborhoods. Loans for the repair of existing structures were small and for short duration, which meant that families could more easily purchase a new home than modernize

an old one, leading to the abandonment of many older inner city properties. . . . The FHA also explicitly practiced a policy of 'redlining' when determining which neighborhoods to approve mortgages in. Redlining is the practice of denying or limiting financial services to certain neighborhoods based on racial or ethnic composition without regard to the residents' qualifications or creditworthiness." Fair Housing Center of Greater Boston, *Historical Shift from Explicit to Implicit Practices Affecting Housing Segregation in Eastern Massachusetts*, interactive timeline, *www.bostonfairhousing.org*, November 10, 2013.

14. Shel Trapp, *Dynamics of Organizing* (2003), 22–23.

15. Ibid., 23.

16. Ibid., 53–54.

17. Trapp, interview by Westgate and Vick-Westgate; this section of the interview appears in Westgate with Vick-Westgate, *Gale Force*, 103.

18. Trapp, interview by Westgate and Vick-Westgate; this section of the interview appears in Westgate with Vick-Westgate, *Gale Force*, 95.

19. Quotations from Don Elmer's interview of Shel Trapp are published here by permission of Kathy Trapp and Don Elmer.

20. Shel Trapp, "Dynamics of Organizing" (1976).

21. From Shel Trapp, *Blessed Be the Fighters: Reflections on Organizing . . . Collected Essays of Shel Trapp* (Chicago: National Training and Information Center, 1986), 14, 18.

22. Quoted in David Moberg, "All Together Now," *Chicago Reader,* October 16, 1997, *www.chicagoreader.com*.

23. Drew Astolfi, comment at National People's Action, "Your Legacy Lives On" (a page that documented stories and comments on Trapp after his passing), October 21, 2010, *showdowninamerica.org/your-legacy-lives* (page no longer available; October 23, 2010 snapshot archived at the Internet Archive Wayback Machine, *archive.org*).

24. Trapp, interview by Don Elmer, n.d.

25. Ibid.

26. Trapp, interview by Westgate and Vick-Westgate; portions of this section of the interview appear in Westgate with Vick-Westgate, *Gale Force*, 86–87.

27. Miller notes that "there seem to be a tension in Trapp's trips to local affiliates. Here he says he was 'selling the issues.' Earlier, he describes himself as listening to, and working on, whatever are the local issues. No doubt Trapp, as would any organizer, sought a balance—sometimes working to support what came up locally, other times pushing NPA's national agenda. It's a balancing act: tilt too far one way or the other and an organizer will undermine people power."

28. NTIC, "Gale Cincotta, 'Mother of Community Reinvestment Act' Dies," press release, August 15, 2001; posted to Colist, the discussion list for COMM-ORG, the On-Line Conference on Community Organizing and Development, by Randy Stoecker, August 16, 2001, *comm-org.wisc.edu*.

29. The previous five paragraphs are from Anne Witte Garland, "'We've Found the Enemy': Gale Cincotta," in *Women Activists: Challenging the Abuse of Power* (New York: Feminist Press at the City University of New York, 1988), 39–41.

30. This paragraph is from Christopher Hayes, "The Good Neighbor: Community Activist Gale Cincotta's Work Was Never Done," *Chicago Reader*, December 21, 2001, *www.chicagoreader.com*.

31. The previous three paragraphs are from Garland, "We've Found the Enemy," 46.

32. Gale Cincotta, "The Next Move," *Disclosure*, April–May 1986, 2.

33. The previous two paragraphs are from NTIC, "Gale Cincotta."

34. This paragraph is from Hayes, "Good Neighbor."

35. The previous two paragraphs are from Liz Enochs, "The Street Fighter: Playing Hardball," *Affordable Housing Finance*, October 1, 2007, at *www.housingfinance.com*.

36. Garland, "We've Found the Enemy," 50.

37. Ibid., 53.

38. Gale Cincotta, "The Next Move," *Disclosure*, August-October 1985, 2.

39. Gale Cincotta, "The Next Move," *Disclosure*, November-December 1987, 2.

40. This paragraph is from Garland, "We've Found the Enemy," 55.

41. This paragraph is from NTIC, "Gale Cincotta."

13

What Every Community Organization Should Know about Community Development (1975)

■

STAN HOLT

Editors' preface: Stan Holt is emblematic of many Protestant clergy of the 1960s. He received his education at Union Theological Seminary, a highly regarded institution, and served both as a local church minister and as a campus minister. The racial justice stirrings of the times and his own commitment to justice led him to CORE (Congress On Racial Equality). He says, "I was an officer in CORE in Cincinnati in [the] late sixties when our chapter was directed to do community organizing. Our first issue was a slum building which was owned by the county republican party chair. Occupants' rents went into escrow. The women got eviction notices. We lost in court; all were evicted. I said to myself 'there must be a better way,' so [I went] off to Chicago with a grant from the Presbyterian Church."[1] He got a job as an organizer in the late 1960s with Organization for a Better Austin (OBA) in Chicago. He was one of several talented people to emerge from work at OBA that was supervised by Tom Gaudette.

Several years later, at Baltimore's South East Community Organization (SECO), where he worked from 1972 to 1974, Holt had his encounter with community economic development. SECO was well known throughout the country both because it brought together under one umbrella unusual allies—African Americans, Polish Americans, and German Americans—and because it won a major freeway fight. Like many community organizations of that period, it decided to engage in community development.[2]

In this essay, Holt provides a classic description of the dangers faced by community organizing groups when they decide to move in the direction of community development. Originally written as a cautionary tale, today it can be read as the story of what actually happened to most of the existing local community organizing groups in the United States. What Holt warned against as a threat turned into the reality.

This essay was first published in *Just Economics*, March 1975, 3 and 9. It is reprinted here by permission of Stan Holt.

A Fable: The Seduction of Community Organization by His Sister—Community Development

One day a factory worker came home after work to his family. He was a lean, clean young man. He worked hard and played hard. He had little money but was independent and strong-willed. He had a fine family and the respect of his fellow workers, neighbors, and friends. As he approached home he saw his sister, who had left the neighborhood three years before, in a big car with some sharp looking boyfriends. She talked about great times, easy money, and easy life. She had rich out-of-town friends who freely spent and asked for little in return, so she said. She convinced her brother to join a local venture with her smooth, professional partners. The young man joined up, schemed, and developed. He made a lot of money for himself and his new partners. Without knowing it, however, he lost the respect of his friends, neighbors, and his fellow workers. He became separated from his family and his integrity.

The initial approach by community developers to community organizations will be as Lady Bountiful. They will come in the guise of a national center which is working on people's problems and neighborhood crises. The center will give money for organizing; of course, the money is welcomed. What community organization doesn't need money for organizers? Once into the organization the center will offer to write and broker proposals. Already, the organization has been had. Proposal writing is worse than death to an organizer. With a sigh of relief the offer is gratefully accepted. Without knowing it, the undermining of the organization is well underway.

The proposals which are written by the center usually have to do with human service programs. The center knows an organizer is naturally suspicious of taking on social services, and, therefore, it uses an appealing rhetoric. The proposals, they say, have enough fat in them that it is possible to skim off administrative money to support the organization. Also, there will be outreach jobs which can be used for straight organizing. Before long an organizer finds himself adopting the line . . . "these programs can accomplish what street organizing can't do."

A Question of Control

The community organization begins to change. A new level of leadership emerges in the organization. They may be old leaders looking for a change, liberals from the rank and file, or middle-class professional committeemen with a nose for where the money is. Good at abstractions and overflowing with planning lingo, the new "leaders" glib talk covers up the fact that they are losing their constituencies, if they ever had any, and their credibility among the neighborhood people. Now the community developers can move in with full force. Talking with the professionals and confusing the working class homeowners, they unveil their incredulous concepts and oblique objectives: "Community development corporations are . . . organizations created and controlled by people living in impoverished areas for the purpose of planning,

stimulating, financing, and when necessary owning and operating businesses that will provide employment, income, and a better way of life for residents of these areas."[3]
Their goals are:

> 1) local control over the means and instruments of development, 2) comprehensive economic development which can also provide for, 3) social good, by tempering economic considerations with social ones and by underwriting the cost of local social services, thus freeing the community from their present dependence on outside institutions.[4]

Got it. . . . It comes in a hundred forms; all with panaceas for community problems. Once the CDC takes hold, here is what happens to a community organization.

1. Cooptation

Successful CDCs depend upon a partnership of city, private business and lending institutions, and the community. Therefore, it becomes essential for a community organization to follow the CDC in massaging city bureaucrats and participating in countless consensus-oriented planning missions with suave commercial money managers. Blue collar homeowners making demands and negotiating settlements with clearly defined enemies is considered old fashioned and crass. Demonstrations are out of the question because pending deals with the establishment may be jeopardized if the organization takes to the streets. A negotiating strategy is the most comfortable for blue collar workers, but when the ball park shifts to the round table, they begin to drop out and leave the organization to the middle class talkers.

Only the best and most experienced leaders can handle the shift in roles from negotiator to planning committee person. Other leaders get confused and end up handling negotiations the same way they do a planning session, or, planning sessions as if they were a confrontation.

2. Change in Goals

The values of an organization shift. What is good for the neighborhood people and what homeowners want gives way to what will attract foundation or investment money. People's perceptions of their needs give way to what will attract foundation or investment money. People's perceptions of their needs give way to what a planning analysis of sociological statistics dictates the people need.

CDCs must make money or at least break even in their ventures to attract investment capital. Therefore, the pervading atmosphere of the organization is "what is good for the Ford or Kettering Foundations is good for the neighborhoods."

3. Financial Dependence

As a CDC begins to generate money it is easy for a community organization to become dependent on it. Obviously when this happens the control of the whole organization shifts to the CDC and, behind the CDC, to those who supply its money. As the saying goes, "He who pays the fiddler, calls the tune." Soon the people will begin to drop out because they will tire of trying to dance to symphonies instead of polkas.

Furthermore, although the money may be without conditions in the early stages, the neighborhoods are losing by not developing their fund raising capacity. . . .

4. *Institutionalization*

It takes a long time to conceive and hatch a CDC project. CDCs require longevity, continuity of membership and a stable climate. With new groups joining an organization all the time, a partial changeover in board members each year, an organization under new leaders may be dramatically reshaped every two or three years. Indeed, if this doesn't occur, something is wrong with the organizing. But what is integral to a healthy organization terrifies a CDC. Change may alter organizational goals and policies. Pursuit of the immediate and specific issues on which community power is built and continually renewed will collide with long established CDC projects. No CDC wishes to subject itself to the unpredictable agenda of a people's organization.

Old leadership which goes over to the CDC and loses its base, or the new middleclass committeemen, fear they have no access to or control over the groups in the organization. Therefore, at the board level of an organization a power struggle ensues. When this happens, any attempt to bring new neighborhood groups into the organization or new leaders into decision-making positions will be considered a threat to the CDC types. CDCs by nature require tight control by a small group of leaders. Commercial money managers and city bureaucrats, the CDC staff says, become extremely nervous when there is talk about decisions being made by the people. Therefore, broad-based decision-making is scuttled in favor of the small corporation.

Any governing board of a community organization which tries to control the speedy smooth car of a monorail on the one hand; and, on the other, a bucking tractor trailer rig, is in for trouble. It can't be done. It will tear the organization apart.

The Alternative

In conclusion, a community-development-community-organization operation will survive only if one of the two factions is master and the other its slave. If the CDC with its consensus style dominates, organizing will become a promotional or service-oriented effort. If community organizing on the people's agenda dominates, with its demand-negotiating methodology, CDC will become a tertiary adjunct to accomplish some necessary rehabilitative projects.

The latter arrangement can maintain an aggressive organizing style and gain the respect and cooperation of city bureaucrats and establishment institutions. If a community organization wants to enter into a CDC or human services, it is necessary to spin them completely away from the organization and to hold them accountable to the agenda of the people. Better yet, as Mike Miller points out in "Notes on Institutional

Change,"[5] a community organization can require city agencies and private enterprise to set up needed projects and then hold them accountable to the people. This has a double advantage; organizing to get the project, and organizing to keep it honest.

Notes

1. Stanley Holt, "Organizer Profile," *Community Organizer Genealogy Project*, Center for Community Change, accessed May 24, 2014, *www.organizergenealogy.org*.
2. Asked by the Center for Community Change's genealogy project to share three lessons he had learned during his years as an organizer, Holt replied (in the typical fashion of his era's male organizers): "(1) Leaders are developed through action. (2) Organizations of diverse ethnic and racial groups are built by finding an enemy they all hate more than each other. (3) Stay clear of movements, they are best left to the bathroom" (ibid.).
3. Geoffrey Fox, *CDCs: New Hope for the Inner City* (New York: Twentieth Century Fund, 1971).
4. Gerson Green, *Community Development: A Review of Experience* (Washington, DC: National Center for Urban Ethnic Affairs, 1973).
5. Mike Miller, "Notes on Institutional Change," *Social Policy*, Winter 1972–1973, available from the author (mikeotcmiller@gmail.com).

14

John Baumann and the PICO National Network

∎

INTERVIEWED BY MIKE MILLER

Editors' preface: Baumann was interviewed by Miller on January 30, 2013. In this first segment, Baumann speaks about the beginning of his career and his training with Tom Gaudette.

I'll be seventy-five in March 2013. When I started Jesuit seminary in 1956, I had not experienced community organizing or social action. I was on a track to be a teacher in one of our Jesuit educational institutions after ordination. In 1966, I was in the process of finishing up the last three years of my thirteen-year Jesuit formation. I entered Alma College [affiliated with Santa Clara University] during the tumultuous '60s, an age of reform and revolution in the country and church. This was an era of many movements: civil rights, hippie, Chicano, anti-war, gay rights, feminist, free speech. Vatican II, which closed in 1965, influenced and impacted how the Catholic Church should interact with contemporary society. The Jesuits held a general [meeting] in Rome which unleashed our imaginations regarding a ministry in doing justice. Challenged by Vatican II and the Jesuit General Congregation, Jerry Helfrich [a fellow seminarian and good friend] and I decided that the time for talking about justice was over; [it was] a time to act.

At the end of my first year of theology in 1967, Jerry and I attended the Urban Training Center [UTC] in Chicago. It was a life-changing experience. UTC was my first exposure to community organizing; it had a three-month program [that included exposure to Saul Alinsky and Fr. Jack Egan.] I was impressed with Alinsky.

My two-month UTC fieldwork placement was at The Organization for a Better Austin [OBA], where Tom Gaudette was the director. Shel Trapp was on staff. Gale Cincotta was just emerging as a key leader, but wasn't yet president of OBA.

Gaudette just had us dive into the work, which was knocking on doors, listening to the people, learning the issues, then organizing action around the issues. When we learned of an issue from a number of people, we'd call them together and go after a target—a landlord or the absentee owner of an abandoned building or some city official who wasn't doing what he was supposed to do. This was the continuous cycle in which we were engaged.

[At organizer meetings that often went on late into the night,] each person would give a report on his door-knocking. Gaudette would ask questions. He wanted to know details. What did a person say? What did you say in response? What did you learn when you researched the issue? Who is the target? What are the handles for action? What's the proposed action? So the learning was both from your own exchange with Tom and from watching his exchanges with others who were around the table.

In '68, Jerry was ordained. He went back to Chicago and was invited to work at the Holy Family parish, which was in the middle of large public housing projects, and was a mixed—Italian, Mexican, and black—neighborhood. In 1969, I was ordained and returned to Chicago and joined Jerry. We treated the Chicago Housing Authority just like we'd treat a private slumlord. There were basics that needed to be done, like fixing broken windows, doors, plumbing, or other things. Some of the buildings were high-rise; others were town houses. Public housing was still a step up for a lot of people, and there were people who'd been living in those projects for quite some time, so there wasn't high transiency. We'd organize meetings like we'd organized a block club, and then take action. Each building had a group. I was there from 1969 to 1972.

There were other Jesuits who were interns in Chicago, several at Holy Family parish, including Rollie Smith [who went on to become an IAF organizer] and Greg Galluzzo, who founded Gamaliel. Tom Gaudette met with us weekly. The staff meetings were like the meetings Tom held in OBA; that's how we were getting our training as organizers. As there were more of us, we expanded to the next neighborhood.

Tom Gaudette

I remember Tom as the organizer and Tom as the family man. He was angry at injustice, and a fighter for justice; he felt people's pain, and wanted to do something about it by helping them to do something about it; he loved people—loved to tell stories about getting people into action and about their lives, about seeing them develop and gain self-confidence when they'd win an issue. He was a hard-nosed organizer. He was also a devout Catholic, and loved the church. His work was deeply connected with his faith.

Then there was the other part of Tom: he was a family man, loved his wife and kids, loved to have people at their home for dinner and to meet his wife, Kay, and then to sit talking and drinking together late into the night. Tom Gaudette was a unique person.

Tom had a break with Saul Alinsky because, I believe, he would not move from Chicago. Tom felt strongly the importance of making a difference in his own city. He loved Saul, and the break hurt him deeply. Tom could spend endless hours telling stories about Alinsky. In 1971, he and Saul met and made peace; he was so happy about that.

Tom was a big influence on me; he was my mentor. He always had time for me. I had a deep trust in him. Something else, Tom was very territorial: you worked your turf; you didn't get into someone else's turf. Turf was a big thing in those days in Chicago. People were very protective of where they were working, and there wasn't any work between organizations.

The Work and the Pacific Institute for Community Organization (PICO)[1]

In 1972, Jerry and I left [Chicago]. We had the idea of settling in someplace in California, within the California [Jesuit] Province. Jerry moved to California during the summer and connected with Fr. Oliver Lynch, a Franciscan, who was pastor at St. Elizabeth's Parish in East Oakland. He was very pastoral and had a strong faith in doing justice: supporting Cesar Chavez and the farmworkers, working in the neighborhood, very pro-organizing. . . . Oliver's provincial knew and agreed with Alinsky, so there was support in the Franciscan order for what he wanted to do. He invited us to come to work in his parish.

With seed money from the Jesuits and Lynch's support, we started the Oakland Training Institute [OTI]. Tom Gaudette's idea was to set up centers around the country so that everyone didn't have to go to Chicago for training. We quickly recognized that you couldn't train people in organizing without having them do organizing. So that was the beginning of Oakland Community Organization [OCO]. It was a relief to be in Oakland because there weren't any turf wars going on; nobody else was doing what we had in mind. So we started organizing block clubs through our OTI trainees, with the idea that we'd develop an Oakland-wide organization, focused in east, west, and north Oakland.

Gaudette was to be our backup consultant. He was doing his consulting under a nonprofit organization he'd made up, the Mid-America Institute, which was really just him. His idea was that he'd consult with regional groups like OTI around the country, and he'd travel to them to meet with trainees, and consult with the people running these regional organizations. He worked with Sister Mary Jordan in New Orleans, Greg Galluzzo in Seattle, Steve Honeyman and Kathleen O'Toole in Delaware. After three years, we expanded to Santa Ana, San Diego, Stockton, and Fresno—all in California.

Our method of organizing was what we learned in Chicago, organizing block clubs. It took us four years in Oakland before we had a founding congress, or convention. It adopted a constitution for the organization, an issues platform, and elected officers, and named the organization Oakland Community Organization. The pattern was what we'd learned in Chicago: [block clubs, block clubs getting together for bigger issues, wider campaigns that involved the entire organization].

In 1981, we were invited to work in Watsonville. A young organizer by the name of David Valencia applied for the job. We interviewed and liked him. But he told us he didn't want to use our "block club model." He wanted to organize based in the churches because that's what he'd learned from Jose Carrasco, who had trained him in the PACT [People Acting in Community Together] organization in San Jose. So, with Valencia, I went to meet with Jose to learn his method of developing an organization through churches. We had many meetings over coffee. Then in 1984 we invited him to come to a PICO five- or six-day staff retreat to present the underlying principles of the church-based model, and go through its organizing process with us. We were interested enough to continue in this conversation. Jose consulted with David in Watsonville, which is pretty close to San Jose, for two to three years. Meanwhile, we were all learning this approach. Jose was very important for PICO in making the transition to church-based organizing.[2]

From 1972 to 1983 PICO implemented the neighborhood model of organizing that we learned in Chicago. While religious congregations were involved, their participation was not central to the work itself. For many community organizers, including myself, "organized religion" was part of the problem, not the solution. After twelve years of organizing it became clear that issue-driven organizing without an institutional base in the community would not develop the permanent organizational and leadership capacity to address fundamental change.

[*PICO then conducted hundreds of one-on-one meetings with leaders in OCO and created a broad consensus for a shift to "faith-based" organizing that would be rooted in congregations. Thus began the transition in PICO.*]

[The] central weakness of the neighborhood model was that it focused almost exclusively on changing "things" rather than changing "people." [It was] issue driven rather than values driven; it failed to understand the role and power of religious faith and values in shaping social action.

The faith-based model gave new life to PICO because it enabled organizers, leaders, and families to relate to one another and act together in a new way. It functioned as a bridge that brought together congregation and community, faith and action, clergy and laity. It is where faith and activity interact. It is about moving faith into action.

In 1984, there was a decision to apply this model in other places within what had become the Pacific [instead of Oakland] Institute for Community Organization [PICO]. We decided to implement the approach in Oakland at St. Elizabeth, where Fr. Lynch was still the pastor. The results were impressive. The turnout at the first meeting was between seven hundred and eight hundred. That was almost as large as the earlier entire OCO citywide actions. Not only that, the entire turn-out was accomplished without flyers; it was done by disciplined one-to-one meetings—a core group of parish leaders talking with people, listening to them, developing relationships with them, earning their confidence. And not only talking with members of the parish, but reaching out to talk with neighbors, and inviting them to be part of the action and part of the core group that we call "Local Organizing Committee" or "LOC." Every congregation was to have an LOC. And a commitment every congregation made was to reach out to its neighbors through the congregation members who initially comprised the LOC. The meetings that were convened included both church members and neighbors.

Jose Carrasco advised us to let the block clubs remain; don't try to disband them. There isn't any need to do that. Over time, a number of the block clubs just stopped meeting and became a part of an LOC. The only people we lost during the transition were the activists who were more comfortable with a neighborhood model of action.

When we organized block clubs we often held meetings in the churches, especially when a block club held an action. We often asked the pastor to announce action meetings or place [an] announcement in the church bulletin. So, Tom felt that there really was no change when we transitioned to the church model. Tom did not want to admit that a transition was building stronger organizations. However, Tom recognized the success we were having with the church model and suggested to groups that he was working with—like New Orleans, Louisiana, and Mobile, Alabama—that they affiliate with PICO.[3] The church-based model answered a lot of questions that were increasingly concerning us. In Oakland, for example, we had the idea that we were going to become a power in the city. But we never could reach the scale required to do that. For example, when we pushed for a "first-source hiring" resolution from the city council, we were defeated. ["First source" means that when public funds are involved, a contractor has to first hire people from within the city of Oakland.] That was a big defeat for us. We knew we weren't sitting across the table from the real power because we hadn't been able to negotiate with the city to get support for this policy.

Part of the shift to institutions was a real emphasis on leadership development and through leaders [to] develop a powerful organization. This work required more skilled staff, which meant we weren't using interns—who were okay at door-knocking if you gave them a little training, but not able to do the process that accompanied the church-based model. Now we were asking leaders to do things that staff used to do. For example, leaders reached out to families in their communities, did "research actions" in which they learned who made decisions affecting an issue and what the policy options for addressing an issue [were], and learned how to plan and conduct actions.

In addition, there was something about the confrontational style of the block clubs that I was uneasy with, and so were others. We sometimes dehumanized targets in the way we treated them. We'd ask someone to come to a meeting, and then hit them with our demands, and if, for an example, a landlord did not comply, we'd go to their neighborhood and tell his neighbors that "Mr. X is a slumlord in our neighborhood." To me it violated the dignity of the individual. In the new approach we were undertaking, we'd have a smaller research meeting with the target and tell that person what we wanted and invite them to come to a community meeting and respond to our proposals. The person knew what was coming. Our expectation was that when they were faced with a large number of people, they wouldn't say no. In one of our meetings like that, we invited Oakland mayor Lionel Wilson. On the day of the meeting he informed the leaders that he would not attend. We went forward with the meeting as scheduled and placed an empty chair on the stage. It was a big news story: one thousand angry Oaklanders wanting their mayor to respond to their problems. He lost the next election, and I think that meeting had something to do with his defeat. People wouldn't forgive him.

With the transition we think of organizing as being about people, with issues following from our caring about people. In our earlier period, we would say that organizing is about issues. We have very intentional conversations with people about the pressures that bear upon them, their families, their neighbors—like crime in the neighborhood, or not being able to afford health care, or the education their children are receiving in the public schools, or how stretched they are economically, and so on. We invite them to think about the world as it is and the world as they would like it to be. We relate their self-interest to their values. We talk about needing an organization that has power—by which we mean the ability to act—to accomplish something on those concerns. We have a very intentional discussion of power. It's something we discuss in depth.

Block club organizing burned out both staff and leaders. When you use action on issues to sustain the organizing, you are under constant pressure. You're door-knocking, having house meetings, doing actions, then repeating more or less the same steps again . . . and again. We couldn't sustain what we had. There was lots of turnover, both of organizers and leaders. And it was very staff intensive.

[*PICO expanded, became a national network, and adopted the "institution-based" approach it learned from Jose Carrasco. Baumann wryly observed that when they started organizing in Oakland, they thought of the church structure as the enemy. Now they seek to renew and revitalize it. Scott Reed is now PICO's executive director; John Baumann remains on the staff as director of special projects.*]

Notes

1. The name was later changed to People Improving Communities through Organizing.
2. Jose Carrasco was a professor of social science at San Jose State from 1968 to 2004. He took several sabbaticals to work in community organizing. Carrasco had worked earlier for the Industrial Areas Foundation (IAF) in Texas and Los Angeles. He started the organization in San Jose that eventually became PACT, which was an affiliate of IAF. After being "independent," PACT later affiliated with PICO. Jose would become a longtime consultant with PICO.
3. See Chapter 11 for a different version of this tale.

15

An Introduction to Dick Harmon

■

VARIOUS AUTHORS

Introduction

I met Dick Harmon in 1966, in Buffalo. For a week before our meeting, I had been in an intense briefing with Ed Chambers on Kansas City, where I was to take over as staff director for an organization that was in trouble. I was somewhat intimidated by Chambers, and thought to myself, "If this is what you have to be in order to be an IAF organizer, I'm not the person to do this." My meeting with Harmon changed that. In both size and manner, Harmon was much more like me, leading me to conclude that IAF organizers didn't have to be in an Ed Chambers or Saul Alinsky mold.

Harmon is the most wide-ranging in his thought of the IAF organizers I have known. He is more willing to speculate on things beyond what might be realized in current struggles; more willing to look at the "big issues" of the day—including political, economic, social, and cultural concerns; and more interested in integrating different strands of thinking to create a small "d" democratic ideology. He isn't afraid to use "the i word"—ideology—and notes that everyone has one whether they acknowledge it or not.

Working with Dick Harmon: A Remembrance

—Ken Galdston

Ken Galdston was one of the IAF training institute's students mentored by Harmon. Galdston went on to a lifetime as a community organizer, working for IAF and then the Citizen Action–affiliated Mass Fair Share before striking off on his own. He now directs the New England region's InterValley Project. Here are some of his reflections.

This chapter was edited by Mike Miller.

One [IAF Institute] workshop I attended by Harmon, on moving from problems to issues, changed my direction, I thought at the time for the next five years, but ultimately for the rest of my working life. In [the workshop] Harmon kept pressing the group to define "issue." After a long round of people offering definitions of the word as a noun, he asked, "Isn't 'issue' a verb too?"

Working from the idea that issues emerge from the community, he then went into a focused, passionate discussion of how organizers need to understand the communities they organize in the way artists need to understand the wood they sculpt, with wonder, intensity, and humility.

Organizers need to immerse themselves in the life of their community, understand its known and hidden history, listen and observe, and, ultimately, work with leaders to fight for it because they and their community are sacred.

Before this workshop I had seen myself as organizing for two years in North Carolina and then returning to school, possibly to pursue a graduate degree in history and a life as an academic teacher. I was so struck and moved by this view of organizing as an art that I walked out of that workshop floating, immediately thinking that this was something I could devote the next five years to. . . .

[After the Institute seminar] I worked with Harmon for six months and then with [Ed] Chambers [see Section E] for six months and then rotated back. Their styles were different—Chambers, the older one by seven years, taller, larger, focusing on the nuts and bolts of power, relationships, and your growth, operating on a blunt version of his own anger. Harmon was closer in age to us, and, for some of us, his interest in national issues and the ways to bring them into the local arena, was compelling. So was his cooler, more intellectual style.

But both were clearly at war with what was going on in the country, and that was how we felt too. After a decade of the civil rights movement, summers of riots in Watts, Newark, and Detroit, assassinations, and the Vietnam War, being in a war with the Daley machine, the utilities, and the banks felt right.

During this formative period as a young organizer being mentored by Harmon, I found his energy—for naming what was wrong and who was profiting from it—inspiring and worth learning from, at times to the point of copying his tone and his style.

His emphasis on reflection as a means of learning was dramatic. I once told him after an action that I had not helped the leaders do an immediate evaluation—I said there hadn't been time. "Goddamit, Galdston, the only reason you do the action is so you have something to evaluate!"

The passion Harmon possessed shines in "Making an Offer We Can't Refuse" [included as the next chapter in this volume]. It led to a cold, strategic anger, especially when one understood that a key element of this war was over which way middle Americans—blue collar people and those just above them economically—would go politically. . . .

It was these families that I was organizing with, [under] the guidance of Harmon and Chambers, in The Midway Organization (TMO), an offshoot of CAP [Citizens

Action Program], organized by the IAF in part as a way to give the student organizers a place to learn their craft.

TMO's neighborhoods at the southwest edge of Chicago were . . . [home to] many police or firefighter families, because by city regulation they had to reside in the city, and this was as far away from the ghetto as they could get and still do that.

The turmoil of the times changed the lives of these working families; rising anger about pollution was an example. This meant that people who lived near factories—where the Midway area was—would no longer accept the bargain that smoke and pollution at least meant jobs.

When TMO leaders decided to fight for the future of their community, the ongoing corruption institutionalized in the Daley machine turned from something perhaps benign, or something that might help you get a job, to your enemy.

Lifting up the corruption behind the decisions that damaged these neighborhoods was an energizing part of organizing there. The corruption had huge consequences—in unabated pollution, redlining, and finally in the proposal to build the Crosstown Expressway down the whole western side of the city, taking scores of churches, displacing thousands of families, and eliminating many blue collar jobs—all laced with deals for Daley machine insiders. And the people could see that.

(During the fight against the Crosstown, I remember our speculating that our aldermen had purchased land in its path long before that path had been revealed to the public, planning an action to expose this if it were true. Leaders found the evidence at the assessor's office within a week.)

It was against this backdrop that Harmon's . . . pieces were written and eagerly absorbed. . . .

Harmon is at once reflecting deeply while grounded in the contours of a particular community—a local bar, a corner store, a major Catholic parish—all senses open, asking: How does this place work? What is its history? Who has the power?

This weaving of elements is so central and so attuned to what feels best about organizing, that I believe ["Making an Offer"] is the single best short piece on organizing written in our era.

At a time now when much of congregation-based organizing is focused on public institutions, rereading the early paragraphs of "Fuelish, For God's Sake" on congregations and oil companies, is a refreshing reminder of how vibrant and energizing private sector campaigns can be. The fact that the most powerful corporate and financial entities dominate governments in this country adds to the importance of these campaigns. . . .

After Chicago, I organized with the IAF in Minneapolis-St. Paul and then in Buffalo, where Harmon served as a supervising organizer for a period. He had a lot of passion for our work there, as his work to create BUILD [Build Unity, Independence, Liberty, and Dignity] there in the 1960s with leaders in the black community was central to his formation as an organizer. We were building a new organization across the city and Harmon helped guide our work. . . .

[Harmon and I] reconnected in the 1980s when each of us had begun to build organizations that exercised power through issue campaigns, but also through the creation of democratically controlled housing and jobs. . . . Harmon had been organizing Brooklyn Ecumenical Cooperatives (BEC), also rooted in organizing, while creating a major credit union and thousands of units of affordable housing. Our exchanges and discussions of our experience around these shared ideas were part of a rich period for me.

While Harmon stepped back from organizing several years ago after organizing in Oregon with the IAF, his writing can [still] inspire this generation of organizers because of his contributions to how we think about organizing. . . .

His work has deepened our approach to institutions, individuals, and the nature and scope of the power we seek through organizing. It has helped many of us stay in this work because it has reinforced the idea of organizing as a path to unfolding growth, if we act, reflect, read and think ambitiously, as well as deeply about our work.

Read together, Harmon's memos combine critical insights on how and why organizers organize every day, with a vision of what we can do if we combine with others to take on corporate as well as public sector targets. This combination of being grounded in the everyday while reaching for the stars is Harmon's overarching contribution to our work.

Selections from Harmon's Writings

—Mike Miller

In this section, I draw from three documents: "What Is BEC About?" which discusses Brooklyn Ecumenical Cooperatives, where Harmon worked as an independent (he was out of IAF for about sixteen years); "Metropolitan Broad-Based Organizing: What Are We Building?"; and "Fuelish for God's Sake: A Memorandum for Clergy and Laity (1974)," which he wrote while he and Ed Chambers were the principal staffers at the IAF Institute. "What Is BEC About?" and "Metropolitan" are both organizational documents that do not officially acknowledge an individual author.

Harmon recently noted that he would make a point of identifying both women and men as the actors in these pieces were he writing them today.[1]

From "Fuelish for God's Sake: A Memorandum for Clergy and Laity" (1974)

In 1974, in the midst of a national energy crisis that was expressed in skyrocketing fuel bills, Harmon wrote "Fuelish," which connected big ideas and big-picture politics to a

The selections from Dick Harmon's "Fuelish for God's Sake: A Memorandum for Clergy and Laity" were originally published by the Industrial Areas Foundation (Chicago) in 1974. They are reprinted here by permission of Dick Harmon.

strategy that was based in religious congregations and denominations—that is, to a possibility of people power commensurate with the challenge posed by the politics of the time. While not written with this purpose in mind, his article was a response to those who say that community organizing only deals with local issues.

Small "d" democratic politics is local because everyday people act locally: they vote in a local precinct, demonstrate in their home town, boycott a product at local outlets where it's sold, strike at a factory or business that is in a locality. The people power question is this: can enough of these locales be assembled into a national or international presence sufficient to affect the bottom lines of decision-makers who think globally? Harmon proposed an answer that was informed by the IAF's several years of experience with CAP.

Here's a sampling of what CAP tackled: redlining, Mayor Daley's major freeway project (the Crosstown Expressway), air pollution, tax relief and reform, political participation, and more. But in every case, there were local handles, even in the case of redlining, which CAP challenged by organizing depositors to move their money from offending banks (a practice called "greenlining"), instead of legislatively. We explore why IAF did not subsequently pursue this "big issues"-of-the-day direction in Chapter 27.

Note as you read Harmon's piece the introduction of possible wins. Note also that it is not simply wins, but an ability to enforce those victories, that is central to the case he makes. Reaching the capacity to undertake Harmon's challenge remains organizing's unfinished business.

Harmon asks, "How can you effectively do something at a local level about a 'national' issue?"

THE CHALLENGE OF THE ENERGY CRISIS
Harmon begins by establishing the extent of the problem of energy costs on the local level.

In a large parish in Philadelphia, the pastor paid $11,570 for fuel oil in 1973. In late 1973 fuel prices jumped 133%. . . . That pastor, in a relatively well-off parish, pointed out last year that he gave $8,563 to charity. . . . "I either pay the oil companies so they can make record profits, or I give to the poor."

The Archdiocese of Chicago has, in the city limits alone, 299 churches, many of them with schools and other separate buildings; 67 high schools; 8 colleges, universities and seminaries; 17 hospitals and special institutions. How many of these buildings are affected by the immediate oil price gouging? [*Harmon observes that every denomination has the same problem, and that energy price increases also affect public institutions, which pay the costs in taxes, as well as affecting homeowners and tenants.*]

CONTEXT OF THE OIL CRISIS
Harmon places the specific oil crisis of the early 1970s in a broader political context, and analyzes it. He argues that public policy during the Eisenhower, Kennedy, Johnson, and Nixon presidencies all fostered policies against consumer interests.[2]

The major oil companies "convinced" a captive U.S. government (which received $5 million in campaign contributions from oil executives in 1972) that there was a major "shortage." . . . What about this business where the federal government is totally dependent on industry figures? That is true—we're supposed to take the oil companies' word for it. . . .

The American public, to regain any kind of public confidence, must see independent government inventories—what is in the ground, what is in the pipelines and railroad cars, the refineries; these reserves and supplies must be examined first hand, and metered, not "seen" through company-supplied glasses.

[*Step by step, Harmon shows how the major oil companies are driving the independents out of business, making extraordinary profits, and paying minor taxes by using the various loopholes they lobbied to create. Citing both government and independent research, he demonstrates that consumers can't expect the electric utilities to fight on their side because "the same major banks that own the oil companies control the utilities." To complete his picture, Harmon shows how the Federal Energy Office is also controlled by the very interests it is supposed to regulate.*

In light of the current state of the economy in 1974, and the deep recession, Harmon foresees that "as prices level off and the economy adjusts, stock prices will go back up. The banks, oil and insurance companies can sell off large blocks of the stock they picked up at the bottom of the market they in large part created." Harmon concludes that they will emerge from the "crisis" with "a windfall profit, and immensely increased economic control."]

What Can We Do?

What can religious leaders and their people do? What are prudent, attainable actions and goals? This is an issue which includes economic justice, empowerment of consumers, and the financial survival of religious institutions. . . .

1. Key local clergy and lay leaders, once they are clear about the factual basis for this "crisis," can pull together a mass meeting of their colleagues. Into that large meeting they can bring the local congressional delegation, the U.S. Senators, and the Governor and the State District Attorney, [and initially demand] a rollback or freeze on the price of heating oil, at least until the federal and state governments complete [an] independent investigation of the real supply and distribution situation. That places an *immediate*, realizable demand on the politicians, and it keeps pressure on the governments to get the facts, and stop being dependent on the oil companies for their information. . . .

   Regular accountability sessions, of equal-size and seriousness, should [continue to] be held with those politicians. . . . Sign *contracts* with those politicians.
2. At the local and state level, the demand can be placed on the District Attorney and Attorney General for subpoena power to get at all the facts. We don't have to

place all our trust in the federal government. It's clear at this point that even the IRS agents are confused. And we need local accountability against price fixing and black marketeering and hidden supplies.

3. In addition, at the local level, every taxing district—the city, county, board of education, sanitary district, etc., will have to pay huge increases in its fuel bill . . . which means tax increases. Heavy pressure should be put on the local politicians occupying seats of power in those local taxing districts to support your program at the federal and state level, and to challenge, on their own, the bids offered for oil and gas by the oil companies. Allies, such as teacher organizations and public employee unions, can be brought into this fight. For if the local taxing districts have to continue to pay for huge oil and gas price increase, there will be no money for necessary and just wage increases.

4. Longer range demands at the federal level include different tax legislation for the oil companies; and—perhaps both at the federal and state levels—the government should set up a corporation similar to the Tennessee Valley Authority, to provide, not nationalization, but a yardstick, to prove that oil or gas can be delivered to the customer at a much lower price than the oil companies currently charge. . . .

5. The stranglehold of control over all our sources of energy which is held by a small group of banks and companies must be broken, both for economic, social and religious reasons. . . . That means heavy, organized, consistent pressure on the politicians to enact—and enforce—laws which benefit local institutions and consumers, instead of obeying the wishes of campaign contributors from the oil companies and the banks that control them. . . .

6. Finally, well organized religious leaders and members can get meetings with top executives of the oil companies and the banks that own them. They are obviously making private decisions which affect the public order and the religious order in massive ways. So they should be brought out into the public light by the leaders of the public and religious institutions.

If those meetings do not yield the required results, then it may in all likelihood become necessary to organize the religious stock portfolios, pension funds, and savings and checking accounts—on regional and national and local levels—to bring economic pressure on the banks and oil companies. Religious institutions and their members have enormous amounts of financial leverage, if they will organize it. Once they organize their own leverage, consider the possibilities of asking unions to do the same, with their pension funds, with their stock portfolios, with the savings and checking accounts of their individual members. Then take it a step further, where organized religious leaders and members, allied hopefully with union leaders and members, place the same demand on local and state politicians, to leverage [public funds] . . . to bring the runaway banks and oil companies into a relationship of accountability with citizen and religious institutions.

This is an elemental question of economic survival for religious institutions. Either organize or go under.

From "What Is BEC About?" (1990)

These selections from the Brooklyn Ecumenical Cooperatives (BEC) organizational document, written fifteen years after the one above, reflect the broad range of Harmon's thinking.

[In BEC] we aim at both civil and economic justice. On the civil side, our communities require security, clean and healthy environment, responsive and effective schools, affordable housing, and health care for all. On the economic side, our communities require capital flows that re-circulate, and new work that expresses our dignity and imagination.

OUR STRATEGIES

1. Civil justice requires civil empowerment, which centers on establishing a new relationship of accountability between our communities and the structures and leaders of government.
2. Economic justice requires empowerment also. Economic empowerment centers on building up new institutions to re-circulate capital through our communities, and on worker-owned enterprises.

[In its "civil justice" work, BEC engaged in issue activities aimed at holding political and economic decision-makers accountable to its justice and civic participation agenda. BEC opened new ground for community organizing in its economic justice work.]

BEC's economic empowerment agenda includes a 2,000 member credit union, with almost $2 million in assets; a housing development corporation; a construction loan company; a bank; a mixed-income housing development; and a worker-owned recycling company. The boards of each of these entities are either directly elected, or appointed by directly elected BEC bodies.

SOURCES OF OUR VISION AND WORK

Here, Harmon covers a wide range of material. It begins with the life stories of the people with whom he is working—the struggles that took place in their countries of origin and in the United States. These stories combine practical life-experience and a cultural/religious context in which they are interpreted. A good organizer pays careful attention to both. In life experiences are found "problems" that can be turned into "issues." The cultural/religious context provides the language to make participation in an organizing effort make sense.

The selections from "What Is BEC About?" were originally published by Brooklyn Ecumenical Cooperatives (New York) in 1990. They are reprinted here by permission of Dick Harmon.

Together these offer a panorama of ideas and ideals that feed into the stream of thought that underlies a broad understanding of a democratic way of life. (In his use of Mexican and Catholic symbolism, Cesar Chavez was masterful at this.)

Reaching deeply into the history of Western civilization, Harmon includes both the Old and New Testaments as well as ideals of the Greek city-states. In them he finds precedents for a fundamental equality among all people, regard for the land as sacred, and deep commitment to popular participation. In Christian texts, he notes participation is without regard to gender or ethnicity, thus providing an early point of reference for feminist historians, whom he also cites.

In American history, he cites Jefferson and Jackson, the abolitionists, the Populists, and the American civil rights movement—all of which give us a picture of full participation in civil and economic life by all members of our society. He draws upon Gandhi, King, and Solidarity (the Polish union whose people power forced the Communist government to negotiate with it), where we see a fundamental commitment to effective nonviolence.

He also delineates the intellectual, cultural, and spiritual roots of his economic ideas. From the Bible Harmon draws "the mutual economic aid provided in both pre-Monarchy Israelite villages and the early churches." In the late medieval craft guilds of Europe he finds extensive mutual aid. Shifting to Populists, he lifts up the story of ordinary Americans across the South and West "organizing . . . to bring economic justice into reality." Looking at the increasingly widely known worker-owned Mondragon cooperatives in the Basque region of Spain, he finds "that worker ownership can be an effective strategy in local communities." Shifting to theology, he draws from creation-centered spirituality: "(a) [The] Sacredness of the universe, including Earth and all its species and processes; (b) The role of the human enterprise is to respond to God's full creation, in awe."

LEADERSHIP DEVELOPMENT

Our [leadership development] process starts with listening and relationship-building. Then it goes to small, local issues coming up through each congregation. It then moves out to larger, more common issues, such as crime, drugs, health, and housing/commercial development and new work.

From "Metropolitan Broad-Based Organizing: What Are We Building" (c. 2000)

This is also an organizational document, for The Organizing Project in Portland, Oregon. From Brooklyn, Harmon returned to IAF and continued his organizing work in the Pacific Northwest. This document more specifically addresses the nuts and bolts of what he was building.

The excerpt from "Metropolitan Broad-Based Organizing: What Are We Building?" was originally published by the Organizing Project (Portland, OR), c. 2000. It is reprinted here by permission of Dick Harmon.

1. **What business are we really in?** We are building power to transform institutions and their cultures so that America's politics, economics and culture are both sustainable and democratic.
2. **Why are we in this business?** We live in a culture that isolates persons from each other, from their institutions (including family), their democratic participation in decision-making, and from nature; and segregates the private and public aspects of our lives.
3. **What are our goals?**
   (a) General Goal: Dis-organize that culture of isolation; de-segregate the artificial walls between public and private; build instruments of effective civil power.
   (b) Specific Goals:
      i. Strengthen the Relational-Action-Reflection culture inside our institutions of religion, labor, education, environment, health and housing.
      ii. Expand the pool of leaders of those institutions, and of the Broad-Based Organizations.
      iii. Build Broad-Based Organizations for the Common Good, capable of negotiating with strategic decision-makers for our region.
4. **What are our objectives?**
   (a) Develop effective Core Teams working in Participating Institutions.
   (b) Develop Reflection Group Leaders through the annual institutes.
   (c) Develop teaching teams through the annual institutes.
   (d) Develop significant relationships among teams of leaders from the "mix" of all the institutions engaged in building the Broad-Based Organizations.
   (e) This Leadership Development process enhances the six capacities of Sustainable Citizenship:
      i. Social;
      ii. Spiritual;
      iii. Political;
      iv. Economic;
      v. Natural/ecological;
      vi. Intellectual.
5. **What are our tools?**
   (a) Individual Meeting/Reflection;
   (b) Reflection Group (House Meeting);
   (c) Action (Negotiation).
   (d) Evaluation.
6. **What are some of the issues that have surfaced over the last two years?**
   (a) Loss of the 40-hour week, causing lack of time for prayer, for meditation, for children, for participation in our institutions.

(b) Flat or falling income for 40–50% of our working people—in the face of exploding housing costs, causing severe family tension, displacement and homelessness.

(c) Public schools suffering from both under-funding and bureaucratic cultures, causing severe stress for teachers, parents, children and principals.

(d) Unacknowledged grief over our relation to nature in this magnificent region, causing unnecessary paralysis and division inside families and among institutions.

(e) Anxiety over toxics in our food, air and water.

(f) Isolation from each other, as the pace and scale of technological change sweep over all of us, causing confusion and difficulty within congregations, unions, schools and our organizations of housing, health and the environment—and within families/households;

(g) Cynicism over the role of big money in electoral politics, causing increasing alienation and powerlessness in our public life.

(h) Fear across ethnic, gender, religious and class lines.

(i) Explosion of temporary employment without benefits, increasing anxiety and family tension.

Notes

1. Dick Harmon, comment to editors, August 1, 2013.
2. This section was moved above the following one.

16

Making an Offer We Can't Refuse (1973)

■

DICK HARMON

Organizing is teaching . . . which rests on people's life experiences, drawing them out, developing trust, going into action, disrupting old perceptions of reality, developing group solidarity, watching the growth of confidence to continue to act, then sharing in the emotional foundation for continual questioning of the then-current *status quo*.

Organizing as teaching has two fundamental educational premises:

1. We learn with our bodies first, not our minds. All understanding starts with bodily perception, primarily of our relationship with other persons and institutions. Even ideas are bodily images, translations of physical encounters and actions. Even the most abstract ideas have a chemical basis in bodily experience with events, at least in the hands of creative initiators. . . . This means that education is primarily in the *action*, but becomes really liberating education only if the person develops the discipline to rigorously reflect on that action.

2. We have to *own* the questions in this educational process. It must be our curiosity that is the engine of this learning process, pulling us into action, then reflection, then more action, more reflection. The major problem with academic education, from kindergarten through graduate school, is that action is not the basis of the learning process. There is no drawing on people's actual bodily experiences, no running with the pulling force of *their* curiosity, *their* questions. Hence, teachers wind up standing in front of passive groups answering questions people are not asking.

(This suggests, by the way, a model of education in which much of the student's time, from kindergarten on, is spent in the community doing real work, dealing with real problems; and the school "building" is the location where teachers and students come together to reflect on that action. . . . This also assumes that teachers have . . . experience in their own communities, have reflected a lot about that experience, and are imaginative [in how they present it to students]. . . .)

The purpose of education is not to transmit the culture—unless you're in a power

This essay was first published by the Industrial Areas Foundation (Chicago). It is reprinted here by permission of Dick Harmon.

position, which benefits from students, teachers and administrators *not* questioning the basis and functions of that culture's institutions. . . . The purpose of education, . . . [for] the organizer[1] working with citizen organizations, is to develop accurate confidence and competence in a person so that he[2] can effectively negotiate his way among the power institutions which affect his life. In other words, education is the development of public skills, so that a person can carry out his potential and purpose. That is power—the ability to act.

Power lies in the relation between energy and structure. Applied to a person, power lies in the liberation of interior energy—usually packed down and driven into warring elements within a person—through a personal structure of confidence and competence, so that the person's full potential and purpose can emerge; that enables him or her to be a full human being. . . .

[*Harmon says most U.S. institutions, ranging from family to church, school, corporation, government and others, make individual persons feel battered, out of touch with reality, like a drowning swimmer in an Atlantic gale. To regain some personal control over our own lives, we have to create power organizations to remold the society's major institutions.*]

So real education is for power. Citizen organizing is mass adult education in political skills. When organizations are good . . . [i.e., *multi-issue, lots of action, large collective leadership, member-based funding, with an organizer who is a first-rate teacher and who is out after three to five years*] then citizen organizations are great universities.

How do people learn in large citizen organizations? What are the steps?

1. *What is the problem?* The organizer usually starts with a potential leader or a small group that has a problem. His task in this first step is to get the leader or small group to talk about the problem, for several reasons. First, to understand as many of the dimensions of the problem as possible. Second, to see how the person or group feels about it, how much of it the group understands, whether there is a glimmer of willingness to go into action on it, and whether it can be broken down into an *issue*—that is, a piece of the problem which can be effectively acted upon. Third, to develop the beginnings of a relationship of trust between the leader or group and himself. Fourth, to try to spot the talent, in either the individual or group, for leadership.

2. *How many other people feel the same way?* This is the first action test—will that leader or that first small group go out and bring together other people faced with the same problem? If that doesn't happen, the organizer knows there is no issue. But if they go out and get more people, then the organizer repeats with this larger group many of the steps he took with the first group: again analyzing the problem, getting everyone in the room to talk about it—in order to spot talent, understand how the persons there relate to each other, see if there is a cautious readiness to go into action, and, through his questions, establish trust.

3. *What precisely do we want?* Mid-way in this second meeting, if the organizer sees that the problem can be made issuable, he starts challenging the group to define exactly and specifically what it wants. This steps up the intensity of relationships in the room, it forces the beginning of the decision-making process, it further clarifies who is serious and who is a nut, and it is the first step in the development of an agenda for the action that is to come. Throughout the process, the organizer presses people to *focus*, to *specify*. People don't go into action over generalities.

4. *Who do we see to get things changed?* Usually, when a group is green, several people will say, "The Board of Education," or "City Hall." But here the organizer has to draw out of the people *who* in the Board of Education, exactly what person in City Hall. Some persons will be afraid: "Let's not make it personal, now." That's especially true among middle class people, who tend to be mainlined with massive doses of politeness. But the organizer can draw from the group the admission that institutions of power are made up of persons, that persons within this particular institution are making the decisions which are hurting the group, and therefore, if the group really wants to get rid of its hurt, then it has to identify that Joe Cullerton—the responsible decision-maker to negotiate with. This step is crucial in bringing people to the edge of personalizing the issue—naturally and easily out of their own experience and common sense.

5. *How many of us should go to see him?* The natural inclination of many groups at this early stage is to "delegate" one person or a small group to "represent us, that's the proper way to do it." They are usually reacting against an image of "confrontation" they have seen in the media. Someone in the group—especially if it's middle class—will even say, "Now, we don't want a confrontation. That is not the way we do things in this city." With inexperienced groups, it's usually fatal for the organizer to throw down the glove and demand, "What's wrong with confrontation?" In some cases that may work, but usually it's much more effective to have anticipated this problem with the leaders in the group, who if they think about it, know they are not prepared to go into negotiations alone, and really want the psychological support of the group. The leaders can then argue, "Look, this problem belongs to all of us here. All of us have to be in on all of the decisions. I'll be glad to be one of the spokespersons, but I for one am not going in there to see Cullerton unless we all go in. I don't want a shouting match any more than you do, but we should all see what he has to say. That's the democratic way to do things. Of course we can be polite, but we should all go in, so we all know what is going on."

The organizer knows this step is essential because he knows that Cullerton's reaction to the group will teach them some basic lessons, and the more people who are there to experience that reaction the better. This separates the business agent or social worker from the organizer. The business agent or social worker is fundamentally interested in solving problems, which means to him that he, with all his professional qualifications, is best qualified to solve the problems of the people. That makes the people dependent on the business agent or the social worker. . . . The organizer, on the other hand, knows that the problems won't really get solved without the people being in on every stage of the process; and further, he is fundamentally committed to the developmental process of people increasing their public skills and experience. Solving problems, to the organizer, is one-third to one-half of what's important. The rest is the political education, in action, of the group he is working with. The purpose of that action, in turn, is to build the organization. Therefore, the more people in on the Cullerton meeting, the more people there are who move along another step in their education. And the vehicle—the organization—is built that can carry them effectively into the next issue. So the point at this stage is to get everyone committed—using a sign-up sheet if necessary—to be in on the Cullerton meeting.

6. *Who will be the spokespersons?* This is where the group begins to choose its leadership consciously. They will agree to pick spokespersons because they don't want a mob scene, a "confrontation." The organizer's problem here is not hard, he just has to be sure that there are two or three people who will consciously do the talking. This is important at early stages because the organizer has no real way of judging the leadership talent in the group until he sees them in action— and he has to see a number of people in action to know who he is to spend the most time with. Also, if there is only one spokesperson, and the tension in the negotiations builds up, it is more than likely that, with inexperienced people, a single leader will feel too much pressure and collapse—which will set the group's development back badly. So the organizer asks the group to pick two, three or four people to do the talking. Then they are the people he spends more time with in meetings before the action, refining who is going to say what to Cullerton.

7. *Are we willing to caucus?* This will be foreign to most people. The organizer starts on this point by getting the group to re-focus on the agenda for the meeting with Cullerton. He then says something like, "You know, it's very easy when we go into the actual meeting itself, to get confused and to forget exactly why we are there. At some point, we may get confused in the discussions, so we ought to be willing to caucus. All we have to do is, any one of the three spokespersons can simply stand up and say, 'Mr. Chairman, I call for a five minute caucus.' Then we all walk out in the hall to clear up our heads, and go right back in." That will make sense to most groups. A caucus has saved thousands of negotiating sessions from disaster. And caucusing has a nice side-effect: It will probably confuse the hell out of Cullerton, at least for a while.

8. *What is the timetable for the response?* Asking Cullerton for a timetable—"When do we get your answer?" or, "When will you act on what we want?"—is the single most effective way to cut through the problem of politeness. For if the organizer can keep the spokespersons focused on the specifics of the agenda, and

on the timetable for an answer or an action from Cullerton, Cullerton will react. And Cullerton's reaction, as any good organizer knows, will teach the group more, faster, than all the organizer himself can do.

The spokespersons do not have to be impolite, just persistent. All they have to do is to keep repeating, "When do we get it?" until Cullerton either caves in and gives them a victory, or blows up and makes himself the enemy.

In middle class organizations, the heart of the educational process occurs when people discover they have real enemies, who regard them as invisible, as niggers or honkies. That discovery is a rite of passage into the real world. That is why the organizer prays, not for rain, but for defecation. When Cullerton throws the bucket of shit in the group's face, they are forced to start grappling with the *real* relations of power between themselves and Cullerton's institution. They discover quickly that issues are always personalized—that Cullerton the person made a decision, Cullerton the person insulted them. And they have to decide whether they're willing to fight for what they want from him.

With people who suffer from politeness, it isn't hard to get them to see the necessity of asking Cullerton for a timetable. After all, every important thing in our lives has a timetable—the mortgage, the car note, the paycheck, the day we start school or work. Asking for a timetable is the professional, middle class way to order our lives. *When* is the critical factor: *when* do we make love, eat, take the trip, die. Once they see that, and once they are in the meeting with Cullerton, the organizer concentrates on keeping the spokespersons focused on the specifics of the agenda, especially the timetable. Here is where his work with the spokespersons before the bargaining session will payoff. And here is where, at a signal, a caucus may be necessary. . . . [*Harmon here lists the many techniques Cullerton may use to avoid responding to "when?"*]

But if the spokespersons stay focused, and remain persistent about the timetable, Cullerton will react. He will call them irresponsible, ignorant, parochial, unrepresentative, a waste of his time. *He* will become impolite. Why? Because sticking to the specifics, to their agenda, *pins* Cullerton, reduces his freedom of movement: exactly the same effect as one wrestler putting another's shoulders to the mat for a count of three. They are reducing his power.

When Cullerton reacts, he will surprise them, insult them, anger them. In a green group, especially in [the] middle class, his reaction will flush up in them feelings they didn't know they had.

When Cullerton reacts, he reveals himself as their enemy. And as their enemy, he becomes their teacher.

9. . . . [*The evaluation must happen immediately following the action.*] The rule here is, never let people go home alone after an action. For the evaluation session has two functions. First, as people begin to talk, usually after some gentle prodding from the organizer, they flush up to the surface those feelings that Cullerton's reaction provoked.

The people begin to discover that each of the group has some of those feelings. . . . And what happens when people share those feelings is the discovery
that they are in the fight together, that it is not terrorizing to support each other.
Their privatization begins to break down. That psychological sharing and support
is the beginning of *solidarity*. It's the breaking into a new depth of relationships
among them. It begins to crack through the loneliness. Life starts to get a hell of
a lot more vivid and meaningful.

Second, as people analyze their feelings and the events of the action itself,
they start to develop an *interpretation* of what happened. They start to make
sense of it, give it some order and meaning.

There are a number of key questions which must be dealt with in an evaluation session: Did we get what we went in there for? What did Cullerton agree
to, if anything? Did we stick to our agenda? What about the timetable? How
did the team of spokespersons work out? Did Cullerton try to take us off our
agenda? Why did he react the way he did? Why did he insult us? What does he
think of us if he insults us like that? And then, questions about the next steps—
where do we go from here? Once people in the evaluation session have aired
their feelings and have analyzed how both sides operated and what that means
about the power relationships, then the question is, who do we tell this story
to? We tell our neighbors, friends, relatives, colleagues, fellow church or club
or association members. In other words, we spread the word to build our base,
because we're going to need more people to get what we want. More people is
our only weapon.

Why is the rule—never let people go home alone after an action—so important? If a person is inexperienced at citizen action, and he goes home full of
undefined feelings, confused about what happened and why, one of two situations will probably develop. Either he will sit at home alone as his confusion gets
worse—which means he gets so frightened he won't come back to another action.
Or, if he (or she) faces the spouse and tries to tell the spouse what happened,
but all that comes out is something very foreign to what they have done before,
the spouse will usually say, "No more of that! *You're* not going to be one of those
rabble rousers!" So it's crucial that he go home feeling good about the sharing of
feelings with the other participants (he's not alone then), and that he go home
with some clarity about what happened and why it happened that way, and what
the next steps are.

One more thing about the evaluation session—the role of the organizer. In
the first actions of the group, the organizer will have to do most of the questioning in the evaluation. It's absolutely essential that his basic posture be to ask
questions, to give a *minimum* of answers. He should give his interpretation—in
pieces—only well into the discussion. The evaluation session has much of the
same dynamics as the first two meetings did, when the group collectively analyzed the problem, decided to act, chose their target and spokespersons, etc.

Everybody should be in on the discussion. Everybody should wrestle with the analysis, and with their feelings. To get the group to move along in the public skill process, the organizer has to "put out" or "impregnate" with his ideas—but only in chewable pieces. His "answers" must be in response to questions that people are genuinely struggling with. The people—or at least some of the people in the group—have to be really hungry for his ideas if they are to take. And they have to be in "pieces" not just because the people may not be "ready" for a full-blown chalk-board chart, but more accurately because they have common sense and dignity and will have parts of the answers themselves. Only a business agent or an ideologue wants to focus all the attention on himself and his "wisdom" by giving all the answers. The organizer wants to draw out of the people *their* feelings, *their* reflection, so the pieces of answers he gives really serve to whet the people's curiosity and their appetite for more action: "You know, this stuff is really interesting!"

Then, as the organization emerges, and the members and leaders get more experienced, the *leaders* lift up the questions for analysis. *They* run the discussion. The organizer then can play a diminishing role, stepping in only when he thinks they are kidding themselves, or ducking a hard fact, or ignoring some of the questions. And if the organizer does his job correctly, the leaders will soon go about the job of training secondary leaders, in part by turning the questions in the evaluation session over to new people they and the organizer want to develop. So the skills spread progressively among a continually expanding group of people; fresh talent enters the process; the pool of leadership expands. The organization grows, its power increases.

10. *Where and when is the next meeting?* This is also decided in the evaluation session. When the participants go out to talk with their networks of neighbors, colleagues, friends, institutional members, etc., they not only have to tell them what happened at the action, but they also have to invite them to participate in the next step. So they bring a larger body of people into a meeting (which should be no longer than 3-7 days after the Cullerton meeting.) When they go out to talk with those other people, to expand their base, they have to have the specific information on where and when that base will come together.

This is not the time to lay out the elements of a good meeting, except to say, in the context of the educational process I'm talking about, that the meeting has two points: Highly focused, colorful action reports on what took place in the meeting with Cullerton; and a vote on a specific action proposal: Either a larger body of people goes to see Cullerton, with media invited; or a large group goes to see Cullerton's superiors. In either case, people in the meeting must be asked to *commit*, by *signing* up for the action.

Then the process is repeated: the collective leadership group that is beginning to emerge meets and agrees on the specifics of the agenda and the timetable they want. The organizer role-plays with them, to "rehearse" them just like any public figure uses his staff to rehearse for an event. They go into the action focused so that the other side again reacts. Another evaluation session, more spreading of the word, a larger mass meeting. They're on their way to building an organization. At each step, their confidence and competence deepens. Their public skills, their ability to act, increases.

What are the elements that people learn in this process? Clarity about institutional power. Clarity about the lack of citizen power without large organization. Clarity about who their enemies and allies really are, which involves the breakup of many stereotypes. How to draw people—their followers—into action, and how to deepen public skills of their followers; in other words, how to lead. Clarity about self-interest. The design and dynamics of actions. How to understand and use the media. How to run meetings. Now to negotiate. How to get a reaction from the other side. How to raise money from the people who are into the process. Finally, personal insight at the deepest level (there is a solid continuum between private and public skills). Insight into the pieces of the person's identity, why he did what he did in the events of his history; his relationships with family, friends, allies, enemies; how and what he communicates through his actions; clarity about his own self-interest, and therefore into his own *real* values; a bodily perception of the relation between energy and structure in all the events, people and institutions around him—in other words, an experiential understanding of power and tragedy.

What does the organizer as teacher get out of this? What does the organizer understand? Why does the good organizer teach?

First, a word about ideology. Any good organizer has to wonder much of the time where all his work is leading. Where is it all going? One reason organizers usually have heavy liquor bills is because victories aren't coming fast enough, organizations aren't multiplying fast enough. That's true in any time, but it seems particularly troubling in the context of Watergate, when the moderates of America are being forced to look at most of the institutions of the country in a new light, and are discovering that none of those institutions, the White House included, are sacred, that there are Watergates in every county, town, and city, that Watergate is not a burglary but a pattern of values that stretches back into World War II.[3] Watergate is a cultural stream, which has washed five presidents and thousands of key politicians, corporation executives, and union leaders. Watergate is the use of the Cold War as a rationale to concentrate power in the Pentagon and its friends, and to protect that power, including all the bureaucracy and apparatus of a mass police state. Government then rests on secrecy, not accountability. Government becomes the private preserve, at all levels, of the corporations. A royal line develops, across the top of government, military, business. That royal line peddles the myth that it is sacred, to be held in awe, unaccountable to mere citizens. Some are more equal than others. Some have no limits, are beyond being judged.

So when Watergate swings open, and it turns out to be the gate to the Presidential toilet, and there squats Nixon shitting just like the rest of us, a reaction sets in among American moderates by the millions. Their awe toward most institutions of government and business disappears, but because we have let our voluntary intermediate institutions atrophy so badly over the past thirty years, most Americans have no effective political option except lethargy and cynicism.

In this context, thoughtful organizers are both alarmed at the prospect that the Watergate mob will fight desperately to protect its position, and exhilarated by the opportunity to organize among millions of moderates who no longer hold tight to many of the old myths. We may be well into what Alinsky called the "reformation" of the middle. But the police state and the runaway corporations with their whore politicians will fight back with every weapon they can grab. We are coming into a number of years of great danger and great opportunity.

In any event, if in the next five to ten years we help build hundreds of major citizen organizations, which in turn transform in basic ways hundreds of corporations and units of government, nevertheless none of us can know what the American system will look like at the other end of that time period. Any ideology which tries to detail what the institutions should look like after a decade of struggle will itself atrophy and drown in the ocean of change upon us.

No, I think the ideology lies in the medium term, in the commitment to develop thousands of new leaders in large, tough citizen action organizations, which can effectively take on the Watergate mob. That ideology means that organizers continually challenge those leaders, continually fight to multiply new leaders, continually challenge them to stay in action, picking more and more powerful targets. The ideology rests on the faith that a continually multiplying group of trained radical leaders and organizers will create and develop mass organizations capable of transforming the Watergate Institutions. In what exact way the Watergate Institutions will be transformed no one can foresee. That is up to the people of the new generation of citizen organizations. Our faith is in the anger, common sense, and public skills of those people.

In the process of going through the action education provided by a large citizens' organization, the active people are transformed. The organizer is an intimate partner in that transformation of persons. That relationship is both intimate and objective, and it is his lifeblood, it is what sustains him.

For in that relationship of continual action and reflection, the organizer acts out the examined life, which is the prime self-interest of the good organizer.

The good organizer's life consists of a continual process of effective action, disciplined reflection, and challenge from other people, which provides for him continual insight into his self and into as many other dimensions of reality as he is capable of understanding. His prime drive is a quest for clarity, which he knows is always in process. . . .

That's the center of the organizer's drive. He knows he can lead the examined life at its fullest only in the teaching relationship among people who are struggling to take effective action in the major power arenas of his time. He knows that in the action, in the disciplined reflection on that action, in the drawing out into clear air continual questions about the always-emerging reality, those people teach him. They help him deepen his clarity.

The quest for clarity—that's the offer we can't refuse.

Notes

1. Harmon's note in the original: By "organizer" I mean catalytic agent, teacher, agitator; even missionaries are sometimes good organizers.
2. Dick Harmon, comment to editors, August 1, 2013: Were I writing today, I would have both women and men identified as organizers, leaders, and participants in this story.
3. Watergate was a scandal during Richard Nixon's presidency that led him to resign. The investigation of the administration's activities would have been in progress when Harmon was drafting this essay.

17

Ed Chambers: The IAF Institute
and the Post-Alinsky IAF

■

MIKE MILLER

There are different versions of the beginnings of the IAF Institute. In mine, it began with a challenge made to Alinsky in 1965 at one of his ten-day Asilomar, California, workshops on mass-based organizing. An activist Episcopal priest by the name of Barry Bloom made the challenge. Alinsky's response: raise $250,000, and we'll start an organizer training institute here, with projects in the largely Latino Mission District and in one of the major black areas of Oakland (in both places, an invitation to IAF was being developed). But it was not to be.

In 1968, Gordon Sherman, heir to the Midas Muffler fortune, pledged $250,000 to Alinsky for the training institute with one condition: it had to be in Chicago. The story is told that on a wedding anniversary he asked his wife what he could do to demonstrate his love for her. She replied, "Do something to help end the war in Vietnam, and something about poverty and racism in Chicago." Sherman met Alinsky through the ubiquitous Msgr. Jack Egan, who had himself only met Sherman a little while earlier. Sherman was eager to meet Alinsky. Egan was hopeful that Alinsky would accept the money and use it for a substantial black community organizing project based in Chicago's Lawndale area. But Alinsky had another idea: the training institute.

The IAF had no experience with something as formal as a training center or school for organizers. It now had to address multiple questions, some that were easily answered, others not. It was clear from the outset that the Institute's "students" were going to be clergy, activists emerging from campuses across the country, and others whose hands were dirty from toiling in the vineyards of some version of organizing work.

There were plenty of applicants. The churches were a natural network to identify, screen, and recruit prospective students. Alinsky hoped that adding Staughton Lynd to his staff would give him an avenue to organizers whose roots were in the civil rights and student movements—Lynd had been a key planner of the Mississippi Summer Project's Freedom Schools, and he was a highly respected New Leftist in northern white student movement circles. The core faculty were Ed Chambers, who was Alinsky's senior organizer, and Dick Harmon, who had successfully developed the BUILD (Build Unity, Independence, Liberty, and Dignity) organization in Buffalo, New York's black community.

Chambers and Harmon developed a thoughtful application for prospective students to fill out. They interviewed those whose written material passed muster. The first class began with thirteen students. By its end, almost a year later, there were four remaining.

The initial curriculum was based on Alinsky's ten-day seminar, including a reading list that Alinsky had developed. It was an eclectic mix that included *Federalist No. 10*, *Alice in Wonderland*, *Democracy in America*, Alinsky's *Reveille for Radicals* and *John L. Lewis*, and selections from the Bible, Mao, and Lenin.

Chambers and Harmon knew that individual conversations with the students would be central to their training. These would probe deeply into what made each of them tick and the source of their commitment, as well as their hang-ups and whatever else might impede success in the demanding job of community organizer.

But something else was needed as well: a fieldwork placement that would provide the experiential base for the conversations, and the on-the-ground implementation for the theory. "Alinskyism" is, if nothing else, a practice-theory, only understood by applying it.

The need for fieldwork placements created a new institutional imperative: the need for organizing turf. In Alinsky's earlier work, sponsor committees had been a key ingredient in the success of a project. Not only did they provide funding, they also legitimized the organizer. They demonstrated that a broad base of people in the targeted community wanted to be organized by the IAF. Before he assigned an on-the-ground organizer to a city, Alinsky would develop a sponsor committee there, through occasional visits to that city. In effect, he performed a huge piece of the organizing work in advance. His process, at its best, created a momentum analogous to that created by a social movement: the assigned organizer, upon his arrival, was swimming with the tide, not against it.

But by 1968, Alinsky was a national celebrity. He was no longer putting together local sponsor committees. He knew it was no longer tenable for a white to play a lead role organizing in black and Latino communities. Further, he had two major new interests: the white "have-a-little-want-more" working/lower middle class, and the mostly white middle-to-upper middle class. He was worried that the former were falling into the hands of a newly emerging racist right wing. The national elections of 1964 (racist Alabama governor George Wallace made big inroads in white ethnic blue-collar precincts in his Democratic primary race), the 1966 congressional elections, and the "Southern strategy" of Richard Nixon's 1968 presidential campaign all demonstrated that "white backlash" was real.

The middle-to-upper middle class, Alinsky was convinced, was in deep trouble, with its members leading, as he put it (quoting from Thoreau), "lives of quiet desperation." His response was "Proxies for People." The idea had been tested in Rochester,

New York, when church proxies were gathered to give FIGHT (Freedom, Integration [later Integrity], Goals, Honor, Today) access to the Kodak annual meeting. The proxies provided Alinsky with the leverage to say to Kodak that if an agreement was not reached they would find themselves in front of Senator Robert Kennedy's anti-trust committee. The idea was far enough along in his mind that he'd asked a young Hillary Rodham (later Clinton) if she would be interested in heading it up. (She preferred being an inside player rather than an outside agitator, but that's another story.) His scenario went something like this: congregations, denominational bodies, and religious pension funds would be the core of a national organization. Others, both individuals and organizations, could join. Carrying the proxies for tens of millions of people, large delegations would descend on corporations' annual meetings with various demands for reform. They would, of course, be voted down by a few wealthy individuals and the representatives of vast financial institutions. What could more graphically demonstrate the contradictions between vast personal wealth and corporate power, on the one hand, and the democratic promise, on the other? Organizations and public authorities could be approached with resolutions to divest from evildoing corporations and financial institutions. Politicians could be asked whether they were on the side of the people or the money.

Alinsky was enjoying himself. Traveling around the country, hosted by religious bodies, major civic organizations, seminaries, and universities, he was the nation's radical agitator. He was no longer interested in the nuts and bolts of either specific organizing projects or putting together an organizer training program.

Chambers, Harmon, and Alinsky knew that the Institute could not simply be focused on African American and Latino communities, both because of the rising nationalism in them and because IAF staff understood that a broader base for significant change was both possible and required. They thought the emerging environmental movement might provide the organizing context if the focus was on air pollution, which affected minority and white-ethnic/blue-collar neighborhoods even more than the population as a whole because polluters were most often located adjacent to those neighborhoods. It was also an issue of deep concern in the middle-to-upper middle class.

The IAF Institute's fieldwork placement challenge was met in an intriguing way. There was not the careful, typically multiyear buildup of a sponsor committee. Alinsky asked a friendly reporter to do an article in one of the Chicago dailies that asked Chicagoans if they wanted to do something about the environment and, if they did, to tell Saul Alinsky; his address was provided. There was an outpouring of mail in response. The story touched a raw nerve.

Thus was born the Campaign Against Pollution (later Citizens Action Program, or CAP) as a single, metrowide, Chicago-area effort, rather than a separate neighborhoods effort. A metropolitan base was required to encompass the different socio-economic groups the IAF now saw as the required constituency for major change in the country. The conclusion was also drawn that it would be more effective to do this within one organization than trying to bring together separate, more locally based organizations. There was now motion in the middle class—both on environmental and peace issues. Blue-collar anger was abundant, though it was moving in racist and conservative directions—a challenge Alinsky wanted to undertake. Minorities needed allies. A wider base would be able to financially support a larger organization, and a wider base was required to place the number of interns who were likely to be in the growing Institute classes. The pieces all seemed right.

Institute students were sent into the metro Chicago area. They might have been asked to work on a CAP campaign, or to develop a new neighborhood organization that would become an affiliate of CAP, or to work with an already existing neighborhood organization that had grown out of earlier Alinsky or Alinsky-related work, or to do something else. Dramatic campaigns were waged and won. The action was continuous, exciting, and demanding.

Tom Sinclair was part of the first class. Here's how he recalls the early Institute assignments:

> We started with a seminar, individual consultation, and fieldwork observation. For fieldwork observation, we immersed ourselves in a Chicago neighborhood and made written and oral reports on what we were learning. I was assigned to a part of Division Street that was in transition to becoming Puerto Rican. I spent three weeks there interviewing people, doing other research, and making observations.
>
> After this initial period, we were either placed in existing organizations, or were involved in creating them. I ended up in the greater Evanston, Illinois, area, just north of Chicago, working with an upper-middle-class, mostly white organization that was attacking air pollution.[1]

Soon it was clear that CAP could not provide sufficient placement opportunities. But there weren't sponsor committees anyplace nearby, nor were there reporters who would front for an Alinsky organizing operation. On the other hand, there was still a sense of motion for change in the country. It was this motion that the Institute's trainees sought to capture, and for which they were to provide direction. And so each class was dispatched: to next-door DuPage County (middle- and upper-middle-class white), to nearby metropolitan Gary (black and blue-collar ethnic), to Milwaukee, to Indianapolis, to the Twin Cities of Minneapolis and St. Paul, and more. And Ernesto Cortes, after a stint in a fieldwork placement in East Chicago, Illinois, returned to his home state of Texas and developed Communities Organized for Progress and Service (COPS).

The simple assignment of organizers to places without the broad-based invitation that Alinsky had earlier insisted upon, combined with the much larger demographic that was targeted for organizing, meant a different kind of organization was being built. It lacked the initial imprimatur of a sponsor committee. It was also more immediately open to challenge by rivals if it didn't prove its breadth of support fairly quickly.

Ed Chambers as a Supervisor

I met Chambers in Rochester in 1966, when he was both directing FIGHT and supervising the IAF's other current organizing projects—Buffalo's BUILD, then directed by Harmon, and Kansas City's Council for United Action (CUA), then directed by Squire Lance, a former lead organizer of The Woodlawn Organization who was in the process of retiring from the field a year and a half before completion of the CUA contract. Chambers picked me up at the Rochester airport on a cold, blustery night and dropped me off at my hotel. "See you in the morning," he said as we parted. That was the beginning of my briefing on Kansas City, which Alinsky had told me was to be my school.

The Ed Chambers I knew was a gruff, cigar-chomping, alcohol-consuming man who was over six feet tall and whose tough talk was interspersed with expletives—vastly different from me. (Luckily, as I describe at the start of Chapter 15, I met Harmon the following week.) In the days that followed, Chambers would dart in and out of my hotel room between his FIGHT and other responsibilities to fill me with information (e.g., mini-lectures and things to read), ply me with questions to audit my understanding of organizing and see how I thought, challenge my thinking when he thought it was required, and share with me his understanding of how organizing ought to be conducted. After two weeks, my brain about to explode, I left Rochester to meet Alinsky at the Newark, New Jersey, airport, where we would both depart for Kansas City and he would introduce me to the CUA leadership. Chambers soon wrapped up his work in Rochester, passed the torch on to a young African American organizer he'd trained there, and moved to Chicago to be full-time supervisor of IAF's projects.

In the year and a half that followed, Chambers was my Kansas City supervisor. From him, I learned an immense amount about putting together a mass organization, ranging from the nuts and bolts of putting together an annual convention (if you did this you knew how the national Democratic and Republican conventions worked in a way that nothing else could teach), to conducting an effective campaign for jobs, to the intricacies of black church politics (CUA president Rev. O. D. Carson once told me, "When the white man divided up power in the country, he gave the black man the church"), to negotiating with public and private power structure people, and everything in between. From my conversations with early Institute participants, he was the same way with them.

Changing Times

In this early Institute period, major campaigns were undertaken. There were often big victories on issues, including a major one that halted Chicago mayor Daley's Crosstown Freeway. Hundreds if not thousands of leaders were identified and trained. Barriers were, at least temporarily, broken down between constituencies that heretofore had been indifferent if not hostile to one another. Catholic and Protestant church leaders—both local pastors and denominational staff and executives—were excited about putting the gospel into action. In some cases there was an institutional payback to churches as well, in the form of more members, more leaders, more income, diminished internal conflict, a deeper connection between faith and life, a pastor learning how to be an effective leader, and more.

But not everything was going well. Some projects were volatile in character: up one week, down the next. Turnover and burnout were high. Money was a continuing problem. While there were victories, it was not clear that serious, continuing power was being built. In this environment, some of the IAF's former students—now project directors—and the veterans Chambers and Harmon began looking at other directions.

Chambers became an institution-builder, something Alinsky had avoided. He gathered a talented group of organizers in the IAF, created the space in which they could build organizations that expressed their own particular creativity in the work, and guided the development of a continuing relationship between local projects and the IAF, and organizers and the IAF.

During this period, IAF organizers were critically looking at their work and thinking about the broader forces at work where they were doing it. Such ongoing evaluation was a continuing process in the organization. They drew some important conclusions.

The first had to do with the erosion of voluntary associations: population mobility, poverty program and foundation funding, women entering the workforce, consumerism in the society as a whole and the privatization of life that accompanied it, and other broad social changes had weakened the autonomous civil society structures that had been the base of older IAF organizations.

The second had to do with what was going on within the congregations that had always been the core constituency of IAF groups: their inner life was weakening. They were not immune to what was going on around them; pastors and core leaders were stretched thinner and thinner; membership was declining; families and individuals were feeling more and more isolated and powerless; and thoughtful religious leaders were deeply concerned about the gap between professed values and the daily practices and thoughts of members, either in their understanding of biblical text or of their tradition's own teachings.

The third had to do with their relationships with one another and with the organizations they were building. Alinsky's old formula for IAF involvement with a project had been three years and out. In some projects, that length of time had been extended, but the extension was seen as a sign of inadequacy. The organizers who were trained to carry out these efforts had little vision beyond the institutionalization of their own project—which meant that they were likely to become absorbed in the administration of programs rather than taking action on the cutting edge of social change.

What emerged from all this?

First, religious congregations became the sole constituent organizations (there were a few exceptions) of IAF projects. Second, IAF organizers mastered the organization development skills of congregational renewal (revitalizing the life of a church), with the added ingredient that action for justice was central to such renewal. In doing this, they based organizing on a conversation about values that made deep connections between the struggles facing typical church members with the larger economic, political, social, and cultural forces at work in the world. Further, they deeply engaged what came to be called "core teams"—bodies of lay leaders—to reach out and listen deeply to what the church's members were thinking and feeling. A specific and elaborate process was designed to do this. Issues came out of that process. Observing the results, Danny Collum called it "reweaving the fabric of community."[2]

To pick up on what the IAF became, I have drawn from interviews Aaron Schutz and I had with three Institute graduates and an important early staff member: Arnie Graf, who spent his life as an organizer and was until recently a codirector of the IAF; Gregory Pierce, who did excellent work that he wrote about in *Activism That Makes Sense* (1997); Tom Sinclair, who left organizing after a stint with IAF and became a lawyer (and chair of my board at ORGANIZE Training Center); and IAF veteran Dick Harmon.[3]

IAF through the Eyes of Graf, Pierce, and Harmon

Graf's relationship with Alinsky started with fighting words:

> I first encountered Alinsky in an Institute seminar. We had a big argument, and Alinsky threw me out of the class. He had been speaking in glowing terms of John L. Lewis. I had read about the United Mine Workers Union, and its general corruption, and was around at the time when Jack Yablonsky—a reform candidate for president of the union—was killed along with his wife and one of his kids by the Lewis old guard who controlled the union. One of his daughters was in the Graduate School of Social Work at West Virginia University where I was a graduate student at the time. The murders deeply shocked people at the school; the later conviction of union president Tony Boyle clearly confirmed the union's corruption. So I argued with Alinsky about Lewis, granting that he'd been a great organizer at one time and was responsible for the CIO, but also wanting to be clear that the union had become corrupt after his death.

Harmon, Graf's mentor at the Institute, told him, "Go back tomorrow; Saul will have forgotten the argument." The next day, there was indeed no problem. A little later, Graf had a three-hour lunch with Alinsky, who came from an apolitical Jewish family. "Saul was upset that there were few Jews in my class of twenty-five or so students— only three or four."

Pierce showed up at the IAF for what he thought was going to be an individual interview. Instead, there were about ten other people there. He describes this first encounter with Chambers:

> We were all sitting there waiting for Chambers. None of us know each other; we've all been given the same meeting time. Chambers blusters in and he sits down and he turns to the first person on his right, "Why do you want to be an organizer," and whoever it was gave some answer and he says, "Get the hell out of here." Next guy [or one of a few women, same question], Chambers says, "Come back in five years." And at the end of the meeting I'm the only one sitting there. To this day, can't remember what I answered. But he says, "Show up January 2; quit that fucking scholarship you have at the University of Wisconsin, and come down here and I'll pay you $100 a week and teach you how to organize." So that's what I did.

Pierce spent some time in Minneapolis, then went to Queens where he built the Queens Community Organization (QCO). Harmon remembers the climate of the time:

> When the IAF Training Institute started, in late '68 in Chicago, we didn't know, of course, what we were doing. Ed Chambers and I spent several weeks crafting teachable units and getting the word out through church and campus networks. Before long, we had more trainees than we could handle.
>
> But we needed "sites" and situations for them to develop experience, and Cardinal Cody was in town. He was tight with the mayor and the Democratic machine, and he was disciplining and exiling "independently minded" priests. So the pastors were in bunker mentality; for the first time since 1940, almost all Chicago Catholic parishes were closed off to organizing. We had no significant institutional base.
>
> The Citizens Action Program (CAP) sprang out of our response to a weeks-long air inversion over Chicago in early 1970. Families in neighborhoods all across Chicago, across all its ethnic boundaries, were choking from trapped air filthy with high-sulfur coal burned by Chicago's utility, Commonwealth Edison.
>
> Trainees from the Institute simply spread out into neighborhoods, invited people into leadership teams; they called rallies and quickly built up into a major cross-ethnic, cross-religious, and desperately angry movement. It was easy because the common interest was so deep, immediate—and there was a clear target—ComEd.
>
> ComEd's top people refused to meet with CAP leaders. So we took up the stock proxy tactic and ran a huge action at ComEd's annual meeting on the first Earth Day, in April 1970. ComEd's CEO agreed to meet, and two weeks later the company announced a deal to buy low-sulfur coal.
>
> Meanwhile, in the national midterm campaign. Agnew was out on the trail, playing up racial division, dismissing environmental problems, driving every wedge in sight.

CAP was proving that on-the-ground reality was very different—people were tense, but still able to cross ethnic lines if the common interests were real and immediate.

After Edison, CAP went on to a short, hilarious campaign against the Cook County sewage disposal operation; and then took on the biggest project on the machine's plate—the Crosstown Expressway. Chicago media loved it, and for a while, CAP was a household word in Chicago.

But the weak part of CAP was that it wasn't self-funding; it became dependent on door-to-door canvassing, mostly in well-off suburbs, for its income. CAP had terrific leadership in Mary Lou Wolf, Len Dubi, and others. But organizationally it was a movement, not an organization, even though the top leadership was deeply committed. Because of the cardinal and his deals, there was no long-term, institutional base.

We had worries about the canvassing from the beginning, but saw no other way to fund it. CAP finally imploded; the canvassing tail was wagging the organizing dog. Chambers had little to do with the CAP work; Peter Martinez and I worked directly with the leaders. Chambers kept asking, "Where's the money going to come from?" We responded, "What else are we going to do with the trainees?" The difficulty that exposed itself is similar to what happened over the last several years, when many Catholic dioceses withdrew from organizing (except for immigration) to tend to the pedophilia tragedy. Without an institutional base, you become dependent on outside money for the bulk of the organizing budget. That's the kiss of death.

In my own memory, there is another version: the IAF and CAP fought over who was to control the canvass. There was another major internal fight between CAP and the IAF over electoral politics. Some of its leadership—particularly Paul Booth, who came from a student movement/New Left background—were much more interested in continuing electoral engagement than the core IAF people were. Harmon says, "From a development point of view, some very good long-time organizers came out of CAP and its allies—for example, Frank Pierson and Steve Pulkinnen. But as a long term effort, CAP couldn't be sustained."

Graf got a ten-week fieldwork placement in CAP, where he was assigned to neighborhood associations in white working and middle-class neighborhoods. He recalls that

CAP assigned me to work organizing working-class, predominantly white, and black students—some were kids, others were older students—on community college campuses. There had recently been no tuition at the community college; now it had tuition and was seeking to raise it. When the IAFers did research on the issue, they discovered that bankers who were on the community college board had a financial profit angle related to the tuition hike.

In this period, the Institute was still figuring out what it was. After the ten-day seminar, the pattern for those who remained was to get a fieldwork placement; write detailed reports on what we were doing in it, our understanding of it, and our feelings about it; and meet twice a week with a mentor to review what we'd written, and what we were going to do next.

At this time, the IAF had no payroll beyond the core Institute staff, and they were looking for fieldwork placements for the Institute graduates. It was a seat-of-the-pants operation, inventing tomorrow today. Beside CAP, there were high-maintenance projects in a number of places surrounding Chicago.

Then in 1972, Alinsky suddenly died. Only months before, in his well-known *Playboy Magazine* interview, he had told the reporter he thought he had another ten productive years ahead of him.[4] Graf says, "For a few weeks, there was a lot of turmoil." Chambers and Harmon both told Graf that Ralph Helstein—a former president of the packinghouse workers union, an old friend of Alinsky's, and a member of the board—had moved himself into the position of IAF executive director. Chambers and Harmon went to the board and said they would quit if Helstein continued as the IAF's chief. The board hired Chambers.

Graf describes what happened next:

> Ed built on what Saul was doing, and elaborated it in new directions. When I went in '71, there was a huge concentration on power and self-interest. [This] earlier notion of self-interest focused on what people want, not on meaning, a person's passion, or recognition. Self-interest was conceived around issue and task. For example, Alinsky thought the way to clergy's self-interest was to think of them as landlords: "They've got a big building they're responsible for," he'd say. "They want to fill it with people so they can pay the bills." There was truth in that, and it opened up a new way of thinking about churches. On the other hand, that omitted another dimension of self-interest—what called someone to become a clergyperson in the first place— and that was a major omission. Harmon wrote about this stuff, but it didn't find its way into the training at first. The training evolved to encompass this, and other material after Saul died.

The training developed more depth over time. Sessions were added on culture; on the distinction between public and private life—aimed at getting people to see clearly that politicians weren't their friends, and that advertising that appealed to their personhood was simply interested in selling products; on strategic planning; and on congregational development. Graf speaks about the expansion:

> A good part of the curricula is post-Saul. "Story" became a much bigger thing— getting people to see change in the world as part of their own autobiographies. Perhaps an elder in the family had participated in some kind of social change

effort; in a nation of immigrants, almost everyone's family had moved to escape poverty or oppression in another country. Or for Native Americans and African Americans there might be family stories of a different aspect of struggle; women might remember an experience where they stood up to sexism. From 1978 to 1985 or 1986 the Cabinet [IAF senior organizers] would get together periodically for a two-day retreat and work on curriculum. People came in with different ideas—how to expand, deepen, change the training. They would read things, discuss them, draw new ideas out that would then be translated into material in the ten-day. It was a deep period of collective development. We role-played new curriculum in front of one another. We were shaping ourselves as a collective.

San Antonio's Mexican American COPS—soon to be the IAF's flagship organization—was an emerging success in the mid- to late 1970s. "We were trying to go beyond a narrow, limited understanding of self-interest," Graf notes.

Graf's first experiences with Chambers were often shouting sessions, with Chambers doing the shouting. "He'd threaten and yell at me; he thought of it as agitation—to make people think, argue. Instead, it simply intimidated some people. Then I met with Harmon, who was totally different in his dealing with the students; Harmon was my mentor."

Graf was subsequently assigned to Milwaukee, where efforts were underway to build three different organizations. He built one of them. As Milwaukee unfolded, there was a great deal of controversy about it. Graf was in conflict with the lead organizer of one of the other two neighborhoods:

> Chambers, Harmon, and Peter Martinez, who had become another IAFer participating in the Institute conversation about Milwaukee, unilaterally decided that the way to "fix" Milwaukee was to merge the three organizations into a single citywide group. This was the occasion of a sharp argument between Chambers and me. While I agreed with the substance of the decision, I was also unwilling to simply manipulate it through the leadership body or announce it as a dictate from on high. I wanted the leaders of the organization to discuss it, and make their own decision.

Merging neighborhood-based organizations into single larger organizations was a policy that IAF had started to pursue with all the groups it was working with at the time. IAF also was beginning to think of itself as a network. Chambers wanted the Milwaukee projects to pay the IAF $5,000 a year. Graf supported the idea in principle, but wanted a year to implement it:

> Chambers and I argued about this as well. I said I'd take the idea to our leadership. Chambers just wanted me to make it happen, however I was going to do it. But there were incorrectly stated available funds as part of the proposed merger. No one

was stealing money, but there was a mistake; they were counting on proposals that didn't get funded. This put the proposed merger in a serious bind. I "mobilized" [*note that Graf says "mobilized," not "organized"—a distinction we elaborate elsewhere in this book*] a successful convention, but left after that because of this disagreement over money.

Now on his own in Wisconsin, Graf tried to build a statewide sponsor committee. There was a six-month hiatus from IAF, but the prospect of a national network was too inviting. Graf reconnected with IAF:

> Fr. Pat Flood, Ed, and I had dinner at Ed's Chicago home; he apologized for Milwaukee, and asked me to return to IAF.[5]
>
> Despite the initial ups and downs in my personal relationship with Ed, I have deep respect and regard for him. On a personal level, when I was fighting cancer with the prospect that I might die, Ed visited me after I came home from the hospital and told me that IAF would make sure that my children were able to go to college. It was a big burden off my shoulders, and there was nothing anyone could have said that would have been more supportive.

Graf's Chambers is very loyal to people; it's a side of him not often seen. Graf considers Chambers the least recognized, and one of the most important, of the major post-Alinsky organizers:

> He fought for the Institute, and said Saul wasn't interested in it. He was the principal architect of the Institute curriculum that defined most community organizing thereafter. Key people who later played important roles in Gamaliel, PICO [Pacific Institute for Community Organization], and DART [Direct Action and Research Training Center] all were schooled in the IAF ten-day workshop.[6] Ed was responsible for 60 percent of that curriculum.
>
> He also was responsible for professionalizing organizing—raising pay so that one could remain in the work and raise a family; establishing health care and retirement funds; developing a career ladder in the field, so one could move from trainee/intern to organizer to lead organizer to regional organizer—who supervised a number of local projects. By letting people remain in a region, it was possible for an organizer to have some family stability because he would be able to keep a home base and supervise projects in the region. Ed ended Alinsky's rule that IAF organizers had to be available to go wherever he needed them, and that they couldn't be in a project for more than three years.
>
> Ed was deeply committed to significant funding coming from the people—first from a sponsor committee that brought an organizing project into being, then from dues of member organizations and events that they put on; he taught the basics of organizing and ownership by leaders.

Ed did more than supervise organizers; he agitated them—and [this is] different. He was a provoker par excellence! He got the Cabinet members to stretch themselves, to think of themselves as mentors to other younger organizers so IAF could expand beyond what could be done by a relatively small group of "have gun, will travel" organizers. This was a major contribution because Alinsky had never been able to make IAF grow beyond the initial organizers he directly hired and related to himself.

At the same time, he gave organizers lots of room for their own creativity; he sought good people, then let them loose and trusted them to take leadership in their respective areas of responsibility. This was made possible by the decentralization of IAF into regions, with regional directors who supervised projects in their respective areas. Ed formed the IAF Cabinet, which was made up of regional directors. The Cabinet was a collective leadership, rather than leadership by an executive director.

Graf's Chambers was great to work for: "He was constantly throwing out new ideas; he agitated you to always be thinking about your work; he mellowed with the years as well. He institutionalized organizing. As a tactician, strategist, and trainer, he was excellent."

Graf also notes some weaknesses, however:

Ed didn't see IAF as more than building more and more local organizations. As new organizations developed, new organizers came into IAF through the local organizations. We could have been more—a convener of something that led to regional or national issue campaigns that had a real base in local communities. There wasn't thinking beyond our ten-day and sending people we thought could become good organizers to fieldwork placements. The whole could have been larger than the sum of its parts. We weren't thinking of a national presence. The argument against was that "it is premature." Ed thought of the United States as several countries, with regional economies. It was too big for us to pull something together. He always said, "We aren't big enough yet," and "It's too big a country to affect the Congress." There were always reasons for not doing what might have been done. Ed simply didn't believe in moving into a national presence. And there were valid arguments he could bring up to support that point of view: whether we were big enough; had enough money; had sufficiently broad presence in the country. I thought I had answers to these objections, but those who were arguing for a national presence didn't think they [received] serious consideration. We thought IAF could get past those things.

As he got older, he became engaged in getting back to Chicago. For five to seven years, he was lead organizer for Chicago—putting together a sponsor committee and building the on-the-ground organization; he was much more engaged in that than thinking about IAF as a whole. He was much happier doing that. We ended up with another lead organizer, not an executive director. The down side was no leadership at the top. We were without national leadership; everyone was doing his own thing; soon we were getting together less often.

Ed's personality both connected with people when he was in good agitational form, but slipped into intimidating people when he wasn't. People would remember him from the ten-day much more than me—both positively and negatively. But they often remembered irritation, not agitation; he bruised people in ways he didn't even intend. He thought he was being provocative in a positive way. When he was irritating, he did that par excellence as well. Maybe it was lack of patience; he was not a patient person. That flashes into anger, and the person has no idea why. That was not a positive. People came away with hurt feelings. But it was a great positive when he was on; he provoked people to think in a great way.

The idea that you had to have a shoot-out with people to agitate them was later challenged. There was a reevaluation of the shoot-out style as unhealthy. We abandoned it. No yelling anymore. Now you work with people; draw them out; Ed saw the merit of this and adopted it, mellowed into it. But he could still revert to old impatience, yelling, and intimidation; his short temper would come out.

The women's movement made a contribution to this reevaluation. We were way off base in how we regarded women. That was part of the machismo culture that characterized organizing in those days. Ed and everyone in the field was in that mode at the time—in the civil rights movement as well as in community organizing. We also reexamined the way we talked; can't use vulgarity the way we used to. Now 50-plus percent of our organizers are women. Those of us who were of a younger generation were marrying professional women who had mastered their own fields, were active in the world, strong, independent. That personal experience was key to our viewing women in a different way. Another thing that changed for Ed was that he married a very talented and independent artist who was the ABC network artist for courtroom scenes, when you couldn't take photos, and he had children. All that shaped a different view of women and the importance of family and private time.

Harmon looks back through a similar lens:

During the mid-to-late 1970s, the best trainees spread out across the country to help build local broad-based organizations; but in this period we also lost a number of talented people. We were all absorbing the cultural, political, and growing economic crisis, which was mirrored in a psychological and spiritual crisis for individual organizers and leaders. Some of us, including myself, lost our moorings. We were besieged by the mass media in ways that got you hooked on the confusion. The mediating institutions were losing their moorings as well. The world we had known, it seemed, was beginning to spin out of control.

I left IAF in '77, took two years out, built Brooklyn Ecumenical Cooperatives [BEC], and came back to IAF in '94. In the IAF network in the late '70s
Chambers responded to the crisis. He expanded the key team. He got Arnie Graf
back into the work; convinced Ernie Cortes to get back to the fundamentals;
Mike Gecan emerged through his great work on Chicago's Northwest Side.
Together they crafted a different way to help organizers develop. In the early
years [the 1960s], we did "cowboy organizing"—send someone out for two years
and see if they made it. We went through a lot of people unnecessarily; there was
no intentional mentoring. It was unnecessarily romantic—an unrealistic view
of how to develop organizers. In the late '70s, we finally matured, and recognized the importance of intentional mentoring in both organizer and leadership
development.

In the '60s work that Ed and I came through, the intentional, relational aspect
of organizing wasn't explicit. In the early '70s, Chambers kept pounding the table,
insisting that issue-organizing did not build a base for the long term. Only relationships did that. It's a nuanced thing; it's not either-or. There was always relationality among the key people, but not intentionality about developing people,
cultivating specific skills in organizers or leaders. It was mostly instinct; mostly
seat-of-the-pants.

It may also have been a product of the worldview of the time—a product of the
Cold War. Our operating assumptions were (a) that you didn't ask basic questions
about the economy because that would label you a "pinko," an ideologue, and
worse. If you raised these kinds of questions, the climate of the time would shut
you down, so you had to be pragmatic. Saul had seen some of his lefty friends shut
out—blacklisted, shunned. And (b) we thought that solid organizations would be
enough to get their leaders a seat at the table. Our people would get their piece
because the economy would automatically continue to grow, making government revenues expand as well. We had no ongoing, fundamental analysis of the
economy, no long-term diagnosis. No one was asking about alternatives to all the
companies moving to the South, Latin America, Asia. We didn't have any alternative except, just keep building organizations.

In my view, looking back, you can argue that you should not introduce ideology into organizing. But I have to point out that "ideology" is present in any
organization, regardless of its mission—it's either explicit or implicit. I think our
ideology was borrowed from the domestic political necessities of the Cold War.
We should have been equipped with better tools for analyzing the economy. That
would have given us a better long view. We were riding on the surface, and we
could do that well. But, at least in retrospect, something was missing.

Part of this, and it's going to sound airy, is that the basic idea of industrial
unionism that Saul absorbed from John L. Lewis was pretty instrumental. The way
that Saul offered was hard-nosed, imaginative, utilitarian organizing. When the
industrial model began to shift off its moorings in the late '70s, and people were

asking, "What's going on here?" there was an opening, a shift in the culture. You didn't have to be as narrowly instrumental, didn't have to be so macho.

Options began to emerge. In Brooklyn, from '78 into the early '80s, I absorbed this opening from the feminists, especially Starhawk on power, from Amory Lovins's ideas on alternative energy, from Larry Goodwyn's portraits of the Populists' cooperatives, and from the Mondragon system. Before that, we stuck with the earlier view of organizing and organizers.

The reality on the ground was that Saul did not want to do the tough, day-in-day-out work of developing organizers. He didn't want to teach in small seminars or one-to-one. He loved the big public lectures, packed with students, on the college circuit. He relished the role of irreverent public intellectual, which in our culture even then, before his death in '72, turned him into a celebrity.

When Harmon left the IAF, the voice that might have consistently advocated these ideas also left. At the same time, it wasn't as simple as that. When I was the IAF's organizer in Kansas City, Chambers proposed that we invite Minister Florence to be the principal speaker at our annual convention. During the FIGHT-Kodak battle, he pushed me to get the Kansas City organization to do a support picket line at a local Kodak outlet. When I objected that we couldn't just spring this idea on the local leadership, he told me we'd never build a national movement if we couldn't do this kind of support for other IAF organizations.

We might have a better, if more muddied, understanding of the IAF if we see an organization in flux, with the same person holding different views at different times. Sometimes the difference was a function of a difference in the times. At other times it was a function of mood, of taking an oppositional view just to clarify one's own thinking or to get another person to clarify his view, or of a conscious or unconscious self-justification of something one had already done in practice.

As we dig into these various arguments, the stories told by various organizers, and the writings of scholarly researchers, practitioners, and journalists, it increasingly appears that we are witnessing an example of the story of the fleas on the elephant, with the description of the elephant depending on where the flea was located.

The Transition to Institution-Based Organizing

From CAP's inception until the late 1970s, the IAF was in flux. Initially the organizations were patterned on CAP. Graf shares his memories of the shift:

The emphasis was on issues and campaigns; there was a lot of mobilizing; an effort was made to bring lots of groups into the organizations. It was a period of experimentation, flux, debate, and discussion. IAF sought to involve white working- and middle-class [people] and minorities to build citywide power. But urban neighborhoods were rapidly changing, and cities were losing their clout. There was the massive exodus from the inner cities to the suburbs. And there wasn't that much that an alderman or councilman could deliver because of tightening budgets, with the result that neighborhoods couldn't deliver much either.

The richness of the discussion of this period is reflected in the papers that we published, particularly "Family and Congregation" and "Standing for the Whole," both of which were written by Mike Gecan but reflected the continuing conversation going on among us.[7]

During this period, Ernie Cortes returned to his home in San Antonio, and built COPS. In COPS, he also started going deeper into the church as an institution; he put the essay "Family and Congregation" on the ground, put it in practice. He built a leadership group from among the different groupings within a parish; it was called a "core team." Core team members were trained to do one-on-ones. The core team reached out into the parish, visiting as many members as it could, including both those who were active and those rarely seen. In some cases, it went beyond the parish. More formal "reflections" were developed—integrating biblical faith with action in the world. I went from Wisconsin, where I'd reconnected with IAF, to COPS as lead organizer, and Cortes went to Los Angeles as part of expanding IAF in the southwest.

The Present and Future

In 2013, Graf spoke about the generations of the IAF:

There were weaknesses in the approach that only built upon religious congregations. It leaves out a lot of people. We're now doing public-school parent organizing, basing organizing in local public health centers, working with unions. In Wisconsin and Illinois, we're working with the National Education Association [NEA] affiliates.

Our IAF generation, including Ed and Dick, and the present older organizers like me, took IAF as far as we could. Now there are both an organizational culture and differing appraisals of current political reality that keep IAF from acting nationally. The culture emphasizes internal development. The views of what's possible are pretty far apart. In 1992, we assembled a couple of hundred leaders from all the different organizations in IAF with the thought that some consensus might be reached when we all got together. But the leadership divided along the same lines as the organizers.

We've now reached as far as we can go; it's up to the new generation of organizers coming along. We now bring the lead organizers together to talk among themselves; the Cabinet members are not present. "It's for you to take the future. You can move this in another direction, or keep going the way we now are." In a week or two, twenty of them are meeting in Chicago—people who are now in their early forties, and another group in their thirties. They're really excellent.

I see IAF as three chapters: first, Saul; second, Ed, Dick, and my generation; third, now a new chapter being written by the new organizers—the twenty or so who have taken over directing the organization.

An Appraisal

Ed Chambers was the principal person who, along with Dick Harmon, took Alinsky's small IAF and built it into an institution. He and they guided this institution through a period of tumult in the country—and the newly emerging IAF reflected that tumult. Evaluating the weaknesses of what they were doing, they took a turn toward rooting their work in religious institutions. They built powerful organizations, transformed many religious congregations, developed many leaders, won important victories, and defined the institution-based organizing that was to be adopted and adapted by DART, Gamaliel, PICO, and other organizing groups.

The new approach had its problems as well. Harmon identifies the central ones:

My shorthand version of what has happened since World War II is that the classic local mediating institutions—congregations, school communities, and local unions—have all been assimilated by capitalism. We've let our institutions be seduced. So they've lost much of the core of their mission; lost much of their core values—their founding stories. For example, I'm critical of many Christian denominations because they've given up on both creation and usury—both of which are primary elements of scripture and at least parts of tradition. They went for adjustment, growth, size, big buildings, and uncritical assimilation of immigrants into this grand new nation and its culture.

When the local institutions that are the most important to a democracy get assimilated to that worldview, they no longer ask questions about fundamentals, such as where corporate capital is taking us. Now, our young people view these institutions as obsolete because they are not dealing with the primary realities of their lives, such as debt, meaningful work that can support families, and climate. They just walk away from the institutions of their parents—into the arms of the corporate social media.

In some ways we have to start all over again. I'm of the mind that we need a new generation of mediating institutions to re-create community. It can't be done with the organizational culture and mind-set of existing institutions. In some cases, this means building something new from scratch. In other cases, it's a new congregation, school community, or local union forming out the shell of the old.

That new generation–work is happening in the "emerging church" in mainline and evangelical Protestantism. In the denominations, we need a re-naming, a re-phrasing, of scripture, theology, and organization. Many Protestants, Catholics, and evangelicals are still boxed into the old view.

Labor doesn't know how to admit it has a set of fundamental problems, so it hasn't yet grown the imagination to create practical alternatives. People organizing on the schools side usually don't have a power analysis, so they don't recognize that a comprehensive corporate takeover of our schools is well underway. Common to all three of the mediating institutions is failure to let go of their hierarchical designs in order to grasp radical relationality and new organizational cultures capable of working effectively in a new matrix.

That adds up to a gloomy assessment. For me, the issue is the awakening of millions of people, here and around the planet—an awakening to the inexorable connection between economic inequality and the ecological/climate crisis. Corporate capitalism is One system, a Whole, assaulting both human beings and the rest of our natural world. The question, in my view, is whether our local mediating institutions can transform themselves so they can equip our people for what's coming at us. Can we develop resilience or even survive? In the U.S., especially, our denial that we have a problem is massive. Right now, the odds are basically against us.

What I want to see is organizers and leaders talking about this.

My Appraisal

Saul Alinsky often said, "In your strengths you will find your weaknesses." That was true about the IAF's leaders. They were presumptuous. If something wasn't done by them, it didn't merit recognition (though if there was merit to it, the IAF would adopt it).

One of the IAF's organizers said to me, "I think we're the gold standard." While there's nothing wrong with thinking you're the best, I prefer an attitude that says "we're among the best" so that others can fit in the space without you saying they don't belong there. In the IAF, the result was a certain sectarianism—something like the fights among Christians before ecumenism, or the battles on the political left over the "correct" understanding of Karl Marx and the road to revolution and socialism. The result was an absence of space for people to work together when doing so might have stopped bad things from happening to people, made more good things happen for people, engaged more people in shifting from being passive objects of history to subjects creating their own history, and built the people power necessary to slow, halt, and reverse present trends and move toward the realization of the country's democratic aspirations. I say more about this in my conclusion to this book.

Notes

1. Tom Sinclair, interview by Mike Miller, February 19, 2013.
2. Danny Duncan Collum, "Reweaving the Fabric: The Democratic Hope of Church-Based Community Organizations," *Other Side* 32, no. 5 (1996): 12–18.

3. Arnie Graf, interview by Mike Miller, February 16, 2013; Gregory Pierce, interview by Aaron Schutz, January 20, 2013; Sinclair, interview; and Dick Harmon, interview by Mike Miller, January 5, 2013. Where not otherwise indicated, all subsequent quotes from these men within this chapter are from these interviews.

4. Saul Alinsky, interview by Eric Norden, *Playboy* 19, no. 3 (1972); republished as "Empowering People, Not Elites: Interview with Saul Alinsky," *Progress Report*, October 23, 2003–September 4, 2004, *www.progress.org*.

5. Fr. Flood had been active in Milwaukee at the time of the dues argument.

6. As noted elsewhere in this volume, however, there are also a significant number of organizers who were in effect trained by Tom Gaudette, especially those involved with PICO.

7. These documents are included in this book as Chapters 18 and 21.

18

Organizing for Family and Congregation (1978)

■

INDUSTRIAL AREAS FOUNDATION

Editors' preface: This was a seminal paper in the development of community organizing in the United States. It expresses the thinking that was the underpinning of the IAF's shift to "institution-based" (or "values-based" or "faith-based") organizing. The paper begins by noting that "the ideas that follow reflect the collective experience of hundreds of lay leaders, clergy, women religious, and professional organizers in twenty cities across the country."

[T]he Industrial Areas Foundation is] developing a possible strategy for families and churches in the war over values. Our country is in the kind of crisis that both Madison and De Tocqueville warned us about. The intermediate voluntary institutions—including churches—are ineffectual in a power relationship with the powerful. As a result, the middle is collapsing, confused. The economic and political middle of this country is being sucked dry by a vacuum—a vacuum of power and values. Into that vacuum have moved the huge corporations, mass media and "benevolent" government. Those institutions in large part created the vacuum because the churches and unions were not prepared for the new institutional arrangements and technologies that have overwhelmed us since World War II. So we have given over control of much of our lives (including many tasks formerly exercised by families) to "experts" and "specialists," who are in fact only fronts for institutions of greed and unaccountable power. Without effective institutional power of their own, the families and churches withdraw, backbite, blame each other, or perhaps experiment with fads—ignoring their history and strength. If families and churches which are clear about their Judeo-Christian value base do not develop the capacity to negotiate institutionally, the masses of American families will continue to feel a decreasing sense of integration, centeredness and confidence in their own relationship to other institutions. Families and churches, as instruments of nurture, clarity and protection for their members, will continue to lose their capacity to be effective. . . .

This document was originally self-published in Huntington, New York. It is reprinted by permission of Michael Gecan for the Industrial Areas Foundation.

[In a section titled "Background and Context," the IAF staff critically distinguished itself from three other approaches it considered ultimately inadequate to solving social problems: (1) the civil rights, anti-war, and women's movements; (2) "the small civic organization," which was too small and parochial to address the larger issues, and (3) the one-man "insider" who curries favors from downtown. According to the IAF writers, the movements "were vivid and dramatic. Each was built on an issue. Each was led by charismatic leaders. Each sought instant redress of grievances. Peace Now. Freedom Now. The tone was loose and rhetorical. Anyone could, and sometimes did, jump into the demonstration or march. . . . The glue of the movement was the issue, the commitment to the issue, the commitment to the cause." They shared central weaknesses, however. For example, "when the cause collapsed, when the war ended, the movement collapsed with it." Overall, they struggled with "a lack of collective leadership, reliance on charismatic leaders, lack of a solid dues base, tendency toward unaccountable action, and the alienation of moderates and conservatives."]

Analysis

[This section begins by identifying "pressures on churches and families," and asks, "Who are the casualties in this values war?" It gives examples of the pressures and how they impact families and congregations.]

. . . The spinal cord institution of our society is the family. The family can be viewed as an organizationally small network of people, with a set of values, and with the ability to generate money through labor. The church is a network of families, with an explicit set of values, and with the ability to generate a substantial budget. The fundamental issue for the future is whether these institutions will survive the pressures being brought to bear against them. These pressures are threefold: economic pressures, community pressures, and cultural pressures.

The modern American family has become a money machine. Month after month it must meet the food bills, mortgage or rent, car and other transportation costs, insurance premiums, non-insured health items, clothing costs, taxes, utilities and fuel, school tuition and expenses, recreation, entertainment and travel, . . . contributions to charity and to churches[, and others]. Churches have similar burdens, plus staggering building maintenance costs, denominational assessments, and staff salaries to pay.

A second set of pressures comes from the immediate physical community. Almost every community is beginning to feel the accumulated corrosive effect of alcohol abuse, drug abuse, pornography. In Houston, Los Angeles, Chicago, New York, and scores of other cities and towns, the air still stinks; and that stench wears at the health and morale of the residents. Crime doesn't respect the boundaries between city and suburb, suburb and town, town and country. . . . These conditions, some subtle, some obvious, combine to kill the spirit. Watch frightened children walk down the middle of a street to avoid a group of toughs. Talk to members of a synagogue who are no longer involved in activities because they are afraid to leave their homes at night. Stand outside a door and listen to the long series of locks and latches that must be undone before you can enter a home. Talk to a Presbyterian pastor who has been robbed four times in eighteen months, robbed of more than his money, robbed of his vitality, of his spirit. Listen to the landlord who wakes up to find graffiti scrawled across his neat two-flat and freshly painted garage—his voice shaking with frustration and disgust.

The third set of pressures is cultural. Television is a profoundly parochial medium with an almost universal range. The networks transmit the simplistic values of the advertisers—basically money, luxury, and sanitized sex—and the blameless violence of Hollywood, backed by $500 million in annual revenues. Television tells people how to eat, how to look, how to love, how to kill, and how to feel. It throws out powerful images of what it is to be human—images frequently destructive of healthy family values. It devours space in family homes—where a TV room is now common—and it devours time that families could use together.

Another form of cultural pressure is the over-scheduling that occurs in schools, in sports and community activities, and in churches and synagogues. Mothers become strung-out chauffeurs. Men and women who begin by wanting to help out at the church or the park get trapped into more and more work. Their free time is soon completely consumed.

The final form of cultural pressure is work—the expectation that work schedules are more important than family schedules, and the pressures that force those parents to work. In half the families with school-age children, both parents must work to fuel the family money machine, to meet the basic costs of keeping the family alive. Too often, what they work so hard for is undone by their own hard work. The child who leaves a struggling school, who walks down dangerous streets, often arrives at an empty, parentless home, or to parents so strapped by the demands of work, the tensions and frustrations of an environment seemingly out of their control, that they have no energy left for the love and care of their children.

Institutional Power

Having briefly described the pressures on families and churches, how do we begin to analyze the sources of those pressures? Where do the economic and cultural and community pressures originate? If we follow where our dollars go, we will find the institutions that shape our daily lives.

Our dollars end up in banks and savings and loans, in insurance companies, in oil companies, in utilities, and in the hands of major manufacturers, real estate developers, retailers, and organized criminals. These people speak with money. Banks, insurance companies, and organized crime provide capital for the others. They buy the second level, the politicians, lawyers, the advertisers, the media. The media live on revenues from these institutions and rarely take the time to investigate and report the truth about the actual power relationships among these institutions. Unions are seldom prime decision-makers in a metropolitan area. At best, . . . [with exceptions], they are at the edge of major decisions. Lawyers and other professionals provide the rationales and jargon to perpetuate the top power institutions and screen them from the public. These professionals also do a lot of negotiating with the government bu- reaucracies and pass back and forth between government and private jobs, especially at the upper-middle levels. . . . Politicians get money, trips, and advance information from the money institutions. . . .

Most citizens' organizing efforts, lacking an accurate power analysis, try to ne- gotiate only with politicians and government bureaucracies. As a result, their energy is directed at the wrong rooms. They end up in "hearings" where they are heard by hearing officers who are paid to hear but not make decisions. Smart politicians, pro- fessionals, and bureaucrats set up elaborate "advisory" hoops for citizen groups to jump through, effectively exhausting the citizens and taking them out of the arena. Meanwhile, the real decisions are sealed months before in elegant board rooms. . . .

Decisions made by primary power institutions—institutions built upon the money of families and congregations—obviously have a major impact on the congregations and their families. If banks, insurance companies, and developers decide to build up a huge suburban area, church planners have to play catch-up ball with demographic trends. Or, if the financial institutions decide to redline city areas, those same church planners and established congregations go through the agony of shutting down and merging churches, or subsidizing marginal operations. Or, when a major manufac- turer such as Westinghouse decides to pull out of a community like Buffalo, thou- sands of church families are hurt badly by the sudden loss of jobs. Or, when the economic establishment of San Antonio prevents industry from entering the area to avoid union organization, they destroy the hope for economic and social stability for thousands of Mexican-American families. When retailers pull out of neighborhoods, or buy into suburban shopping centers, family values, habits, and travel patterns are all affected along with the stability and future of the local churches. When organized crime, estimated to have a $26 billion annual take, sells hard drugs in or near a school, or introduces pornography and prostitution to a community, or pulls the money of working people into sports betting and numbers, neighborhoods and churches and families suffer.

The point is not that all executives of all banks and corporations in America are bad men. Rather, the point is that profit is the bottom line value of their institu- tions, and that "the system" is blind to the destruction of churches and families. So long as families and churches exhaust themselves with the middle-men, so long as families and churches struggle with the politicians and the bureaucrats, the align- ment of power will remain the same. The deterioration of family and congregational life will continue. The economic, cultural, and community pressures will increase to an intolerable point. The institutions that cause those pressures, mammoth ma- chines lacking eyes, ears, and sensitivities, will continue, by instinct, to stamp so- ciety in their own images.

Broad-Based Citizens' Organization

Outward Signs

How does a collection of families, a church or synagogue, or an alliance of churches, a citizens' organization, break out of the materialist pattern? How do they arm themselves for a values war? What strategies do they employ? How do they train their leaders and deploy their forces? . . .

[*The paper then describes local efforts in major cities in which the IAF organized and people used their combined institutional and individual purchasing power to leverage agreements with corporate decision-makers.*]

These are some victories, the outward signs of institutionally-based citizens' organizations, organizations which re-arrange the relationship between families and churches on the one hand, and the major money and power institutions on the other. They recognize that power tends to come in two forms: organized people and organized money. But what are the elements of such an organization, and what goes into the process of building one?

Elements of an Organization of Institutions

. . . One of the largest reservoirs of untapped Power is the institution of the parish and congregation. Religious institutions form the center of the organization. They have the people, the values, and the money. Without church people, moderates and conservatives as well as liberals, citizens' organizations tend to be controlled by activists.[1] Without church values, citizens' groups can get sucked into movements or relationships which can actually weaken family life or church life. And without the money, a solid dues base that builds from year to year, organizations spend most of their time raising money. The citizens' organization of this type respects and builds on the traditions and patterns of the community. It is a systematic patterning and sewing, much like a quilt, of the pieces of diversity and differences among people and their institutions.

Money

The initial seed money for a two-year organizing drive is raised from the local churches, regional church bodies, and national denominations. It is a mix of money. As the number of local churches in the organization increases, the organization becomes increasingly self-sufficient. By the end of the second year there should be less national and regional church money, and more and more dues money coming from local member churches and institutions. They must become financially self-determining or go out of existence.

For a two-year organizing effort, the locally controlled sponsoring committee must raise between $160,000 and $250,000. In larger metropolitan areas three years should be secured. This money is used to employ trained and competent organizers and for intensive leadership training both locally and nationally under the supervision of the Industrial Areas Foundation.

Trained, Skilled Organizers

This is where the bulk of that money goes—not to renting a storefront, or to printing fancy brochures, or to hiring a lawyer, but to attracting the full-time efforts of professional men and women who have one crucial skill: the finding and developing of a strong collective leadership. It takes three to five years for a good organizer to develop. And the organizer's tools are not mere instincts picked up on the street. He or she must be systematically trained, just like a surgeon or a top-flight coach. The organizer's job is like a tutor's—to share insights, to teach methods of analysis and to provide tools of research, to challenge citizens to sharpen their public skills, to develop their ability to reflect and to act. The organizer is hired and fired by the local organization.

Collective Leadership

The core of the organization, depending on the size, is 50–200 leaders representing institutions. By leaders, we mean men and women who have a following and who can consistently deliver that following. Most so-called leaders are isolated individuals, either self-appointed, or fronts promoted by politicians, the media, or outside economic interests. Responsible elected leadership maintains its quality and reliability through a disciplined system of mutual accountability. The system is simple: If you can't deliver either people or dollars to the organization, you are not a leader of that organization. If you are not committed to an internal training process in which the central value is to teach primary leaders how to find and in turn teach other leaders, you don't belong. These leaders recognize that leadership is not by nature a form of individual aggrandizement, but rather a means continually to expand the number of their fellow-leaders in the interest of collective power.

Leadership Training

Leadership training focuses on developing lay leaders, but the participation of the church staff and religious education people is absolutely essential. What are the specific skills leaders learn through the training process? There are a number of them: how to make clear to yourself your self-interest; how to be an initiator rather than a reactor; how to listen to and affirm other people; how to distinguish between leaders and followers; how to identify and proposition current and potential leaders; how to run a meeting; how to hold members of your own networks accountable; how to hold other leaders accountable; how to raise money; how to analyze institutions (both your own and those you're up against); how to negotiate with other decision-makers; how to run an action; how to run an evaluation of an action; how to pick issues so that you're not running into the biggest issues at the start; how to plan issue campaigns; how to develop realistic schedules; how to view and accept tension; how to live and grow with a *process* of dealing with issues rather than with the particular issue or task; and how to invite in new institutions and develop allies.

Multi-Issue Program

We start with the family and the local church and ask, What are the institutions pressuring and breaking up the family and church? We are engaged in a war on many fronts: economic, cultural and community. Initially organizers and leaders will select and engage in battles that can be won. This means dealing at first with several small issues. This is partly for the sake of the concrete results of these fights. Most importantly, it is done to expand the pool of experienced leaders, to season people in victory rather than discourage and scatter them in defeat.

Research

Prudent people will not go into action unless they are sure of their facts. The best way to guarantee that new leaders feel secure about the facts is to take them through the research process so that they themselves discover what the facts are and who the decision-makers are. Research focuses on two elements: who makes the decisions, and who gets the money. Out of the on-going research process comes a first-class power analysis. Leaders put together a chart of the institutional power patterns and institutional decision-makers that are affecting the life and work of their families and local churches. As this analysis emerges, as this map gets drawn in greater and greater detail, so collective leadership develops a basis for making strategic decisions about campaigns, about schedules, about allies, and about opponents.

Action

Action has a two-fold significance for a citizens' organization. On the most simple level, the action is the focusing of organizational energy to effect certain results—police attention to neglected drug traffic, favorable insurance rates, building a branch bank in a neighborhood that needs and wants it. More importantly, action fuels the organizing process. Action is to organization what oxygen is to our bodies. Without the action, the process is reduced to a sociology class or navel-gazing. Action is the womb of discovery—discovery of self, of values, of power. In the actions new sides of current leaders emerge. New leaders come to the fore; talkers evaporate. And actions create reactions from opponents which require flexible and factual decision-making by the collective leadership. Action enables the organization to grow, to deal with increasingly complex issues, to win more substantial victories, and thereby again increase its growth.

Reflection

Action for its own sake has no place in a citizens' organization of this type. Only action in the context of reflection is valued here. Highly developed, highly disciplined reflection and evaluation enable the leaders to execute aimed actions over a sustained period of time. On-going evaluation is simply elementary, but is usually overlooked in the heat of the issue. So many battles are lost which need not be. It is important to take the correct amount of time with each fight or skirmish so that the leaders have a chance to evaluate and integrate their experience. Action campaigns can run from 10 days to 9 months, so they must be planned. Leaders and staff have to develop daily and weekly schedules which permit them to plan and to think. Otherwise they will burn out. In addition to obvious organizational benefits, such careful planning and reflection enable leaders to integrate organizational life with family life. The organization will not squander the valuable time of its leaders, time which can be spent with the family.

[*The paper then elaborates "The Organizational Process," which outlines the steps to implement the above. Briefly, these are:*

- *formation of a local sponsor committee;*
- *congregation decisions to join and organize, which involve both dues and the creation of a leadership organizing team of eight to twelve laypeople led by the pastor;*
- *individual ("one-to-one") meetings with laity, with listening being the key element (interested people may later be invited to join the organizing team so that it grows in size);*
- *house meetings (or congregation meetings) to discuss what has been lifted up in the individual meetings;*
- *learning how to research issues;*
- *small "actions" to get answers to questions from "downtown";*
- *sharing of findings, and development of a power analysis that describes how things really work in the city, county, or other unit of analysis;*
- *growth and consolidation into leadership bodies that encompass all the participating congregations/parishes;*
- *identification of actionable issues and taking action;*
- *reflection and evaluation based on what is being done and learned; and*
- *a final formation of the federation at a large meeting (of 3,000–5,000 people) that puts the organization "on the map."*]

Conclusions

We began by talking about families, churches, and institutional power. We've also introduced the broad-based citizens' organization. It is the alliance, the vehicle, the *instrument* that can be used by families and congregations to fight this value war.

What can a citizens' organization do? What can be won by such an instrument? Much can be won in the community, in the parish or synagogue, and in the family.

In the community, a well-organized alliance of churches can win favorable rates from redlining insurance companies; can use organized dollars, millions of dollars, to leverage banks to branch *into* a community; can drive drug dealers off a corner and out of a community; can get abandoned buildings demolished; can pressure advertisers that promote violent television shows; can initiate housing redevelopment and humane commercial planning; can open up the doors of corporate America and government bureaucracy so that citizens can enter the board rooms and meet the men and women who make major decisions, enabling citizens to see that there is no special mystery, no air of sanctity, about those people and those places. The citizens' organization, in the process of winning these victories, serves as a forum for city-dwellers and suburbanites, blacks and Hispanics and whites, transforming words like *ecumenicity* and *racial equality* into flesh and blood realities.

Within the parishes, congregations, and synagogues equally important victories can be won. If the religious men and women and lay people of the community work out a sophisticated analysis of who and what is hurting their institutions, if this research has been done, if some victories have been won, then the mood of the institutions begins to shift, to improve. The church is no longer a helpless victim. The institution, through its leadership, understands its relationships to others and is in a position to act, not just react.

Again, if the process of interviewing is done well, if the pastor and key lay leaders listen closely to the congregation, the team begins to grow. In so many cases people who have been interviewed end the session by saying, "Thanks for dropping by. You're the first person from the church who took the time to listen to me."

When the team begins to research and act on some small local concerns, the cautious moderates, the skeptical conservatives soon see that this is not just a new cover for an old 1960's tune. They begin to see that two institutions, the congregation and the family, are the central concerns of the team. The test of any issue in a congregation is how many members will participate in its resolution. If the issue is close to home, well researched, and approached without hysteria, the center of the congregation will begin to get active.

Additionally, the church begins to see the interviews and issues, the research, action and evaluation, in the context of education. At its best, the organizational process offers a new experience and new methodology for religious education. One example comes out of a Pennsylvania city where several congregations are fighting a conspiracy of crime syndicate figures, city officials and developers to steal highly valuable land for condominium construction. After six months of heavy involvement by laity, clergy and sisters, the principal of the local Catholic high school developed a curriculum for her high school seniors called, "Neighborhoods Just Don't Die." Her ideas call for seniors to go through the same research, action and reflection, under her supervision, as their parents do with the organization. And their parents came into class to help teach.

Organizational activities and victories can also be seen in the light of the congregation or synagogue's tradition. The *present* struggles of a people of faith to preserve and enliven their values can be celebrated in prayer and liturgy.

Finally, families benefit from this organizational process. Skills are acquired, practical and creative skills. The leaders learn to listen consciously and effectively. The leaders understand their own self-interest and the self-interest of others. The leaders look at the community, at the line-up of decision-makers, in new ways. The leader in the context of other leaders must commit himself or herself to a curriculum of growth and accountability more demanding than any school work.

The organization enables family members to participate, not spectate. This helps break through the alienation that comes from doing nothing as a family but buying things. As parents go into action, they can't help but tell their children about it. Many organizations encourage parents to bring their children along on actions so the children can see for themselves. Children witness their parents as much more significant, as heroes or heroines instead of passive victims. They see their parents as more than someone who goes away to work or someone consumed by television. They can become curious about the struggles and stages of their parents' lives and lose their fear of asking. They begin to see their parents as stronger, more real than Kojak or Charlie's Angels.

Dealing directly with opponents instead of through experts or television means that a central value of family life becomes the taking of action and accepting the consequences of those actions. A sense of competence and confidence grows as the person gains small victories. The organization teaches adults how to negotiate effectively, how to win. Those skills, as they are shared among family members, enable parents to clarify and transmit values they hold strongly to their children, not in words, but in actions.

Action cannot be based on hot anger or impulse. It must be planned. This requires cold anger, research, shared reflection. When a family participates in an effective action against an unscrupulous auto repair shop, or a deteriorating school, or an exorbitant supermarket, the family members all discover that it is all right to risk, that it is all right to be straight, to be blunt, to deal from strength, not anxiety. This enables family members, both with each other and with outside people, to go ahead and be honest, to cut through the mores of politeness, reticence, and fear.

The process and skills we have sketched here are not developed in a few weeks or a few months. The birth and growth of a first-rate citizens' organization takes several years. It is nurtured by pastors, organizers, rabbis, lay leaders, women religious. It is subject to severe tests. Will the religious leaders of a community assume initial *ownership* of this organization? Will the lay leaders move in and *lead*? Will the early leaders step aside and open positions for new leaders? Will the organization be a forum for adult education in the survival skills necessary to cope with the late 70's and 80's? Will the central values of dignity, self-determination, and justice be kept in focus by the leaders and members of the organization? Will participation in the organization *change* people, *move* people fundamentally and profoundly? Will the organization have the courage to weather the attacks from without and from within? Will there be the money, the energy, the vision to sustain these groups?

These are difficult rites of passage, difficult tests. Difficult because the development of a first-rate citizens' organization is as complex and critical as the raising of a family, as the growth of a congregation. In isolation, families and congregations have no chance. With the citizens' organization as a context and as an instrument, families and congregations can move with dignity and confidence into the arena of institutional power. Families and congregations can fight for their values. Families and congregations can win.

Notes

1. In organizing parlance, "activists" are people who participate in "actions" but don't organize for long-term power.

19

Relationship and Power
An Interview with Ernesto Cortes Jr. (1993)

■

NOËLLE MCAFEE

ERNESTO CORTES JR.: We are trying to recreate a public square, a public
space, an assembly where ordinary people can participate effectively on
issues that affect them, such as education, employment, health care, and so
forth. By so doing, we can recreate and reclaim for the twenty-first century a
substantive concept of politics. Now, we would like for that not to be just for
people who are affluent, well connected, and have access. We would like to
develop a vehicle whereby ordinary people can so participate. Our purpose is
to create "mini-universities," whereby people learn about politics—politics in
the generic sense—which has to do with discussion and debate and decision
making about issues that affect families, that affect properties, that affect
education.

NOËLLE MCAFEE: Do you think that people have to overcome their self-
interest, become altruistic, for politics to work?

CORTES: No, in fact part of what we are trying to figure out is a different way
of understanding what a self is, because we see a self, or the notion of self-
hood, as defined in relationships. I am who I am because of my relationship
with my wife and my children, my relationship with my family. We are situated concretely in time and space. We are not ahistorical or acultural beings. I
was born Mexican and I was born in San Antonio; that has do with what my
self is. Understanding my interest has to do with understanding also my history, my situation, my relationships with those people who are important to
me. A proper understanding of self-interest—being rooted in the Latin word
interesse, to be among and between—involves that which the self is among
and between, with which the self is involved, that in which the self is invested, which the self is connected to and related to. A proper understanding
of self-interest leads to being your brother's and your sister's keeper, because
then you begin to recognize that those things that are really important—for
me, the kind of environment my children grow up in, the kind of school they

This interview was first published in the *Kettering Review*, Summer 1993, and reprinted by the Civic
Practices Network (*www.cpn.org*). It is reprinted here by permission of Ernesto Cortes and Noëlle
McAfee.

go to, whether or not I can have meaningful work, interesting relationships, good friends, a conversation which is convivial—do not occur in isolation; they require relationships that are meaningful and interesting.

MCAFEE: I am glad you gave that explanation. Now let's start at the beginning—with the state of politics.

CORTES: Well there is something seriously wrong. *We don't do politics anymore.* We do elections; we do electioneering. Every four years, we do what I call a quadrennial electronic plebiscite. It has very little to do with real politics, even though on occasion—and this last one was better than most—you see some discussion of issues. For the most part, the center-pieces of the campaigns are about marketing strategy. Professor Kathleen Hall Jamieson, who is an expert on presidential elections, has said that if you want to know about elections that are going to be proficient and ef-fective, don't study political science. Political science will teach you about Montesquieu and the Founding Fathers, but what you really need to learn about are marketing strategies: direct mail, 30-second spots, nega-tive campaigning, how to do different commercials, how to understand market segments, scripts—all these kinds of things, which really have to do with manipulating people's preferences. Elections have become sub-jective expressions of preference, preference as opposed to judgment. So the focus is on election day—what happens that one particular day, what you're feeling and what your disposition is at that moment.

Now that would be all right if voting was the culmination of a process of judgment whereby people went about the business of debating and discussing and came to some sort of consensus about what they thought, so that the election was a ratification of that consensus. If that was what the politics of our elections were, the ratification of a national consensus-building process, then it would be great. But I don't think that's the case, because of the roles money and image-making play. You really don't have any serious ongoing discourse taking place between potential candidates and organizations of real live people. That's what is fundamentally wrong.

I consider myself a reasonably intelligent person. I try to keep up with stuff and try to read. But my reaction to a particular decision may or may not be competent. In fact, I find that, left to myself I am not real smart. I become more interesting and smarter to the extent that I engage in discussion and debate and get feedback, get reactions, because then I realize that there are things that I have not thought about or considered. People are going to make decisions by themselves, but they don't need to do it in isolation. They can do it in relationship with other people, where there is discourse, conversation, argument, and debate with real listening. And I think it is important also that they have access to information. Now, if we deliberately withhold things from them or worse, bombard them with so much that they can't make any sense out of it, then you render people incompetent. It is not that they are incompetent; but we can all be rendered incompetent by not having access to interpretation, or access to context or a frame of reference in which we make judgments. We can also be rendered less competent by not having access to other people's reactions to whatever happens. It seems to me we place so much focus on "what an individual thinks, left to himself or herself" that we have forgotten that there is a deliberative process that requires a public forum and a public debate—public discourse—in order for people to make an informed judgment. We need to create institutions that will enable people to undergo that kind of process before they make judgments.

MCAFEE: Institutions for the public?

CORTES: Institutions not only for the public, but that are organic, are not artificially created, have come out of families, have come out of churches, congregations, institutions that reflect community. I don't want to suggest a sectarian religion, but the word *religion* does mean literally to bind together, to reconnect. We don't do that very well; we don't make those kinds of connections, unless there is something that transcends our own situation. When we do that secularly, we don't do a very good job. We get into trouble when we try to do it as secular beings, as they found out in Europe: the Nazis tried to do it; and that's what the communists tried to do—to create community outside of a religious context. They tried to develop symbols and civil systems that transcended an individual's experience. But the result was horrible.

MCAFEE: In conventional politics, we tend to look for a few good leaders whom the rest of us can follow. What effect does this idea about leadership have on public life?

CORTES: We need to recognize that leaders come in all shapes and forms. In our organization, we always talk about primary, secondary, and tertiary leaders, understanding that the definition of a leader is someone who has a following and can deliver that following. We presuppose that you can't be a leader unless you have a following. There has to be a relationship. That is not always clear, because we sometimes point to people as leaders when they have no evident following, no constituency behind them. They're our leaders because TV recognizes them, or the newspapers recognize them, or politicians recognize them. What they are saying is, "These are people whom I admire and respect, or I use to advise me, but they have no real following in their particular community." Thus Governor Ann Richards might say, "Well, Ernie Cortes is a great leader and I like him and so I am going to designate him as a leader." But the difficulty with taking me out of the context in which I am now is that I might have absolutely no one following me. So all of a sudden, she may decide, "He wasn't so good after all." Then my leadership is gone. It's only been derived from her thinking. There has to be an organic constituency connection to make leadership possible.

Think about the qualities that we ought to look for in a leader. Number one, leaders have to be relational. Number two, they have to be reciprocal and disposed to being reciprocal. And number three, they have to be interested in conversations, which means listening, arguing, interpreting, and informing their constituents. More importantly, they have to understand politics, and they have to be interested and be involved in developing politics. Beyond that, they ought to have some other qualities: passion, a sense of humor, and what we call anger, which is rooted in a real understanding of relationships and an understanding of injustice. The Gospel says, Jesus saw the widow and he was moved; and the word used suggests he was moved in such a way that his bowels were disrupted; he felt physical discomfort. And it was not just a stomach ache: it was sorrow. He felt the woman's situation not just because she had lost a son, but because she was now vulnerable, because in that tradition if the woman was not in relationship to a male relative, anybody could do anything they wanted to with her. She had no protector; she could be killed; she could be robbed; she could be raped. You could do anything you wanted to her and there would be no one to take any revenge or protect her. She was alone—isolated. That was what moved him: her vulnerability, her wretchedness—because being poor, with no one to be your advocate, to protect you, you were isolated, at the margin.

That notion of identifying with people who are at the margin, who are vulnerable, who have no one else to speak for them, who everyone else dismisses, is a quality the Hebrews thought important, a quality that leaders ought to have.

MCAFEE: Why do you think people yearn for others to lead them? Or do they? Is it that people don't have the energy for politics or do they truly want other people to make decisions for them?

CORTES: That's a very complicated question. I would ask you to read a chapter in *The Brothers Karamazov* called "The Grand Inquisitor," which has a view of leadership that I don't particularly subscribe to, but it is interesting psychology. Christ came back to earth. . . . He was immediately recognized by both the crowd and by the grand inquisitor who has him thrown into jail in the dead of night. The grand inquisitor comes to see him. He asks him, "Why did you come back? We tried it your way. We tried the way of freedom, we tried to give people choices, we tried to provide hope and opportunity for people to challenge them, but it didn't work. They didn't want that; they wanted to be dependent; they wanted to be taken care of; they wanted to be fed. After years of trying it your way, we had to go over to the other guy and we made a deal and we offered people magic, mystery, and authority . . . and we've had to keep this terrible dark secret among the few of us."

That perspective is prevalent for a lot of people and most of our institutions. It is the way our institutions come at people: they teach people to be helpless; they teach people to be dependent. The universities, corporations, even the churches sometimes, teach people dependency; they teach people to be passive. The best workers are those who mind their own business, work in their own particular slots, don't ask too many questions, and don't make any trouble. When you have an organization or institution that teaches that kind of dependency, that kind of learned helplessness, then it's not unreasonable for people to take to a pattern of behavior like that. They're always looking for somebody to tell them what to do. Now, I think there is another way of teaching people. People have the capacity to be initiatory and have the capacity to be self-governing. The people have to have institutions, mentors, and teachers who will teach them confidence in their own competence, so that they learn by doing. I don't think people yearn to be told what to do; I think that's what they have been taught.

MCAFEE: What do you think politics would look like if citizens thought of themselves as leaders?

CORTES: I'm not trying to say that we are all the same: not all of us are leaders. I am not arguing for the kind of system where everybody's opinion is the same as everybody else's. That's what television does for us. We already have that, so to speak, and that kind of system can lead to the worst abuses. Hitler created a mass man; the communists created a mass man. There is no intermediate institution or no intermediate leadership. It's all—you know—we all owe allegiance to the great father or the great leader. I am arguing for a different system. I am arguing for a system where there is structure, where there are intermediate institutions, where there are all kinds of leaders and everybody who wants an opportunity for leadership gets an opportunity to play a role at some level. I'm asking for a restructuring of political attitudes in the same way that corporations—the best ones—are getting to be restructured and beginning to empower people at the bottom to make decisions. I understand that means you must also enable people to have confidence and competence and resources. If you tell people at a plant that they are in charge and responsible for what happens and then you don't give them the resources and the authority to make decisions or influence decisions, you're being cruel. And if you tell people "I'm empowering you" and then you don't recognize that they must be able to fail, that they must make decisions, yet be able to make mistakes, then you're teaching cognitive dissonance. You're like a parent that tells his kids, "I want you to learn; I want you to grow and want you to understand"—but never lets them make a mistake and always smothers them.

MCAFEE: We think of leaders as people with certain kinds of power, charismatic power, financial power, the power of legality, of coercion. What kind of power can citizens have?

CORTES: We have to understand power. Power is the ability to act. It requires two or more people with a plan. So anytime you get two or more people together with a plan, they could have power. Now, the question is, how to teach them to get enough power to do the things they think are important. Ten people by themselves may not be able to do much, until they coalesce with a hundred other people—in other words, until they begin to build coalitions with other people and learn the rules of politics. This means that they are going to have to be reciprocal. When you don't feel you're being ripped off, and I don't feel I'm being ripped off, and there is some way of maintaining or checking our perceptions of what's going on, then we can begin to learn how we can eventually get what is important to us. Not just by grabbing it, but by having the subtlety, the nuance, and the sophistication to be able to bargain first with each other, then with other people. I help you on yours and you help me on mine; I can't do mine by myself—I need the both of us—and that means that I have to be disposed to be in an ongoing relationship. You teach people, ordinary people, that kind of process, that kind of understanding, then they can be effective. We don't teach: "*You* don't have to do anything; all you must do is say what you want and choose *me*—and I'll do the rest. Let me do the rest for you." Then they will come back and tell you they didn't get what they wanted. That is a debilitating, frustrating experience. All it does is teach you periodically to choose someone else who is going to get you something you want: find another Santa Claus, find another maternal uncle who is going to deliver for you.

This proves not helpful in developing people's ability to act on their own behalf. It creates dependency; it corrodes human dignity. We have what we call the Iron Rule: never do for anybody what he should be able to do for himself. Anything that makes people dependent is negative, because we all have the inclination to be selfish. That's part of our nature. But we also have—Niebuhr taught us this—the capacity to be just; we have the capacity to reach out; we have the capacity to be relational and to be connected and to be reciprocal. So the question is: Can we create institutions, can we create leadership that builds on our strength, our capacity to be just and to be relational and all the while recognize our limitations? There is nothing worse than civil innocence, a romantic misunderstanding of what people can do, without proper training, without institutions that cultivate their development.

MCAFEE: I am trying to imagine what these institutions would be like in any given community.

CORTES: Well, here's the kind of institution we are trying to build in Dallas right now: sixty congregations—African-American, Hispanic, Unitarian, Spanish, Jewish, United Methodist, Lutheran, Episcopalian, Roman Catholic, Friends Service Committee, Quaker—fold onto that some labor unions, fold onto that some future organizations, fold onto that some other social organizations we create, and you begin to create a kind of extraparliamentary institution that enables people to mobilize. The institution is committed to teaching people, developing their leadership and their understanding of public policy.

That's what the big city political machines used to be for. They had their limitations—they were corrupt—but they also enabled people to participate effectively, as labor unions also used to do. This is a way of mobilizing our energies and imagination and our curiosity. That's the center of what we are talking about—how you activate and mobilize people's energy, their curiosity, their imagination. *What people can't imagine, they can't do.*

MCAFEE: My family was given an Afghan hound when I was a kid, and the owner said, "This dog can jump your eight-foot fence; but it's okay. Your dog doesn't *know* he can jump this fence."

CORTES: That's right. People can only do what they can imagine they can do. People need also to have in mind that there is a place that they can go to, a forum where they can talk about things that are important. That there's a mechanism for taking those private, personal pains and translating them into some kind of public action. People learn that they have serious problems, and that these problems have to be broken down into issues—which means they can affect other people but can't be resolved in a short period of time. Then they learn to be realistic in their assessments of what can be done, and they don't go off like Don Quixote, fighting windmills. Even though we are trying to stimulate their imagination, we also must recognize their strengths and limitations. That's important.

MCAFEE: Former President Richard Nixon once said, "A leader must be willing to take unpopular stands when they are necessary and when he does find it necessary to take an unpopular stand, he has an obligation to explain it to the people, solicit their support, and win their approval." How would you assess this remark?

CORTES: On the face of it, I would not necessarily quarrel with that; but the problem is that what I think he really means, and wants, is for leaders like himself to get television wizards to help them convince people to support what they are going to do. Such a statement presumes incompetence on the part of the people, and presumes that they don't have anything to say to him, that their job is merely to give their assent or deny their assent. It reduces people to a passive, tepid role. I think that's dangerous, potentially.

We have spent so many years destroying the institutions that had taught people how to participate—labor unions, political machines, political organizations, other volunteer associations. We have spent so much time destroying those—that it is clear to me that there are lots of people who want to participate effectively. It is also clear to me that potentially their participation could lead to some cynicism, if it doesn't happen correctly.

By that I mean, we need to figure out ways to connect people to the kind of institutions that can teach them, guide them, and mentor them. We need to recognize that people have to learn new ways of thinking, new ways of acting. They have to learn how to operate collaboratively with other people—and that is not something they know very well. They've been taught to be individuals; they've been taught to be isolated; they've been taught to be unilateral; they've been taught to be passive.

MCAFEE: Would you say that an IAF organizer is a leader?

CORTES: The role of the organizer is to develop leaders: people who are willing to take positions on these issues in order to become the leaders of networks; to be the spokespersons; to be the decision makers. Now, that's an important point because when people are insecure, they want to make every decision. Where you sit, who goes to the bathroom, you know what I mean. Your best managers know that there are only two or three decisions that really matter in a year and the fewer they make the better. That forces and challenges other people to make public decisions. The more powerful you are in an institution, the fewer decisions you've chosen to make. The Iron Rule—never do for anybody what he or she can do for themselves. That means having real conversations.

I do a session where I talk about the difference between communication, which is subject to object, and conversation, which is subject to subject. We are trying to teach conversation, whereas when most people talk about politics they want to talk about communication, an objective transfer of facts and figures and ideas. We are talking about something, we hope, much deeper than that. We are talking about political relationships, public relationships. They are not private; they are not about intimacy; they are not about being lovers; they are not about being spouses; they are not about brothers and sisters. They are about how you develop relationships so that you win people's respect, so that they might become your friends, your colleagues—because you've worked together, you've collaborated. But there is still a boundary; it's not a marriage. I can engage with other people and still respect my own relationship to my private commitments.

MCAFEE: You mentioned what you call the Iron Rule: never do for someone what he or she can do for himself or herself. What are some of the things that people can do for themselves, that no one else should do for them?

CORTES: They can try to figure out what relationships are important to them. They can develop some curiosity about themselves. They can develop some imagination about what the possibilities are. They can develop capacity, and they can develop competence. Somebody can't make you competent; and somebody can't be competent for you. Somebody can't enhance your capacity for learning: someone can't learn the violin for you, they can't learn a language for you; those things you have to learn by yourself. Someone can't learn how to drive for you; someone can't learn how to raise your kids for you; those are things you have to do for yourself.

The worst thing that happens is for leaders to see their roles as servicing. They become gatekeepers, or they become service centers, or they become business agents. One of the problems with big city political machines is that leaders become just people who distribute favors for fifteen other people; think in terms of "you come to me and I give you a job." For these people the leader is nothing more than an informal service provider; and there is an informal welfare system that emerges out of the political party or the labor union.

The role of leadership is to guide, to challenge, to agitate, and to teach people how to be their own best advocates and understand their own situation. We are trying to recognize the role mediating or intermediate institutions have played historically in enabling people to figure things out and understand what's going on. There is no civil society without mediating institutions. But now those intermediate institutions are either attenuated or imploding—they are collapsing: family, church, neighborhood, communities of all kinds. So, what we are trying to do is to take the families and the churches and other institutions and make one huge, big intermediate institution, which then becomes effective in transmitting culture and values and traditions and an understanding of what the community is.

20

A Call for Organizing, Confrontation, and Community Building (1995)

■

REV. JOHNNY RAY YOUNGBLOOD

I appreciate the invitation to speak with you today. I'm the pastor of St. Paul Community Baptist Church in East New York, Brooklyn; the co-chair of East Brooklyn Congregations, a fifteen-year-old organization of fifty congregations and associations built with the assistance of the Industrial Areas Foundation; and a key leader of Metro IAF, our new coming together of eight New York IAF organizations and the other IAF organizations in the northeast and mid-Atlantic region.

The theme of this luncheon program is "A Call for Collaboration, Coordination, and Community Building." I do believe in community building. I have spent my life doing it. As a pastor, as a minister who has spent intensive time ministering to black men, as a leader in a multi-racial and multi-faith organization, I'm in the business of building meaningful public relationships. And because I spend my life doing that and believe so strongly in building successful communities, I'm suspicious of most collaborations and partnerships. So I would title my remarks differently: "A Call for Organizing, Confrontation, and Community Building."

Thirty Winters Ago . . .

I was still a teenager in a Roman Catholic high school in Louisiana, heading toward college and seminary, and a career in ministry. Wherever we were, we were all witnessing some of the key early struggles of the civil rights movement in this country. We were thrilled by the calls for wars on poverty and discrimination. In the summers before that winter thirty years ago, millions mobilized and marched, scores of thousands worked, and many decent men and women died for their beliefs. It was a time of disciplined demonstrations, civil and mostly civilized disobedience, and under-financed but independent freedom schools.

Thirty winters later, there is a paid pinstripe army of agency executives, economic development advisors, academic researchers, public authority bureaucrats. There are

This speech was delivered at the Boston Area Meeting of the Neighborhood Funders Group, December 1995. The text is archived at the website of Christians Supporting Community Organizing (CSCO), *www.cscoweb.org/young.html*. It is reprinted here by permission of Rev. Johnny Ray Youngblood.

thousands of agencies and programs and development corporations and so-called job training efforts. There are hundreds of conferences and reports and studies. But no war, no battle, no front fully engaged against the forces of deepening poverty and hardened discrimination. Thirty winters later, what used to be called "pockets" of poverty are now wide swaths of cities, metropolitan areas, regions. And these swaths seem immune to the imagined magic of the market; immune to the supposed corrective effects of multiple government programs; immune to the newest placebo: a partnership of the failed market and failed government sector. Thirty winters later, the aging cities of the northeast and rustbelt have replaced Appalachia and the Deep South as the most dramatic and most resistant homes of poverty, depression and isolation.

What is the response? We in the IAF have identified at least three that we believe don't work: One response is what we call the outside-in response. This response says that cities and regions can only be saved by those who don't live within them—by tourists, shoppers, sports fans, theatergoers, casino gamblers, and conventioneers. This response calls for cuts in social spending and hikes in subsidies and tax breaks to build the business and entertainment centers capable of attracting those who live outside the cities. One of the largest and newest convention centers in Philadelphia lost "only" 6 million dollars this year, was anticipating an even larger loss next year, and was reported to be "on a roll." (As a pastor, I marvel at this accounting and public relations miracle. If John Heinemeier[1] or I got up and told our people we had lost only 6 million dollars last year, we, too, would be "on a roll"—rolling out of town!) People who promote this response see cities as museum districts, profit centers, pleasure places— their public faces grinning at commuters, their backs to their own citizens.

A second response says that we just need more and better programs. As a leader who has been familiar with the Job Training Partnership Act travesty for more than six years, I am as skeptical of this response as of the first one. A Federal study of JTPA showed that young, minority men (African-American, Hispanics and other ethnics) made seven percent less after participating in one of the JTPA programs than those who never did. Think of this: Young black men and Hispanic men make seven percent less if they go through one of these job training efforts. In New York, we have pressured for other studies. Each has shown devastating failure. IAF tried to bring this failure to the attention of both Bush's and Clinton's Labor Secretaries—Lynn Martin and Robert Reich—to no avail. The traditional liberal response to cities—multiplying and tinkering with bureaucratic programs—is dead, as dead as the Democratic Party that still sometimes promotes this approach. The difference between George Bush and Bill Clinton, if you live in an impoverished community, is zero.

A third response is that we need more public-private partnerships. This response has a long history. Partnership and collaboration usually involves the private sector and the government sector, with a token community advocate or preacher on the board for window-dressing. This kind of response tends to be tame and non-confrontational. Let's not point fingers, we're told; let's get something done. It tends to be led by professionals and planners. It tends to be small in scale. It tends to be acceptable to funders and grant makers. And it tends not to have very much impact. (I know there are a few exceptions to what I've said, and I'm sure some of you will want to point them out to me; but, after fifteen years in the public arena, I stand by what I say.) Most of these partnerships and collaborations are feel-good, but of little consequence. And they are a far cry from the heart, soul, and guts of the civil rights work done thirty winters ago.

The IAF Response

If these three mostly don't work, then what? Here's the response we in the IAF in the north-east have developed: First, start inside, not outside. Start with leaders, ministers, pastors, rabbis, coaches, teachers, mothers, uncles, families of all kinds. Start with the institutions and associations that have remained through all the residents, political party shifts, Reagan fads, Bush fads, Clinton fads, Dole fads—parishes, congregations, and others. Build legitimate, independent, power organizations—as we have in East Brooklyn and Baltimore and San Antonio and Los Angeles. Train and develop local leaders. In short, build power in the third sector capable of dealing with the public and private sectors. In short, organize. Go back to many of the basics of thirty winters ago (adding in all we have learned in those three decades and remembering to do much of what others have forgotten or rejected). Children, families, congregations, cities—they grow, for the most part, from the inside out.

Second, redeem the notion of work from the social theorists and market fundamentalists, and demand that workers receive a living wage. Where we started in Baltimore is by pressuring cities and states that contract with vendors for various services to insist that those vendors pay their workers a living wage. In Baltimore, the first living wage bill was passed through the leadership of our IAF BUILD organization and AFSCME (*American Federation of State, County & Municipal Employees, AFL-CIO*) last year, raising the wage of all city contract workers from $4.25 to $6.10 an hour, with increases each year.[2] A living wage paycheck is better than any program. A living wage paycheck is as good to a family if it comes from a public sector employer as it is if it comes from a private sector employer. As long as people do real work for a real wage, we are on the right track.

Third, increase the opportunities for ownership (of homes and businesses) and equity for working poor families. Our 2,200 EBC Nehemiah homeowners are all employed at a living wage, all paying less for a new home than they paid for their rental apartments, and all building equity. These three elements—the power of an organization like EBC, a regular paycheck at a living wage, and opportunities for ownership and equity—help expand what we in the IAF call "the critical mass class." They are the group in the millions, black and Hispanic, Asian and white, long-time resident and new immigrant, ready to move from poverty or semi-poverty to working-class status. If there are enough of them, they create a critical mass. When they reach critical mass, there are all kinds of other constructive chain reactions that counter the current chain reactions of poverty, violence, dependency, and death. These positive chain reactions include saving money, getting more education, finding stability, developing more self-respect, having time for organizing, praying, action, voting, thriving in the fullest sense. These positive chain reactions make us more than customers of the market or clients of the government. They make us full citizens of a decent society.

What's Next?

This may seem too simple, too basic, for some of you. I don't know what to say about that. There are plenty of complicated battles ahead. In this region we have to attack and dismantle the great public authority racket—large authorities like the so-called Urban Development Corporation in New York which raises and squanders more than $2 billion each year. Up and down the northeast, these authorities have multiplied and grown and wasted money and allowed public and private sector executives to live off the remaining fat of the land. We have to attack and dismantle those government programs that do no good and use those funds to create dignified public work that pays a living wage. We have to pass living wage legislation in every major city and state so that the government does not subsidize worker poverty by allowing contractors to pay depression-era wages. And we have to find others where they are, I don't really know who, to begin to think strategically and creatively about this region of ours. We who live between Boston and Washington live in one of the world's great centers of education, technology, finance. Someday we'll make better use of our resources and see that the workers of this region are paid fairly and treated respectfully.

What do you as funders do? Be skeptical of anything with partnership or collaboration or collaborative in the title. Be skeptical of elaborate procedures and structures and bureaucracies—anything the Kennedy School finds attractive. Be skeptical of anything that sounds too good. Be skeptical of anything that doesn't create tension. Support those who do direct organizing with the unorganized, those who have talented leadership, those whose name and intent create discomfort and unease. If you were around then, remember what it was like thirty winters ago—exciting and dangerous, deeply challenging and stirring, full of tragedy as well as joy.

I thank you for your time today.

Notes

1. CSCO editor's note: Former leader of East Brooklyn Congregations; now pastor in Boston.
2. CSCO editor's note: $7.70 in 1996.

21

Standing for the Whole (1990)

■

INDUSTRIAL AREAS FOUNDATION

> Political virtue is the commitment to, knowledge of, and ability to stand for
> the whole, and is the necessary condition for democracy.
> —[Charles Douglas] Lummis, *Democracy*, Fall 1982

We who lead and organize with the Industrial Areas Foundation may be considered presumptuous for talking about "a commitment to, knowledge of, and ability to stand for the whole." If you added up the budgets of our 28 affiliate organizations, the total would not reach $5,000,000 per year—a pittance by corporate, church, union, or political party standards. All of our full-time organizers and support staff number no more than 75. Our offices are in some of the most neglected and devastated corners of America's central cities and written-off rural areas. And our names do not appear with any regularity in the political or social or celebrity columns of major newspapers. Yet, we *do* presume to describe our commitment to, our knowledge of, and even our ability, to stand for the whole. Here's why.

Our organizations are made up of 1,200 congregations and associations; tens of thousands of ministers, rabbis, pastors, lay leaders, and nearly two million members and associates from Brownsville, Texas to Brownsville, Brooklyn. Our members are black and Hispanic, Asian and white; individuals on the edge of homelessness as well as families in stable middle-class communities in the San Fernando Valley or Prince Georges County. We are Democrats and Republicans and Independents, most of us in the moderate middle of the political spectrum. Taken together, with our millions of hours of practical nonpartisan activity, our range and depth of experience; our growing ability to employ the full range of relational public skills (listening, presenting, agitating, confronting, negotiating, compromising) and our mix of patience for the pace of political development and impatience at the conditions that stunt and stifle growth—we are as diverse, as determined, and as vital a network of related and relating citizens as exists in our nation today.

This document was originally self-published in Chicago. It is reprinted here by permission of Michael Gecan for the Industrial Areas Foundation.

Before trying to define who we are and what we believe, we are going to take the time to say who we are *not*. We are *not*, fundamentally, materialists. We don't believe greed is good. We don't worship profit. Wall Street isn't sacred, and stock transfers aren't liturgy. We don't see the profound transformations taking place in Eastern Europe as triumphs of the commercial spirit (consumers starved for shopping malls going over the wall), but as triumphs of the human spirit. In Eastern Europe, men and women are demanding that the state and the economy serve the interests of the most important sector of any healthy society—what Peter Drucker has called the third sector. This sector of voluntary associations—family, congregation, and other institutions—gives the market its meaning, not the other way around. This sector is most precious to the majority of Americans. This sector is where we grow and see our children grow. This sector is the soul of the whole.

Nor are we citizens who worship another false idol: the bureaucratic state. We *don't* want a society of empty programs and do nothing administrators. We don't believe that bigger government is always better. We don't value paper and procedure and patronage. *We* are the ones who have suffered the most in cities staffed by political hacks and process junkies. Those are *our* children who have not been educated. Those are *our* blocks which have not been rebuilt. Those are *our* loved ones who have died on stretchers in overloaded emergency rooms or who have watched their life-blood drain away while waiting for an ambulance that came too late. We reject the building of bureaucratic kingdoms—whether the Republican version (cost-plus defense department contracts), the Democratic version (cost-plus social service programs), or the socialist version (both).

We are also not people anxiously awaiting a charismatic leader—a savior who will lead us to a political promised land. We value leaders who aren't "naturals," who have difficulty speaking, people without sound bites ready for the press. We believe that *no one* leader is needed, but a collective of leaders. We believe *no one* person should stand for us and speak for us and broker for us—thus depriving us of our dignity and our stake in our own futures—but that we should learn to stand and speak for [the] whole ourselves.

Finally, we do not see ourselves as another faction or party or sect, not another issue group or special interest or lobby. We don't view the public arena as a piece of limited turf, or as a cramped apartment with only three small rooms. We are not trying to squeeze one of our leaders into one of the rooms where power people currently meet. We see ourselves as trying to build a large enough room, with a big enough table, to accommodate as much of the talent and creativity and variety as we know still exists in the shattered cities and towns of our nation.

Then who are we? We will try to answer this by describing what we believe, what we teach, what we do, and why we do it.

1. We believe in what we call *the iron rule*: never do for others what they can do for themselves. *Never*. This rule, difficult to practice consistently, sometimes violated,

is central to our view of the nature of education, of leadership, and of effective organizing. This cuts against the grain of some social workers and program peddlers who try to reduce people and families to clients, who probe for needs and lacks and weaknesses, not strength and drive, not vision and values, not democratic and entrepreneurial initiative. The iron rule implies that the most valuable and enduring form of development—intellectual, social, political—is the development people freely choose and fully own.

2. We believe that most leaders—hundreds and thousands and millions—are *made*, not born, and that the majority of men and women have the ability to understand, to judge, to listen, to relate, to speak, to persuade, to confront, and to resolve. We find in our congregations and our blocks; in our public housing projects and barrios, a vast pool of citizens, able-bodied and able-minded men and women. They are often untrained and untaught. They are ignored by almost everyone. They are even redefined as a new class or underclass, but time and again they have proven their ability to grow and develop if invested in. The heart of our organizing is the finding of talented potential leaders, the inviting of those leaders into training and relationship, and the enabling of people to decide whether they want to develop, and where, and when, and how fast. Creating the context for leadership development is the core of our work.

3. We believe in a sense of ownership of our own development and ownership of our institutions. We believe in dues. We believe in paying our own way. We neither solicit nor accept governmental monies for our central organizations. Without financial independence, there is not true political independence.

4. We believe in an educational process that has little to do with traditional classroom approaches. In local areas, every night and most weekends, scores of local national training sessions take place, analyzing public agencies, tracing the connections between public and private power players, designing strategies, planning action. We also conduct 10 days of training three times a year, where several hundred leaders and organizers systematically probe the central issues of democratic politics and effective action. But the greatest percentage of learning and tutoring takes place in the field, in the City Halls and housing agencies, in state legislatures and bank board rooms, in T.V. studios and editorial boards. The materials that we and our fellow leaders use are the unlimited examples of failure in our cities: the bankrupt programs and grounded pilot projects, the political fixes and insider deals. We don't have to look far for issues. They surround us.

5. We believe in the individual meeting. By individual meeting, we mean a contact that is face to face, one to one, for the purpose of exploring the possibilities of a public relationship. It is a thirty-minute opportunity to set aside the pressures and tasks and deadlines of the day and to probe another person, to look for their talent, interest, energy, and vision. The other person's

perspective is of primary value. Their stories and insights and memories are more important than a name on a petition or contribution to a cause. The modern leader and organizer is not a peddler of issues—an activist Fuller Brush man—but an initiator of individual meetings and builder of public relationships.

6. We believe in building for power—power that is fundamentally reciprocal, power that is tempered by the teachings of religious traditions and exercised in the context of ever changing relationships with our fellow leaders, allies, and opponents. We value the public sphere; we want to build a larger table in a more spacious room, but we don't kid ourselves about the tone of discussion that will take place at that table. We accept the tension, emotion, conflict, and uncertainty that are part of political life. We are prepared to argue, listen, revise our views, and compromise in exchange for respect and a willingness to compromise from those who now hold power. What matters to us is not consensus, but a stake in the ongoing dynamic of controversy, resolution, and change. We do not want to dominate. We do not want to *be* the whole. We want and will insist on being recognized as a vital part of it—and as capable as others of standing for it.

What exactly do we do?

One way to answer this is to say that we build a new kind of organization. It is rooted in families, congregations, and associations. Our organizations are dues based. Our organizations have very small professional staffs. Our organizations are fueled by the hundreds of thousands of volunteered hours of talented men and women in local communities. Our organizations work on a wide range of issues—from getting cities to replace stop signs to getting states to restructure and refinance their school systems; from pressuring to get a drug den demolished, to rebuilding entire neighborhoods with new affordable homes; from reducing exorbitant water rates to figuring out the financing for a new water and sewer system.

Another way to answer, equally true, is to say that we try to construct a classroom without walls where the truly best and the brightest citizens of our republic—parents, teachers, teenagers, factory workers, bus drivers, garment workers, secretaries, nurses, dignified people on public assistance—come and learn through their own experiences how to translate their values and dreams for themselves and their communities into concrete reality. We use issues as *means* to advance our knowledge of the whole, and how that whole works and fails to work, and how that whole may be bettered.

A third way to answer is to say that we see ourselves as building and rebuilding a vital, powerful, voluntary third sector. That sector will confront, compete with, and collaborate with the partisan public and private sectors at different times. We challenge the public sector—undermined by privatization, corruption, celebrity-worship, and a loss of citizens' confidence—to redefine its role in the 1990s.

Why do we do what we do?

The answers are as diverse as the individuals who comprise our organizations.

Some of us organize and lead because our faith, our religious belief, impels us toward this work. The words we read in the Old Testament or New Testament or Koran haunt us as we walk the streets of our cities. We are compelled by their injunction to relate, to reflect, to take action and risk to make the dry bones of our shattered communities rise up, connect, and live.

Some of us organize out of anger—out of the root meaning of that word, grief. We move into the public arena grieving for all the opportunities lost and to be lost, for all the careers stunted and shortened, for all the hopes and dreams denied. We have looked into the eyes of undamaged children and looked again, years later, to find those eyes deadened by drug addiction or dimmed by inferior schools or degrading work. We have looked in the mirror and seen ourselves isolated, disconnected, spectators watching the play of public life on a TV screen, and have looked again and seen the same selves engaged in the drama of pressure and progress and change.

We organize because there were moments in our lives—often long buried—that told us that we could lead, moments like this moment described by one of our fellow leaders:

As a young girl in North Carolina, my sister and I began to attend the local Roman Catholic Church. In those days, blacks sat in the back pews. Now I was a very large young girl, rather heavy, and so was my sister. When we went to that church, I saw no reason why my sister and I should sit in the back. So one Sunday we went right up and sat in the first pew. The pastor and ushers were upset. The pastor came over before Mass and asked if we would please sit in the back, like all the other blacks. I was as scared as I could be, but I just couldn't see where God would care where we sat, and so I said no. Finally, the ushers came and carried my sister and me to the back. Carried us right down the aisle of the church.

On the next Sunday, my sister and I sat in the front pew again, and the priest came and the ushers came and they hauled us off again, them huffing and puffing, to the back. On the third Sunday, the same thing happened. By this time, we were pretty well known. Two black girls who got carried to the back of the church every Sunday. My family, my mother particularly was frightened at what we were doing, but said that we were doing the right thing.

On the fourth Sunday, the priest and the ushers didn't do a thing. The Mass started, the choir sang, we took our seats, and from then on we sat where we wanted in that church and in any Roman Catholic Church we ever attended.

We organize and lead out of love and stubbornness, out of joy and near-despair, out of clarity of purpose and, sometimes, simply, because we don't see who else will do what needs to be done.

We organize and lead because we know, or sense, that there won't be a whole—a whole nation or whole city or whole community greater than the sum of its parts—unless many millions of Americans feel that the land is theirs, ours, that we are in it, of it, and willing to know it, commit to it, and stand for it.

We organize and lead because we see our participation as a necessary condition of a healthy democracy and a dignified life.

PART III

DIFFERENT DIRECTIONS

Section A
Heather Booth, Midwest Academy, and Citizen Action

22

An Introduction to Heather Booth, the Midwest Academy, and Citizen Action

■

AARON SCHUTZ, WITH COMMENTARY
BY MIKE MILLER

Heather Booth's route to community organizing was via the northern student, civil rights, labor, and women's movements of the 1960s. She also participated in the 1964 Mississippi Summer Project. Her involvement in the emerging women's movement began at the 1965 conference of Students for a Democratic Society (SDS), where women walked out in response to sexism and held the "first major independent women's movement meeting."[1] She participated in a women's group with noted feminists Shulamith Firestone, Jo Freeman, and Naomi Weisstein, organized the Action Committee for Decent Childcare, cowrote position papers for the movement, and according to Jo Freeman "was responsible for more early [women's] groups than any other single person."[2]

In the 1970s she and several associates created the Midwest Academy organizing training center, and later developed the multistate Citizen Action coalition. After work in the civil rights and women's movement, Heather Booth started an organizing training center, Midwest Academy, with money she won from a back pay suit for labor organizing. She has directed or consulted with organizations including NAACP National Voter Fund, immigration reform campaign (Alliance for Citizenship), financial reform (Americans for Financial Reform), MoveOn, and others. She ran and consulted with many election campaigns and was the training director for the Democratic Party.

Midwest Academy and the Alinsky Organizing Tradition

In 1970, Booth's husband, Paul, previously a key leader in SDS, became cochair of the Citizens Action Program (CAP) in Chicago (see Chapter 17). It was the IAF Institute's effort to engage the energy of the environmental movement and translate it into a powerful metrowide, multi-issue organization in Chicago. In 1971, she attended the IAF Institute's organizer training, whose seminars were led mostly by Ed Chambers and Dick Harmon (she met with Alinsky only once). Only months after she finished the seminar, she began running her own organizing workshops, drawing upon her own experience and what she saw as the best aspects of Alinsky's organizing. Midwest Academy (MA) followed quickly afterward.

Booth remembers wanting MA to become a "national training center for leaders, activists, and organizers, to teach skills of mass-based organizing." At the same time, she sought to provide "a cultural integration of people who were active," extending her own antisectarian agenda—responding to growing sectarianism in both the student movement and sections of the women's movement.[3] MA quickly became a well-attended organizing training center, later publishing its widely read manual, *Organizing for Social Change*. Today, thousands of people have gone through MA workshops.

There was also a substantial departure from what was envisaged in the Saul Alinsky Institute. The IAF seminar was the entry point in what had been initially envisaged as a yearlong experience, with the "training" taking place in a fieldwork placement under the mentorship of a senior IAF staffer, and resulting in a growing but not large cadre of highly skilled organizers who could put together a CAP-like organization with continuing supervision from the IAF's core staff.

MA had a different approach and strategy: organizers, leaders, and activists would come to its weeklong workshop, and then return to their own home-based organization—whatever it might be—and might (but it wasn't part of the package) engage in a continuing consultation with MA. A question remains about how much "organizing" can be taught in just one week without a longer assignment in the field as part of the training (although MA has periodically offered internships to a few of its students).

The original version of the MA manual focused on organizing women in particular, with an introductory chapter written by Booth. It's included in this volume as the next chapter because it represents one of the most comprehensive statements of her early intentions for MA.

Booth notes that when she wrote the manual, it was "both a time of exciting new movements, the consumer movement, and the environmental movement" and "a time of great transition and confusion," as old movements were fracturing.[4] MA represented an effort to intervene in this space of uncertainty: to infuse these movements with lessons she drew from Alinsky, and to ensure that their energy and potential were not dissipated in unproductive internecine conflict.

Booth attended the IAF training because she "was very impressed with what IAF was doing in terms of their routinizing and consolidating a lot of different information and also [the] incredible experience they had" with organizing—something she had seen in CAP. The highlights of her IAF training included:

- Analyzing "the specifics of how you do an action"
- Encountering "the discipline of learning organizing," as opposed to the more freewheeling approach of many movement folks
- "Taking winning seriously"
- "Seeing that there are reforms that matter and that building people's leadership also matters"
- "Understanding conceptions of self-interest"
- Discussing the roles of leaders and organizers, and recognizing "that there are different functions" for each role.
- Going over "the histories of specific case studies of how [the IAF] won various efforts."[5]

She was also impressed with key elements of their approach to training, which included role play, one-on-one consulting, and the expectation of participants "to report and be accountable."[6] She emphasizes that she is indebted to the Alinsky tradition, and that she is still learning from it. She is "very grateful to what the Alinsky folks did," and stresses that "a lot of what I've learned I've learned from their approach." Many aspects of her vision of effective social action "are built on what Alinsky did."[7] As a result, she is somewhat uncomfortable with being placed in the camp of critics of the Alinsky tradition.

Criticisms of the IAF Approach

However, she did have serious criticisms about what took place at the training, and about what she thought was missing from the overall vision. She had "very specific differences on . . . style, culture, constituency, conception, approach, values, techniques," and more.[8]

She was offended by their approach to women and pragmatically disagreed with two of their claims: that organizing was a man's job, and that women shouldn't be organized as a separate constituency. She came to the training already having stated in her application that she was interested in training women. She remembers that there was

> a kind of mystique: "Well, boy, so and so is a great organizer. Can I be a great organizer like that? What's involved there?" Drinking hard, smoking hard, having a, you know, an f-you attitude. But suddenly there were going to be women around. [*Laughs*] You know, I asked, when I was at the IAF, "Well, what would your advice be? I'm organizing women around day care. What would your advice be for organizing women?"[9] They said, "Well, what about the nuns?" And while that's actually a very good point for institutional support, it is not about the organizing of women

with children, so, it is kind of a funny point. It's an answer that shows not a full understanding of what a vital women's movement is developing.[10]

The trainers "took a posture in class, I think, to toughen me up," which "ended up being an attack on why would I be organizing women," including "arguing that women couldn't be organizers." There are two distinct points here: first, the IAF was arrogant toward women, and toward the possibility that they could be organizers. Along with this, it had a machismo style that was a "who can be the biggest and baddest guy on the mountain top, and who's going to try to knock him off." On these points, Booth was ahead of her time, but certainly prophetic: all the organizing networks today count women among their most talented organizers, and they are increasingly abandoning the macho style as well.[11]

While she understood the importance of challenging organizers, activists, and leaders to do their best, Booth's experience told her that, especially at that time, many women would come to sessions with more "lack of confidence" than most men, something the IAF approach "didn't understand or acknowledge." In her own training, then, Booth tried to take a different approach to training and leadership, exploring the "relationship[s] between support and challenge," which she describes as "very complicated."[12]

Booth later organized other trainees into sending a joint letter to the IAF, asking it to hire a "part-time woman teacher for future training sessions." Their letter noted that "there are many organizing styles, and women must develop ones that are appropriate for them. The styles offered in the school, if incorporated by women, might isolate them from the very women they may want to relate to." They further noted a lack of respect for the ways women tended to discuss issues in "consciousness raising" groups and elsewhere.[13]

In addition, what the IAF saw as a strength, Booth saw as a weakness: the workshop was designed for organizers, not organizers, leaders, and activists. While the IAF saw leadership education as central to the organizing role. Booth wasn't convinced this would happen. Booth wanted to end what she saw as a "secrecy and the mystique" involved in organizing. She wanted to emphasize that it was not just that there are "these great organizers, but [that] you can also do it."[14]

The IAF thought the organizers would train leaders, and that there could be neither effective leadership nor organizer training in the absence of the proper organization that was the context for each. Booth, and later MA, thought that the workshop, advanced workshops, retreats, possible continuing consulting, and other means would allow activists, leaders, and organizers to return to a wide variety of organizations with sharpened concepts and skills that would make all of them more effective.

In taking this step, Booth also departed from Alinsky, who thought that the good organizer was a rare find, and that it was a central responsibility of the good organizer to be a teacher who did his work in the "mass organization" that he created. While Booth wanted to train organizers, leaders, and activists from all kinds of organizations, the IAF wanted to train organizers who could build mass organizations, within which they would train and educate leaders.

Because her focus was initially on the workshop, she thought it important to break complicated ideas into easily communicated parts. That led to a codified approach to strategy, exemplified in MA's now well-known "strategy chart"; a revised version of it appears in MA's *Community Organizing for Social Change* manual. The initial 1973 version was a series of five columns: "Vision (longer range goals, principles)," "Organizational Considerations," "Constituencies (both members and allies)," "Targets," and "Tactics." The chart was meant to help organizers and leaders relate these different categories with each other, moving between the overall vision on one side to the specific tactics on the other. This has now been simplified into three core concepts: winning victories, developing the competence and self-confidence of people, and altering the relations of power—a good summing up of organizing.[15]

Other areas of concern with the IAF training were what she saw as its lack of positive consideration of movements; its focus on narrow self-interests, instead of seeing them in addition to the more deeply held values that motivate people; its lack of interest in working with unions; and, later, its opposition to electoral organizing. She also wanted to emphasize organizing that helped to build institutional and structural or systemic change in society (looking beyond a single community or city or metropolitan area). Moreover, she was concerned that the IAF's approach—at that time— was not collegial to other organizing efforts.[16]

Note that the IAF also "wanted to emphasize organizing that helped to build . . . systemic change in the society."[17] But the IAF drew a very different conclusion from its experience with CAP and its counterparts—namely, that these groups were not sustainable, and that action at a statewide or national level was premature because there was insufficient people power to seriously engage in it. Mike Miller returns to this issue below.

Movement Contributions

Because of Booth's commitment to the social movements of the period, she wanted less emphasis on organizational structure and defined roles, and more of what she called an "open source" approach to collective action—an approach that drew upon various sources available to find what was best. She looked in part to the fluidity of the social movements of the time as a counterweight. She remembers that "you'd throw out ideas and then people [would] figure out, well, what can we do? There was an involvement of volunteers and lots of different creative alternate tactics. There was a context of thinking about making history and understanding economy, understanding politics. There was seeing that your struggle is related to other struggles [while] some of the community organizations became narrowed."[18]

Ironically, Alinsky had several concerns about narrowness himself. First, growing rhetorical and tactical militancy were isolating various movements of the day from their own respective constituencies. Second, various movements were pursuing their own particular interests in isolation from each other, so broad-based power could not be built. Third, the white lower-middle and middle class had to be part of building people power. The reaction he feared was exemplified electorally by Republican Richard Nixon's presidential victory in 1968, and the subsequent crushing defeat of McGovern in 1972. Booth was a voice of sanity in the context of the movements, continually arguing for broad-based effort. The IAF concluded that the best way to move forward was to work on strengthening stable civil society institutions, particularly the church. Booth, on the other hand, was interested in putting labor, religious, civil rights, environmentalist, women's, and other organizations and movements together around big issues that affected them all.

Booth also sought to replicate in her work "the vitality and joy of the movement"—singing, dancing, a spirit of collectivity and sisterhood, and more.[19] Finally, Booth seemed to approach social struggle in general from a more "movement"-oriented perspective, looking for big issues that could draw large numbers of people into mass action.

Before Midwest Academy: Workshops and Manifestos

The earliest description of a workshop I could find in the MA archives was that of a "Direct Action Organizing Class" for women led by Booth and Kathy Blunt in 1971, only a few months after Booth's attendance at the IAF training. It argued that it was time for women to move beyond seeking media coverage and engaging in consciousness-raising to "develop a base of power and implement changes." Booth and Blunt wanted women to take action on real issues in the world. They wanted to "develop a sense of unity among women" while "challeng[ing] their [limited] sex roles."[20]

They laid out the three key criteria that Booth repeatedly emphasized over these years. They proposed an approach that, in their words,

1. alters the existing relations of power (taking power from the ruling elite)
2. gives people a sense of their own power (having won rights and not given them at the whim of gov't, etc.)
3. wins reforms that materially improve the conditions of women's (people's) lives.[21]

And they focused on the importance of mapping out the power structure and finding realistic intervention points. While discussion was important, it was not sufficient. "Changes in consciousness," they argued, "will come through [women] directly experiencing changes." Further, they stressed the importance of focusing in on self-interest as a core motivating principle.[22]

Drawing selectively from the IAF, Booth and Blunt concluded their description with pragmatic and concrete criteria for ensuring that issues "relate to all aspects of women's lives," "convert a vision into a specific activity," "can be broken into parts to be fought for as [discrete] reforms," and "can . . . develop a mass organization."[23]

While running workshops, Booth and Blunt worked on position papers, encouraging the broader movement and the women's movement in particular to regroup around a more coherent, strategic approach for achieving specific reforms.[24] They argued that those at the two basic poles of the women's movement—groups focused on personal change and groups focused on structural issues—needed to come together and integrate their different insights.

Writing the Women's Manual

According to Booth, it was sometime in 1972 when a "social work group contacted me and asked me to write a manual on training for women."[25] Prior to this, she and her colleagues (e.g., Blunt, Day Creamer, Paul Booth) seem to have oriented their workshops with a collection of five typed pages of notes. The pages were titled "Theory and Strategy," "Leadership," "Tactics," "How to Do an Action," and "Media."[26] Early on, she realized that the task of writing the manual was more than she could handle herself, and brought in Steve Max, whom she "had known from the student movement and who was a good trainer." Then "over a week or so [we] designed the basic curriculum that became the Midwest Academy curriculum."[27]

In the first section, Booth covered the core concepts of her vision. Max largely wrote the second and third sections, which focused on the specifics of planning actions and running campaigns as well as on economics and the history of social change movements, with examples from labor, civil rights, and the student movement. In February 1974, the first edition of the manual was complete.

As readers will see in the next chapter, it reflected ideas she had been working on in the preceding years. It began with a reference to the ways women in the movements had been relegated to subordinate positions, making phone calls and licking stamps instead of leading, even though women had long been "organizing" many aspects of their family lives. Equality, Booth argued, would only come when women stood up and took equal roles in social action efforts.

Anticipating concerns that women readers might raise about her focus on power and confrontational action, she argued that "power as such [is not] evil." Only "power unfairly held, undemocratically exerted, unaccountable . . . is evil." Part of women's avoidance of confrontation, she argued, arose out of a fear of failure and, at the same time, a contradictory fear of success: the worry that "winning" will somehow be seen as "unfeminine."[28]

She laid out a few key principles for working with women: accepting different cultural and personal styles; caring "for women as people," with concern for "their well-being" and "self-respect"; and helping women to understand that what may seem like personal problems are really shared social ones.[29]

Booth concluded her chapter by speaking directly to the "difficulties of being a woman organizer" acknowledging the risks involved in moving beyond traditional roles, and addressing fears of being attacked around "sex and sexuality." She argued, however, that "women can turn these negatives into positives." They could bring special skills for sensitivity and relationship-building that are crucial for strong organizations. Ultimately, however, only victories and successful experiences as organizers will lead to a change in women's social expectations.

Like all the other documents in this collection, Booth's chapter for the women's manual emerges out of a particular historical moment. There is not space here to adequately address the nuances of the second-wave women's movement, or the particular contextual issues that Booth was responding to in her chapter. It is important to note that in a women's movement generally dominated at the time by middle-class white women, she and her colleagues spoke in their writings about the importance of drawing in women across these boundaries, and that she did just this in her work on child care and elsewhere. At the same time, however, one can still detect implicit assumptions about the particular audience of women her manual chapter is addressing. As black, working-class, and other writers would argue, non-white and non-middle-class women did not necessarily face the same challenges with respect to "confrontation" or fears about "winning" that Booth emphasizes in her manual chapter.[30]

From Midwest Academy to Citizen Action

Booth sought a way to bring the different strands of social action she had experienced together—the student, civil rights, and women's movements, labor organizing, and CAP. Her idea was to use a big issue that clearly no one of these groups could tackle alone to build coalitions in which each would build power based on their respective organizational strengths and cumulative numbers. She also drew from her CAP experience with door-to-door canvassing, believing that young activists could solicit funds, do educational work on an issue, and mount political pressure from grassroots constituents on power structure decision-makers:

> We wanted to consolidate all these various constituency groups [that were] developing [into] statewide multi-issue organizations. And we had five statewide organizations that we developed [in the] mid '70s.
>
> [And then] I thought, well, there's got to be a way to build a bridge back to labor that had been ruptured from the Cold War era, and was ruptured in the '60s. Could we build an alliance between labor and community?[31]

Booth hoped that applying the concrete tactical and organizational lessons she'd learned with the IAF to the contexts of labor, social movements, and community groups could strengthen all of them and create vehicles to win substantive victories on important issues. Citizens/Labor Energy Coalition (CLEC) was the first expression of these goals. At the time, utility and energy prices were rising rapidly, with residential utility bills sometimes exceeding rent or mortgage payments. Anger about rip-off utility and oil giants was palpable. And, indeed, substantial victories were won.

Door-to-door canvassing, Booth thought, could free up organizations from their dependency on foundations, as well as from the limitations of member-based fundraising (such as, for instance, its inability to reach the scale required for larger, more powerful organizations). Further, canvassers were a built-in source of talent for other positions within a large-scale coalition organization—organizers, researchers, publicists, clericals, administrators, and others. Specialized units of the canvass could go into communities and generate a sudden deluge of night-telegrams that would appear on a state legislator's desk the next morning—often turning a "no" or "uncommitted" vote into an affirmative one.

Booth's next step was to take the lessons of CLEC and turn them into multi-issue, statewide organizations that came together in the MA-related Citizen Action network. From the beginning, Booth envisioned MA as more than simply a training site for organizers in different silos. She wanted to break down these silos and use MA as a base for experimenting with new strategies and new approaches to building broad-based coalitions. Beyond the workshops, MA also sought "to provide a cultural integration of people who were active" through "Academy Retreats" in the summer "to talk about what we should do."[32] Booth and her colleagues began with a focus on training women, including the leadership of the National Organization for Women, but soon expanded that focus.

The energy coalition was the predecessor of the multi-issue, multistate coalition Citizen Action (CA; not to be confused with CAP). While Booth had earlier supported electoral work, she had not been focusing on it. But in 1980 (after Ronald Reagan was elected), Booth "gave a talk . . . that said, look, we've been fighting with one hand and we need every tactic we can have. . . . We need to move into the electoral arena."[33] CA took the idea of door-to-door fundraising and membership canvasses and spread it to a range of other organizations. Booth remembers how MA spearheaded new "organizations that would put into practice the models that we were developing. It was like a hothouse, and it was really very exciting, and you could see it every day; it made a difference [with] people learning these skills. The sessions were fabulous."[34]

Among the beneficiaries of MA's spreading the word was the Citizens Action League (CAL) in California, to which Booth introduced door-to-door canvassing. This paved the way for Mark Anderson to establish a CAL canvass, which played a key role in winning "lifeline" utility rates, local tax assessment reforms, a major environmentalist victory over a huge development project, and other accomplishments.[35] Mike Miller was, at different times, both chairman and executive director of CAL during this period.

Direct Action, Mass Action, and Organizing

In her manual and elsewhere, Booth often spoke about the importance of "organizing for mass action." In California and elsewhere, drawing from her movement experiences, she focused on developing broad issue areas, like energy, that could draw large numbers of people into participation. As she noted in her women's manual chapter, she was aiming to organize not a "few hundred or even thousands, but millions."[36]

Booth began from a movement-oriented perspective. Her initial aim was to bring lessons from organizing to movements that she and others worried might otherwise disintegrate. "We fear," she and her colleagues said at one point, "that the women's liberation movement may die."[37] Her perspective on the Alinsky tradition—what she saw as most important to draw from it and how she thought different aspects could be used—seems to have been deeply affected by this fear.

She stresses, however, that

> there were many aspects of this organizing, not one rigid model. There were overall statewide multi-issue organizations composed of . . . existing organizations. Some of those organizations were doing on the ground organizing in neighborhoods or with farmers or with congregations. Some were issue-based organizations working on senior or consumer issues. There were unions. There were faith-based institutions. Many had a canvass through which new leaders and activists were identified and which provided a broader base of public and financial support for the organizations.[38]

Overall, there was a sense in the manual and elsewhere in Booth's writings during the 1970s that she and her colleagues believed that they were in a "movement moment." Booth's writings at the time implied that, given the right issues and organizations, she and her colleagues could draw effectively enough on people's "felt needs" to foster long-term mass participation. She notes that they understood they "could not create a movement," aiming instead, in part, to "create the leadership and structures to seize the moment when a movement might arise."[39]

The pluses and minuses of this approach are still a matter of debate among organizers, social movement scholars, and others.

Commentary on Booth

—Mike Miller

The world of organizing is filled with efforts by organizers and organizing groups seeking to distinguish themselves favorably from other organizers and organizing groups. It is our version of sociologist Thorstein Veblen's "invidious distinction"—a comparison designed to establish superiority. There are many pressures leading to this: Funders ask, "How are you different from (and better than) ____?" Potential recruits, whether staff, leaders, or members, want to know why they should join you and not someone else. Third parties (journalists, researchers, public interest advocates, politicians, denominational leaders) whose opinions may be important for an organizer or his/her network ask similar questions. An organizer's own deep belief in the efficacy of a particular approach tends to lead him or her toward a belief that it is The Way.

We have yet to reach a stage of ecumenism or nonsectarianism that is essential if we are to move forward with the greatest possible people power. In this world, Heather Booth is one of the most ecumenical people. I admire her for that. But she, too, is human and susceptible to the Veblen trap. (I am too. During the existence of the CLEC, Tim Sampson—my CAL coleader—and I disparaged it by saying that "zero plus zero still equals zero.")

Booth says she builds on the strengths of Alinsky. If she had said that she takes from Alinsky and social movement sources to do something different, I would have no problem. But her formulation implies that she's adding new strengths and deleting weaknesses. She makes important points about the macho style and antagonism to women organizers (which I believe was there, and she correctly called the IAF on that), as well as conveying her interest in a closer exploration of electoral politics and her appreciation of the importance of a broader values conversation. But I think she omits important Alinsky strengths and adds some of her own weaknesses. They are the weaknesses of activists and activist-shaped organizations that have less than substantial connections with the majority of the people in whose interest and name they speak and act.

When then-Booth colleague and coauthor Harry Boyte interviewed me years ago for one of his books, he asked, "How many organizers would you say you've trained?" I replied, "Maybe a half a dozen or so." He laughed. "Midwest Academy says they've trained hundreds." (ORGANIZE Training Center, which I direct, and MA started at about the same time.) Booth and I had different understandings of the term "organizer." In this field, those differences are important.

Activist organizations and issue-based coalitions can be counted upon to be there on the social, environmental, and economic justice issues of the day. They may win important issue campaigns; we did in CAL. What is more problematic is the depth of their people power.

An illustration is the role of door-to-door canvassing. For an activist issue-based coalition, or a major electoral campaign, canvassing is no doubt an excellent tool. But for in-depth organizing, which requires periods of *inaction* (or, more accurately, a *different kind of action*), there are deep tensions with canvass operations because they require action and media attention to raise money. Further, there is pressure to make canvasser the entry-level position leading to organizer, despite the fact that the canvass experience teaches mobilizing or sales—excellent for an issue or candidate campaign, but not for organizing. The very large staff associated with canvass operations requires downtown offices and other accoutrements that are different from the more-accessible-to-local-people neighborhood offices that characterized organizing. Finally, canvasses create a large number of "paper members"—analogous to all the "members" claimed today by various internet organizations.

The distinction between "organizing" and "mobilizing" is central. It was developed initially by the Student Nonviolent Coordinating Committee (SNCC) to distinguish its work from that of Dr. Martin Luther King's Southern Christian Leadership Conference (SCLC). SNCC people (I was one of them) believed that we organized while SCLC mobilized. By this distinction, SNCC meant that its local organizers used a slower, more developmental process to build local units of people power that could subsequently come together in statewide organizations. It was this distinction that led the IAF away from these big-issue efforts. (Note: SNCC's distinction omitted the fact that often SCLC mobilizations were through the black church—the most stable and indigenous organization of the black community.)

But having someone else do the big-issue campaigns could have been a positive. In California, for example, San Jose's People Acting in Community Together (PACT) endorsed and brought hundreds of its members in the state capitol for CAL's lifeline utility rate campaign. PACT, whose lead organizer was an IAFer, made sure that its organizational identity was protected, but it also saw the campaign as both a way to express its members' anger at rising utility rates and to build itself. The art involved is to build an organization in the context of a wider issue mobilization.

What Alinsky called "mass-based organizations" (now called "broad-based organizations") are slower to act and often cautious when they do. They want to move moderates and some conservatives as well as liberals and progressives. They focus on breadth and depth of base, and identification and development of new leaders. And here's the key: organizations can mobilize, but mobilizations don't necessarily build organization. A core group can use external threats to mobilize people to engage in various actions. Whether the group then builds and nourishes a democratic infrastructure and a culture of participation from the mobilization is a separate question.

In the organizing world as it ought to be, activist groups and individuals would be a force pulling these organizations toward action, moving them toward the confrontation that IAF leader Rev. Johnny Ray Youngblood calls for in his speech in this volume (Chapter 20)—an example of how diverse strands can be brought together rather than being viewed as antagonistic. In this ought-to-be world, organizers and leaders in broad-based community organizations would be friendly to the causes lifted up by the activists. At the same time, they'd warn of the dangers of isolation from the majority of Americans who, in the final analysis, must become engaged if we are to realize the hopes and dreams that animate us all.

Heather Booth and Midwest Academy were, in the period focused on here, voices of reason in a movement world that was going crazy. They sought to build bridges across constituencies, and to get activists to look behind them to see if there were people following. But her formulations in this book indicate that she and MA had some significant blinders on. Our understanding of issues is different. "Issues," in my terms, are only issues if you've got the power to do something about them. If you don't, they are problems and people are suffering with those problems. An "issue" arises when you take action that creates a reaction—i.e., an adversary disagrees with you, so there is a conflict. To create issue coalitions that challenge centralized and immensely wealthy corporate power invites the dangers of being ignored. Defeat, demoralization, and despair are likely, as well as a shrinking army rather than an expanding one. Actions tend to become media-oriented rather than aimed at getting good-faith negotiations because the coalition lacks the depth to force those negotiations. The recent national coalitions that formed to push health care reform and immigration reform illustrate the problem.

Booth's discussion makes clear the gap between her understanding of 'organizing' and IAF and Alinsky's. 'Electoral organizing' mobilizes to support candidates. Lobbying mobilizes to support a legislative issue. Canvassing's strengths lend themselves to mobilizing, not organizing. CA and the strand of organizing that followed went from mobilization to mobilization. Ongoing organization at the base—central to people power—was not built. That said, let me acknowledge that the other side of the coin is when ongoing organizations refuse to engage in large mobilizations—whether to make a difference on an issue or in an electoral outcome. This too is a problem. Both organizing and mobilizing are important.

Craig Merrilees came out of the mid-to-late 1970s student movement. After several years of neighborhood organizing and local electoral campaigns, he left California for Chicago. He recalls meeting Booth in 1980: "She was part of an impressive group of leaders involved with the Midwest Academy and Citizen Action network. In 1981, Heather hired me as a staffer at Citizens/Labor Energy Coalition [CLEC]. We were turning out thousands of people who were angry about skyrocketing utility costs." Merrilees then discusses a division between the so-called chapter-based/nonpartisan and coalition/electoral models:

> Heather [and her associate] Ira Arlook were interested in aligning the Citizen Action network with electoral political campaigns. They were saying to progressive politicians, "We can be your troops on the ground—before the campaigns, to help get you elected, and after to help implement your agenda."
>
> Citizen Action groups were taking notice of Tom Hayden and the California Campaign for Economic Democracy [CED], which was a political campaign organization, not a community organizing/base-building effort like many Citizen Action groups had initially developed.[40] CED staff were focused on winning electoral campaigns; they were dealing with pollsters, direct mail experts, and political consultants. They identified, trained, and developed candidates, and trained people to manage campaigns, do media work, and organize field operations. But all this was very different from the slow, patient work of leadership development, and involvement in collective action that community organizing espouses as the path to power.
>
> In the early 1980s, Heather and Ira were advocating what was described as a "coalition" or "electoral" approach, based on a canvass that did double duty for fundraising and political outreach, plus a network of progressive organizations (labor, church, etc.) with resources, credibility, and some base, and usually a

political action committee [PAC]. Of course, a canvasser who contacts someone at their door can't possibly offer a transformational experience for members—it's more transactional. There's only the briefest trust and relationship established, very little discussion of ideas, and no leadership development. But this limited "grass-roots" canvassing was still deeper than the direct mail and phone banking used by most electoral campaigns.

These groups could operate with far fewer staff and a smaller budget than the base-building groups—but still brought enough talent, staff resources, and base to be players in the political world. Some of the organizations depended on smoke and mirrors to hide the thinness of their base and resources. Heather was saying, "Getting deeply involved with electoral politics says we're serious about power."

Jimmy Carter's defeat in 1980 had a major impact on the thinking among Citizen Action leaders, and although there was no consensus, many felt that we had to be more involved in electoral politics—because the consequences of a Ronald Reagan victory were too serious and urgent for the slower base-building approach. In 1981, Heather was identifying progressive political operatives and arranging for them to do training sessions on electoral tactics and strategy for staff and organizers at the Midwest Academy, and Citizen Action affiliates. The Democratic National Committee [DNC], Democratic Congressional Campaign Committee [DCCC], and Democratic Senate Campaign Committee [DSCC] were desperate to find resources to win back power, and they liked what Heather, Ira Arlook, Bob Creamer, and other Citizen Action leaders were offering—if funding could be arranged, which seemed possible from these political sources who were intrigued with the pitch that CA could help unite labor, religious, senior, consumer, [and] environmental groups into state and national electoral coalitions with electoral clout.[41]

What looked initially like slight differences in emphasis between MA and the IAF led to a pretty wide divergence as the two paths were extended. From my perspective, what was offered was not power, and certainly not changing the relations of power, but the possibility to win some issues and elect some better politicians. Further, IAF's emerging institution-based approach—as contrasted to organizing block clubs—took fewer, not more, organizers, so needed a smaller, not larger, budget.

Stan Holt, who spent two years as the director of organizing at Mass Fair Share (a CA affiliate), describes the experience:

I brought them the idea of block clubs, of grassroots organizing. We got a lot of college students from Clark College. A number of them were very lefty-progressive and wanted to change the whole world, but we got some good organizers out of it. We combined the political organizing on the state level with local organizing at the grass roots. The organizers worked 80 percent of their time on neighborhood issues, but would then get their leadership into the state issues the other 20 percent of the time, so they'd turn out the local people for a big action at the state capitol or something like that.

In other CA groups, they just skimmed the activists and liberals that came off their canvassing. It was a time of a lot of liberal energy among young people and adults. CA tapped into that. I don't think it ever really built a good grassroots structure that had any lasting power or depth in neighborhoods. I don't think [Fair Share staff leadership at the time] really appreciated the grass roots, what the grassroots people were doing for the organization. They kind of put up with me. I would train these organizers who came out of college in this organizing perspective. These progressive kids were all into the issues, but not into the work of producing people. When it came time for action, they couldn't produce. They were in Boston neighborhoods, so they didn't have to travel far for an action at the state capitol, which is in Boston. But kids who were doing the real grassroots organizing in the working-class suburbs could turn out troops. I'm not sure the original organizers of Fair Share really understood or appreciated this. It was still an organizer-run organization. They picked the issues; they designed it; they found statewide leaders who would pick up the issues. Some of these people had a base, and some didn't. The potential was there for a sustained grassroots organization.[42]

Mary Ochs, another longtime, very experienced, and highly regarded organizer, says this:

I've read the Midwest Academy organizing manual, and know some of the Academy's principal people. I respect their work deeply, but I saw it as somewhat different. Generally, I think they made activists more effective and were adept at building broad coalitions. I felt they were not as strong on the mechanics of building deep organizations. I felt there was much to learn from both but I viewed them as different.

In that period, their views on electoral politics were different. IAF said that the important thing was to be powerful enough to deal with whomever was elected. MA wanted to influence who was elected and gave that greater importance.

IAF and MA spoke differently about self-interest. I never thought IAF was talking about narrow self-interest. There was an emphasis on self-interest, but they were trying to focus people who came in with big Left ideas on self-interest as a prime tool for organizing. I had no problem with that. In that discussion there was sometimes a loss of the "enlightened" part of self-interest, which is the way Alinsky thought about it, let alone the broader question of values, which is what Heather and MA talked about. IAF's emphasis on values came later. Heather and MA spoke accurately about "too much emphasis on narrow self-interest," but I put that in the context of IAF trying to get people to go beyond their big Left ideas to the practicalities of organizing large numbers of people and not just those who were already politically conscious.

I was at a later meeting at which Ed Chambers, Peter Martinez, and others started talking more broadly about values. And some of the IAF analysis was radical without using words and language of the Left.

IAF had a critique of "movements" not being organizing. My response was, "I don't have to think that, but I can use what they are teaching to build real organization while keeping the idea of having a 'movement quality' to what we were doing."

I knew Lee Staples, one of the founders of Mass Fair Share, from WRO [Welfare Rights Organization] days. That got me to Fair Share. Michael Ansara was just taking over. There seemed more discussion of politics than how to organize. It was inspirational in some ways, but not a lot on how to build broad and deep organization. Fair Share did some of that, but I think that was the influence of individual organizers who were brought in who had other experiences—initially Lee and Mark [Splain] and Barb [Bowen], and later Ken Galdston, Jeanne DuBois, and others went out there and built something on the ground. But the dominant feeling in Fair Share was big-issue campaigns and not much deep leadership development. The big issues were viewed as superior to the local base-building work. There were waves of leader and organizer revolts.

There were exceptions, but some of the CA organizations were coalitions and/ or primarily canvassed members that didn't seem to have a deep leadership base.[43]

It need not be either-or. There is a tension between the two. It can be healthy or debilitating.

Since no one has yet made the revolution, a bit of humility should be offered on all sides. The country is better off as a result of the work Heather Booth, Midwest Academy, and Citizen Action did and do. And, in important ways, the country is in worse shape than it was when we all started on this road forty-plus years ago. There is no people power force now capable of slowing, halting, and reversing the growing poverty, deprivation, and economic insecurity in the country. Nor is there one capable of transforming the concentration of wealth and power in the hands of the few and creating a genuinely democratic social order. The task ahead is to see if a new generation of organizers will be able to discern a path that will take us where we need to go.

In 2013, I spoke with Miles Rapoport, who was close to MA, spent two years as a CAP organizer, and went on to direct a CA-affiliated organization in Connecticut. His observations seem right to me:

As I look back upon it now, the amount of energy invested in fighting people two or three degrees to the left or right of you astounds me. Incredible amounts of energy were wasted. There were far better ways to invest our time. In CAP, the real divisions were with other networks—not so much within CAP.

The rivalries were deeply intense. The differences pale when contrasted with the common agenda that could have been created. Had there been a will to find a common agenda, greater willingness to collaborate among the organizing groups, there could have been a citywide organization that covered more territory, represented different ethnic and racial groups, had a deeper base, etc. There could have been a real citywide coalition that would have been a powerful force in Chicago. CAP had an impact. So did NPA [National People's Action—see Chapter 12]. But together much more could have been possible, and more sustained.[44]

In his conversation with me, Rapoport criticized how the IAF tried to muscle a vote through CAP, which echoed what Arnie Graf says in this volume about the IAF telling him to deliver a vote in Milwaukee. In Rapoport's opinion, "What IAF wanted to accomplish was a reasonable thing to try to do, but not the way they did it."[45]

I once asked Alinsky why the Chicago groups didn't get together. He responded with one word: "Egos." Rapoport thinks otherwise: "I don't think it's as simple as egos. It wasn't simply one macho guy fighting another macho guy. It had more of a tribal cast to it: 'We do real organizing, and they do bullshit.' There are a lot of reasons, but in general I don't think they were about serious philosophical organizing differences. The key thing was not ideology."[46]

I will return to these questions in my conclusion to this volume.

Notes

1. Ronald J. Grele, "Reminiscences of Heather Tobias Booth: Oral History, 1984," 66, Student Movements of the 1960s Project, Columbia Center for Oral History, Butler Library, Columbia University, New York, 33.
2. Jo Freeman, "On the Origins of the Women's Liberation Movement from a Strictly Personal Perspective," 1995 (shorter version first published in *The Feminist Memoir Project*, edited by Rachel Blau DuPlessis and Ann Snitow [New York: Three Rivers, 1998], 171–96); available at "About Jo," *www.jofreeman.com.*
3. Heather Booth, interview by Aaron Schutz, July 26, 2012.
4. Ibid.
5. Ibid.
6. Ibid.
7. Ibid.
8. Ibid.
9. The questions Booth asked bring up an important substantive point that Alinsky addressed on other occasions when people raised questions about one issue or another. Had the IAFers been interested in having respectful conversation with her at the time, they would have probed "organizing women around day care," and asked whether it wouldn't be better to organize women around their powerlessness, and then see if in a particular context a campaign for child care programs might build their power. Her reply might have been,

"That's what I was attempting to do," but the evidence we have isn't clear. Alinsky raised the same point with clergy who were "organizing against urban renewal" but didn't have the power to affect urban renewal policy in their city.

10. Booth, interview.
11. All quotes in this paragraph are from Booth, interview.
12. Booth, interview.
13. Booth et al., untitled letter, n.d., box 251, folder "Saul Alinsky Industrial Areas Foundation July August 1971," Midwest Academy Records, Chicago History Museum.
14. Booth, interview.
15. Heather Booth, strategy chart, 1973, box 43, folder "Campaigns—Mapping a Campaign," Midwest Academy Records, Chicago History Museum.
16. Heather Booth, comment on early draft of this chapter, February 9, 2013.
17. Heather Booth, comments on early draft of this chapter, February 13, 2013.
18. Booth, interview.
19. Ibid.
20. Heather Booth and Kathy Blunt, notes for "Direct Action Organizing Class," October 4, 1971, box 80, folder "Coalition of Labor Union Women," Midwest Academy Records, Chicago History Museum.
21. Booth and Blunt, notes, 1.
22. Ibid., 1–2.
23. Ibid., 2.
24. Heather Booth, in conversation, February 8, 2013, referred to "Blue and White Papers" presented at a conference in California around 1970, but we were not able to locate copies of these.
25. Booth, interview.
26. Booth et al., "Theory and Strategy," "Leadership," "Tactics," "How to Do an Action," and "Media," box 80, folder "Coalition of Labor Union Women," Midwest Academy Records, Chicago History Museum.
27. Booth, interview.
28. Heather Booth, chapter 1 of *Direct Action Organizing: A Handbook for Women*, 3rd ed., by Heather Booth and Steve Max (Chicago: Midwest Academy, 1974), box 46, folder "Organizing—Direct Action Organizing," Midwest Academy Records, Chicago History Museum.
29. Ibid.
30. An example was the women leaders of the National Welfare Rights Organization, which we mention in Chapter 24 and which was fading out just as Booth was writing her manual. See also Premilla Nadasen, *Welfare Warriors: The Welfare Rights Movement in the United States* (New York: Routledge, 2004).
31. Booth, interview with Schutz.
32. Booth, interview with Grele, 66.
33. Ibid., 70.
34. Booth, interview with Schutz.
35. Note that we were interested in building a "majority constituency" organization and resisted the idea of lifeline being limited to low-income people, which the phrase "lifeline rates" usually now refers to. A lifeline rate provides a basic amount of gas and electricity at the lowest per-unit price. We also defeated the idea of "utility stamps" (like food stamps) for the same reason.
36. Booth, chapter 1 of *Direct Action Organizing*.
37. Ibid.

38. Booth, comment on early draft, February 9, 2013 or February 13, 2013.
39. Booth, comment on early draft, February 9, 2013 or February 13, 2013.
40. CED was founded by Hayden in 1976 after his surprisingly effective—albeit unsuccessful—Democratic Party primary campaign for Senate.
41. Craig Merrilees, interview by Mike Miller, February 18, 2014.
42. Stan Holt, interview by Mike Miller, May 20, 2013.
43. Mary Ochs, interview by Mike Miller, July 30, 2013.
44. Miles Rapoport, interview by Mike Miller, August 25, 2013.
45. Ibid. See Chapter 17 for Graf's account of the Milwaukee incident.
46. Rapoport, interview.

23

Direct Action Organizing:
A Handbook for Women

Chapter 1 (1974)

■

HEATHER BOOTH

While women have long done the office work and leg work for most organizations, they have usually been denied the roles to develop skills of strategic planning and organizational development. Among most activists, there is frustration in struggling for power in earnest for lack of experience and training.

To address these kinds of problems, the Midwest Academy has been formed. It is a school designed to train organizers and activists in political and economic theory, strategy and action. . . .

This summer the school will be taking applicants primarily interested in organizing with working women.

—Heather Booth, "Chicago Women's Liberation
Union and National Organization for Women
Announcement of Midwest Academy," n.d.

Editors' preface: The initial draft of this manual was written fairly soon after Booth's attendance at an Industrial Areas Foundation workshop, where, despite learning a great deal, she believed that women's issues and women organizers were not treated with sufficient respect or seriousness. This manual represents one of her early comprehensive efforts to imagine concretely how women and the energy of the women's movement (among other movements of the time) might be brought together with her own understanding of key aspects of the Alinsky organizing approach. It also reflects her concerns about the limits of the approaches to social action and social change prominent at that moment in history in the women's movement. She draws on her extensive experience working in the movement. Subsequent editions of this manual dropped the focus on women and became the Organizing for Social Change manual still published today by Midwest Academy; Booth is no longer listed as an author of that manual.

This document was first published as chapter 1 of *Direct Action Organizing: A Handbook for Women*, 3rd ed., by Heather Booth and Steve Max (Chicago: Midwest Academy, 1974). It is reprinted here by permission of Heather Booth.

Why a Training Guide for Women?

Women have been the backbone of most organizations. They make the phone calls, lick the stamps, ring the door bells. Yet women have not often played major roles in strategy mapping and decision making. As a result, they have not learned many of these crucial organizational skills. More importantly, many of the real concerns of these women are not put into the programs because they lack central and unified influence in the organization. A mystique has developed about organizing itself, so that it often frightens off the women who could most use its methods. While many women are capable enough to organize households, raise five or more kids, and involve people in all sorts of tasks, few women think of themselves as "organizers."

Organizing is a creative process, but one that is based on skills and accumulated experience. Getting people together and helping them build an organ to express their concerns is a talent. It involves understanding the social context for specific grievances and providing the resources by which individuals can *win for themselves* their rights through a planned series of events.

If ever there is to be a society in which men and women live as equals, women must have the skills and experience to organize for significant social change. For those women who are willing to take the leap and become organizers, for those who recognize that this is what they have been doing all along, and finally for men or women who will be organizing with women—for them, this handbook has been written.

This is a handbook on the fundamentals of direct action organizing. It is not the only form, nor the only right one. Service, education, legal and many other types of work have advanced our movement. Of all the forms of political activity, direct action is the most difficult. In other forms, partial achievements are the rule. If you service one person in health referral you feel you have helped out. If you educate one person in a liberation school you can feel you are making some one's life better.

BUT in direct action organizing, victory means actually affecting the relations of power. Victory at any one stage may be inadequate at another. Organizing implies a long range strategy. Its satisfaction comes from the fact that its victories, when achieved, are the most significant in terms of offering real alternatives for women. All the alternate service institutions and counter-education curricula cannot meet the needs of the majority of the population. Only demanding and winning from existing institutions changes for all of us, as our rights, will provide real alternatives. Direct action should be related to these other essential projects, services, and consciousness raising methods of our movement. It is focused on here because it is the least practiced and the one with the most potential right now.

Strategy Planning

Strategy is the overall plan of how to achieve your goals. It involves knowing where you are going, where you are now, and what steps you may take to help you achieve that end. Often women have been hesitant to approach a strategy because it implied heavy analysis. This has allowed them to be used in other people's strategies, because they had no agenda of their own.

Planning is the conscious preparation of alternatives; preparation which makes the unexpected into the expected and controlled. Women have often relied on "intuition" and "spontaneity" to know what to do. But our instincts often were just ways to keep us from consciously recognizing the abilities we had and the ways in which we could increase our skills by focused attention and planning.

There will always be spontaneous, unplanned aspects of our actions, but to the extent that we can, especially because people's lives depend on it, we must plan.

Organizing does not have an exact start or an exact end. It is a process using pre-existing resources and shaping those conditions into new elements. It involves more than one event with a beginning and end. Effective organizing is made up of a series of *campaigns*: planned activities in sequence, each one building on the strengths of the one before. They go from investigation to strategy planning, to build up for first action, to partial victories, and hopefully to final victory on a particular issue. But even here, a campaign does not end. From that victory, a group can build for even more significant change and remain ever vigilant to protect the rights that are won. . . .

If you have three people interested in working on a project and have a long range goal of involving hundreds, the first step is developing those three into a good working group by holding a meeting under their leadership. The next step may be having the recruits from that meeting go see the head of an agency. The next step a public meeting; and not 'till the tenth or later action, a victory. Think in terms of campaigns heading toward goals, rather than one-step actions. . . .

Principles and Goals

We should never lose sight of why we are organizing. This seems so obvious, yet caught in the press of daily events (each of which seems so urgent) one can lose sight of WHY they should be done. All the knowledge of technique is worthless without understanding what it is all for. The successes, when they are achieved, need to be worthwhile. This is true whether the achievements are concrete goals, like better health care or more amorphous ones, like more self-confidence and more women aware of their potential. There are long-range goals, like the end to discrimination, Equal Pay for Equal Work; and short-range ones, like getting out the next mailing, and setting up a good meeting. More difficult to set are *intermediate goals*, that are desirable and do-able. Intermediate goals are the key to successful realistic strategy.

We need to recognize the principles on which we are organizing: the broad social goals. This will help us define what we will mean by success. Effective organizing should develop from these basic points.

1. *Win Reforms That Improve People's Real Conditions.* This means meeting people's needs, serving their self-interest and being seen as a winner and a realist. It means changing the regulations or priorities so that women have child care or better health facilities. This begins to help in the real problems that women feel directly: their material conditions.
2. *Give People a Sense of Their Own Power and Potential.* This can only be done through an organization. Only an organization can be the bearer of past successes and have force greater than the strength of its individual members. Only organizations will make clear that problems are social, not just personal. If they are social we need social solutions to overcome them. Through this, reforms achieved are not seen as the "gift" of some "beneficent" ruler, or a privilege given through the goodness of the heart. Reforms are seen as rights struggled for and won through the power of women united.
3. *Alter Existing Relations of Power.* This means weakening the real power of those now exercising arbitrary control. It can be done most effectively through winning new structures for popular control. It might mean truly democratically controlled review of child care funding and licensing, or participation by women's and patient's groups in the planning of maternity services, as two examples.

    It is the most difficult of these three criteria for organizing, but will be the most important to insure the permanence of victories.

All these points need to guide us. We may emphasize one more than another on any specific issue. Keeping the principles in mind we will be more able to set priorities for our work. We also must know what victory looks like, to claim it when we win.

Organizational Self-Interest

An *organization* is a self-sustaining, powerful, growing unity that is the tool of its members. It is their organ for expression, strength, and direction on the issues it works with. The reason for organizing should be to build an organization. Only this will give people authentic power. However, this is often forgotten in unrealistic attempts to rush into activity or unsure coalitions.

THE NEEDS OF THE ORGANIZATION, THE REALITIES OF THE ORGANIZATIONAL SITUATION MUST BE CONSIDERED AT THE START.

Are you beginning to build up from scratch? Is the need now for uniting unrelated members? Integrating new people? Training leadership? Supporting veteran

members? Do you now need to expand and find new resources? These considerations will determine how you decide to work and on what issue, how large or small
the campaign will be. Organizational resources are precious womenpower, leadership, staffing. Plan ahead.

After such questions, the general organizational situation should be studied. Are
these other groups working in the arena? Must you work with them? Must they work
with you? What is the basis for alliance? Organizations need to have a strong sense of
self-respect in order to convey that sense to [their] members.

Constituencies

The constituency is the people who are affected. First ask, "Whose problem is it?"
Then ask, "What do they see as their stake in the problem?" People will join a voluntary organization because it gives them something they need. These needs (self-
interests) must be understood, in the following ways:

1. Every possible constituency should be listed and considered, even those which
   seem unlikely. Then see where interests overlap. For example, on the childcare
   issue, while it is clear mothers might be interested, it might not be so obvious
   (yet more likely in fact), that small day care center operators will want to organize to make more realistic licensing and funding requirements.
2. Organizability of the constituency must be considered. This often turns a likely
   group into a difficult one. For example, young mothers with several children
   needing childcare may be very interested in the issue, but lack of childcare
   may be such a burden that they will not be able to attend meetings, or keep
   up with the organizing tasks.
3. Importance of the concern to the individuals. If the same mother who has
   no time is so hopping mad about how she is abused, she may well bring
   her child to the action and overcome problems of illness, time, money and
   immobility.
4. How much risk is there? Employees might want to join a picket, but would not
   want to risk their jobs. Risks must be weighed against possible achievements.
5. Social needs, desire for power, friends. All bind people in a group and should not
   be overlooked in building the core. Relationships between people as well as the
   issues give group cohesion.

For women, especially, in the cities, one consideration must be physical danger (real
and imagined). Meetings at night are more difficult in areas of high rape rates (though
this fact might make a rape project an important alternative). Targets need to be
picked within the physical and psychological reach of the constituency. Women especially have been trained to fear authority, or at least to be polite and obedient because

they lack the power to do much else. We need to develop actions to meet and raise the expectations of the membership.

In general, the issues should be significant, affecting large numbers in deeply felt ways, and ones which they believe [are] conceivably winnable. Our organizations need to build up self-confidence. This will best be done if we show people they are actually accomplishing something.

Institutions and Targets

You must be looking for HANDLES on an issue. They help people grasp a situation. Handles make good ideas into do-able projects. The key question is: WHAT SOURCES OF POWER CAN YOU EXERT OVER THE INSTITUTION THAT IS YOUR TARGET?

YOU NEED SEVERAL HANDLES AND ISSUES, NOT JUST ONE SLOGAN.

Understand the many ways in which the institution and its parts touch people's lives: federal, state, local levels; executive, judicial, legislative, and regulatory bodies; business and board connections; social and personal affiliations.

For example, if you were concerned about meat prices in one chain store you might develop tactics at the store as well as around:

- price commissions, city councils, then members of each body
- churches, clubs, cultural endeavors, especially of the highest ranking store executives
- branch stores, local managers

Look for who has the power, controls the money, etc. See what decisions are coming up, what planning meeting is to be held. Look both for forums for your position and for places where you can gain power from the weakness of the enemy.

You need to match your resources to the weakness of the opposition; this is the oldest tenet of military doctrine.

Don't attack where they expect. They will develop a "channel" for you that ends in bureaucratic mazes. Go to bodies that have power in an area, but are not used for making these decisions.

For example, if you are fighting a rate increase of Bell Telephone you will find the state regulatory agency is accustomed to absorbing such conflicts in its hearing procedures. But they might not be used to a hearing on discrimination cases and regulation. On the other hand, state legislators might be used to a hearing on issues of discrimination, but not on issues of rate increases.

Identify their self-interest, play one off against the other: Democrat vs. Republican, upstate vs. downstate, in-group vs. out-group. Your enemy's enemy may be your ally. Your potential ally may be a target until it is definitely your active ally.

YOU MUST MAKE DEMANDS ON INSTITUTIONS IF YOU EXPECT TO ALTER RELATIONS OF POWER.

On Power and Struggle

Power for us means primarily our numbers (or as customers—our dollars, as employees—our labor, as citizens—our votes). We have not won the power to participate as equals. We must organize for that power, democratically. To shy away from that organizing is to endorse the conditions as they are. To deny that the issue is one of power—where people have to choose sides—is to play into the hands of those currently, illegitimately exerting their power over us.

Women, powerless for so long, often fear attempts to win power and therefore to effectively win their rights. Sometimes this is the fear of failing. But this can be overcome by designing initial actions which are more assured of victories, as it has been by all groups entering into struggle for the first time.

More difficult to deal with is fear of succeeding. Sometimes this is couched as fear of being un-feminine. This can really be overcome only when the anger is great, and the possibility of reward from achieving the victory is sufficiently attractive. Thus we must constantly provide *desirable, realistic* alternatives for people. Our movement should not appear [to be one that is] just for outcasts. It should appear to be one that can be a majority movement with benefits for all women.

When arguments are raised about "femininity" it is sometimes useful to remember the words of Sojourner Truth, an ex-slave woman active in the early Suffrage and Abolitionist movements. When she heard some men saying that fighting for one's rights was not women-like, she said, ". . . I could work as much and eat as much as a man—when I could get it—and bear the lash as well, and ain't I a woman? I have borne thirteen children and seen most of them sold into slavery. And when I cried out in my mother's grief and none but Jesus heard me . . . and ain't I a woman?" Femininity may all be in the eye of the powerful. The ability to define ourselves is an issue of power. We can be, in Helen Reddy's words "strong . . . invincible . . . woman."

Sometimes, the fear of going for power is couched as not wanting to play men's games. To the extent that institutions have not been controlled or influenced by women, they have excluded us from having power over our lives. This does not mean that power as such is evil: but power unfairly held, undemocratically exerted, unaccountable—that is evil. This is what we need to change. Whether we like it or not, equality and an end to discrimination are questions of power.

There will be some who fear winning because they are so used to co-optation (that is, used to movements being bought off with half successes). Reforms without ongoing struggles and organization can just strengthen the hand of those in power. The war on poverty did this in many cities—starting as a popular struggle in the streets, and ending as a source of patronage with minimal social service. Avoiding co-optation depends more on the manner of the struggle and organizational strength, than on the reform itself.

It is indeed an illusion to think that any one struggle will yield a final victory. Nor will the liberation of women, or any group, come from the building of victory

on victory. "Liberation" involves a more revolutionary re-ordering of society, a quali-
tative change

But reforms are intermediate steps. They prove to people that we are working for
good, here and now. They build self-confidence. They can weaken the arbitrary power
of those that now rule.

As important as any one of the reforms is the struggle that builds together a
working organization. The struggle teaches people how to work in a united fashion.
The organization is thus as important as the reforms, because it is necessary for
checking on the targets, building our solidarity, and taking on new ideas.

Forms of Direct Action

Anything might be a good tactic if it builds your strength, and weakens the opposition. Be flexible and creative. Tactics are just a reflection of your power (numbers,
prestige, appeal, etc.). . . .

[*In the rest of this section, Booth listed different forms of direct action, including confrontation, negotiation, public hearings, embarrassment, guerilla theater, mass demonstrations, exposes, civil disobedience and arrest, legal disruptive actions, accountability sessions,
and educationals/teach-ins.*]

Guidelines

Developing these and other types of actions, we need to be sensitive to the specifics of
the situation, as well as to general principles. We should remember:

- to be especially sensitive to people's personal styles and choices, knowing it is
  hard for women to survive. Wearing makeup or bras does not determine whose
  side you are on in the most important struggles.
- we need to really care for women as people, and be concerned about their well-
  being. But the basis of concern needs to be self-respect.
- we need to understand and demonstrate that problems women most often feel to
  be personal are really social in nature.

This means:

1. they are not the only ones feeling it,
2. they are not alone to blame for it, and
3. the solution must also be social.

For example, the women who feel they are or would be bad mothers, because they
need to or want to work, need to find support while they demand child care centers.

If we are interested in organizing for social charge:

- it means we want to reach out and join with most women. We cannot be talking about a few hundred or even thousands, but millions.
- if we are talking about millions of people with jobs, families, skills and interests, we must provide *divisions of labor* in movement activities. Everyone cannot make the leaflets, run them off, give the speeches, and make sure the microphones are on—all this in addition to a personal life.
- if we are talking about such a division of labor we need to establish solid organizations that hold people together beyond feelings of sisterhood or personality.
- if we are to build organizations we must demonstrate by our activities, as well as our words and person, that alternative social relations are both desirable and POSSIBLE. THIS CAN BE DEMONSTRATED THROUGH ACTIONS THAT MOVE TOWARD SOCIAL GOALS.
- if we are serious about these goals it means we must be able to win victories. Women have been losers too long. We are not used to winning. If we are asking people to take risks, at least we must show we have the possibility of success. And we must show our success is significant.

For all this we need direct action organizing for power for women.

Difficulties of Being a Woman Organizer

The organizer is not a neuter role. All of the real and emotional factors weighing on most women, also weigh on the organizer to some extent. She is a woman venturing beyond established roles, in a risky position.

Being trained and more used to "polite" if not passive roles, women often lack the self-confidence to push ahead. This makes them vulnerable to problems of organizational and individual complaints. If she is seen as the strong person, that may lead to focus on her for gripes and complaints which she may not be accustomed to handling. It is a struggle to maintain emotional balance and be both sensitive to people and strong enough to have complaints and attacks roll off.

For a women organizer, her sex and sexuality will likely become an issue. The aggressive styles so necessary to maintain oneself may make her seem a "bitch" to some. If she is less aggressive, she may seem unserious and less secure. She will have to contend with attitudes of men organizers, often hostile to women. Because women are defined as sexual objects, she stands to lose either way. She has less credibility, even when she does succeed because this is not supposed to be a woman's field.

Women can turn these negatives into positives. Where she may be vulnerable, she is also often sensitive to personal interaction. With this awareness she can keep in touch with the relationships which provide organizational glue: make the group stick together. Particularly important is the fact that she may be more sensitive to the needs of the women in the group and help them develop into leaders.

As with most contexts where women are breaking into new areas, the solution to these problems depend on winning victories which will build both her confidence and her organization. It is likely she will also need support groups amongst friends and co-workers to provide encouragement and perspective. There must be a situation in which she does not have to feel that she is organizing. As more and more women are trained in these roles, the pressures on any one organizer will be that much less; the support that much greater.

Finally, what will build a woman organizer's self-confidence is successful organization, seeing women coming into their own, and feeling their power. In this, united struggle, lies the real meaning of sisterhood.

24

An Introduction to Wade Rathke and ACORN

■

AARON SCHUTZ

The roots of the Association of Community Organizations for Reform Now (ACORN) in Alinsky are a bit indirect, but clearly there. Here I trace what is more a "dotted line" than a direct connection, and explore some of the similarities and differences between what started in Syracuse and what ended up as ACORN.

The Community Action Training Center

The story begins in the early 1960s, when Alinsky supporter and Syracuse University professor of social work Warren Haggstrom managed to get the federal War on Poverty's Office of Economic Opportunity (OEO) to directly fund a university program he ran called the Community Action Training Center (CATC). It brought together about half-a-dozen graduate students in Syracuse's Master of Social Work (MSW) program and half-a-dozen "trainees" (who were not official students) drawn from different branches of the civil rights and northern student movements. Some of them, including Rhoda Linton and Bill Pastreich, later became key organizers in the movement of welfare recipients to obtain increased benefits and decent treatment by welfare bureaucracies and social workers—this movement led to the National Welfare Rights Organization (NWRO). Their work deeply influenced Wade Rathke, ACORN's founder.

The CATC program combined seminars on organizing with extensive fieldwork and an associated research effort. The students worked under the direction of Alinsky organizer Fred Ross Sr.; Alinsky himself was a regular lecturer in and consultant to the program.

Ross trained the students to implement organizing drives such as those he'd done in the Community Service Organization (CSO; see Chapter 8). They were sent to different locations to form local organizations. From door-knocking and house meetings a series of issues emerged, which led to a large meeting. At that meeting, issue committees and a constitution committee were created, and voter registration took place. The issue committees worked on particular challenges like housing and parks. A number of local organizations emerged as part of the Syracuse Community Development Association (SCDA), a low-income individual and family membership organization.

As might be expected, there were soon confrontations with the powers-that-be, including the mayor of Syracuse (a Republican), who was furious that federal money was paying organizers who were behind attacks on him (coming largely from Democratic areas). The mayor, along with mayors and local officials from across the nation, as well as members of Congress, mounted an attack against the federal agency—the Community Action Program (CAP)—that funded these activities. Syracuse became a poster child during congressional hearings on the dangers of funding organizations without going through local elected officials. CAP's rules were soon changed, giving existing local authorities more control over local Community Action Agencies (CAAs). Under pressure from donors and officials, the university increasingly restricted Haggstrom's control of CATC. The federal government ultimately defunded CATC in early 1966.

Nothing better illustrated the difference between the War On Poverty and Alinsky's projects than the Syracuse experience. In his *Social Solutions to Poverty*, Scott Myers-Lipton writes, "OEO hoped that CAP would empower the poor and thereby lead to poverty solutions and to a more democratic society as the poor became active citizens rather than passive recipients of aid."[1] What Syracuse made clear was that the government wouldn't fund serious reform that involved challenging the government. Based in large part on the Syracuse experience, Alinsky wrote a paper titled "The War On Poverty: Political Pornography."

At the same time, internal tensions led to confrontations within the CATC. A full accounting of these events has yet to be written; it seems clear that there were a number of causes. First, the students and trainees within CATC didn't share goals or tactics. The trainees had come out of the civil rights movement and the New Left and were used to a more egalitarian and "fluid" movement organization. Ross also had very clear ideas about how organizing was to happen, intent on applying the approach he had used in the CSO. He saw himself as the director, and he expected the staff to follow his lead. Ross said to Miller at the time that the students wanted to "experiment with different and new approaches." He replied, "I told them that was fine, but they first had to learn how to do the basics. Picasso first learned to render."

Pastreich remembers that Ross was also opposed to militant demonstrations. A protest that drew over two hundred people to a welfare office "turned into a shouting match, you know, just a whole big to-do, which in welfare rights days" was not a big deal. But "Ross then had this meeting with us just to say, 'What is the matter with you people?' He bawled us out for not having control. It didn't strike me that he was saying you shouldn't have demonstrations. It sounded at the time that he was saying you should always have this thing under control and you didn't just let people go wild." But Pastreich also later came to believe "that Fred really did not do [disruptive] demonstrations. He really believed in the vote and having numbers would convince government to do stuff."[2]

A key moment came when Students for a Democratic Society (SDS) was holding a conference in Newark on a range of national and international issues, including Vietnam. Some of the organizers asked their leaders whether they wanted to go, and when they said yes, the leaders went—over Ross's objections. "The students," Haggstrom noted, "said that they had only brought up the Newark conference to their organizations as information, and after that merely followed the maxim to: 'Let the People Decide.' Fred Ross had told them not to weaken the joint organizational effort by pulling leadership elsewhere, nor to divide the organizations within and among themselves by injecting into them the SDS stand against the war in Vietnam."[3] As a result, the three organizers who went to the conference were fired.

This brought on even more internal dissension, as well as protests by some of the local organizations to defend "their" organizers. Amid university administrative pressures, and an abortive effort to get the federal government to reverse its funding decision, the organization slowly died.

Welfare protests in Syracuse, however, were a harbinger of the future. In fact, Pastreich organized the first Syracuse welfare protest, around Easter clothing. (In that period, there were various specific discretionary benefits recipients could claim; their existence was buried in the small type of welfare regulations.) When the protestors won, the idea spread across the different organizations associated with CATC, leading to the protest that so inflamed Ross. Near the end of its existence, the CATC "hosted a Poor People's War Council on Poverty, . . . the first national convention of the poor, . . . [gathering] over six hundred delegates from twenty-one states, including civil rights veterans, welfare recipients, and a range of middle- and working-class people who had fought the local battles of the War on Poverty."[4] Attending was George Wiley, who would later head the NWRO.[5]

After Syracuse, Linton moved to New York and began working on welfare issues. Pastreich went into the Peace Corps to avoid the draft.

The Massachusetts Welfare Rights Organization

When Pastreich got back to the United States, he first worked with Ross in New York, organizing the grape boycott there. But after six months he left "to become the first paid field organizer of the NWRO" in Massachusetts. The story of the genesis of the NWRO has been explored extensively elsewhere.[6] Here we focus on the Massachusetts Welfare Rights Organization (MWRO).

Pastreich and Linton, who was still in New York, developed the strategy now known as the "Boston Model," which Pastreich applied to the creation of a statewide organization with fifty-five local organizations and five thousand members.

Lawrence Bailis called the approach "a cookbook for community organizers" with "a detailed set of instructions to guide the neophyte's every step." The core premise of the Boston Model was that welfare recipients could be mobilized quickly only with "believable promises to bring about changes that would have a direct, tangible impact upon people's lives."[7] Organizers went door-to-door with a local recipient in a new neighborhood, talking to residents about the concrete benefits they could receive if they collectively approached the welfare office. The door-to-door work was almost always assisted by a list of welfare recipients in the neighborhood, whose names were acquired by more or less nefarious means—from "sympathetic case workers," local CAAs that "catered heavily to welfare recipients," and recruiting tables at local stores on "check day," when recipients received their checks.[8] The aim was to get people to a large meeting, from which they would then walk with their demands to a local office.

According to Pastreich, Ross said that "old leaders are just going to be in the way. The question is whether you'll fight them in the beginning or later, not whether you'll fight them." Pastreich did try to neutralize opposition from local leaders. To avoid having local leaders spread negative information, a welfare rights organizer would make "persistent efforts to win the sympathy of a few community leaders." But an organizer "did not attempt to recruit any of them for leadership roles in . . . [a] new group."[9] As we note in Chapter 2, however, Ross did look for "informal leaders"—the people without titles who were respected by local people—and it was through them that he did his organizing.

Pastreich departed from both Alinsky and Ross: formal leaders were bypassed, and informal leaders weren't particularly sought. When asked why MWRO eliminated the house meeting, he explained that this change was, first, a result of a lack of staff (although Wade Rathke would use volunteer "organizing committees" later in Springfield). Second, in contrast with Syracuse, MWRO leaders already knew what their issue was and what they wanted people to do—so they didn't need to hold house meetings to generate issues from their constituency.[10]

As Bailis explains, this approach was less focused upon leadership development. The organizers really mobilized people with the promise of immediate material benefits if they came to a meeting. Then the organizers and a few activists they'd been working with more closely led people out of the meeting on a march to welfare department offices. As long as there were repeated payoffs, this approach could work. The governor soon announced that the system would change to a "flat grant" system. This was a major victory, because it raised recipient income and eliminated the paternalistic discretion of a welfare worker, but it also eliminated "the special needs grant provisions" that the Boston model depended upon.[11]

Other, difficult challenges began to emerge. On the welfare system side, "a stiffening of Welfare Department responses to MWRO demonstrations . . . cast doubt on" the ability of the Boston model to maintain itself.[12] At the same time, the organization was in the thick of a major internal conflict between old and new leaders and staff that was never resolved, and that affected leader-staff relations as well. By 1970, the orga-nization had lost most of its strength, and it did not have the capacity, institutional structure, or strong local leadership necessary to sustain itself.

Wade Rathke and the MWRO

The new chief organizer who faced the conflicts described above was none other than the future creator of ACORN: Rathke. Pastreich had originally hired Rathke out of a local CAA and sent him to Springfield on the recommendation of Rathke's former supervisor. Rathke was given almost no training beyond reading the Boston Model document and whatever NWRO pamphlets he could get his hands on. A result was that he ended up having a somewhat different experience than Pastreich had in Boston. One significant change—although he didn't realize it at the time—was that instead of focusing in on one organizing drive, he organized in multiple locations at the same time. Since he was organizing by himself, this meant that he was dependent upon "organizing committees" in these different locations to do much of the work themselves.

Events also intervened. During an early protest at a welfare office for winter clothes for adults, his group faced stiffer resistance than they had usually encountered else-where. Police moved in, arrested Rathke and others, and then tricked the women sitting-in into leaving the office. As John Atlas describes it, one of the women leaders saw the police pushing one of her organization's members, and "she crashed through a glass door and into the welfare office. Although other welfare rights demonstra-tors stayed disciplined, someone in the gathering crowd threw a rock at the paddy wagons, and a riot ensued." Atlas adds, "The incident touched off two days of unrest in Springfield and the destruction of property worth millions of dollars."[13]

Rathke first saw the protest as "a complete debacle," but at the next meeting he held, he discovered that people actually felt empowered. Their loyalty to the organiza-tion intensified through this experience. People not already on welfare began to join MWRO, and Rathke moved beyond the focus on welfare, organizing "a successful campaign around free school lunches for poor children." The membership was multi-racial, and included blacks, Puerto Ricans, and whites. Lacking much background in organizing and without significant training, Rathke had nonetheless already begun—almost accidentally—to develop the outlines of his own approach.[14]

By the time Rathke took over the Boston office, he was concerned that the single, narrow-constituency "welfare rights" approach "might be a dead end." He was also worried that the focus on getting immediate benefits was too limited. He "began formulating a more audacious strategy to help the poor."[15] After Boston blew up, Wade made a deal with Wiley to create a new kind of organization in Arkansas, where Wiley hoped to build power in the backyard of powerful politician Wilbur Mills, who was on a key Senate committee related to Wiley's goals.[16] Thus ACORN (originally *Arkansas* Community Organizations for Reform Now) was born.

The Creation of ACORN

Rathke's aim was to move beyond the focus on welfare recipients to "organize a constituency organization of low and moderate income families." He had come to the conclusion that a wider base than welfare recipients was required to exercise serious power in American politics. He was interested in a multiracial and ethnic, multi-issue organization, for what he began to term "majority constituency organizing."[17]

His approach to ACORN was almost completely informed by his experience in Massachusetts, especially his somewhat unique experience in Springfield. He took what worked and reacted against what didn't work. "I thought," he notes, "the door-to-door work [in the MWRO] was exceptionally strong. I thought the [ACORN] model needed to be built on an organizing committee because that was the only way I'd obviously been able to work." Otherwise, "much of what I saw as the components for building ACORN when I moved to Arkansas were in reaction to things I thought did not work in Massachusetts and welfare rights. If that was up, this was down. This was to the right, this would be to the left."[18]

As described in the ACORN model document, included in this volume as Chapter 25, the approach Rathke developed for an initial organizing campaign in a neighborhood was fairly straightforward and designed to be easily replicated by novice organizers. Rathke associate Gary Delgado summarized the outline this way:

1. Research and analysis;
2. Initial contact work;
3. Establishment of an organizing committee and specifying the issue for the campaign;
4. Preparation for the neighborhood meeting;
5. Holding the neighborhood meeting;
6. Initiating collective social action;
7. Evaluation.[19]

Also key to organizing successfully was how the organizer assessed who would be appropriate members of the organizing committee—i.e., their capacity for leadership.

After research on the neighborhood, initial contact work was done to identify the initial members of the organizing committee (OC). These leaders were identified through a range of potential strategies, including following up on names uncovered during other ACORN drives or found on voter registration lists, chatting with folks at a local gathering place, running a "safe petition" (i.e., one that almost anyone would sign) to get names and engage in conversation, and even just going door-to-door. As Rathke describes it, the OC

> would be a combination of some of the early leaders and some people who caught fire on the doors who you'd been able to pull out with real interest or enthusiasm

or skill because of their commitment to the issue or their effectiveness on the doors. And they became the workers, the twenty, thirty people who did the work of the drive. If a drive was six or eight weeks, there would be six to eight of these [OC] meetings held throughout the neighborhood that would help funnel the various decisions around what were the priority issues we were hearing about.[20]

The OC selected the initial issue for the drive, signed a letter sent out to membership prospects across the neighborhood, collected dues, worked with the organizer on door knocking, and helped prepare for the neighborhood mass meeting. During the early organizing meetings, the organizer was mostly in charge, but then slowly faded back so that when the final mass neighborhood meeting took place, the OC members ran everything. "Not surprisingly, many of them were elected as the first leaders of the group, because they had this ability and had built a base throughout the process of the organizing drive."[21]

New organizers were trained through an organizing drive with a skilled organizer. Essentially that meant going with the organizer wherever she or he went, watching, imitating and learning. After that, the organizer-trainee did his or her own organizing drive, with the skilled organizer watching everything she or he did. If that was successful, the organizer-trainee was now an organizer supervised by the skilled organizer who had done the initial training. Soon, the new organizer was replicating that process. It was an amoeba-approach to organization growth. Rathke notes that "although we would be pushing through the door-knocking process into the organizing committee meetings, [those holding the organizing committee meetings in their homes would] also for fear of embarrassment and personal prestige be pulling neighbors and friends and others in that neighborhood into that meeting at their house as well."[22]

The goal was a turnout of 15 to 25 percent of the contacts who would elect leaders, adopt a platform, affiliate with ACORN, and move from their meeting into nonviolent direct action—typically on a small issue they could quickly win. The small victories provided leadership training and a sense of efficacy and self-confidence. Chapters quickly connected with other chapters—in their city, region, state, and later the country—to work on bigger issues. These chapters would meet monthly to work on local issues and connect with regional and national campaigns.

Like Ross's groups and the MWRO, ACORN was an individual member–based organization. Institutional leaders were sought to support campaigns early on, to give legitimacy, and to neutralize potential opposition, but, in part because they did not usually live in these neighborhoods, they were not sought as leaders in the organizations. But the organizers did seek out people who had relationships—those who were respected by their neighbors in the neighborhoods. Rathke notes, for example, that "if I'm out on the doors in the East End of Little Rock, and if I ask who else do you think might be interested in joining ACORN, I keep hearing Rose Washington's name, I'm going to find Rose Washington, and see if I can in fact either recruit her into the organization or neutralize her so she's not opposed to the organization. Because obviously she has a base." Rathke was also careful to control the early agenda development of a chapter. It was local issues that were widely expressed and quickly winnable (rather than the particular interest of a single leader) and the ACORN larger issues (regional, state, national) that he and his organizers wanted to use to shape the chapter. Rathke notes that

> there's always a history of struggle. And if there are people that have been involved in a history of real struggle and have a base—they may not have an organization, in fact they probably don't—often they've been beaten and had their teeth handed to them. We would categorically try to find those people. We wanted those people as part of an ACORN organization. They would bring the local legitimacy on the ground, they would build the respect they had from whatever that legend or tradition might be, and that was a more important blessing for the organizing effort, if you will, than a letter from a bishop downtown, or the head of the Arkansas AFL-CIO or whatever it might be.[23]

In ACORN, organizers had a great deal of control, both in their "selection" of leaders for the initial organizing committee and in framing what ACORN is about and what it should be doing. Rathke called how he ran ACORN "tight-loose." On a few key things, control was tight. (There was, for example, no question about Rathke's authority to hire and fire organizers.) Otherwise, it was fairly loose. Rathke notes that individual groups "had absolute autonomy in terms of deciding on the issues and tactics, but if it went past your area to another neighborhood or a citywide issue, you had to coordinate."[24]

While Miller and I don't have extensive information about membership turnover in ACORN, reports from former ACORN organizers indicate it was a problem.[25] As I noted earlier in this volume, Shel Trapp struggled with turnover in his somewhat similar block club–based approach. It seems likely that for ACORN, membership turnover on the local level was similarly a challenge in most cases. In ACORN, conflict generated by a campaign or action (such as participation in a voter registration drive) provided a different kind of relational base among the members who engaged in it—in the same way that participation in a strike builds solidarity among the workers who walk the picket lines.

While in the MWRO members had paid minimal dues, ACORN dues in the early years were significant enough to provide more than half of the organization's income. Rathke was a student of H. L. Mitchell and of the Southern Tenant Farmers' Union (STFU) of the 1930s, one of the first integrated labor unions in the United States. Rathke notes that he "tracked down" Mitchell in 1973, who told him "STFU died because of its inability to collect dues. Believe me, I never forgot that."[26]

Rathke reports that the organizer-to-neighborhood organization ratio was initially one to eight, but later this declined to one to three, and the process became increasingly staff-intensive (and more dependent on outside money). The organization attempted early on to create "ACORN representatives" who would act essentially as volunteer organizers in individual groups, but this approach found only limited success, and increasingly fell out of favor.[27]

ACORN in Arkansas soon became a significant voice for low- to moderate-income people there. Not only that, but drawing from his experience in Springfield, Rathke managed in that southern state, in the early 1970s, to bring white and black working people into the same organization. It got into electoral politics, electing school board members and briefly taking over a very large county-elected board in Arkansas. The earlier drives started in white communities, because Rathke believed that you could move from white to black but not the other way (although sometimes you could organize simultaneously with both).

ACORN became an effective voice for low- to moderate-income people. Over time, however, its constituency became increasingly African American and based in the cities.[28] It was able to capture the imagination and energy of dedicated and talented young people as its organizers, and by creating a relatively simple and replicable organizing model, it continued to grow until its unfortunate demise at the end of the first decade of the twenty-first century. ACORN grew from its 1970s beginnings into a nationally recognized organization within a twenty-year time span. Its combination of local autonomy and centralized control gave ACORN an extraordinary capacity to adopt and move quickly on national campaigns in which it made a difference—whether the target was the political process or corporate exploitation. ACORN became particularly prominent for its large-scale voter registration/get-out-the-vote drives among low- and moderate-income voters, especially African Americans who would otherwise have been unlikely either to register or, if registered, turn out to vote. While ACORN was nonpartisan in its work, this was, of course, a constituency that voted heavily on the Democratic Party side of the ballot. That opened the door for alliances with key segments of labor and "progressives" among the Democrats. In its later years, ACORN entered into alliances with various other Alinsky-tradition groupings as well. An internal scandal and a relentless effort by the Republican right wing put ACORN out of business.[29]

Over the years, major criticisms have been raised about how much depth ACORN had "at the base." By selecting a relatively small neighborhood—sometimes as small as five thousand people—in which to build a chapter, and saturating that neighborhood with ACORN contacts and information in the organizing drive, ACORN sought to achieve depth but in a small area. How well it succeeded, and for how long it was maintained over time, is a matter of dispute. Miller and I are satisfied that at least in some areas, where a combination of good organizers and leadership existed, the local organizations had substance. And in other areas, they didn't.

As I noted at the outset of this chapter, the connections between ACORN and Alinsky are weaker than those of the other examples in this volume. The MWRO "Boston Model" was developed by Pastreich and Linton, two people trained by Ross, but the approach left out key aspects of Ross's vision—especially Ross's focus on house meetings and the development of local leaders. Rathke developed his own unique approach to organizing with the MWRO while left largely to his own devices in Springfield. Yet Rathke was a careful student of everything he could learn about organizing—from individuals and books—and was deeply influenced by his MWRO experience. The tenuous links to Ross and Alinsky along with his own experience and research together allowed for the development of something new in ACORN.

Key References

For the CATC and MWRO:

Bailis, Lawrence. *Bread or Justice: Grassroots Organizing in the Welfare Rights Movement*. Lexington, MA: Lexington Books, 1974.

Haggstrom, Warren C. "The Power Bind" (unpublished manuscript). N.d. *www.gatherthepeople.org*.

Kornbluh, Felicia. *The Battle for Welfare Rights: Politics and Poverty in Modern America*. Philadelphia: University of Pennsylvania Press, 2007.

Lancourt, Joan E. *Confront or Concede: The Alinsky Citizen Action Organizations*. Lexington, MA: Lexington Books, 1979.

Linton, Rhoda. Interview by Aaron Schutz, January 29, 2013.

———. "Why Social Action? A Study of Motivations and Objectives of Social Action Organization Students and Trainees in the Syracuse University School of Social Work Field Placement and the Community Action Training Center (1963–64; 1964–65)." MSW thesis, Syracuse University, 1965.

Miller, Marjorie. "The Pastreich Principles of Organizing . . . An Argument for Community Organizing." Undergraduate thesis, UC Santa Cruz, 1977.

Pastreich, Bill. Interview by Aaron Schutz, January 17, 2012.

Schechter, Danny. Interview by Aaron Schutz, January 23, 2013.

For ACORN:

Atlas, John. *Seeds of Change: The Story of ACORN, America's Most Controversial Antipoverty Community Organizing Group*. Nashville: Vanderbilt University Press, 2010.

Delgado, Gary. *Organizing the Movement: The Roots and Growth of ACORN*. Philadelphia: Temple University Press, 1986.

Rathke, Wade. Interview by Aaron Schutz, February 14, 2013.

Russell, D. M. *Political Organizing in Grassroots Politics*. Lanham, MD: University Press of America, 1990.

Swarts, Heidi J. *Organizing Urban America: Secular and Faith-Based Progressive Movements*. Minneapolis: University of Minnesota Press, 2008.

Notes

1. Scott Myers-Lipton, *Social Solutions to Poverty: America's Struggle to Build a Just Society* (New York: Paradigm Publishers, 2006), 216–17.
2. Pastreich, interview.
3. Haggstrom, "Power Bind," 5.
4. Kornbluh, *Battle for Welfare Rights*, 35.
5. Interestingly, Wiley was originally a chemistry professor at Syracuse and worked with CORE. However, he left Syracuse for a position with CORE just as the CATC began to be put

together. Therefore, he never worked directly with Ross or Alinsky, as far as Miller and I can tell. By the time of the War Council he had left CORE for the Citizen's Crusade against Poverty. See Nick Kotz and Mary Lynn Kotz, *A Passion for Equality: George A. Wiley and the Movement* (New York: Norton, 1977).

6. See, for example, Kornbluh, *Battle for Welfare Rights*.
7. Bailis, *Bread or Justice*, 19.
8. Ibid., 31.
9. Miller, "Pastreich Principles," 9.
10. Pastreich, interview.
11. Bailis, *Bread or Justice*, 15.
12. Ibid., 14.
13. Atlas, *Seeds of Change*, 15.
14. Ibid., 15–16.
15. Ibid., 17.
16. Pastreich, interview.
17. Rathke, interview.
18. Ibid.
19. Delgado, *Organizing the Movement*, 65.
20. Rathke, interview. Delgado listed the number of OC members as between ten and fifteen. (*Organizing the Movement*, 67).
21. Rathke, interview.
22. Ibid.
23. Rathke, interview.
24. Ibid.
25. See Swarts, *Organizing Urban America*.
26. Wade Rathke, e-mail to Aaron Schutz, August 1, 2013.
27. Rathke, interview.
28. See Atlas, *Seeds of Change*.
29. See ibid. for a detailed discussion of the downfall of ACORN. For a brief introduction to the demise of ACORN, see Heidi Swarts, "Organizing Through 'Door-Knocking' within ACORN," in *Collective Action for Social Change: An Introduction to Community Organizing*, edited by Aaron Schutz and Marie G. Sandy (New York: Palgrave Macmillan, 2011), 137–54.

25
ACORN Community Organizing Model (1973)

■

WADE RATHKE

Editors' preface: This document was distributed by Association of Community Organizations for Reform Now (ACORN) in 1973, only a couple of years after the organization began. It was designed to provide novice organizers with a standard approach to setting up and running an organizing drive, taking them from the initial entry into a new neighborhood through founding an ACORN chapter and all the way into a first campaign on a neighborhood issue. We have made some minor edits to the document, such as correcting typos and omitting aspects of the model that were abandoned in subsequent practice, but overall, we believe that it gives a good sense of how ACORN generally initiated its new organizers.

GOAL: To build a mass community organization which has as its primary principle the development of sufficient organizational power to achieve its individual members' interests, its local objectives, and in connection with other groups, its state interests. The organization must be permanent with multi-issued concerns achieved through multi-tacticed, direct action, and membership participating in policy, financing, and achievement of group goals and community improvements.

I. **Role of an Organizer:** The organizer is the key component in developing an unorganized and apathetic community into a viable organization. Someone at every step of an organization's history must fulfill the roles of an organizer.

There are vast numbers of roles an organizer plays in ACORN organizing. The most simple is that he brings in members and keeps them there. Other roles include:
- Responsibility for keeping the organization active and democratic.
- Responsibility for keeping the leadership independent and responsive to the membership of the group.
- Responsible for running the organizing drive. . . .[1]
- Responsible for setting up the contract between the local group and ACORN.
- Responsibility for maintaining an agenda ahead of the organizations he works with at all times. Without an agenda, you are not organizing.

- Responsible for building the organization and maintaining self-discipline, responsibility, organizational priorities, loyalty, and structure.
- Responsible for the total goals of ACORN even above and beyond the local group goals.

II. Setting Up the Organizing Drive

A. *Analyzing the Macro-area: City, Town, County*

1. *Geography and Landmarks*: Take a telephone book and list all the primary organizing landmarks: union halls, city hall, court house, post office, welfare office, housing authority, public housing projects, OEO [Office of Economic Opportunity], school board offices, neighborhood centers of any kind, etc. Then systematically go through the city with a map in hand, checking the locations of the landmarks in the area, and noting those areas which seem to contain neighborhoods in your organizing constituency. Chances are usually excellent that our natural organizing areas are in some proximity to many of the landmarks. A census tract can be helpful. Note whatever is unique or uncommon.

2. *Contacts*: [*These were to be made* before *the formal organizing drive began.*] The whole process of making contacts is built on a pyramid theory. Make one that leads to others. The purpose of contacts is to gather information and resources, and to build power. There are three types: hot, warm, cold. The hot contacts are people we have met before at some point in the organization's history. Check the bio-graphical file in the state office. Warm contacts are those we have not met but know something about in order to build an edge, i.e. we have an opener or a handle for the conversation—something they did, someone they know who we know, some reason to believe we can hit the core. The cold contacts are those people we must meet for some reason, yet we have no lead to them. The only edge there is simply an organizer's skill in prying information and setting up his ego in order to loosen his tongue in person or on the phone. It's a skill to be perfected, if you're greasy, you are in the hole.

    Contacts give you several critical elements for setting up the plan. Be careful though that contacts move on your agenda, and not you on [theirs] . . . ; many contacts will attempt to influence your eventual organizing plan to serve their self-interest and not ACORN's.

    (a) Raw information on the area in terms of their analysis on what makes the area move.

    (b) Ability to get things; resources, office, lawyers, tips, other con-tacts on the pyramid model.

    (c) A constituency to use to build power in the greater area, i.e. they will know the behind-the-scenes roles ACORN is playing in the community in making things happen and making the agenda. They will be the insiders. They will compare the changes from the time you arrive through the period of the organization, and your ability to do what you said you would and could in terms of the reality. Our ability to alter their conceptions of how things move in the community will build their view of ACORN and will get them to then build the organization's influence with their contacts and assumptions. Obviously, if you fail, the same thing happens.

(d) Your contacts also give you your invitation and legitimacy in the area, since you are initially talking to them about the possibility of organization rather than the fact of it. The suggestions they have for ACORN give us the mandate to be there. As residents and factors in the community life they have the ability to protect us against many forms of indirect attack. They can vouch for us in conflict.

(e) They can, if needed, write organizing letters for the operation which allow us to borrow their power and influence until we have some of our own.

WARNING: With external-contacts always guard against being used for their self-interest if it is not in our self-interest. As a general rule of thumb in all phases of organizing, give on your agenda only when it doesn't matter, never give easily, and never give where it matters.

3. *Press*: Read the paper carefully and every day for a source of current issues and ideas for issues. Analyze it in terms of how it handles stuff similar to ACORN's potential style and issues. Paper conservative or liberal? Editorial policy? Does it slant? What do you need in tactics or issue content to make good placement? You will also need a reporter to call who you can deal with for your first issues. Find out who usually covers our kind of stuff or general community events. Find out who is the best reporter. If we can pull it off, give him a tip on the first action—background, etc. The only deal is not to quote the organizer or run the story before the action.

4. *Politics*: Learn the names of the public officials and the rumors and facts behind who really runs the area. The question always is—who is behind what makes the city really move: individuals, interests, and issues. What are the party officials like, what are the local officials like? What real power does the mayor or county judge have, and how do they execute it? In many ways first campaigns are directed at getting on their agenda. Makes sense to attend some of their meetings and get a feel of how they operate, handle a public request, or a

negotiation. If it's a ward system, pay special attention to whose ward covers constituency neighborhoods.

5. *Race*: Get a feeling of the percentages, and where whites and blacks live. In most areas in setting up a broad-based, long-term organizational effort in the area, the first drives are going to have to be all white or predominantly white. Pick up the black with subsequent drives once you have established the image of the organization. It is nearly impossible to do the opposite. Find out what role race played in the political and social history of the area in the '60s and '70s, as a guide to these problems. Your better contacts will know and say. How you handle the racial stuff in the initial drives will largely be determined by this history, as well as what kind of drives you need to settle out with your contacts. Only go black first if you never want a white membership in the area or if the area is all black.

6. *History of the Issues*: If you do not know the history you duplicate previous errors, or build a "me too" group without realizing it. The only reason to ever go into an old issue in the area is if you (a) know you can win (b) are "forced" by the adamancy of the membership; or (c) have a new wrinkle on it (time or tactics). It is always necessary for your contacts and your potential membership to establish the uniqueness of ACORN. Old issues are usually already encrusted in the communities' viewpoint. How, who, and what happened in old issues will also give you an edge in knowing what to expect from the external factors and the community leadership.

7. *Previous or Current Organizations*: You need to know what the competition is—to avoid them, freeze them out, and not tread on "their" issues until after you have built your base. It is also important to know how they lived, died, how long, who put them together, and whether they are still around. Look for established groups: unions, NAACP, ACHR [Arkansas Council on Human Relations], etc. for a record. The most interesting ones are those that were exclusively local. Little things that happened and then faded away.

8. *Office*: You are not looking for an office, so much as you are looking for space, a phone, and someone to handle your messages. Sometimes your contacts can lead you to such a place, sometimes they can provide it. . . . You can't take just anything you are offered. Some places you might pick could define your effort differently than you want the group actions to. You also want a place you can trust and where you can control your information. A lady in one of your neighborhoods who can answer the phone would be better than letting yourself get forced [into a problematic space].

9. *Lawyers*: Always make sure that one of your contacts is a lawyer. In state organizing it's like insurance. If you do not find one, then know where ACORN's closest lawyer is. You can never tell. A good contact lawyer might also do minor local issue research for you, or, if necessary, file suit.

10. *Services*: Know what variety of social and community services exist in an area, how they work, and their effectiveness.

11. *Buses*: Know what transportation is like in case part of a tactical organizing plan ever involved a mass action flowing out of your neighborhoods. Know the costs.

B. *Analyzing the Micro-area: Neighborhoods*

1. *Geography*: Go through all the neighborhoods that are in your potential organizing constituency. Get a feel for their size and their diversity of housing, etc., and where they are in relationship to the rest of the city.

2. *Landmarks*: Note everything that seems potentially relevant in the drive. Churches, grocery stores, agencies, parks, neighborhood centers, schools, projects, businesses, industrial or commercial encroachment, zoning patterns, highways or freeways, real estate activity, etc. are all organizing landmarks.

3. *Race*: If white or black, where does the other housing begin? If so, which is dominant? Our goal is building power for people to achieve their interests in an organized fashion. We are not interested in just making people like each other. People coalesce around power; anything else is social work acclimating people to what exists.

4. *Income*: Determine from census information, housing, streets, etc. what the general income range in the neighborhoods are.

5. *Visible and Historical Issues*: Driving or walking through a neighborhood you can often spot visible issues—streets, open ditches, drainage, bad lighting, condemned or dilapidated housing, curbs, gutters, sidewalks, litter, domestic and commercial eyesores, weeds and overgrown lots, lack of parks or recreational facilities, bus routes, and a number of other issues. Depending on the situations, all of these things are potential organizing issues. With historical issues find out from your community and external contacts whether or not solutions have been actualized, what progress has, or has not been made. Historical issues are important—if the history was good, build on the increased and unfulfilled expectations. If the history was bad, it may be an even better history to build upon since if your issue is good you build the expectations.

6. [*This section discussed "discounts" with local businesses, which did not remain a long-term part of the ACORN strategy.*]

7. *[Initial] Contacts*: The key element in setting up the neighborhood
    is the quality and quantity of your initial local contacts. These are
    people for the most part who live in the area, know people in the
    area, and are your potential members. These people will also be your
    best feedback on local organizing issues.

    (a) *Community Leaders*: Always be wary and careful with people who
         are seen as community leaders in the neighborhood. Some are
         good and some are bad; but they are always potential problems
         in terms of their agenda versus your potential organization's.
         They have the ability to define your group. Community leaders
         always bring the past history of the area with them; our purpose
         is always to organize against that past history. If that's not where
         they are at, keep them away from where you are. Ministers and
         OEO personnel and others often define themselves as commu-
         nity leaders.

    (b) *Churches*: Ministers, in general, and especially of smaller, neigh-
         borhood churches, often can tell you who some good people are
         who have not been overly active. He can also give you names of
         people in the church who have had low-income problems and
         might be naturally more sympathetic.

    (c) *Grocery Stores*: Small grocery store owners and personnel can
         often give-you a sense of the area and some names. They are
         often community institutions where people talk freely depending
         on the owner. They know their customers. They know who has
         lived there the longest.

    (d) *Larger Grocery Stores or Shopping Centers*: This is an effective
         though more at random method to get contacts. Set up a table
         in or outside of the store with the permission of the owner or
         manager. Use a sign which catches the eye and interest of the
         passerby. Have flyers, or something to give them, on the orga-
         nization, or the drive, or what could be done in the area. The
         key is to aggressively go out to people, give them a flyer, and
         engage them in conversation concerning the neighborhood.
         Have a list to have them sign with their name, address, phone
         number, etc.

    (e) *Community Centers*: Any kind of center will have some knowl-
         edge and names in the area, no matter how scarce. Recreation,
         day care, neighborhood centers are examples.

    (f) *Hang-outs*: Places where people meet could give you a contact
         if necessary. Examples: union halls, food stamp lines, welfare
         offices, public meetings. Most of the contacts made this way
         are sloppy. Bars are always a waste of time. People do not go to

talk, [and] when they do, they do not remember it, or they will always associate you with it.

(g) *Newspapers*: Selling some newspapers could give you a way to meet people and a reason to talk to them. Just make sure you get the names down.

(h) *Lawyers*: Names of clients in our constituency or neighborhoods.

(i) *Doorknocking*: If no other alternatives are present, hit some names at random from your list.

(j) *Petitions*: Circulating a "safe" petition at random could give you contacts from a gathering place. This is not a raw list of contacts, because at least you know they can be interested in something enough to do something about it.

(k) *Mailing*: If necessary send a "feeler" out in the areas of the neighborhood to involve individual responses. This is only used in forcing a drive.

8. *Lists*: Without a list there is no drive. The priority on lists is the names, addresses, and phone numbers. Your lists should be as comprehensive as possible, in order to make the final decision on which neighborhood to enter on your initial drive. Lists can be built from a variety of sources:

(a) *City Directories*: Once you have sketched out the geography in your neighborhoods with the corresponding border addresses, you can find the name, address, and phone of every individual house. It also shows you who owns and who rents.

(b) *Voter Registration Lists*: Once you know the streets and the precincts or whatever political subdivisions exist in the area, you can find the name and addresses of everyone in your area who is registered. Should be public information.

(c) *Criss-Cross*: Names and addresses in one section and phones and names in another. If you match them up, you have a good list.

(d) *Phone Book*: If the area was rural and small enough, you could get it straight from the area phone book.

(e) *Supplemental Lists*: Add up the bits and pieces from your contacts or store tables or whatever. Additional lists might be obtained from food distribution centers or any list you have gotten from specific sources, Title I lists, etc.

(f) *Computer Cards*: Put them all up for labels and to keep a record for later.

C. *Decision on the Organizing Plan*: Consolidate all the diverse information you have accumulated in and outside of the neighborhoods. Once the plan is made you will have to live with it, so make it good and tight, and take the time to do so.

1. *Contacts and Lists*: The better they are the better your chances of a tight drive. But, if the other factors fit better elsewhere, this should not be your criteria for the drive.

2. *Issues*: They must be realizable, specific, immediate, and have multiplier effect. With a good enough issue you can make a drive anywhere, although you will have to do more cleaning up on it.

3. *Size*: The size of a neighborhood to be organized [. . .] should be determined by natural boundaries, contacts for the organizing committee, area of the issues impact, etc. If the size is unwieldy for one drive, then [. . .] smaller units on the drive should be considered. [. . .]² Another component in the size question is density, Four hundred on a list is manageable, but if they are spread out to the extent that people do not feel the issues or identify with the area, it would be easier to have 1,000, if it were more concentrated. Never make a drive bigger than you can run and control.

4. *Timing*: Much of your organizing plan revolves around its ability to create a happening—momentum. A drive that runs past a month can become almost anti-climactic, as well as deteriorate the stability of your work forces. You cannot lose your immediacy, or you will lose your issues and their appeal. It would be better to cut the list if pressed than to lose the immediacy, since you can clean one up but not the other. [*By "cleaning up," Rathke means going back and contacting people who don't make it to the initial organizing meeting to try to bring them into the organization.*]

5. *Agenda*: Make it complete and be thoroughly comfortable with it. If you are not, you will be unable to move people without great difficulty.

6. *Politics*: In organizing, politics is everything that makes things move. Direct your organizing plan to as near as we can get to the core of it. Neighborhoods are not organized [by ACORN] to solve [individual neighborhood] problems, but to build power in that area for the [entire] organization. If the plan is oriented to the core, it can accomplish all the goals. If it is organized just to the specific [problems of individual] neighborhoods, it may not even enter into the arena. Nearsightedness is the fatal weakness of any organizing plan. The entire future of the organization is not built from the action or from the drive, but from the very beginning.

III. Running the Organizing Drive

A. *Establishing the Organizing Committee (OC)*: The organizing committee is your manpower on the drive, your legitimacy, your potential leadership, and the focus on the issues. The group can be made or broken depending on the quality of your committee. [Everything prior to this point is prepa-ratory to beginning the actual, focused effort to organize the neighborhood through a "drive."]

1. *Making the meeting*: The OC is organized from the [initial] contacts you have made in the neighborhood, as well [as] anyone else they bring in with them. You want to hold it at one of their houses or if necessary, at a central location. You will have already set up the basic agreement of creating an organization to deal with the issues in the area before the meeting. You want strong people who will work. You want to cut away possible conflict or disagreement. You want a cross section of the neighborhood. Sometimes it is helpful to get the person holding the meeting to help in the final invitation process [to the first OC meeting].

2. *Holding the [OC] meeting*: Invariably the organizer will end up guiding the OC meetings, especially the first one. Draw people out to take roles in moving and running them. You will always have to maintain a complex dynamic in the OC, which allows for "testing," digressions, humor, enthusiasm on the issues and events, and con-sensus on the techniques, responsibilities, and commitments which members of the OC will be forced to make. These [OC] meetings should be held weekly during the drive.

3. *Agenda for the Organizing Committee*:

    (a) *Introductions and Purpose*: You are only cement in the [initial OC] meeting. Make the introductions. Decide when to start it. Lay out what the meeting is about and why. Play it off against the person whose house it is.

    (b) *Issues*: Test the visible-issues and those issues which people have mentioned to you. Get response. Anticipate other issues and differing emphasis than you had expected. Get consensus on the first issue and the first campaign [at this first OC meeting]. This part of the meeting usually takes 50% of the time.

    (c) *Elections*: The group must be democratic. Election of officers must be agreed upon from the first meeting. [Initial, temporary officers for the neighborhood, however, will be chosen at the first mass meeting.]

    (d) *Organizing Letter*: Have a sample from another drive and pass it around. Get agreement on the format and the based wording. Get agreement on their signatures.

    (e) First [mass neighborhood] meeting: Get a date and time.

    (f) *Membership [Dues]*: Stress it. If you forget, people will feel deceived at the first meeting. It helps to have them sign up at the OC meeting.

(g) *Name*: Have one ready; do not be willing to concede on one which is ridiculous, or duplicates.

(h) *Contract*: Make clear what they can expect from ACORN (services, research, assistance, contacts, political power, literature, etc.), and what ACORN expects of the group (dues, affiliation, news distribution, etc.). Define your role, as well as the future independence of the group.

(i) *Doorknocking*: Get agreements on when, not if [the OC members will doorknock with you or by themselves].

(j) *Future OC [Meetings]*: Set the time, place, and dates [for these]. At future meetings go through the progress, other issues, expand on your original themes. On the last meeting, prepare an agenda for the first big meeting.

B. *First Mailing [to Residents in the Neighborhood]*:
[*This is the point, after the first OC meeting, at which the concentrated, day-to-day doorknocking of the four- to six-week organizing drive begins, supported by the work of the OC.*]

   1. *Organizing Committee Letter*: The organizing letter has several purposes: to give the drive local "neighbor-to-neighbor" legitimacy, to define the first issue [which was set at the first OC meeting], to serve notice of the doorknocking, to create a receptive visit on the doors, to turn people on, to invite them to join the committee, and to notify them formally of the first [mass] meeting. Must be signed by all the organizing committee. Do not mail it to those people you want to exclude. (Appendix A)[3]

   2. *Flyer*: This should be your basic identifying card, consistent throughout the drive. It should be brief and to the point (25 words). It should highlight the time, place, date, and issues. Doing flyers is not art, but it is *an* art. A sloppy one will kill you and make the drive look amateurish. There is no excuse for it. Where you bunch words, type it. (Appendix B)

   3. *Organizing Letters*: Depending on whether you need it to get in the door, or to get people to the meeting, you should use an organizing letter here for your credit card. Select the letter to use depending on your constituency and what problems you predict.

C. *Doorknocking*:

   1. *Reason*: There is no substitute for personal contact in convincing people to become active in the organization. Doorknocking does it best. It gives the doorknockers a chance to answer questions and create the impressions of the organization. It allows you to bring people in, and define some people out. It gives organizers a feel of

what the meeting and organization will be like, and whether you need to make any special plans or adjustments.

2. *Teams*: Doorknocking in teams mutes the outsider role of the organizer and reduces the foreign experience of an organizing drive when you are using local people. Men and women teams are best, women teams second, and men teams third in neighborhood organizing. Having two people on the doors is also insurance against forgetting important things which need to be said. Alone is never good, but better than nothing. It's not so bad if a single is from the area, and not an organizer.

3. *Techniques*:
   (a) Get in the door whenever possible.
   (b) Keep it less than fifteen minutes. You were not invited, so do not make yourself unwanted. Avoid being trapped into coffee and socializing—primarily, you are there for critical, though not somber, business.
   (c) Know the name, it makes all the difference.
   (d) Do not set yourself off past common understanding, or within common stereotypes in dress styles and delivery.
   (e) Keep your organizing cards to yourself. It turns people off to think they are one of the millions in their own organization.

4. *Rap*: You have to do many things with little time, so plan it carefully. Brief your doorknockers carefully and plan out who takes what pieces of the rap.
   (a) *Set the scene*: What's happening, when, where, and what about.
   (b) Pull them out on the issues and find out what moves them. Engage.
   (c) Stress power; people, pressure, accountability, change; what organizations have done and what they can force people to do.
   (d) Give them a good sense of exactly what is going to happen at the [mass] meeting: election, dues issue discussion, agenda, plans for action with examples. If people know what to expect, they won't be surprised and the meeting will be smoother.
   (e) Explain ACORN and never forget to mention membership dues.
   (f) Get the phone number, if you don't have it.
   (g) Get a commitment on attendance at the first [mass] meeting.
   (h) Give them a flyer to remind them of the facts behind the meeting and when it will be. Give them whatever other materials you have prepared as well.

5. *Organizing Cards*:
   (a) Make a card out for everyone on the list with name, address, and phone number.

(b) Mark their response on the attendance with yes, no, or maybe
     from your analysis of the meeting and the nature of the com-
     mitment, not from what they say. Put it in the upper right hand
     corner.

(c) Put any relevant comments on the bottom of the card. Example:
     other issues, special problems, need for transportation, etc.

(d) Make sure you keep them organized so that you know whether
     you have seen them, or they were not at home, or whether you
     still have to do them, or whether you are dealing them.

D. *Second Mailing*: If the second distribution is through the mail, send it
    during the last week as near as you can time it to arrive before the first
    [mass] meeting without risk. If done by hand, do it the day before.
    This mailing constitutes a reminder. In some cases it will be the first
    mailing that some people on the drive have ever seen, so don't under-
    estimate it. . . .

E. [*In this section, Rathke discussed house meetings, which were ultimately not
    used as a strategy.*]

F. [*In this section, Rathke listed a range of media options, including distributing
    flyers, pursuing radio advertising, and getting stories into the press.*]

G. *Telephone Calling*: The last night or two (depending on the size of your
    list) have your organizing committee call your list. Remind them of time,
    place, etc. and get a commitment on attendance, Identify yourself; be
    brief. Be careful of overkill. Get a count on your cards. Make sure you
    checked during the doorknocking on the correct numbers with the people;
    that way they also expect this call.

H. *Developing Leadership*: Your organizing committee will in many cases
    end up being the primary leadership of the group. Make sure you spend
    enough time with them so that they understand what a drive consists of
    and what we do.

I. [*In this section, Rathke referred to the ACORN representative.*]

IV. First [Mass] Meeting

A. *Time*: Almost invariably the best time for the meeting is at night (or pos-
    sibly the weekend), since the vast majority of our constituency works.

B. *Place*: Location should be central and positively defined. Concentrate
    on churches, union halls, schools, etc. which all have positive or neutral
    connotations.

C. *Numbers*: You have to know what to expect in terms of a crowd, simply
    in order to be prepared. Having a hundred cups of coffee for ten people
    devaluates the ten—and you'll need them to build on. Most ACORN
    community organizing drives will net 15–25% of the list. Numbers are

important because this is a mass organization directed at political power where might makes right.

D. *Materials:* [*In this section, Rathke listed supplies to bring to the meeting location, including the meeting agenda (see Appendix C), an attendance list, blackboard and chalk for elections, extra pencils, relevant ACORN literature, and refreshments.*]

E. *Membership:* Membership is $1.00 to join and $1.00 per month, except if they pay for 6 months in advance it is $5.00, or an entire year in advance is $10.00. You want everyone to join and you want them to join in advance. Collect the dues as people come in and go by the organizing table to sign the sheet and pick up materials. Have an aggressive member of your organizing committee to do the job. Make it part of your agenda to catch everyone who slipped by the table during the meeting. Dues tie in our people and are our life blood, so collect them when your opportunity to do so is highest.

F. *Forms and/or Petitions:* As a general rule of thumb, forms are for membership actions and petitions are for pre-membership or non-membership. Forms give you bulk and individuality of request. It helps to have something that constitutes action right from the first meeting and forms/petitions can do some of it. We don't want people just to sit and listen, unless it's a funeral. (Appendix I [not included in this volume])

G. *Elect Temporary Officers:* Temporary, until you are sure they are stable in the group and are good enough to run the organization. Basic officers are Chairman, Co-chairman, Secretary, Treasurer [*or Dues Collector*].

H. Leave most time for discussing the issues and getting agreement on a definite, specific plan of action on the issues. If people don't see that something happened at the first meeting, they won't be back.

I. Introduce the members of the organizing committee and have them take parts in the agenda.

J. Opening the meeting with prayer produces order in the meeting, sets off uncertain expectations, and gives legitimacy to your purpose.

K. *Committees:* Committees are not something to be entered into lightly. They can divide the activity and identity of the group. They take a lot of time to function. Interest is usually low in committees and elections on first meetings, because of the diverse reasons [for why] people came. If you do committees, make them specific with realizable tasks.

L. *Next Meeting:* Remind people of the date and time for the next meeting. It should be on the bottom of the agenda.

V. **First Campaign:** The plan was made during the drive, so now it is organized and ready by the time of the first meeting.

A. *Analyzing the Issues*: Remember the importance of being multi-issued, so that the group doesn't over extend itself on just one. Have the second issue ready to go. Keep the issues specific, concrete, and realizable. If the issue develops as long term, fill the gap with something immediate.

B. *Analyzing the Tactics*: You always want an action of some kind. The membership either has to go to the target, or the target has to come to them. Tactics are as endless as your imagination. Judge them on two levels: (1) what will they do to advance the issue, (2) what effect will they have on your long-term goals. We don't want our tactics to be a question of winning a battle and losing the war. Take conservatism of your membership and the community as a general assumption. If you want to use more hard-hitting tactics, build your membership up to them as the campaign escalates. In choosing specific tactics, remember that public meetings are open forums with their own given legitimacy of mass action. Petitions, public hearings, dramatizations, demonstrations, etc. are all standard tactics. Choose carefully and focus on the particular situation. There is nothing wrong with a tactic which ridicules a target, rather than running him over.

C. *Leadership*: Prepare your leadership carefully to handle the action and the issue. Warn them of the possible responses. They should be organized, not only on the goal of the campaign, but also on where to settle in negotiation or action. If they aren't, you may stumble and win, but more probably, you will lose.

D. Make sure there is always a direct and clear view of what you want, and what you expect to achieve. If there isn't you will be hard pressed to define the action once it is over as a win. The action is always defined in the mind of the membership after it is over, not while it is in progress, so keep your perspective.

E. *Target*: A crucial organizing mistake is often made in how organizers pick the target, or if there is more than one, how they pick the order of setting up the targets for the campaign. Know something about him and his structure, so you can determine the difference between concessions and smoke screens.

F. *Timing*: If you lose momentum, you lose. Don't wear out the campaign, the press, or your members. Remember if the question is between the issue and the organization, sacrifice the issue with whatever you can get out of it. Two weeks is ideal, a month is pressing it, more means you better start injecting the second issue.

G. *Other Factors*: Obviously, we set up most campaigns on the principle of numbers and their potential power. Our ability to utilize the maximum number of variables against the target supports this concept.

   1. Our ability to use the press to keep the issue a public concern is important.

2. Our ability to seem "morally" and actually right on the issue or campaign is key. (Appendix J [*not included in this volume*])
3. Our ability to change the tactics from the target's expectations.
4. Our ability to exploit the political situations.
5. Ability to escalate the campaign, makes us appear reasonable and justified, and maintains momentum.
6. The threat is more powerful than the action, although you must at some point prove your strength and your ability to actualize the threat.
7. Ability to go to court if forced, if for no other reason as an exit on the campaign.

H. *Models and Histories*: On any campaign make sure you have checked with the [ACORN] state office to see if there is a history on a similar issue or campaign, or a guide model on the elements of such a campaign. These are not the Ten Commandments, but they could help you see what the critical factors are, what past mistakes have been, and how to avoid them.

I. *Research*: Having sufficient and correct information is essential on all elements of the campaign especially on the information your membership supplies you. Always remember that your first (or any) campaign can be your last. It is not nearly as defeating to lose on an issue of merit, as it is to beat yourself.

VI. Cleaning Up the Organizing Drive: Too often the later stages of building an organization are neglected in the relief of the drive's end, the climax of the first [*mass*] meeting, and the pressure of the first campaign. We pay for neglecting to clean up the drive [*i.e., following up on people who expressed interest but didn't show up*] in maintenance problems, low membership, poor dues collection, and loss of some of the group's potential.

A. *Maybes*: After the first meeting get back to the "maybes" [people who said they might come to the mass meeting but didn't] developed in the drive. The later you wait the more improbable the task becomes. People will feel the structure is set. They will be hung up that they didn't come when they said they would. They will lose contact and interest. Furthermore, if you win, they will get the benefits without effort, making their membership seem irrelevant. Use the new officers for this; especially if they were not part of the OC. Send them [the maybes] a mailing for the second group meeting after this contact.

B. *Attendance List*: Get back to the people who were at the meeting in order to (1) collect their dues, (2) increase their information and involvement, (3) define the meeting, and (4) feel them out on what they want to see and problems they had.

C. *Executive Board*: Get the board together to go over the meeting and their roles in order to build leadership.

D.   [*In this step, Rathke refers to the ACORN representative.*][4]

E.   *Computer Cards*: Transfer the relevant information on your organizing cards to the computer cards in the [ACORN] state office as a permanent record of the drive, etc. Don't make flippant judgments which you will regret a year later or [which are] irrelevant in dealing with the person later.

F.   *Biographical*: Take the cards on the external contacts and transfer them to the biographical system in the state office for use in other campaigns, research, and general information.

G.   *Secondary Leadership*: The cleaning up process will enable you to bring out and spot potential leadership outside of the elected structure. If they aren't hooked up and involved early, you will lose what could have been the backbone of the group.

VII. Maintenance: The beginning always predicts and prejudices the end. At this point, 90% of the fundamentals of the group have been laid. The process does not simply repeat, but becomes more sophisticated.

A.   *Issues*: You always want the group to be moving on some issues and projects which involve the maximum number of your membership. . . .

B.   *Attendance*: The majority of first meetings are the biggest meetings that groups will ever have, depending on the quality of the issues. Build a core which you can depend on for consistency in the group in both size and quality. This is a natural organizational event. You must convince the group, though, that they never have enough people to be satisfied, but don't allow numbers to depress their activity or stability.

B.   *Leadership and Membership*: Leadership is built in actions; talk is never an adequate substitute. Transferring vast numbers of organizer roles to the membership is critical, so these roles must be clear and simplified for effective execution.

C.   *Politics*: If you don't move your membership into the political arena, the long term goals of the organization will never be realized. People relate to the elective process, so use it as a power-building vehicle. Their role and potential impact in this arena should be understood and planned for by the group. The membership needs to move on the political agenda when the time comes, so prepare them from the beginning and throughout their history.

E.   [*In this step, Rathke refers to the discount system.*]

F.   *Maintenance and Historical Models*: Check with the [ACORN] office for what is available and useful to your group in terms of future campaign guides.

G.   *Research*: Most of the research for the group will be handled out of the [ACORN] state office on any issues and activities the group is interested in pursuing.[5]

Appendix A: Organizing Committee Letter

March 2, 1972

Dear Neighbors:

For years we have been talking about the problems in Garden
Homes. Now we feel it is time for us to get together and do
something about them. Our community needs a neighborhood park for
our children, better drainage, and an end to the heavy traffic coming
through our neighborhood.

We have decided to form a Garden Homes Community Organization,
with the help of ACORN, and with everyone in the neighborhood working
together we can solve our problems. ACORN is a statewide organization of over 3,000 families who work together to solve their own
community problems. ACORN is not supported by any government agency.
It is run entirely by its members who pay membership dues to meet their
expenses.

On March 16 at 7:30 p.m. at the Welch Street Baptist Church
Education Building on Roosevelt and Welch, we will have our first meeting. At this meeting we will:

    1. Elect officers
    2. Discuss our organization and what it can do
    3. Plan how we can get a neighborhood park
    4. Discuss some good news on the drainage
    5. Explain ACORN

Before the meeting, one of us will visit you to talk more about
our community organization and to find out what you would like to see
done. If you would like to help, please call one of us.

Mrs. Shirley Burks   Mr. Morris H. Rhoads
1700 E. 21st   1724 E. 20th

Mr. & Mrs. Jack Deese   Mr. & Mrs. William N. Quick
1816 Security   1718 E. 16th

           Mr. & Mrs. Edward W. Short
           2008 Security

ARKANSAS COMMUNITY ORGANIZATION FOR REFORM NOW
523 W. 15th Street   Little Rock, Arkansas 72202   376-7151

Appendix B: Flyer Example

WE ARE ORGANIZING THE:

<u>ARCH</u> TO <u>SPRING</u> <u>NEIGHBORHOOD</u> <u>ASSOCIATION</u>

ZONING!

PARK?

ABSENTEE LANDLORDS!

FIRST MEETING

WEDNESDAY
JULY 5TH

7:30 PM

OLD
CENTRAL PRESBYTERIAN CHURCH

20TH & ARCH

LITTER!

COMMERCIALIZATION

PUBLIC NUISANCES

WE CAN IMPROVE OUR COMMUNITY,
IF WE WORK TOGETHER!!

AT THE MEETING:
1) Discuss affiliation with ACORN.
2) Elect Officers.
3) Discuss Neighborhood Problems, Especially Re-zoning of Broadway.
4) Make Plans to go to the Planning Commission.

<u>PLEASE COME</u>

Questions or rides: 376-7151   Prepared by ACORN

Appendix C: Mass Meeting Agenda Example

UNEMPLOYED AND WORKERS ORGANIZING COMMITTEE (UWOC)

AGENDA

September 22, 1971

I.   Prayer -- Rev. Poindexter

II.   What is the UWOC? What is ACORN? Wade Rathke, Head Organizer, ACORN

III. Introduction of Organizing Committee members:
      Harold Hedlock   Horace Bratcher
      Tom Lovelady   Gene Gibbons
      William Chilliest   Glynn Starkey
      Ronnie Peters   Wainright Coppas, Jr.
      Rachel Hampton   Ester Bell

IV.   Election
      A) Chairman
      B) Co-Chairman
      C) Corresponding Secretary
      D) Recording Secretary
      E) Treasurer

V.   Discussion and Plans
      A) UWOC Petition -- date to present it. Harold Hedlock
      B) Jobs -- Emergency Employment Act, ESD Tom Lovelady
      C) Benefits -- Harold Hedlock
      D) Private Employment Agencies -- Wade Rathke

VI.   Selection of Committees:
      A) Jobs
      B) Private Agencies
      C) Legislation
      D) Grievance
      E) Recruitment

VII. Adjournment

REFRESHMENTS FOLLOWING

NEXT MEETING

> UAW Union Hall
> Wednesday, Oct. 13
> 1408 Rebsamen Park Rd
> 7:30 pm

ACORN

Affiliated with: Arkansas Community Organizations for Reform Now
523 West Fifteenth
Little Rock, Ark. 72202
376-7153

Notes

1. We have removed references to the "ACORN representative," a position that was originally conceptualized as a kind of leader/organizer in groups, but which did not ultimately work out.
2. The deleted section discusses "block clubs" as a strategy, but ultimately this was not pursued.
3. We have included only a few of the numerous examples appended to the original document.
4. See Note 1.
5. In the original document, this section was followed by more instructions on the ACORN representative, which we have omitted.

26

The Story of an ACORN Organizer

Madeline Talbott

■

INTERVIEWED BY MIKE MILLER

Editors' preface: Madeline Talbott grew up in the family of an Army engineer. Her father was active in World War II, Korea, and Vietnam; her mother "an iconoclast" who didn't flinch from challenging ideas around her. In Talbott's Catholic education, she was "involved in the ferment" of post–Vatican II teachings, introduced to The Feminine Mystique, and exposed to migrant labor camps. At Radcliffe, she joined a strike against the Vietnam War, attended rallies for tenants' rights in Cambridge, and decided "that I ought to go into an occupation that could lead to eliminating lead paint, not treating its symptoms."

Still a student, she went to Chelsea, Massachusetts, "and worked with women in that working-class town. They wanted to get a day care center so they could go to work. The warmth of Chelsea was a striking contrast to the coldness and aloofness of Radcliffe/ Harvard." She took a year off from Harvard, moved to Chelsea, took a minimum-wage job, and continued doing neighborhood work. She went to a community organizing seminar, and "discovered there were groups doing this, and people were getting paid to do it—that was exciting." She heard ACORN's Steve Kest, who "wasn't too macho for me" (others were).[1]

In the rest of this chapter, Talbott's words are in plain text, and Miller's commentary in italics.

At Steve Kest's invitation, I went down to Arkansas to see if people actually did pay dues to have their own organization—and learned that they did. That's how I came to ACORN—from a vague place that was very interested in social change, but had no ideological underpinnings for it. When I started at ACORN, I had some "helping people" experience, and a little organizing in the day care issue.

The desire to help, of course, is often what starts people down a path that leads to organizing. The great problem with "helping" is that you do for people what they can do for themselves, or you put Band-Aids on cancer. Helping has a place, but it doesn't change things.

I started in Dallas when Texas was opened up. I went there in September 1975 to do one of the first [organizing] drives. Steve Holt was the head organizer, and [ACORN lead organizer] Wade Rathke was around a lot. Wade ended up [being my trainer], but it pretty much consisted of him taking me out on the porch of where I was staying, and telling me "knock on doors, find out people's issues, ask them to join at $16.00/year or $1.50/month, sign up a member a day." Steve Holt filled in the blanks, and Meg Campbell was there also, so I'd ask her questions as well. That was about my training. The standard of "a member a day" was a high bar; only a few had accomplished it, but I didn't know that. I believed what I was told—so I went out and did it.

Putting together my first ACORN chapter had a big impact on me and my life. I was very anxious. The first day out, I knocked on the door of a new resident in the neighborhood—a gay guy who was eager to become part of his neighborhood. He joined to be part of a neighborhood improvement organization. That gave me a little bit of confidence about what I was doing. Steve and Meg told me I should have three times the number of "yes" responses to the actual turnout goal, but I didn't believe that. I got sixteen yeses for my first house meeting, known as an Organizing Committee [OC] meeting, and worried that I had too many people to fit in the small living room. The host couple and two other people, one who was a bit drunk, showed up; that was it. Steve came for moral support. I had expected sixteen people, and almost none of them came.

I concluded that people were liars, and I wasn't going to do this again. If people didn't want this, I wasn't going to do it. The next day, Steve took me to the neighborhood. "Go back to the people who said yes, and tell them it was a great meeting, and get them to join, and then organize another meeting." So I did that. At the next meeting we had 10, then 17 at another meeting, then 150 at a founding meeting. It was a good experience.

One guy, "Big Jim," said if I got more than one hundred people to the founding meeting he would join. I told him, "Then you have to help." He did, and he helped me with the drive. So I learned the work, believed in it, and believed in myself as well.

When you get people together in the first stages of organization development, there is excitement at being in the same room together. People who had been telling me that "the other" was the problem now discovered that they were involved in the same concerns. They were excited to be working together. They remained racist when they left the room. But, over time, you could break that down. I discovered in the first drive that you had to get diverse groups together so they could discover the excitement at the same time. The first OC meeting is a kind of spiritual experience—"I'm not alone; there are other people who feel the same way I do"; it's a magical moment of community. If you discover that with "the other," then you start to make some progress on race.

The experience of each door was magical to me as well. People would invite you in. The experience of the OC was the same: people seeing each other as "like me," wanting to create something better in the neighborhood.

You were looking for people with energy, charisma, the ability to create a following if not already having one. I was looking for people who had "good politics," but I found out that was not necessary. I was generally not looking for white males. I noticed when Steve Holt came in, he went after some of the white males, and brought them in. I think his expectation was that if an organization didn't have white male leadership it was not going to be respected in the wider community. At the founding meeting, I was surprised that a white male was elected, not a woman I'd expected to win. Steve was clearly looking for someone with a following, or who could have a following.

I read the [ACORN] model [document] (see Chapter 25), and referred back to it a lot. But I thought its tone was obnoxious; Steve got a big kick out of that. I didn't like the part about race—that you had to start white, then go black; not that the content was wrong, but the way it was said. I thought there was arrogance in the tone, but I learned a lot from the detail.

I went into both black and white communities, and built chapters there. In one Arkansas area, I got a phone call from a neighborhood known as white racist. They said, "We saw what you did with the niggers; would you do the same with white people?" I also worked with racially mixed groups. But in Arkansas, there were complex realities around race. There was an integrated history and tradition there, in the Southern Tenant Farmers' Union [SFTU] and populist history of black-and-white organizing there, and some memory of it. But it was difficult to find a place to meet, and some whites were worried about what their neighbors would think if they were in a mixed group, etc., etc. You couldn't assume anything.

I now began to pay attention to Fred Ross [see Part II, Section A], his use of house meetings versus Alinsky, and his work through existing organizations. While people were acting like there were different and mutually exclusive styles, it all made sense to me. Of course you would visit leaders of existing groups. Of course you would go door-to-door. You didn't just do one or the other. House meetings were important; organizing committees were important; existing leaders were important. If you didn't have existing organizations because they were all conservative, then door-knocking was essential for the community building process. Where there were conservative institutions—like block clubs or improvement associations—then you had to go underneath them to build something that better represented the community. I realized there were different kinds of organizing, but that good organizing came down to the same thing. Good organizing was what delivered organized communities with leadership that moved on issues with some success.

It got harder as you tried to keep [an organization] going. After 90-120 days into the work, there was a slump; you now had to learn how to maintain a "built from scratch" organization while at the same time building others. Maintenance required a great deal of effort, and sometimes work we just didn't know how to do. We knew we had to build a lot of organizations if we wanted to reach scale—to become a national or statewide force. We were already working very hard; now we had to work harder.

Key to maintenance was identifying big, exciting campaigns that everyone from all the groups could be involved in because all of them were affected. In Pine Bluff we created a structure in each neighborhood group where the officers ran their neighborhoods, with block captains who had a couple of blocks. They were responsible for phone lists and flyering. It was a lot of hard work.

But structures alone don't do it for you. People drop out if there's nothing going on that gives people an interest. We had things going on that provided the interest. We ran big campaigns that really mattered to people—stopping a highway through their neighborhood and homes, building sanitation sewers, installing drainage.

As I stayed longer in places—five years in Detroit, thirty in Chicago—I saw turnover more often. It had a huge impact on me. I did things so that we wouldn't lose leaders, members or staff. If you had to re-create those things, it would have a huge [negative] impact.

Over time, I began to work more to make sure that leaders were running things and making the decisions. In my earlier years, I was "guiding" their decisions. Even Wade, who also was a control freak, told me I was an obstructionist. I'd get into battles with leaders. What Wade was trying to tell me, and what I learned from people voting with their feet, was that the organization had to be a vehicle for everybody's dreams, not just mine. Out of necessity, I became more committed to democracy, and to the organization being a vehicle for all our dreams.

What I came to see was that the key component to the work, maybe the key goal, was developing the leaders and the organizers. It was developing a community of struggle—with the organization being the vehicle. A commitment to the development of the people was central. I think that's what I became known for. I learned that if you didn't do that you'd lose people at a faster rate than you could develop them. As I looked more carefully at the work, I saw that development of people was the key.

For a long time, I believed in simply marching forward and not being distracted. I was just wrong about that. [Gamaliel organizer] Mike Kruglik stopped in to see me and told me he was going to organize the churches in Englewood, where we had an ACORN chapter. I said, "OK, you do that and I'll organize the individuals in the south suburbs, where your organization is, and we'll see who does better." We started talking; I told him I was interested in what he was doing because I saw he was moving a couple of thousand people to come to a convention. He told me he was interested in what I was doing because I was moving a couple of hundred people with militancy, flexibility, perseverance, and consistency in fights until we'd win an issue. We agreed we had something to learn from each other.

[After going to a Gamaliel workshop], I concluded I wanted to do training sessions. Wade said, "They're about building loyalty to the organization, not teaching anything." I didn't know that, but I kept it in mind. So I created a list of readings for people who'd been organizing in ACORN. I sent out this list, and people complained about organizing being intellectualized. But I saw that it was possible to reflect on things and that it could help you in the work. Then Wade started an advanced series, with a whole lot more reading, and people learned more. Warren Haggstrom said that the way you learn the work is case studies of the work of good organizers, and see what you can glean from them.

I started a leadership development program in Chicago. The text the leaders wanted to read was the Bible. We had a series around biblical texts and liberation theology. [*Case studies of organizing were read as well.*] All of that came out of being jolted into being open to doing the work well. For years, I'd thought that you just had to work harder. I began to realize that there was an important role for conversation, reading, reflection. Prior to that, I'd been great at going after a target and getting him. I was good at that, but limited to it.

The impact of biblical reflection on members was a revelation to me. When they could relate what they were doing in ACORN to their religious passion, it felt so good to them. Prior to that, they had two facets of their personality that weren't related to each other: they cared deeply about church, and they cared deeply about ACORN. Once we helped them connect the two through a revised version of liberation theology, it made a big difference for them. Making this connection was a huge relief; an integration of their personalities. Action was now for their religion as well as for their community. Prior to that, they were criticized by neighbors and friends, and didn't have a good way to talk about what they were doing.

This was a jolt to the ACORN culture itself, which was really based on action. It was jolting to people that they would have to read hundreds of pages before coming to a weekend dialogue. This transition took place in the early '90s. That became an addition to the culture; this was a big change in ACORN.

I was slow to be able to articulate what I was doing, why, and how. Perhaps it was because I was alone—the only organizer—so much of the time in the early days, without anyone to share ideas with. Perhaps it was because there was so little formal training in those days—so little reading and reflection and discussion. Later, beginning in Detroit, I interacted with organizers who had more background in the work. Things became clearer to me, and I became happier in the work. When I could explain what I was doing, I felt good and more committed to it.

It wasn't until many years later that we were systematically analyzing and trying to figure out where we fit in. Only years later did we make this part of our organizational culture.

If you're looking for an opportunity to make a difference in the world, consider this an invitation to become an organizer yourself.

Note

1. "ACORN" originally stood for "Arkansas Community Organizations for Reform Now" and later became "Association of Community Organizations for Reform Now."

PART IV

27

The State of Organizing

■

MIKE MILLER

Saul Alinsky was surrounded by a swirl of controversy throughout his life. The debate over his work polarized Catholic and mainline Protestant churches, activists, civil rights leaders, the political Left, and others. I think he was more on target in his views than those who opposed him. With hindsight, his cautions against the super-militancy of the later 1960s, and the failure of its social movements to root themselves deeply in the constituencies for which they claimed to speak—i.e., to build real people power—were correct. So were his interests in preventing the growing white working class turn to the Right and racism, and in organizing the middle class.

Values and Theory

Alinsky rooted organizing in the American small "d" democratic tradition and the social and economic justice teachings of the world's great religious traditions. He took both the tradition and the teachings seriously, and engaged leaders and organizers in discussing them. His ideology comprises these two sources of values, an understanding of democratic theory and practice, careful power and constituency analyses to find out what was possible in any given time and place, and a set of organizing methods.

Power, he said, gravitates to two poles: organized money and organized people. He was on the people's side. Organized people could break out of their privatized self-blame and feelings of powerlessness (internalized oppression). They could discern, define, discuss, deliberate, and debate their own problems and the solutions to them. If decision-makers in the power structure wouldn't meet or engage in good-faith negotiations, organized people could use their numbers in strikes, boycotts, nonviolent disruption, public shaming, mass lobbying, and electoral engagement to force such negotiations. There was a cycle: seek negotiations; fight if you don't get them; negotiate when your power forces the other side to "the table"; compromise judiciously because there aren't

311

100-percent victories, and leave room for your adversary to save face; make agreements work—i.e., engage with implementation; use your position at the negotiating table to "up the ante" by proposing solutions that reach more deeply into problems of social and economic inequality or political injustice; and when recalcitrance arises—as it assuredly will if you haven't been co-opted—repeat the cycle.

While he personalized the opposition, he understood that there was a *system* of which individual decision-makers were representatives. He hated injustice, not the people who were its perpetrators—a distinction of central importance to his religious supporters.

Tactics for him were important only in the service of larger principles. Alinsky was sharply critical of tactical excesses—either in action or rhetoric. He warned—very correctly, it turned out—against creating a reaction bigger than our sides' capacity to overcome, fearing this would lead to setbacks for civil rights, economic justice, and democratic participation, and victories for racists and for conservatism more broadly. He correctly feared a reaction that would lead to setbacks for earlier victories and to repression.

His Contribution

Alinsky invented a new social form: the mass-based community organization. The organizations formed by the Industrial Areas Foundation (IAF) during his lifetime made substantial contributions to the quality of life for the people they represented. They engaged tens of thousands of everyday people in civic life, and trained thousands of people to become effective leaders—people who would say about themselves, "I never thought I'd do something like this."

Alinsky also engaged in an entirely different level of organizing—the transformation of U.S. (and international as well) Catholic and Protestant understandings of the role of the church in relation to democracy and social and economic justice. In his speaking and writing, he pounded away at this theme: "If you want justice, organize!" Within the churches, the struggle over "Alinskyism" continues to this day, with an endless litany of conservative Catholic and Protestant criticism of his views. Ironically, the political counterparts of these religious conservatives incorrectly paint moderate President Obama with the Alinsky brush because he was for a brief time a community organizer.

For the most part, Christendom in the United States dealt with poverty by offering charity. At the same time, there were significant voices coming from the church who believed that charity was not a substitute for justice. These Christians were typically "advocates"—that is, they spoke publicly in behalf of justice, making a moral witness in its behalf. The common phrase used was (and is) "speak truth to power." Alinsky's teaching modified that phrase to "speak truth with people power to incumbent power." Alinsky taught Christians how to use mass-based people power.

Finally, Alinsky's emphases on the centrality of civil society, and of continuing and active citizen participation, are central to both our understanding of what meaningful democracy is and what is required now to reclaim it. That understanding is as central today as when he first uttered these ideas. Frank Pierson is a recently retired thirty-year veteran of the IAF. As he puts it, "Conventional wisdom has it that IAF-style face-to-face organizing is outdated and outmoded—a kind of political blast from the past. From the point of view of political instrumentality [new high tech tools for communicating are] a grand success. From the point of view of deepened democratic practice they [are] short term, shallow, deceptive and ultimately disheartening for legions of participants."[1]

Weaknesses

I'd like to focus on two of Alinsky's weaknesses: his understanding of how to reach national power, and his relationships to the social movements of his day.

While Alinsky fully recognized the need for national power to address major injustices, he did little to create mechanisms that might develop it. He could have organized a national sponsor committee of public intellectuals and theologians, celebrities from the entertainment and sports worlds, writers and artists, leaders in the professions, and institutional leaders from higher education, labor, politics and other spheres of influence to give broad legitimacy to his organizing work. In addition to raising seed money for various projects beyond the core budget of a local community organization—for example, yearlong intern-trainee stipends for potential organizers—the sponsor committee could have added its voices to his and the religious community's in the national debate then going on about organizing.

Nor did Alinsky create a national temporary organizing committee to bring together leaders of local organizations. Among other things, this body could have helped organize in new places by visiting them and sharing local stories of their own successes. It could also have envisioned policies or programs to pursue as the power to do so became a reality. It could have used this envisioning to inspire and sustain commitment to more organizing—including converting skeptics with the power of a realistic vision. It might have made possible an alternative to co-optation by the community development corporation approach to institutionalization.

Alinsky's strategic weaknesses in relation to building national power are connected with his critical commentary on social movements. Movements, he and his associates said, were single issue, led by charismatic leaders, and only capable of mobilization, not organization. It was an incomplete analysis, and only partially true. The civil rights movement engaged in a wide range of issues affecting the black community. In hundreds of communities across the country, there were local black organizations that saw themselves as part of "The Movement," and that were locally led by more than one leader. The Student Nonviolent Coordinating Committee (SNCC) built some in the Deep South. Even the Southern Christian Leadership Conference (SCLC), led by

Martin Luther King (who was indeed a charismatic leader), had other leaders at the core of the organization, and certainly in its local affiliates. In large part because it was rooted in local black churches, the Montgomery Improvement Association (MIA) sustained an almost-100-percent-successful bus boycott for a year, during which there were bombings, arrests, fines, and other attempts by the local power structure to disrupt and destroy it.

The Question of Vision

Alinsky was vulnerable to the charge that he lacked a vision any greater than getting excluded groups to the table where they could get their piece of the American pie. Actually, his democratic vision—articulated in *Reveille for Radicals* and elsewhere—was far broader. But he refused to discuss policies and ideas that might have elaborated a mid-twentieth-century understanding of substantive—i.e., beyond procedural—democracy.

Why didn't his local organizations sponsor worker- and consumer-owned cooperatives? (Dick Harmon did this in his independent organizing work in Brooklyn.). I do not understand why Alinsky did not say, "A national organization of people power organizations could look at options to replace the current concentration of wealth and power in the hands of corporate and financial elites. These might include various forms of publicly owned companies, like the Tennessee Valley Authority (TVA) or the state bank of North Dakota. The present monopolies and oligopolies that now run the economy could be broken up into competitive smaller units. A legislative and financial base could be created for wider worker-ownership. And that's just a start." He could have added his warnings about big public bureaucracies that tend to grow beyond democratic accountability. He simultaneously could have insisted that his calling and priority was to build the effective people power organizations that could meaningfully discuss and pursue these alternatives. And, he would have added, it was not his role, nor should it be any organizer's role, to define the people's program. That's something they should and would do.

While "activists" who are impatient with the requirements for building real people power tend to dominate most social movement organizations, they do often make substantial contributions in issue campaigns. Alinsky might in the mid-1960s have initiated some state or local campaign that invited the participation of the activists and their canvassing and media mobilizing tools, along with other organizing networks, with each delivering in mutually agreed-upon areas. In ongoing evaluations of who was delivering and who wasn't, of what was going to enforce a victory once it was won, and of the possibilities created by not reinventing the wheel each time you engaged in a major campaign, there might have been opportunities for IAF organizers to teach and learn from activists and other organizing approaches. Organizing in a mobilizing context is possible, and can expand organizing.

Work

When Alinsky organized in Back of the Yards, a vital labor movement was growing, challenging corporate power, providing dignity in the workplace for its members, and vastly improving wages, hours, and benefits for workers. In the political arena, it was a central force in all the progressive legislation of the period. But by the mid to late 1940s, Alinsky concluded that unions, while important to democracy, were not the central organizing vehicle for its realization. Essentially, he saw their agenda as limited by the sector of the economy of which they were a part.

From that time until today, the scope of labor's agenda in the workplace and its authority and power in civic life have been radically reduced. In part, this is a result of self-imposed limits. More importantly, it is the result of a relentless assault on labor by corporate power and its political allies—in both political parties. But work remains a central dimension of humanity. Community organizers need to address it.

The centrality of work for the human condition is established in Pope John Paul II's *Laborem Exercens* (Encyclical on Labor), but it is by no means only the Catholic tradition that makes this case. Reading the encyclical can be a challenge for the typical layperson—Catholic or not—so Catholic Charities of St. Paul and Minneapolis published "notable quotations" to get a broader audience to read it. Here I quote from their document.[2] (The numbers refer to sections within the original *Laborem Exercens* text.)

Human work is the key to the solution . . . of the whole "social question." To consider work is of decisive importance when trying to make life "more human." (3)

We must pay more attention to the one who works than to what the worker does. The self-realization of the human person is the measure of what is right and wrong. . . . (6)

Work is in the first place "for the worker" and not the worker "for work." Work itself can have greater or lesser objective value, but all work should be judged by the measure of dignity given to the person who carries it out. (6)

But above all we must remember the priority of labor over capital: labor is the cause of production; capital, or the means of production, is its mere instrument or tool. (12)

Workers not only want fair pay, they also want to share in the responsibility and creativity of the very work process. They want to feel that they are working for themselves—an awareness that is smothered in a bureaucratic system where they only feel themselves to be "cogs" in a huge machine moved from above. (15)

The justice of a social and economic system is finally measured by the way in which a person's work is rewarded. A just wage is a concrete measure—and in a sense the key one—of the justice of a system. (19)

History teaches us that organizations of this type [unions] are an indispensable element in social life, especially in industrialized societies. (20)

Awareness that our work is a sharing in God's work ought to permeate even the most ordinary daily activities. By our labor we are unfolding the Creator's work and contributing to the realization of God's plan on earth. The Christian message does not stop us from building the world or make us neglect our fellow human beings. On the contrary it binds us more firmly to do just that. (25)

Workers are the people who are on the front line. They can ensure that their products or services are appropriate, effective, of good quality, and efficiently provided. All work can be organized to be meaningful work. The social technologies now exist to make this happen; in some enterprises, that technology is now being implemented—usually by forward-looking managers and owners who often also have a "union-free environment" agenda. That agenda should not obscure the possibility of making all work meaningful.

The public policies are now available to make it possible for all who want to, should, and are able, to work. Whether this is done by government as the employer of last resort, by absorbing workers who are unemployed in one sector into another sector that requires more workers, by diminishing hours to take in the unemployed (as the Mondragon cooperatives do in the Basque region of Spain), or by some other method, this is not a utopian notion.

The wealth now exists in advanced industrial countries for all people to receive good pay and benefits through living wage and social insurance public policies, redistributive programs such as earned income tax credits, and other means.

Whether it is in alliances with existing unions, in agitation within them for a broader agenda, or by forming new unions outside the present framework of traditional unions, the agenda of the workplace needs to be part of the agenda of community organizers and community organizations. That will require a new relationship with members of the New Left (who are now an older Left) because some of the best worker organizing is being done by them.

The IAF and the New Left

The IAF that followed Alinsky's death, led by Ed Chambers and Dick Harmon, sought to provide leadership in the social movement climate of its day, using environmental issues as their initial organizing tool. In these pages, Aaron Schutz and I have presented weaknesses that the IAF identified in its Campaign Against Pollution (later

Citizens Action Program, or CAP) and similar organizations in the multistate region surrounding Chicago. On the other hand, there were tremendous strengths in CAP, and if anyone could have captured them and built upon them it was the core of organizers at the IAF. That would have required a different attitude toward the New Left.

By then, however, the die had been cast and the polarization between the IAF and the social movement people was near-complete. The IAF's macho style, organizational arrogance, dismissal of "movements," avoidance of any coalition that it didn't organize, unwillingness to look at mutual aid as a strategic organizing tool that could lead to the development of substantial worker- and consumer-owned cooperatives and credit unions, and other shortcomings made inevitable the creation of alternative organizing centers that would emphasize what the IAF neglected.

Could there have been something different? Monday-morning quarterbacking is always easier than playing the game, and hindsight, as the saying goes, is 20/20. Here are some possibilities to consider.

During the Crosstown Freeway fight, CAP produced a flyer that asked politicians in the 1972 national, state, and local elections which side they were on: the people's or Mayor Daley's. From the lowest-level local office to president, candidates had to respond with a yes or a no to the question, "Do you support the Crosstown Freeway?" The absence of a reply, candidates were told, was a yes, so there was no room for evasion. There were three responses that deserve careful attention. George McGovern, the Democrat's very liberal presidential peace candidate, was a yes—testimony to the mayor's power in the national Democratic Party. So was Edward Hanrahan, the Daley-supported candidate for re-election to state's attorney; Hanrahan was also being groomed by the mayor at the time to be his political heir—and he was the man in charge of the raid on the Chicago Black Panthers that led to a police murder of two of its leaders. Incumbent Republican governor Richard Ogilvie was also a yes. In the freeway corridor, where thousands of jobs and affordable housing units would have been destroyed, CAP mounted a massive voter education, registration and get-out-the-vote (GOTV) drive. The vote in that corridor defeated Ogilvie and Hanrahan (who lost to a reform Republican in spite of the Democratic machine).

The logic of self-interest led people of color and white ethnics in the freeway corridor into an otherwise unlikely alliance. Might the CAP activists have been persuaded after this success that a time-out was now required from issue campaigns in order to consolidate something at the base that could challenge the Daley machine, which was as racist and corrupt a political enterprise as there was in the United States at the time? Part of consolidation could have involved mutual aid (i.e., the founding of small co-ops, buying clubs, babysitting pools, credit unions, and other forms that could later become an association, and larger groups as well)—following and elaborating the way the Mondragon cooperatives began and grew. Consolidation could have added depth and infrastructure to the otherwise fragile structures of block clubs, tenant associations, and "civics," as well as new structures developed within or supported by congregations. Might serious membership dues for such local "built from scratch" associations have given them deeper commitment and substance? After all, Cesar Chavez insisted on what in today's dollars would be about $25 a month from farm-workers in California, and the CSO created from scratch chapters up and down the state of California with only a few full-time organizers. Might a meld of the Fred Ross, Tom Gaudette, and Shel Trapp approaches to individual meetings, door-knocking, block clubs, and house meetings have been added to "institution-based" organizing?[3]

And here's the big leap: what if a multi-issue approach had led to a people power congress or convention attended by 25,000–50,000 delegates and alternates who would have adopted a program that emerged from deep within the multiplicity of old and new and large and small organizations that in combination were a majority con-stituency base in Chicago? Might such an approach have built at the base a voluntary people power machine to compete successfully with the Daley patronage machine?

In dozens of metropolitan areas across the country, similar conventions and con-gresses could have taken place, on a coordinated basis, thus creating a real basis for a national people power agenda. Such gatherings would have made possible a presence in almost every precinct in a region. And it would have made possible both boycott and nonviolent disruptive direct action tactics that could have commanded good-faith negotiations with the corporate/finance sector and forced into the political arena the question, "Whose side are you on?" but on a multi-issue rather than single-issue agenda.

In their appraisal of what happened in CAP and its counterpart organizations in the multistate region around Chicago, the IAF concluded that none of this was pos-sible, or at least that it wasn't worth the effort. I think they threw the baby out with the bathwater.

That the people about whom Schutz and I write achieved what they did is cause for celebration and a bit of awe. Against what might have seemed insurmountable odds, they built and sustained significant voices of people power. Despite this, their legacy is not sufficient for the crisis the country today faces. Here are some tentative thoughts for the future.

On the Current State of Community Organizing

The legendary Msgr. John "Jack" Egan was a close associate and friend of Saul Alinsky's, an organizer in IAF Chicago projects, one of the principal figures in the development of the Catholic Campaign for Human Development (a major funder of community organizing over the last forty years), and the person most responsible for raising the money that launched the IAF Institute. In a late 1990s conversation with me, Egan observed about good community organizing that a central goal was to involve *everyone*. He was criticizing the religious congregations–only period that organizing was going through at the time. But his comment had a broader meaning as well, and he lived it. When he didn't see room in community organizing for labor-religion alliances, he worked with Kim Bobo to form Interfaith Worker Justice; when there was no room in the kind of community organizing closest to him for big-issue coalitions, he worked with Heather Booth and supported the Midwest Academy. A Catholic priest, he was also small "c" catholic in his desire to engage *everyone* in the struggles for social and economic justice and the work to create a living democracy in the United States. Egan's spirit should haunt all of us who think we have The Way to go about doing this work.

A Scenario

Organizers want to "do with" rather than "do for"; their rule is "do not do for others what they can (and should) do for themselves." Unless organizers want to ignore these principles, they cannot "stand for the whole" without engaging the whole. They need to remember Jack Egan's lesson. This means developing an organizing effort that the majority of Americans come to know—as they knew the farmworker boycott and the Deep South civil rights movement—and identify as their own; about which they will say, "that's my voice"; in which millions of Americans will be actively engaged. Such a voice might emerge out of a social movement—as the CIO (Congress of Industrial Organizations) did out of the industrial union movement of the 1930s, and as SCLC and SNCC did out of the Deep South civil rights movement of the 1950s and 1960s. But such a voice might more intentionally be formed by a conscious alliance of organizers and organizations that builds it—which, in fact, is also how the CIO was built.

Imagine a group of organizers and leaders meeting together with the intention of starting a campaign whose purpose would be to slow, halt, and reverse the present plutocracy, and create a real democratic alternative to it. They recognize that a lowest significant common denominator "people's platform" focused on, for example, quality education for all, economic justice, and global warming issues, is the tool to accomplish this. But the door is not shut to other platform ideas. They identify issues that resonate with 80 percent of the American people, such as a major expansion of solar power and public transportation to provide good jobs in a sustainable economy and slow global warming, paid for by steeply progressive taxes and by closing multiple corporate loopholes.

The moral imperative for such an effort is clear. Every major religious tradition provides grounds for it. So does the democratic theory that underlies the Alinsky organizing tradition. In political terms, this would be a center-to-left counterpart to the Tea Party, with a capacity to shape both political parties and, if need be, to initiate a new one. Might a new secular small "d" democratic story of citizenship provide a deeply meaningful cultural myth and create for those who are unchurched a bond similar to that engendered by religious faith? It worked for the Populists and the Nonpartisan League, and was part of the cultural myth of the CIO industrial unions (which drew upon both secular and religious language for meaning and sustenance). While no doubt strong, religious faith is not the only faith to sustain people in democratic struggle. The religious bases for this approach are abundant. There need not always be the poor among us. Nor is there a faith-based basis for excesses of riches.[4]

U.S. Supreme Court justice Louis Brandeis put the issue clearly in 1938: "We must make our choice. We may have democracy, or we may have wealth concentrated in the hands of a few, but we can't have both."[5] The campaign envisaged here would make economic equality and the illegitimate power of concentrated wealth the central issues of the day. There can be no serious democracy, nor can there be economic security and well-being, sustainable development, or social justice for the American people if these questions of wealth and power are not addressed.

Equally important, these organizers and leaders would need to recognize that their own initial "exploratory committee" has to be representative of the diversity of constituencies whose participation would be required for a "unity in diversity" majority. Thus the faces of the campaign would be those of men and women; black, brown, yellow, and white; gay and straight; old, middle-aged, and young; from urban, suburban, and rural places in every nook and cranny of the country. And these faces would be directly or indirectly representative of the voluntary member-based associations to which these constituencies now give their allegiance. To accomplish this purpose, representatives of the constituencies that are now divided by right-wing fear campaigns and stereotypes of "the other" must be engaged at the beginning of this exploration process. They have to agree on the "draft" of a "lowest significant common denominator" program. And that might mean agreeing that certain issues are too divisive to be included in this initial effort.

This committee, in turn, would seek sponsorship from a combination of national institutional and organizational leaders, as well as "notables" whose names carry weight with everyday Americans, such as celebrities from the entertainment and sports worlds, prominent members of major advocacy, constituency, and other groups, and anyone else who might give the effort legitimacy and raise its initial budget. With this support, the exploratory committee would expand to become a national "organizing committee" that would invite local groups to join a metropolitan, state, or region-affiliated campaign committee. The local groups would include long-established religious congregations and labor union locals and a wide variety of other groups. They would include newly formed "from scratch" organizations as well as already existing ones. Each stage—exploratory committee, sponsor committee, organizing committee—would be part of a "go/no-go" process. If the right exploratory committee cannot be put together, the project is abandoned or postponed; if things move more quickly than anticipated, the campaign speeds up. Ditto for each subsequent organizational phase. The collective wisdom of those engaged in the effort would make the determination.

Of central importance would be money for the actual campaign coming from the bottom up—contributions from affiliated organizations and grassroots fundraising activities would pay for the core budget. Perhaps a door-to-door canvass operation would be part of it, including a combined "canvass-organizing" effort in which canvassers raised money three days a week, and organized the other three days of their work week—an approach used by the Citizens Action League in the 1970s, but never copied.

The ideas here are intended to be suggestive. No person sitting at a computer can anticipate what will emerge out of the necessary conversations that would be preliminary to such an effort. I hope these thoughts inspire some organizers to begin that effort. Note that without the right people in the room such an organizing campaign cannot be undertaken. Further, this is no overnight, single-election-cycle undertaking. I imagine a time frame of eight to ten years. And I imagine electoral, legislative, *and* direct corporate-targeted (boycott, corporate campaigns, nonviolent disruptive direct action, etc.) efforts.

Big Picture versus Local Organizing?

An important assumption underlies this scenario: local issues are manifestations of global inequities; global issues are manifestations of the absence of local power. If you can't get a decently funded education program at your local school, it is because of national misallocations of money that favor the rich and powerful. If parents and their allies can't hold school districts accountable, it is because of the lack of powerful local organizations. If you can't get a decent education program passed by Congress, signed by the president, and implemented by the U.S. Department of Education, it is a sign of the lack of local powerful organizations of parents and their allies coming together on a national agenda. The common juxtaposition of local versus national (or international) is a straw man. There are tensions in timing, strategy, and tactics between the two, but they are not either-or.

Can such a campaign be won? Asked once by a farmworker whether it would be possible to attain an objective dear to him, Cesar Chavez replied, "There is nothing we cannot do if we have enough people." The more difficult question is whether organizers, leaders, and organizations will do it. When SNCC "field secretaries" (organizers) Charles Sherrod and Charles Jones organized the Albany (GA) Movement, they were frequently asked by the churches and other groups that became part of it, "What's going to happen to our independence, autonomy, and visibility?" These were legitimate questions to which the organizers had to have acceptable responses. But the answer that finally was convincing was this: "Everyone's going to have to give up a little of those if we're going to win."

Organizing and Mobilizing

This is a mobilizing campaign. An organizing campaign aims at putting together a coalition that can win campaigns. I earlier discussed the distinction between mobilizing and organizing. Here's an example of how they were mutually supportive. Dr. Martin Luther King and the SCLC planned a march from Selma to Montgomery whose purpose was to demonstrate support for the Voting Rights Act. The march drew people from across the nation. Its route took it through Lowndes County, one of the most repressive places in the south. SNCC was critical of the march, as it was generally critical of SCLC "mobilizations." But Stokely Carmichael (later Kwame Ture), one of SNCC's best organizers, marched.[6] As he passed through Lowndes County, Carmichael spoke with local black residents who lined the highway to cheer the marchers on, bring them food and drink, and otherwise indicate support. He wanted their names and contact information because he and a small group of SNCC organizers were going to return to Lowndes and develop a local black organization there. They did that. A process of one-on-one visits, during which the organizers listened to, challenged, and thought through with people what could be done, led to the formation of the Lowndes County Freedom Organization, which became a flagship of SNCC organizing. Organizing can be done within the framework of mobilization. Community organizations and labor unions that participated in such an effort would be able to build their own power as a result of it.

In Mississippi in 1963 the groundwork was laid for the Council of Federated Organizations (COFO). It was an organizational vehicle that made it possible for the Congress of Racial Equality (CORE), the National Association for the Advancement of Colored People (NAACP), the Southern Christian Leadership Conference (SCLC), and the Student Nonviolent Coordinating Committee (SNCC) to work together in the state. It created space for national rivals and local organizations to work together in a commonly agreed upon structure, each with its own "turf," and each national organization able to claim credit for its portion of the overall program. COFO laid the basis for the Mississippi Freedom Democratic Party that, in turn, made sharecropper Fannie Lou Hamer an internationally known spokeswoman for racial and economic justice. There is no comparable movement today. But there is a presence of organizations that could mobilize the simmering discontent in the country; such mobilization would parallel a more spontaneous movement.

Strategic Balance

We can with relative ease make "either-or" cases about one or another of the points made above. I have argued for or against them myself, so am familiar with how to do it. But as I look at where the country is today, and the relentless growth of the plutocracy that now governs it, I am persuaded that a different approach is called for—one that is more small "c" catholic in its orientation.

A "both-and" conversation needs the assistance of the idea of strategic balance. The concept suggests different times for different things—a time to focus on mutual aid, another times to do a boycott, still another time for disruptive direct action to polarize (clarify) what the issues are, and yet a different time for electoral activity. And, within each of these, organizers must also find time for reflection, interpretation, internal education, and celebration (to create a new history, new leaders, and a new counterculture)—all aimed at building people power.

Community organizers can make mistakes in either direction. One danger is becoming absorbed in national campaigns with content and timelines over which they have little or no control. The danger, of course, is co-optation in the name of "realism," combined with increasing estrangement from the base. The opposite danger is avoiding the challenge of national (or even international—as a boycott might be) efforts. The result is equally damaging. "People power" will become a joke as the pain experienced by everyday people continues despite organizers' claims about their "powerful organization," and as divide-and-conquer strategies and tactics split people apart. One likelihood in this case is that those everyday people will withdraw into apathy or, worse, drugs and other escapes, or pursuit of alternatives like crime to "make it." Others will resort to scapegoating: in the Rust Belt, for example, many working people blame the loss of good jobs on unions—not the corporations that moved their plants to enjoy cheap labor in antiunion environments; similarly, immigrants are accused of taking "our jobs"—I've heard both arguments from whites and American-born blacks. There will be a growing national vacuum, and the increased danger of demagogues who seek to fill that vacuum.

If we want to build serious people power capable of achieving transformational change—i.e., capable of building a real democratic society—leaders, organizers, and activists need to move among and between different approaches. An eight- to ten-year cycle is a good way to think of the time period within which this motion could take place.

All Organizing Is Reorganizing

I think it was from Nick von Hoffman that I first heard the idea that organizing is really reorganizing—people live in social patterns. When these patterns violate or diminish the dignity of human beings the task is to undo them—to reorganize them. That means not only challenging the dominant power structure, but—and this is more difficult—it means challenging the patterns of leadership among oppressed people. Leaders who acquiesce to the dominant status quo need to be challenged either to change or to be pushed aside. New leaders will arise to better express the constant quest for freedom, equality, community, security, and justice for all.

The various networks of organizers and organizations that now exist each tap a different stream of energy for change. Separate, none of them has the capacity to significantly impact the direction in which the country is going. Together, with additional allies that I've discussed, they might. The question is whether a form for being together can be found that both builds power and recognizes the legitimate organizational interests of those whose participation is essential if that power is to be built.

The Choice

We are in dark times. People power organizing is a major antidote to the darkness. Its growth over the past roughly fifty years, despite setbacks and failures to realize some of its earlier optimistic projections of success, is one of the few hopeful signs of our times. If we fail to rise to the challenge, what Sheldon Wolin calls "inverted totalitarianism," what Bertram Gross called "friendly fascism," what C. Wright Mills calls "The Power Elite," and what G. William Domhoff describes in his *Who Rules America* as "the success of the wealthy few in defeating all of their rivals (e.g., organized labor, liberals, environmentalists) over the course of the past 35 years" will become ever-more accurate descriptions of the state of the nation.[7]

The American People Are Ready—The Problem Is Us

An online document, "An All-American Agenda," includes this prefatory note: "What looks like middle ground in Washington is not middle-of-the-road for most Americans. It's critical to remember that the Republican Party's far-right positions are out of touch with the center-left agenda of the vast majority of Americans."[8]

"An All-American Agenda" presents findings from a variety of reputable polling sources on a number of issue areas important to the American people:

- Taxes: 6 in 10 Americans say that what bothers them most is wealthy people paying too little taxes. 3 in 4 voters say that corporations pay too little in taxes and support eliminating corporate tax loopholes. . . .
- Immigration: Nearly 9 in 10—including 9 in 10 conservative voters, and 7 in 10 GOP primary voters—support creating a real road to citizenship in immigration reform.
- Social Security: Nearly 9 in 10 Americans want to maintain or increase spending on our Social Security system and more than 8 in 10 believe that current Social Security benefits are too low. . . .
- Climate Change: More than 9 in 10 Americans believe that we have a moral obligation to future generations to leave them a planet that is not polluted or damaged. . . .
- Jobs: Almost two-thirds of Americans want Congress and President Obama to make jobs the top priority for the nation.
- Inequality: 3 in 4 Americans believe that today the rich are getting richer while the poor are getting poorer, and more than 6 in 10 believe we need to dramatically reduce inequalities in wealth.
- Medicare: Medicare is extremely popular. 9 in 10 Americans want to maintain or increase Medicare funding. . . .
- Poverty: 9 in 10 agree that our society should do what is necessary to make sure that everyone has an equal opportunity to succeed, and that reducing poverty and inequality should be a priority for Congress and the President.
- Education: 9 in 10 Americans want to increase education in funding or at least maintain it—not cut it.[9]

The problem is us, not the American people. Is there anything more that needs to be said?

Notes

1. Frank Pierson, private communication to Mike Miller, December 2013.

2. John Paull II, quoted in Catholic Charities of St. Paul and Minneapolis, "Notable Quotations from the Papal Encyclical *Laborem Excercens* (On Human Work)," accessed May 27, 2014, *www.cctwincities.org/document.doc.* The website text was compiled from John Paul II, *John Paul's Encyclicals in Everyday Language*, edited by Joseph G. Donders (Maryknoll, NY: Orbis Books, 2001); the numbers refer to sections within the encyclical.

3. When I spoke with Jim Drake in Boston, where he was the IAF's lead organizer, he worried about the narrowness of experience that characterized many of the new organizers coming up within the IAF's ranks.

4. To be sure that I was on firm theological ground with this assertion, I asked Rev. Paul Buckwalter to review it. Buckwalter—an Episcopal priest for fifty years, a recently retired statewide organizer for the IAF's Arizona Interfaith Network (a post he held for eight years), and a founder of the IAF's Pima County Interfaith Council—concurred. I asked theologically conservative Presbyterian theologian Rev. Robert C. Linthicum—leader of workshops on the theology of organizing for various organizing groups, and author of *City of God, City of Satan* (Grand Rapids, MI: Zondervan, 1991) and *Building a People of Power* (Colorado Springs: Authentic, 2006)—what he thought; he concurred as well. United Methodist Rev. Stephen Charles Mott, former professor of Christian social ethics at Gordon-Conwell Theological Seminary, concurs too. He is the author of *Biblical Ethics and Social Change* (New York: Oxford University Press, 2011 [2nd ed.]), and *A Christian Perspective on Political Thought* (New York: Oxford University Press, 1993). Both Linthicum and Mott are evangelicals who, among other things, hold a high view of scripture.

5. Attributed to Louis D. Brandeis; see Irving Dillard, *Mr. Justice Brandeis, Great American: Press Opinion and Public Appraisal* (St. Louis, MO: Modern View Press, 1941).

6. In late 1966, at a United Methodist church in Detroit, Carmichael and Alinsky were billed as having a "debate" about "black power." Alinsky opened his remarks saying, and I paraphrase, "If you came here looking for disagreement, you're in for a disappointment. We don't go into a black community and come out with pastel power." During the session, Carmichael was accused of being "hateful." Alinsky jumped into the discussion before Carmichael could respond, saying, "You are looking at a man motivated by love for humanity, not hate." According to someone who was there, tears welled up in Carmichael's eyes after Alinsky spoke. Later that year, Carmichael addressed a FIGHT meeting in Rochester, New York, to support the IAF project's jobs battle with Eastman Kodak. He got a standing ovation when he said, "When Minister Florence [FIGHT president] says 'jump' to Kodak, Kodak will respond, 'How high.'" A relationship between the IAF and SNCC was close, but at a meeting in early 1967, the SNCC Central Committee decided not to proceed with it (meeting notes, January 20, 1967, author's files).

7. Sheldon Wolin, "Inverted Totalitarianism," *Nation*, May 19, 2003, *www.thenation.com*; Bertram Goss, *Friendly Fascism: The New Face of Power in America* (Cambridge, MA: South End Press, 1987); C. Wright Mills, *The Power Elite* (New York: Oxford University Press, 1956); G. William Domhoff, *WhoRulesAmerica.Net* (online supplement to Domhoff, *Who Rules America? The Triumph of the Corporate Rich*, 7th ed. [New York: McGraw-Hill, 2013]), 2014, *www2.ucsc.edu/whorulesamerica.*

8. Franklin Forum, "An All-American Agenda," August 12, 2013, *thefranklinforum.org*, republished at *www.uslaboragainstwar.org.*

9. Ibid.

28

Thinking beyond the Present

■

AARON SCHUTZ

The period covered by this volume, from roughly the end of the 1950s to 1980, was one of great creativity in the field of community organizing. While there are a few important books that came out after Alinsky rose to prominence in the 1960s, and while there has been a great deal written about Alinsky, in general the details of organizing during this period are not well discussed in the current literature. Few works compare and contrast the different approaches, and fewer place them in a wider context.

In organizing today I think it is fair to say that congregation-based organizing, sometimes inclusive enough of other institutions to be called institution-based organizing, has become ascendant, driven by a range of networks that includes the Industrial Areas Foundation (IAF), People Improving Communities through Organizing (PICO), Direct Action and Research Training Center (DART), and the Gamaliel Foundation. David Walls seems largely correct when he argues that while the IAF, for example, "refers to its organizing activity as 'broad-based' rather than 'congregation-based,' this is something of a misnomer. . . . By 'broad-based' IAF means"—or, from my perspective, at least predominantly means—"that it includes a variety of religious congregations"[1] Important exceptions include some work with groups in, or engaged with, schools, unions, and health centers, that can bring in a range of people from outside congregations. And other creativity continues: in individual affiliates of the congregational networks, a few of which are quite diverse; in alliances with other groups, like unions; and in other groups, including the statewide organizations that hopefully represent the rebirth of the once national network of Association of Community Organizations for Reform Now (ACORN), National People's Action, and others.[2] It's difficult to know exactly what's happening because there is no clear map of the field beyond largely anecdotal evidence.

Beyond Congregation-Based Organizing

I am a supporter of the congregation-based approach—I have worked with one of these organizations for more than a decade. But I worry that the congregation-based approach, by itself, is not *enough*. I worry that it is unlikely to be able to generate the power that poor- and moderate-income people need to survive in a nation with our vastly increasing income gap and increasing corporate control. In my city, there are actually two separate congregation-based organizations. They don't work together, but even if they did they would not have, nor are they ever likely to have, the capacity to significantly change the "relations of power" in my city. I believe the congregation-based approach, *by itself*, will not prove sufficient to build the kind of people power we need in America.

Why not?

In his conclusion (Chapter 27), Mike Miller reports that in a discussion about the congregation-based approach, Msgr. John Egan asked him, "Aren't we supposed to get *everyone* in these organizations?" One limitation of the congregation-based approach that emerges in the available research and in our conversations with organizers is that they generally don't. They tend to succeed in the more established mainline churches. Poorer people and the unchurched tend not to be touched by organizations limited to congregations.[3] This problem has intensified as churches become less geographically based. The old parish churches that drew everyone in a particular area are growing weaker.[4] It's hard to make the church and the community become one, as Tom Gaudette (Chapter 11) imagined, when so many people in the church don't come from the surrounding community.

Churches have long been segregated by class.[5] As Heidi Swarts and others have shown, congregation-based groups tend to draw from more middle-class segments of the religious community.[6] Organizing networks have been unable to attract Pentecostal/Holiness and evangelical churches in significant numbers, including those with poorer congregations.[7]

Many studies have shown that the issue of class is crucial in the development of internal cultures of organizations. Middle-class people tend to exert control over dialogue in the organizations they participate in, and they tend, as Dick Harmon notes in Chapter 16, to be more aversive to conflict, something noted by other observers about congregation-based organizing.[8] These cultural mores and power issues are difficult to address even with the most expert facilitation.[9]

At the same time, the power of religion to hold people together has continued to fade in America. For a range of reasons the Catholic Church is no longer providing the support for organizing it did in Alinsky's day, and the old mainline Protestant churches are declining under pressure from the more conservative evangelicals. I worry that the congregation-based groups may be fighting a losing rearguard action against these tendencies.

There have been efforts to engage the churches in the organizing networks more tightly with residents in their local communities. And it may be that this will end up leading to new and more robust forms of neighborhood organizing. Through the work on this book I have become less sanguine about this possibility, however. I share Gaudette's early worry that organizers who focus most of their training on working within mainline churches, with their unique institutional structures, are not well prepared to engage with the very different dynamics of what I (and some of the practitioners) refer to as "neighborhood organizing." (This includes individual membership efforts like ACORN and "from scratch" institution-building like Shel Trapp's block club approach, which build local chapters that can come together in larger congresses of different kinds to build power.)

When Gaudette and Alinsky were organizing in churches, they were not as focused on intervening in the internal workings of these institutions, likely in part because these institutions were working fairly well at the time (some of the shift to a focus on institutional renewal in the IAF and elsewhere was driven by worries about the increasing challenges faced by churches since the 1960s). While the skills that leaders learned in their mass organizations were certainly often translated into the internal workings of their congregations, this was not an explicit focus.

I also worry about efforts to combine middle- and low- and working-class people together in the same organization for the cultural reasons noted above.

Because of this, in this world of congregation-focused networks, I am increasingly convinced that "neighborhood-based" and "congregation-based" organizing have progressively become very different kinds of activities. It may be that we need different kinds of organizations—working together in coalitions. And I think both sides have something to learn from the other. Congregation-based groups may be pushed to be a bit more nimble and confrontational; neighborhood groups may learn strategies for maintaining themselves together without the constant action that leads to leader and organizer burnout.

But We Can't Do Neighborhood-Based Organizing Anymore

Many arguments have been raised against neighborhood-based organizing outside of stable institutions like churches. Perhaps the most prominent is that it requires too much organizer person-power. Block club organizations like those developed by Shel Trapp or the chapters developed by Rathke's ACORN required larger numbers of organizers than one generally needs to sustain organizations of relatively stable institutions like churches. How would you ever pay all these people?

The problem with this argument is that groups like ACORN were able to pay larger numbers of organizers. Further, in organizations like Organization for a Better Austin (OBA), a good number of the organizers included an odd collection of interns, ministers on six-month and longer releases, long-term volunteers, and others. And there is the example of Fred Ross's Community Service Organization (CSO), which ran more than thirty chapters statewide with only a few full-time organizers.

I agree with Mike Miller, who notes that

the professionalization of organizing leads to ignoring the value of sacrifice—something central in, for example, Cesar Chavez's and SNCC's thinking. The organizers who were central to the CIO in the 1930s were often young people. The "professional" dismissal of youth, low pay, and sacrifice should be taken as a self-serving rationalization, not as an analysis of reality. ACORN was built by young people; so can other relatively simple approaches to building base units of organization be built by young people whose ideals lead them to make economic and other sacrifices.[10]

It may be, as some have said, that in the movements of the 1960s we had lots of people who really wanted to participate in social change, and today that's just not true. And there are plenty of young people doing "organizing" that either don't know much about the Alinsky tradition, or (think of Occupy) reject it. Maybe the nonprofit industrial complex has just sucked all the people who might otherwise have been organizers out of the picture.

I don't believe this is true. I believe that, if provided with sufficient support to live at a basic level, enough young people could still be attracted to organizing as a way to contribute to social change. This is especially the case at a time when jobs are not easy to find.

Yes, we need some organizers who are "professionals" in some sense, but much neighborhood organizing could be done by interns on small stipends and others in short-term (two-year) training programs—the best of whom would become professional organizers themselves. The rest would go on to other careers, but would be deeply informed by their time in the trenches.[11]

Finally, there is the argument that the old neighborhood as a viable base for organizing simply no longer exists: more middle-class people have moved to the suburbs; poverty program funding has destroyed independent organizational infrastructure; drug and crime are even more pervasive in inner-city neighborhoods; etc. As with most arguments, there are important truths in this one. But it is also the case that disaffection about the nonprofit industrial complex has become greater as problems in these neighborhoods deepen. There are also a growing number of people now pressed by social and economic problems as public services decline and job opportunities disappear. There is apparent anger to be tapped—it is routinely reported on in stories about people reacting to the latest drive-by shooting, closings of inner-city schools and other issues. And the structure of the central city is complex—even after the 2008 meltdown that decimated homeownership among the poor, there exist relatively stable areas that could provide a foundation for organizing.[12] Further, there are long-term tenants, small business owners, neighborhood residents who become volunteer coaches for youth teams, and others who could provide community leadership and who might not be found in churches.

The Emergence of the "Truth" in Organizing Networks

An interesting pattern emerges across the different readings in this book. If you look closely, I think you will see that different organizing groups tend to arrive at their organizing "model" fairly early in their existence. Then, once they have found their "truth" they tend to perpetuate their truth to others in the network.

Shel Trapp (Chapter 12) himself rails in these pages against the idea of a correct model for organizing, and he was one of the most flexible of the key organizers we discuss in terms of approach. At the same time, however, organizers I've talked with who worked with him generally agree that he basically arrived at a default "block club" approach in his early days in OBA, was quite vehement in his distaste for church-based organizing, and never really seems to have changed his core convictions or his default approach in most cases.[13] One can see the core outlines of ACORN's model in Rathke's almost accidental discoveries during his first significant organizing experience in Springfield, Massachusetts (Chapter 23). Fred Ross, for his part (Chapter 8), decided in the 1940s that the "organization of organizations" model didn't work, and never moved away from this conclusion. As Ross described it, after he developed the "house meeting" approach, he quickly decided it was the "right" way to organize. The story of the IAF (Chapter 17) is more complex; it struggled to find a working model after Alinsky's death. But once the IAF leaders found their congregation-based/relational approach, they grabbed hold of it with both hands.

While the IAF and other congregation-based groups have tried to reach beyond their congregational base—sometimes with great effect, as in their work with parents in Texas—it is unclear whether these forays have been part of a general view of how to build power.[14] The congregation-based networks have sought coalitions with other groups, as did ACORN, especially with unions, but this coalition work with other organizations that do not actually join an organizing group as a member has not necessarily required them to rethink their own core approach to organizing within their own networks.

There are, of course, many examples of individual organizers being extremely creative in adapting the basic approach they have started with. And every organizer who builds something is creatively adapting general principles or a model to the particularities of a local context. The problem is when the rigidity of principle or model precludes seeing things that would otherwise be important to building people power. And there seems to be a common core "truth" around which each of the different branches of the tradition circle and tend not to move very far away from.

Perhaps I should not be surprised at how quickly a firm commitment to a particular approach seems to set in. Most "organizing" fails. As von Hoffman notes in "Finding and Making Leaders" (Chapter 7) most people wander into communities, accomplish little, and then leave. I've done this myself. So when you find an approach that actually *works*, well, that's golden. You can hear this astonishment in Ross's voice when he recalls figuring out the house meeting approach. *Why fix something if it isn't broken?* Sure, maybe it doesn't do *everything* you may want it to do, but most approaches don't do *anything*.

Dangers of "Truth" in Organizing

Today, most organizers get trained within the core "truths" of a particular network. They are generally trained to be IAF, PICO, DART, or Gamaliel organizers, or ACORN organizers, or the like. It is that network's culture that defines their understanding of organizing. They do not usually get exposure to differing approaches. As networks have increasingly defined "models," they have gone beyond Alinsky's rule that there are no rules, only core principles. These more-or-less replicable models provide guidance to a new trainee. They also create blinders to what might be more appropriate approaches in new contexts, or additional approaches that would extend power by opening up new constituencies.

Of course, to some extent, a commitment to a particular approach to organizing has always been the case. For all of von Hoffman's talk of going into an area with a "tabula rasa" when he went into Woodlawn, he did have a sense of how to build power, how to pull organizations together, and so on. And yet, I think von Hoffman makes a key point: "If you have something in the back of your mind already, you will not see things, or you will not hear things. And also you will think you see things and think you hear things that aren't there."[15] When organizers go into a particular area to create an ACORN or IAF organization, they know what they are supposed to do; they have, however unintentionally, learned to ignore other potential options.

While more sophisticated organizers have taken their groups in unpredictable directions, most people aren't as sophisticated as the people discussed in this book. If you teach most people to build a particular kind of organizing group, they are likely to do what you teach them. If they see this approach working—even if it doesn't build as much power as they might if they had more tools available to them—they seem likely to stick with it.

I think it's important to acknowledge that there is some ego involved in this. There has been a tendency in organizing to decide that one's own "truth" is better than someone else's. In some cases, this is surely correct. And yet, across this volume we display a range of approaches that differ in significant ways from each other and nevertheless proved effective in their own ways. Each, I believe, has its own strengths and limitations.

The congregation-based groups are more stable. But even with the add-on of a union here and there, parent organizations, and schools or other groups, they seem generally less willing to move into confrontation and may organize those at a higher income and stability level than what I'm referring to generally as "neighborhood-based" approaches. Since many lower-income people are in conservative evangelical and Pentecostal churches that won't participate in community organizing, the problem is heightened.

As the writing in this book indicates, "from scratch" neighborhood-based groups generally need to be constantly "reorganized." Yet they have a capacity to organize closer on the ground and reach down deeper into the working class. They are more likely to pull in a more comprehensive membership from a particular area—an increasingly key issue as churches have lost membership where they are located. And in many cases neighborhood-based organizing groups seem to have been more willing to engage power aggressively (for good or ill in particular cases).[16] In fact, those we interviewed repeatedly noted that the key "issues" for their organizing would emerge out of neighborhood-based organizing work. We also need to acknowledge that without new organizing "from scratch" there never would have been industrial unions. Without new organizing from scratch, people who didn't go to church (and those who went rarely) would not have had opportunities to participate in ACORN, the CSO, block clubs, building associations, parent organizations, and other forms of organizing.

The IAF and later PICO decided that the neighborhoods were too fragmented to be organized effectively outside of religious congregations. As the success of many block clubs, tenant associations, parent groups, and ACORN chapters demonstrates, if a careful analysis is done of where the organizing is taking place, effective "from scratch" organizing is possible.

And, in fact, the challenge of fragmentation in neighborhoods that led the IAF and later PICO to abandon it was nothing new. Von Hoffman actually recommended initially against organizing in Woodlawn because he thought the South Side was too disorganized. Trapp developed the block club approach to deal with this very problem in South Austin. And it's important to remember that when it was created, The Woodlawn Organization (Part II, Section A), was made up of churches, collections of block clubs, building associations, business organizations, and other forms, with an understanding of the limits of each of these. (In my interview with him, von Hoffman spoke of constantly having actions for the block and building clubs to work on to keep them viable, just as Trapp later describes doing for his organizations.) Von Hoffman and Alinsky and their co-organizers used whatever they could find on the ground to build power.

There is a question here, as well, about how much "form" matters—to what extent are there important differences among what is accomplished by different neighborhood-based organizing approaches? In these pages we have described approaches focused on building relationships in very particular geographical areas (block clubs), organizing individuals across a larger geographical area (the ACORN approach), pulling together multiple local organizations and individuals in a particular area (Gaudette's "civics" in NCO), and leveraging existing relationships between individuals which may or may not be in the same area (house meetings). I am inclined to think that there are real differences in what is created and what impact these different approaches have on neighborhoods, and that each may be more or less relevant for different kinds of local realities or aims.

Let me emphasize that I am not anti "networks" per se. We do need organizing networks that are experts in a particular approach or set of approaches to organizing. In fact, as I have noted, it increasingly seems likely to me that congregation-based and neighborhood-based organizers, broadly understood, speak different "languages" of organizing, and these likely need to play out in separate spaces. But I would like to see networks that understand their own strengths and weaknesses, see the strengths in other approaches and the ways these strengths may balance out their own weaknesses, work in tight-knit collaboration with organizations working out of different traditions, and are led by organizers that have a breadth of understanding of the power and problems with different models of organizing. To the extent that existing networks already do, that's great. To the extent that they don't, it's a significant challenge to the development of real "people power" in the United States and elsewhere.

Imagining a Different Way to Train Organizers

As I note in Chapter 24, Rathke seems to have developed key aspects of his ACORN model in Springfield essentially by accident. He wasn't given much training, so according to him he didn't know that he *wasn't* supposed to be organizing in multiple areas at the same time. If he had been well "trained" in the welfare organizing approach, he wouldn't have made this "mistake" and there might have been no ACORN.

The IAF experimented for years with different approaches before they came up with their core principles that focus, in part, on intentional work to build relationships within congregations.

Let me try a "thought experiment," meant *not* as a concrete proposal but as an effort to begin to think differently about how to educate new organizers. What if our goal is to create *flexible organizers* who have a developing ability to build power in a way appropriate to the concrete setting in which they find themselves?

What if, in my city (Milwaukee), we found enough money to hire *one* highly experienced and ecumenical mentor-organizer—someone who understood different ways of building power from what I call the neighborhood approaches to the congregation-based ones. What if we had enough money as well to provide room and board and a stipend to ten to twelve intern organizers, recruited from around the United States (you'd lose some to attrition), who made a two-year commitment to learn how to organize?

This could be linked in a loose way to a university program, where they would learn the best current research on urban issues, culture, social movements, and the like, and read extensively in democratic theory, the history of labor and community organizing, the history of democratic struggles in our nation's past, and so on. Perhaps small scholarships could be provided as well.

The organizing group would need to be a formally separate agency—a 501(c)(3) or 501(c)(4)—creating a firewall between the university and the activity of organizing.[17] The actual decisions about how to organize would take place in meetings with the mentor-organizer. The university would not be *running* an organizing effort, it would be providing courses to students who happened to be participating in an organizing group (and who might or might not get credit for "fieldwork" in this work) and collaborating with the mentor-organizer. This arrangement would prevent the program from getting killed—as Haggstrom's was in Syracuse, by outside pressures and university politics (see Chapter 24). This also means that the actual details of the effort, only sketchily imagined here, would be very dependent upon the particular person hired to serve as the mentor-organizer.

My own department actually already has a relationship like this with a small community organizing program, where a small number of students do extensive work with the organization and take university courses; they often have outside jobs as well, and receive little actual credit for their fieldwork (which saves them tuition money). Providing room and board and a stipend (at some level we would need to determine) and perhaps even some scholarships for young people willing to throw themselves into an effort like this would make it possible for a larger number of students from a range of class levels to participate.

What if we sent them in teams into a neighborhood, much as Alinsky sent von Hoffman and Lester Hunt into Woodlawn, and asked them to immerse themselves in it?[18] How does it run? Who is in charge? What organizations exist? What local leaders are there? After a period of research, the interns would work to build power organizations in these neighborhoods under the direction of the mentor-organizer. They would make mistakes, and discover new things. Experienced organizers from outside would be brought in to talk with them about different visions. Later on, individual organizations would be brought together into a larger citywide or regional umbrella. The interns might also work for some time with existing congregation-based and other groups to get a range of experience, to the extent that these groups are willing to participate—in my city I am fairly certain that at least one congregational group would cooperate.

Over time, you would rotate "graduating" organizers out and new interns in. You might have more established organizations for them to work with, but it would be a long time before there wouldn't be neighborhoods left to organize (and even then, some of the organizations would deteriorate and need to be rebuilt/rethought).

The goals would be twofold: first, to educate a new generation of organizers in a diversity of thinking about building power; second, to build power in a city where, frankly, there isn't much to resist barely-elected politicians, business leaders, and others. By the end of two years, interns would be able to work within existing institutions as well as to build new "from scratch" ones that emerged from either door-to-door or house meeting approaches.

Note that the actual cost of such an arrangement—with a single full-time employee and low-paid interns—would be relatively low. With a combination of membership dues, limited donations, and foundation funding, it might be possible to maintain the arrangement over time.

Those who go on to become organizers would likely work within established approaches. But they would bring with them a breadth of experience and this would likely result in innovation (as some of the more experienced organizers whose work Miller and I have examined have described doing across their careers).

Just a Thought Experiment

I have focused on two core issues in this essay: one about the practice of training in particular models of organizing, and another about the importance of what I am calling neighborhood-based organizing at a time when congregation-based organizing seems ascendant. My thought experiment is not a fully fleshed-out solution to these issues, nor am I certain it would actually work as described. The point of a thought experiment is to push us to think beyond what already is. And what already *is* is not sufficient.

Overall, I hope that this volume encourages the field to think outside of established ways of doing things. It is meant as a contribution to this larger discussion about the future of organizing—the future of efforts to build power for those who, today, are invisible to those who control our futures.

A great deal of important work remains to be done. The histories of many important organizing efforts over the last thirty years have yet to be written about in any detail. The different approaches and conceptual understandings that informed these efforts are in danger of being lost with the passage of time, the loss of those with personal experience in these efforts, and the tendency of important documentary material to end up in the trash instead of in professional archives. Similarly, with respect to organizing today we need a broader understanding and tracking of the more creative thinking and experimenting going on out there. There is more being done than is known beyond fairly close networks of organizers, whose knowledge is mostly focused on what is going on in their own networks. And little has been documented in any detail. The more I discover as I begin a small part of this work myself, the more enormous the task seems to be.

In fact, I would like to see a broad-based, interdisciplinary effort to conduct research on organizing, perhaps grounded by an open-access online journal (to supplement the outstanding work already contributed by Randy Stoecker's Comm-Org [*comm-org.wisc.edu*], Rathke's *Social Policy*, the National Housing Institute's *Shelterforce*, and other publications) and perhaps by a yearly conference to bring academics and practitioner/scholars together for dialogue and collaboration across different networks and practices. We need to move out of our silos (within different academic fields, within different organizing networks, between academia and practice) and develop more common spaces to work and converse together. From my perspective, a key aim of this work should be to honestly document the strengths and weaknesses of different aspects of the field in rich detail so that we can all learn from what has gone before and what is being done today.

I look across the neighborhoods in the center of my city and, while there are a few effective organizations, compared to the need I despair at the limited organizing going on. The lack of significant counterbalance in most cases to established power means that city officials can usually do what they want. In this most segregated city in America, with the most segregated suburbs in America, most of the suffering of the poor is essentially invisible to those with privilege. For change to come, we need new ways of thinking about how to organize, ways that draw on and extend the diversity and creativity of visions represented within these pages.

Notes

1. David Walls, *Community Organizing: Fanning the Flame of Democracy* (New York: Polity Press, forthcoming). In June 2014, I conducted a "back of the notebook" look across the websites of IAF, Gamaliel, PICO, and DART affiliates, looking for representation of noncongregational members. I skipped websites where the actual membership was not clearly stated. What I found seemed to support Walls's statement, with IAF being the most diverse (especially in the Northwest) and DART the least. Even in the IAF I found only a small number of affiliates that looked truly "broad-based," with most largely congregational (although Miller tells me that the IAF spends organizing staff time cultivating relationships with unions). The congregational groups seem increasingly likely to enter into alliances with other groups, which is heartening, but this doesn't seem to have changed their membership make-up significantly, at least so far. See also the recent study of the state of the field by Richard L. Wood, Brad Fulton, and Kathryn Partridge, *Building Bridges, Building Power: Developments in Institution-Based Community Organizing* (New York: Interfaith Funders, 2013). While they argue for the "institutional" name, their evidence also seems limited in terms of indicating whether there has been a significant shift away from a dominant focus on congregations. Including religious-based nonprofits, over 80 percent of the membership of these organizations is religious. Neighborhood organizations make up only 2.9 percent, and one wonders how many of these are standard 501(c)(3) organizations, whose capacity to really engage in organizing without threatening their funding base is limited. Only 3.4 percent are unions. More work needs to be done on how noncongregational members participate in these organizations, and beyond my back-of-the-notebook examination, there simply wasn't time to do more investigation.
2. See the discussion in Walls, *Community Organizing*.
3. See, for example, Heidi Swarts, *Organizing Urban America: Secular and Faith-Based Progressive Movements* (Minneapolis: University of Minnesota Press, 2008).
4. Tellingly, in 2000 Albert Farnsley found that only 36 percent of members of African American churches in Indianapolis came from the local neighborhood (*Rising Expectations: Urban Congregations, Welfare Reform, and Civic Life* [Bloomington: Indiana University Press, 2000], 52). These numbers have likely continued to fall. See also Robert J. Sampson, *Great American City: Chicago and the Enduring Neighborhood Effect* (Chicago: University of Chicago Press, 2010), chapter 8, on the limited impact of churches in general on their local communities. Of course, congregational groups make an argument for and have actually facilitated more participation.
5. Timothy Nelson, "At Ease with Our Own Kind: Worship Practices and Class Segregation in American Religion," in *Religion and Class in America: Culture, History, and Politics*, edited by Sean McCloud and William Mirola (New York: Brill, 2008), 135–46. See also "Income

Ranking by Religious Group: Median Annual Household Income in 2000 (in U.S. Dollars),"
a chart published in Ariela Keysar and Barry Kosmin, *Religion in a Free Market* (New York:
Paramount Market, 2006) and available at *commons.wikimedia.org/wiki/File:Income_Ranking_
by_Religious_Group_-_2000.png*. Interestingly, Philip Schwadel, John D. McCarthy, and Hart
M. Nelsen have shown that with rising income levels of parishioners, in Catholic churches,
long a key support for organizing, lower-income white members have tended to fall off
in participation, except in Latino churches, where there is more likelihood of a relatively
homogeneous "ethnic" and class makeup ("The Continuing Relevance of Family Income for
Religious Participation: U.S. White Catholic Church Attendance in the Late 20th Century,"
Sociology Department, Faculty Publications, Paper 80, University of Nebraska—Lincoln, June
1, 2009, *digitalcommons.unl.edu*). In other words, participating non-Latino Catholic churches
have become more middle-class.

6. Swarts, *Organizing Urban America*. Brian D. Christens, Paul W. Speer, and N. Andrew
Peterson found in a survey of five PICO congregational organizations that educational
attainment among their members was significantly higher than that of the overall population,
with 53.7 percent holding a college degree or higher (the U.S. average is around 30 percent).
A full 26 percent had a graduate degree, compared to 10.6 percent nationally ("Social Class
as a Moderator of the Relationship between (Dis)empowering Processes and Psychological
Empowerment," *Journal of Community Psychology* 39, no. 2 (2011): 170–82; see U.S. Census
Bureau, Table S1501, "Educational Attainment," *2012 American Community Survey 1-Year
Estimates*, accessed February 21, 2014, *factfinder2.census.gov* for data on national educational
attainment). Overall income attainment in the Christens, Speer, and Peterson study by
household looked close to the national median, with 52 percent making over $45,000, but
only 17.2 percent made less than $24,000—representing a lower percentage of lower-income
families than the national percentage of close to 25 percent, while 23 percent made over
$70,000 a year. See also Michelle Oyakawa's recent analysis of an important PICO affiliate
where she formerly worked as an organizer. She noted about this organization, which she
gave the pseudonym ELIJAH (although it is not difficult to identify), that "individuals
who participate . . . are predominantly white, educated and middle class, although there
are African American churches and leaders involved, and the organization is attempting to
become more multiracial" and referenced "the complex racial dynamics in ELIJAH, which
is a predominantly white organization working on racial equity issues" ("'Turning Private
Pain Into Public Action': Constructing Activist-Leader Identities in Faith-Based Community
Organizing" [MA thesis, Ohio State University, 2012], 19, 71, *etd.ohiolink.edu*).

7. See Omar McRoberts, *Streets of Glory: Church and Community in a Black Urban Neighborhood* (Chicago: University of Chicago Press, 2005). In the early 2000s, Miller was actually
part of an effort, Christians Supporting Community Organizing (*www.cscoweb.org*), to try
to bring these churches into the organizing fold, but the effort was largely ineffective. Note
that the evangelical church is too complex to describe it simply as the church for the poor—a
complexity reported on in the *New York Times* (Laurie Goodstein and David D. Kirkpatrick,
"On a Christian Mission to the Top," *New York Times*, May 22, 2005, *www.nytimes.com*), but
key segments of it are.

8. See Aaron Schutz, *Social Class, Social Action, and Education: The Failure of Progressive
Democracy* (New York: Palgrave, 2010); Chapter 1 of this volume; and Mike Miller, "Saul
Alinsky in the Democratic Spirit," *Christianity and Crisis*, May 25, 1992, 180–83; John
Baumann references this issue of a reduction in confrontation and the shift to congregation-
based organizing in his discussion of PICO in Chapter 14.

9. See, for example, Schutz, *Social Class*; and Eric H. F. Law, *The Wolf Shall Dwell with the Lamb*
(St. Louis, MO: Chalice Press, 1993).

10. Mike Miller, personal communication to Aaron Schutz, August 22, 2013.

11. See, for example, Rose Starr, Terry Mizrahi, and Ellen Gurzinsky, "Where Have All the Organizers Gone," *Journal of Community Practice* 6, no. 3 (1999): 23–48, for evidence that community organizing training has an impact on the perspectives and activities of those who are not directly employed in community organizing.

12. See, for example, Sampson's work in *Great American City*, which maps out the different levels of "collective efficacy" in different neighborhoods somewhat independent of poverty and race.

13. For example, Schutz's interviews with Bruce Gotschall (September 24, 2013) and Roger Hayes (October 4, 2013), among others.

14. See Dennis Shirley, *Community Organizing for Urban School Reform* (Austin: University of Texas Press, 1997).

15. Nicholas von Hoffman, interview by Aaron Schutz, January 18, 2013.

16. In some cases, in fact, congregation-based groups may fall in a gray area between organizing and "advocacy" groups. Of course, few groups organize those who are struggling the most—the homeless, for example, or recently returned prisoners. Even neighborhood groups, in the anecdotal evidence I have seen, often seem led by and largely populated by more stable members of the neighborhood.

17. The details of how to work this out would be highly dependent upon local contexts. But this agency would likely be formed from scratch for this purpose, and have a very small board of directors made up of people who "got" the program and who were used to taking political heat. The agency would pay the organizer and the interns, handle any scholarships that might exist, but otherwise mostly stay out of the way of the mentor-organizer. The board would not, for example, act as a "sponsoring agency" legitimizing the organizing—such sponsor groups would be developed within individual areas as they were organized (as in the case of ACORN, for example).

18. The effort would struggle with a tension between Ross's vision of learning the basics and letting students experiment. Do we really want to teach organizers the "truth" and *then* introduce them to other ways of thinking? I'm inclined to think "no." I think of Gaudette getting mad at Stephanie Gut when she did what she was told instead of following her own instincts (see Chapter 11). But on the other hand, is it realistic to have very different forms of organizing running in different neighborhoods? Likely not. This too would need to be worked out if something like this was attempted.

Index